D1560282

Philosophy
and the
Darwinian Legacy

Philosophy and the Darwinian Legacy

Suzanne Cunningham

UNIVERSITY OF ROCHESTER PRESS

First published 1996

University of Rochester Press
34-36 Administration Building, University of Rochester
Rochester, New York, 14627, USA
and at P.O. Box 9, Woodbridge, Suffolk IP12 3DF, UK

ISBN 1 878822 61 6

Library of Congress Cataloging-in-Publication Data
Philosophy and the Darwinian Legacy / Suzanne Cunningham.
p. cm.
Includes bibliographical references (p.).
ISBN 1-878822-61-6 (hbk. : alk. paper)
1. Evolution. 2. Philosophy, Modern—20th century.
3. Darkwin, Charles, 1809–1882—Influence. I. Title.
B818.C89 1996
116—dc20
95–46560

British Library Cataloguing-in-Publication Data

A catalogue record for this book
is available from the British Library

This publication is printed on acid-free paper
Printed in the United States of America

For
George

Contents

Acknowledgments

This book was begun in 1985, during my term as a Fellow at the Institute for Advanced Studies in the Humanities at the University of Edinburgh. Since that time, colleagues and students too numerous to mention by name, have contributed to it in various ways. Some of them suggested materials I ought to look at, some offered encouragement, some proposed objections that I ought to consider. My thanks to each of them.

I owe a special debt of gratitude, however, to those professional colleagues who read all or part of earlier versions of the manuscript and provided me with enormously helpful comments and suggestions: Elizabeth Eames, Garth Hallett, Mark Johnson, William Rowe, and Tom Carson. Whatever problems remain in the text, they are of course mine.

Portions of the manuscript have been presented at meetings or colloquia of various sorts: at the Institute for Advanced Studies in the Humanities at the University of Edinburgh; the Philosophy departments at the University of Helsinki; Seoul National University; Ewha Women's University in Seoul, Purdue University; and the University of Florida; a Symposium on the Philosophy of Mind at Rochester Institute of Technology; the Illinois Philosophical Association; the Indiana Philosophical Association; the Society for the Advancement of American Philosophy; and the Philosophy Colloquium at Loyola University of Chicago. I am grateful for the many helpful comments I received at each of those sessions.

My thanks to Kenneth Blackwell and the staff at the Bertrand Russell Archives at McMaster University for their assistance while I worked at the Archives and for their generosity in providing me with copies of the correspondence between Russell and Julian Huxley. Thanks, too, to Nancy Boothe, Director of the Woodson Research Center at Rice University, for giving me access to portions of the Russell-Huxley correspondence. I am indebted as well to Michael Ruse who generously provided me with a copy of his manuscript, *Monad to Man*.

Special thanks to my own Philosophy department and to the administration at Loyola University of Chicago, who supported my work on this project during two research leaves of absence.

Portions of the manuscript have been previously published elsewhere. Part of Chapter Five, on Husserl and Classical Modern Philosophy, first appeared as "Modern Philosophy," in the *Encyclopedia of Phenomenology*, copyright 1995 by Kluwer Academic Publishers and is reprinted with permission. Chapter Seven contains a version of "Perception, Meaning, and Mind," which first appeared in *Synthese*, 80:223-241, copyright 1989 by Kluwer Academic Publishers and is reprinted with permission. Chapter Seven also contains a version of "A Darwinian Approach to Functionalism," which first appeared in Journal of Philosophical Research, 16:145-157, and is reprinted with permission. Special thanks to the editors and readers at the University of Rochester Press for their many helpful suggestions.

Finally, my deepest gratitude to my husband, George Dickie, without whose support and encouragement this project would never have been completed.

Note: Endnote numbers with asterisks are an indication to the reader that the endnotes contain more than simply a bibliographic reference.

Introduction

What biology has rendered probable is that the diverse species arose by adaptation from a less differentiated ancestry. This fact is in itself exceedingly interesting, but it is not the kind of fact from which philosophical consequences follow.[1]

—Bertrand Russell (1914)

Understanding where we are philosophically sometimes requires a look backwards. By considering some of the choices that have been made in the past, at various forks in the intellectual road, we can get our bearings not only with respect to our current direction but also with respect to other directions we might have taken.

One of the most significant choices made by the shapers of twentieth-century philosophy concerned the status to be accorded to Charles Darwin's theory of evolution vis-a-vis philosophy. It is that choice, as it appears in classical analytic philosophy and in early phenomenology—that choice and some of its consequences that are the focus of this book. My central claim is that the complete exclusion of evolutionary, and particularly Darwinian, insights by the founders of those two philosophic traditions has had unfortunate repercussions in significant portions of twentieth-century philosophy. I shall be particularly concerned to trace those consequences in certain theories of mind and of perception.

It is common knowledge that near the turn of the century, philosophy was undergoing dramatic redefinition. Rapid developments in science during the eighteenth and nineteenth centuries had motivated a sharp split between philosophy and the domains of natural and social science that had formerly belonged to it. Both the method and the content of philosophy were put in question.

In Great Britain the search for a new understanding of philosophy was further intensified by dissatisfaction with the versions of Idealism that had dominated the scene during the late nineteenth century. In Germany, on the other hand, the growing success of Naturalism was taken by some philosophers to pose a threat to the very possibility of philosophy.[2]* By contrast, in the United States there was a self-conscious movement on the part of a number of important thinkers to integrate the findings of the new sciences with philosophy. In spite of differing motivations there was, in virtually all quarters, a growing conviction that a new conception of philosophy was imperative. The crucial question was where one should turn for a new framework, a new method, a new account of the content of philosophy.

One might expect that works like Charles Darwin's *Origin of Species*, published in 1859, or his *Descent of Man*, published in 1871, would play a significant role in shaping the new conception of philosophy. Darwin's views, after all, had a considerable impact on intellectual life in both Europe and the United States, and in addition they had profound implications for an adequate understanding of human nature. Such, however, was not to be the case for two of the dominant new schools of philosophy that emerged, analytic philosophy and phenomenology.

The leaders in the development of analytic philosophy, G.E. Moore and Bertrand Russell, were in agreement that biological theories of evolution had little or nothing to do with philosophy. They were even more vehemently opposed to "Evolutionism"—a name given to various efforts made by thinkers like Herbert Spencer and Henri Bergson to combine philosophy with evolutionary theories. For Edmund Husserl, the founder of phenomenology, evolution theory could not be relevant to philosophy because it was the task of philosophy to provide the epistemological *foundations* for all of science, including evolutionary biology. Including it within philosophy would be viciously circular.

In exploring this important period of the reshaping of philosophy, I shall take Moore, Russell, and Husserl as my central cast of characters and this for two reasons. First, each of them explicitly addressed the issue of the relevance of evolutionary views to philosophy, and secondly, each of them played a leading role in shaping the direction that one of the major "schools" of twentieth-century philosophy would take.

My account of things does not pretend to be a complete description of the philosophies of Moore, Russell, or Husserl. Many aspects of their philosophies will be omitted. Neither does my account provide their intellectual biographies. Rather, my story will focus largely on their stated attitudes toward evolutionary views and on the consequences those attitudes had for the new directions in which these men were to take philosophy—in particular, for the approaches to perception and mind that developed under their leadership.

One significant consequence of the omission of evolutionary insights from philosophy was the formulation of theories of mind and perception that paid little or no attention to the role played by mental states in satisfying the needs of living organisms. Mind was often treated simply as an abstract set of cognitive functions, in virtual independence of any relation to the interests and needs of individual living organisms. Perception theories were dominated by concerns about skepticism and about the ontological status of perceived objects. Again, little attention was paid to the role that perception regularly plays on behalf of the well-being of the perceiving organism.

These consequences persist in some of our current theories of mind and perception. One of the current and popular philosophies of mind, Machine Functionalism, for example, continues to argue that adequate theories of mental states can be constructed in total abstraction from their relations to a living organism.

In what follows I argue that this divorce of perception and mind from the concerns of the living organism has been a pivotal misstep in philosophy. And I trace that misstep to philosophy's exclusion of evolutionary, and particularly, Darwinian insights near the turn of the century. A philosophy that takes Darwin seriously, can hardly overlook the close connection between living organisms and their mental capacities—adaptations that assist them to preserve their lives and to provide for their well-being.

The book has two goals: one historical, the other constructive. The first six chapters are largely historical. I begin by exploring some of the background factors that might have influenced the decisions that Moore, Russell, and Husserl made with respect to the philosophical relevance of evolution. Then I consider the explicit reasons that each of them offered in support of those decisions, arguing that they were for the most part open to question.

I should note that the issue here is not simply *Darwin* and his account of natural selection. All three philosophers excluded *any* biological theory of evolution—Lamarckian, Darwinian, and the rest. For them, the problem lay not with a Darwinian versus some other version of evolution but with the whole class of biological theories. Biological considerations as such, and evolutionary ones in particular, were judged irrelevant to genuine philosophy.

After examining the reasons offered for this judgment, I go on to examine the theories of perception and mind that developed under their leadership in the analytic and phenomenological traditions. Again, I argue that both sets of theories were problematic.

Several themes recur in the historical portion of the book. One is the relationship thought to exist between science and philosophy; another is the status of logic and necessary truth; a third concerns the foundations of ethics, and more generally, the status of certain socio-political values. Attitudes toward all of these issues obviously bear on the question of the nature of philosophy and philosophic method. The stance that the three philosophers took on each of these issues affected, and was affected by, attitudes toward both Darwin and Evolutionism. It hardly needs to be said that views about the philosophical relevance of evolution were not the only influences that shaped the emerging philosophies; they were, nonetheless, among the significant ones whose import has yet to be fully measured.

In the second and shorter portion of the book, I sketch some positive proposals about how our current philosophical accounts of perception and mind might be altered to take account of certain basic Darwinian views. What I offer amounts to little more than some suggestions about directions that need further investigation. I provide nothing approximating a theory of mind or of perception. Nonetheless, my proposals indicate some basic philosophical assumptions that need reconsideration in both areas.

The core of my concern is not Darwin's account of *natural selection* as such, but rather his claims about the importance of recognizing that a *struggle for existence* goes on among living organisms. I explore what he means to include in that notion of "struggle," and I conclude that our capacity for perception and for other mental states, both cognitive and non-cognitive, plays a crucial role in that struggle.

A comment may be in order on the time-frame within which my discussion falls. In the historical portion of the book I focus attention primarily on the period between the mid-1890s and the mid-1930s. Naturally, it is not possible to specify a given year as the time in which evolutionary views were assimilated or put aside by philosophers. But G.E. Moore's most explicit statements on the subject began around 1898 and continued through 1903. Edmund Husserl's occurred primarily in a series of lectures in 1905. And while Bertrand Russell's concern with evolution begins in the late 1890s, his most extensive and probably his most influential discussion of its relation to philosophy appeared in 1914. Russell's comments on Evolutionism and its adherents continued, however, well beyond 1914. Furthermore, all the various theories of perception and of mind that were formulated by these philosophers had their impact by the mid-1930s. Hence my choice of a time-frame. I shall make occasional reference to the later works of these men, but the bulk of the historical investigation will center on the first third of the century.

There are several additional reasons to cut the period where I have. The first is simple expediency; even a cursory discussion of those early years will require considerable space. The second is more substantive. I am convinced that the attitudes of those early years had a decisive influence on the philosophy that ensued. One commentator makes an even stronger claim about the early influence of Russell and Moore: "The whole character of modern British philosophy (and that portion of recent American philosophy which shows its influence) goes back to the revolutionary consequences of the thought of Russell and Moore at Cambridge in the nineties."[3] He had in mind, no doubt, their revolt against Idealism, but the point about the extent of their influence on the future character of philosophy remains.

Finally, by the late 1920s new leaders were beginning to emerge in both analytic philosophy and phenomenology. Ludwig Wittgenstein became an increasingly influential figure in the analytic tradition. With the publication of his *Tractatus Logico-Philosophicus* in English in 1922, his views assumed increasing importance as Moore's, and particularly Russell's, began to diminish in influence. On the phenomenological side, Martin Heidegger published some of his most influential work in the late 1920s and early 1930s, as he began to take phenomenology on its existential turn.

Nonetheless, whatever changes in method or theory that Wittgenstein and Heidegger brought to their respective traditions, they did not alter the judgment that had been made by their predecessors about the irrelevance of Darwin and Evolutionism to philosophy. So much for the time-frame.

One final caveat. The title of the book may mislead. Not all of philosophy has ignored its evolutionary and Darwinian heritage. There was one group of philosophers who, at the turn of the century, took Darwin's views very seriously indeed, and took pains to incorporate them into their new philosophic framework. They were the American Pragmatists, in particular William James and John Dewey. Their views, however, did not come to dominate the philosophic theories of perception and mind that emerged in the English-speaking world of the twentieth century. So the story of their relationship to Darwinian insights provides the material for a different book.

And there is another group of philosophers, important on the current scene, who have also made significant contributions to the integration of evolutionary and Darwinian views into their philosophical work. These include philosophers like Robert Brandon, Richard Burian, Helena Cronin, Daniel Dennett, Marjorie Grene, David Hull, Philip Kitcher, Elizabeth Lloyd, Michael Ruse, Elliott Sober, and William Wimsatt, as well as scholars like Ernst Mayr, to name just a few. Given such a distinguished list, one might well wonder if there is any reason to write a book about philosophy and Darwin. There are at least two reasons. First, in spite of the fine work done by these philosophers, evolutionary views are far from dominating contemporary philosophy. Many current theories of mind and perception continue to function within the timeless, anonymous framework bequeathed to philosophy by Plato and Descartes. Machine Functionalism is just one of the more obvious examples. And secondly, the particular changes in our theories of perception and mind that I shall suggest in my final chapter differ in important ways from the proposals that have been offered until now.

So, in spite of the occasional exceptions, I believe that twentieth-century philosophy continues to be heir to a pre-evolutionary, pre-Darwinian view of itself and its world.

Chapter 1

Darwin's Relevance
to Philosophy

*With the one exception of Newton's 'Principia,' no single book of empirical science
has ever been of more importance to philosophy than this work of Darwin's.*
—Josiah Royce (1892)

History is filled with accounts of momentous scientific theories and discoveries that have transformed our ways of thinking about the world. The works of Copernicus, Galileo, Newton, and Einstein are among the obvious examples. Why, then, focus attention on Darwin? What is so special about his views? And why should philosophy be more affected by him than by the others? The views of Copernicus and Galileo, for example, have transformed our ways of thinking about the physical universe and our place in it. Newton undid our notions of a fragmented world by giving us unifying laws that govern its motions. Einstein revised our ways of thinking about some of our most basic temporal concepts. Each of these men has profoundly altered our approach to some aspect of philosophy, most notably perhaps, issues in cosmology.

But there is a sense in which Darwin's views strike even more deeply at the roots of the philosophical enterprise. It is true that along with Galileo and the others, his theories ask us to reconsider certain views we have about portions of our world. But more fundamental than that, Darwin has also offered us a new account of *ourselves*. He has argued that human beings, along with the rest of nature, need to be understood as the product of completely natural forces. And his theory asserts not only the natural origin of our bodies, but also the natural origin and development of our mental powers and our moral sense. To this extent, I suggest, his views have a singular significance for philosophy.

I shall not be concerned here to provide a detailed defense of Darwin's account of *natural selection* against the many objections that have been raised against it in the century and a half since it first appeared. From Darwin's point of view, natural selection explains a great deal that otherwise remains unclear, making use of a version of what William Whewell called "consilience of inductions."[1] That is, it brings under one unifying principle many disparate areas of investigation (e.g., embryology, extinction of species, genetic similarities between certain species, etc.). Having that sort of explanatory power gives natural selection considerable plausibility. But rather than begin with an extended defense of Darwin's views, I shall take his claims about natural selection to be generally right.

For purposes of this work, however, my primary interest lies not with natural selection, but with Darwin's claims about the *struggle for existence*. I shall be concerned with the difference those claims should have made to philosophical theories of perception and of mind.

It will perhaps be helpful to begin by recalling some of the highlights of Darwin's views. Later in the chapter I shall suggest a couple of the background factors that very likely played at least an indirect role in shaping the decision of our three philosophers to bypass Darwin and evolution.

Darwin's Account of Evolution

In his book, *The Origin of Species*, published in 1859, Darwin proposed natural selection as the mechanism by which species emerge and fade. The basic argument of the *Origin* was rather simple. As Darwin summarizes it in the sixth edition of that work:

> If under changing conditions of life organic beings present individual differences in almost every part of their structure, . . . if there be, owing to their geometrical rate of increase, a severe struggle for life at some age, season, or year, . . . then, considering the infinite complexity of the relations of all organic beings to each other and to their conditions of life, causing an infinite diversity in structure, constitution, and habits, to be advantageous to them, it would be a most extraordinary fact if no variations had ever occurred useful to each being's own welfare,. . . . But if variations useful to any organic being ever do occur, assuredly individuals thus characterised will have the best chance of being preserved in the struggle for life; and from the strong principle of inheritance, these will tend to produce offspring similarly characterised. This principle of preservation, or the survival of the fittest, I have called Natural Selection.[2]

There are, the argument runs, variations among individual organisms; some of these variations have proved useful to the organisms that have them, giving them an advantage as they struggle to cope with a given environment; those organisms that are successful in that struggle are likely to pass on their favorable variations to their offspring; this is natural selection. Over time the inheritance of these variations will alter the character of the population that has them, and gradually new species will emerge. (Variations that are disadvantageous in a given environment will be eliminated, and extinction is likely to ensue. Variations that are neither advantageous nor disadvantageous will play no role in natural selection.)[3]*

So the great diversity among living things is to be explained by the random occurrence of variations, some of which are advantageous and can be inherited. These variations are, as Darwin says, "accidental, as far as purpose is concerned (of course not accidental as to their cause or origin); . . . "[4] Species, then, are not fixed but are temporary stabilizations in a very slowly changing population.

Two rather clear consequences of Darwin's view are relevant to traditional philosophical concerns. Most obviously, a platonic account of species is no longer needed. And the fit between organisms and their environments need not be seen as the product of intelligent design but can be explained by natural processes.[5]*

After stating the basic argument for natural selection, Darwin devotes the bulk of *Origin of Species* to explaining the meaning of the central terms in the argument, adducing numerous examples in support of it and discussing possible difficulties with the theory. In this first book, he focuses largely on issues that relate to the non-human organic world, only hinting at the consequences of his views for our understanding of ourselves. In the well-known sentence near the end of the book he says, "Light will be thrown on the origin of man and his history."[6] Darwin himself sheds that light in his later book, *The Descent of Man and Selection in Relation to Sex*, published in 1871. But before turning to that book, it will be useful to consider Darwin's views on the nature and importance of the struggle for existence.

Struggle for Existence

As I have said, my arguments will not center explicitly on Darwin's views of either natural (or sexual) selection as such. Rather, my focus will be on one of the crucial presuppositions of the processes of selection, namely, the *struggle for existence*. The importance of this notion for Darwin is made clear in the following passage from the *Origin*:

> Nothing is easier than to admit in words the truth of the universal struggle for life, or more difficult—at least I have found it so—than constantly to bear this conclusion in mind. Yet unless it be thoroughly engrained in the mind, I am convinced that the whole economy of nature, . . . will be dimly seen or quite misunderstood. . . .
> . . . as more individuals are produced than can possibly survive, there must in every case be a struggle for existence, either one individual

with another of the same species, or with the individuals of distinct species, or with the physical conditions of life.[7]*

As Darwin acknowledges, he has taken the notion of the struggle for existence from Thomas Malthus.[8]* But Darwin is also careful to point out that he uses the term " . . . in a large and metaphorical sense including dependence of one being on another, and including (which is more important) not only the life of the individual, but success in leaving progeny."[9] So the notion of what Darwin has in mind is not simply nature "red in tooth and claw."[10] It includes, rather, all the efforts made by an individual organism to provide for its own life and that of its progeny.[11]* And these efforts may involve fighting with or killing other organisms, but they may also involve relations of dependence and cooperation. As he puts it,

> Two canine animals in a time of dearth may be truly said to struggle with each other which shall get food and live. But a plant on the edge of a desert is said to struggle for life against the drought, though more properly it should be said to be dependent on the moisture.

And a bit later,

> As the mistletoe is disseminated by birds, its existence depends on birds; and it may metaphorically be said to struggle with other fruit-bearing plants, in order to tempt birds to devour and thus disseminate its seeds rather than those of other plants. In these several senses, which pass into each other, I use for convenience sake the general term of struggle for existence.[12]

So for Darwin, the struggle for existence may involve competitive, cooperative, or dependency relations of one individual with another of the same species, with an individual of a different species, or with conditions in the environment. My primary interest is in the role played by the mental states of the *individuals* who are involved in that struggle.[13]*

So when I speak of the "struggle for existence" I shall, in the spirit of Darwin, mean all the efforts (great or small, conscious or unconscious, mental or bodily) made by an individual to provide for its own continued well-being, and that of other individuals who are related to it in certain ways. And I shall make no attempt to distingush between those efforts that are supported by the genetic endowment of the individual and those that have been influenced by cultural context. I take it, then, that an organism that is scrutinizing its environment—whether it is looking for food, a mate, or signs of danger—is struggling for existence. Furthermore, two organisms—female lions, for example—who are cooperating in stalking prey, are struggling for existence by their cooperative hunting as truly as by their killing of the prey and by their providing some of it for their offspring. "Struggle," then is not to be taken exclusively in its physical and violent sense. Darwin's broad, metaphorical sense does include physical and violent activities, but it also comprises all the mental and cooperative activities (as well as a large range of intermediate cases) that contribute to an organism's success in coping with its environment.[14]*

And that success is defined not only in terms of mere survival and reproduction, but also in terms of the general well-being of the individual. As Darwin puts it in his *Descent of Man*, the goal is to rear individuals in "full vigour and health, with all their faculties perfect, under the conditions to which they are exposed."[15]

The human struggle for existence has, of course, been greatly expanded and refined through the development of culture. We cooperatively build structures that will protect us from freezing temperatures, from floods, from enemy fire. We trade the products of our specialized occupations— food, clothing, housing, etc.—in order to provide for our various needs. We learn to be alert in potentially dangerous situations, whether the danger might come from a wild animal, a mugger, or a disease. We have even come to learn that certain psychological states, like affection for another, can contribute to our survival, while states like loneliness or depression can work against survival.

The human struggle for life, then, is neither habitually violent nor always solitary, neither purely selfish nor always competitive. Whatever we do, singly or collectively, could alert us to potential threats or could assist us in providing for our various needs—all these things are part of our struggle for existence. In order to highlight this broad sense of the struggle for existence, I shall frequently speak of our efforts to survive and to provide for our well-being.

One gets a better idea of Darwin's notion of the struggle for existence by considering the analogy between it and the struggle to succeed. Both *can* be violent and ruthless. But both can also involve constructive hard work, problem-solving through intelligent planning, establishing cooperative networks, being alert to capitalize on opportunities, etc.

So in addition to asking us to reconsider some of our long-standing beliefs about the origin and nature of living organisms, Darwin is telling us something quite significant about human beings: many of our capacities and activities need to be understood within the context of our continuing efforts to provide for our own survival and well-being and that of our progeny. There are, then, good reasons for thinking that the theories of Charles Darwin have at least as great, and in some respects greater, relevance to philosophy than do some other scientific theories that one might consider.

I turn now to consider of one of the most important capacities that assists human beings in their struggle for life, namely our mental powers.

Darwin on Mental Powers

In *The Descent of Man* Darwin is concerned to provide a completely natural account of the origin and development of the human body, human mental powers, and our moral sense.

Early in the book Darwin notes:

> We have now seen that man is variable in body and mind; and that the variations are induced, either directly or indirectly, by the same general causes, and obey the same general laws, as with the lower animals. . . . The early progenitors of man must also have tended, like all other animals, to have increased beyond their means of subsistence; they must, therefore, occasionally have been exposed to a struggle for existence, and consequently to the rigid law of natural selection. Beneficial variations of all kinds will thus, either occasionally or habitually, have been preserved and injurious ones eliminated. . . .
>
> Man in the rudest state in which he now exists is the most dominant animal that has ever appeared on the earth. He has spread more widely than any other highly organised form; and all others have yielded before him. He manifestly owes this immense superiority to his intellectual faculties, his social habits, which lead him to aid and defend his fellows, and to his corporeal structure. The supreme importance of these characters has been proved by the final arbitrament of the battle for life. [16]

It is clear from this quote that Darwin means to credit human mental as well as bodily capacities for the remarkable success that the species has enjoyed in its struggle for existence. (Darwin's inclusion of "social habits, which lead him to aid and defend his fellows," is, as we shall see in Chapter 2, a reference to the moral sense.)

In the second chapter of his *Descent of Man* Darwin begins a detailed discussion of human mental powers. There are three distinct claims that he makes about these powers:

(i) they have a natural origin;
(ii) they are the product of natural selection; and
(iii) they function on behalf of the organism that has them.

First, their natural origin. Darwin introduces the topic by noting that while there is a great difference in the mental powers of humans and other animals, it is not so fundamental as one might suppose. The difference in the mental powers of humans and those of other primates is, he says, less significant than the difference between the mental powers of some of the non-human primates and those of less highly developed animals like fish. He goes on to point out the numerous similarities between certain mental states in some of the higher animals and in man—for example, both exhibit curiosity, attention, memory, and both are given to imitation. He says that even reason ("Of all the faculties of the human mind, it . . . stands at the summit.") is possessed to *some* degree by these animals. They "may constantly be seen to pause, deliberate, and resolve."[17]

Darwin has been accused of operating with a naive kind of anthropomorphism in his views of the mental states of non-human animals. And his critics may be right. But for our present purposes that issue is not relevant. Whether or not Darwin's evidence was adequate, more recent experiments have, indeed, suggested that certain animals—among them some of the other primates, dolphins, etc.—have the capacity to learn, and show varying degrees of curiosity, attention, memory, and the like.[18] So Darwin's general conclusion, whether or not it was based on adequate evidence, seems to be right.

And perhaps more to the point here, it is clear that on Darwin's view, our mental powers have the same natural origin as do our bodily structures—they are developments from simpler versions of the same basic powers in other animals. That is to say, he is arguing against a Cartesian account of mind—an account in which mental powers are understood as belonging to a wholly different kind of reality from that of the physical body. I do not mean to claim, of course, that Darwin had Descartes and his views in mind here. He says in his *Autobiography* that he knows very little about Descartes.[19*] What he argues against is any non-natural account of mental capacities.

The second claim that Darwin makes about mental powers is that they are the product of natural selection, along with "use and disuse".[20*] For our purposes, the important point is that in spite of his unfortunate addition of this Lamarckian notion of use and disuse, *both* of the mechanisms to which Darwin appeals give a purely natural account of the development of human beings and their bodily and mental capacities.[21]

> Every one who believes, as I do, that all the corporeal and mental organs (excepting those which are neither advantageous nor disadvantageous to the possessor) of all beings have been developed through natural selection, or the survival of the fittest, together with use or habit, will admit that these organs have been formed so that their possessors may compete successfully with other beings, and thus increase in number.[22]

For Darwin, then, *mental functions* of various sorts need to be understood as adaptive capacities that are the product of natural selection ("together with use or habit"). Not everyone would agree with him on the role of natural selection here. There are some theorists today, even among those who agree that mental powers have developed through completely natural processes, who would not agree that such powers must be seen as the product of natural selection. It has been argued, for example, against certain evolutionary epistemologists, that mental powers might be the result of "drift" or "hitch-hiking" effects—they might be simply accompaniments of *other* features that have been selected for.[23]

The outcome of that particular debate, however, need not concern us here. What is crucial for my purposes, and does seem clearly to be the case, is Darwin's third claim—that mental functions provide an important service to the organism that has them. Whatever natural processes ultimately explain their origin, it can hardly be denied that they assist organisms to pick up information about their environment and about themselves, store it, manipulate it, and put it to use in their efforts to survive and provide for their well-being. Mental functions are, for the most part, adaptive.

Mental functions are not, of course, infallible; they can even occasionally work against the best interests of the organism. But this is equally true of the immune system, and that fact does not prompt anyone to deny that the immune system provides an adaptive service to an organism. So in spite of the possibility of error, the capacity to perceive one's surroundings, to remember what one has perceived, to activate portions of oneself to behave in ways relevant to what has been perceived—these are unquestionably capacities that normally function on behalf of an organism in its efforts to cope with its environment.

Darwin clearly thought that the mental capacities of human beings were efficacious in the human struggle for existence. He says:

> Of the high importance of the intellectual faculties there can be no doubt, for man mainly owes to them his preeminent position in the world. We can see that, in the rudest state of society, the individuals who were the most sagacious, who invented and used the best weapons or traps, and who were best able to defend themselves, would rear the greatest number of offspring. The tribes which included the largest number of men thus endowed would increase in number and supplant other tribes.[24]

And while those mental capacities can, in the long run, benefit the group to which an individual belongs, they function in crucially important ways for the *individual* that has them. It is the individual that will survive and perhaps reproduce if its mental powers are adequate to the demands of the environment.

Darwin also appears to agree with a view expressed by Alfred Russel Wallace that the development of man's intellectual (and moral) qualities would have minimized the need for changes in bodily structure because human beings would be able to adapt themselves to changes in their environment or would be able to alter the environment to suit their needs simply by using their mental powers. These mental capacities, he thought, would continue to improve through the agency of natural selection, but the latter would no longer have much influence on the body. I call attention to this claim, not to evaluate its truth, but to highlight the enormous importance that Darwin attached to the development of our mental capacities in connection with our struggle for existence.

On a Darwinian view, then, human beings are living organisms that are heavily invested in providing for their own continued life and well-being. Their mental functions need to be understood in the context of their efforts to provide for that life and well-being. If that is right, then any effort to deal with mental functions in a way that completely divorces them from their relation to the living organism will be misguided. More on that later.

Perception and Mind: Preliminary Considerations

How is this Darwinian account of human mental capacities relevant to philosophical theories of perception? Among the mental powers that assist their possessors to compete successfully in their environments, perception clearly has a pivotal place. But in order to provide such assistance, perceptual data must be interpreted as more than impersonal information about the environment. That is to say, perception cannot be understood as simply a process of generating true but impersonal beliefs about the world; it must be seen as a process that is capable of integrating information about the environment with the experienced needs, expectations, fears, etc., of the perceiving organism. The organism needs to be able to see things as fulfilling or frustrating those needs or expectations, confirming its fears, etc. That is to say, an organism needs to be able to interpret perceptual data in light of some of its own psychological states—both cognitive and non-cognitive—if perception is to function as a help in its efforts to preserve its own life and to provide for its own well-being. Without this connection to its own states, it would be virtually impossible for an organism to generate effective behavior.

Paradigm cognitive states like perceiving, remembering, believing, etc., clearly provide an important service to the organism in its struggle to provide for its continuing life and well-being. The *content* of a particular state may not always have a direct or obvious role to play in such a struggle, but the capacity to have mental states of this *type* is crucial. An organism incapable of taking in and storing data about its environment, unable to relate this data to its own needs and interests, unable to generalize on the basis of such data, or incapable of generating useful behavior in response to it, will be enormously disadvantaged in competition with an organism possessed of such capacities.

Paradigm non-cognitive states like fear and sexual attraction are also clearly adaptive. Obviously, such states are normally affected to some extent by cognitive states like perception, belief, and memory. One is attracted to or afraid of what one sees or remembers. But there are good Darwinian reasons to suppose that those cognitive states are similarly affected by non-cognitive ones. For example, in the case of states like fear or sexual attraction—perceptions can clearly be altered by their presence. Such states frequently *direct* perception, motivating the organism to look for or listen for certain things in its surroundings. They can also *heighten or diminish* perceptive awareness. Furthermore, non-cognitive states often contribute to the way that one actually sees or hears things (e.g., as frightening or attractive or threatening), which in turn can alter the behavior that follows. This link between non-cognitive and cognitive states has clear survival value.

Some of our non-cognitive states can also act as "early warning systems" that alert us to look more carefully for relevant data about an object or event before we have formed coherent beliefs about a situation. One can have a feeling that something is amiss (or perhaps "right") before one has a fully formed belief about the relevant circumstances.[25]* The utility to the organism of such a backup system is clear. One begins to look for or listen for things that might explain the feeling of uneasiness or might dispel it. Or one might simply act on the basis of the feeling. Again, the issue is not the infallibility of either the cognitive or non-cognitive states, but rather the possibility that their cooperation can avert disaster for the organism.[26]*

Someone might object that while all this may well be true, it is not relevant to *philosophical* theories of perception. Philosophy, it might be argued, is concerned with issues of truth and justification in relation to perception. The rest belongs to psychology or physiology.

In attempting to respond to such an objection, one wants to avoid taking a position that relies on one particular, and probably moot, characterization of philosophy. There are many competing ways of understanding the nature of the discipline. One runs a similar risk when one assumes one particular definition of perception. Does its *concept* include only issues related to justification, or is it broader than that? An adequate response to the objection needs to avoid begging important questions here about the "true" character of either philosophy or perception.

But there is a less direct route by which one can argue that these broader, Darwinian, considerations have a place in a philosophical account of perception. Theories that concern themselves solely with justificational issues, and limit themselves to a consideration of only the cognitive elements in perception, generate what I believe are faulty models of the mind. In particular, they suggest a model of the mind in which mental states can be treated in complete isolation from their function on behalf of the living organism, and they assume that cognitive and non-cognitive states can be treated by theories that are wholly independent of one another. In fact, much of contemporary philosophy of mind (seeing itself as a part of *cognitive* science) appears to operate with just such a model.

Perhaps it is possible for a *partial* philosophical account of perception to focus exclusively on issues of justification. But even in this case the theory should take account of the *artificial* separation that is being introduced between cognitive and non-cognitive states, and among the various interrelated functions of perception. However, if such a partial story is taken for the whole of the philosophical account of perception, misleading models of mind are virtually inevitable.

In sum, whatever definition one prefers for philosophy or for perception, I take it that when the scope of one philosophical theory generates distortions in other areas of philosophical inquiry, then revisions are needed. If I am right in thinking that this is precisely what has happened with most current theories of perception and mind, then we need not only an expanded account of perception, but also some revisions in our philosophical theories of the mind. I shall sketch some positive proposals in that direction in Chapter Seven. For the present, my purpose has been to argue that there are indeed good reasons to incorporate some of Darwin's views into twentieth-century philosophy of perception and mind. In addition to providing us with a natural, non-platonic framework within which to construct a metaphysics, they urge us to understand ourselves, with all our mental (and moral) powers, as products of a set of natural processes. If those mental powers are indeed capacities that enhance our ability to cope with our environment in ways that are generally conducive to our survival and well-being, then that fact ought to figure prominently in our philosophical theories about them.

In this brief account of Darwin's views, I have tried to highlight three of his principal insights about human beings: his insistence on a natural framework for understanding human beings with their mental and moral capacities; his recognition of the importance of the broad notion of the struggle for life and well-being on the part of individual organisms like human beings; and his claim that human mental capacities function on our behalf in that struggle.[27]* Each of these will form a significant part of the background for the rest of the book.

Before proceeding with an examination of the twentieth-century philosophical response to Darwin's views, I want to consider two sets of circumstances that very likely formed part of the backdrop for that response. The first of these is the attitude of some nineteenth-century philosophers like John Stuart Mill, Herbert Spencer, Friedrich Nietzsche, and Karl Marx to evolutionary views. The second is the cluster of disagreements among biologists themselves—the biometricians, the Mendelians, the Lamarckians, and others—early in the twentieth century, about the status of Darwin's account of evolution.

One does not find explicit reference to either of these factors in the writings of Moore, Russell, or Husserl in connection with their decision to bypass evolutionary views. Nonetheless, there is good reason to think that one or both of these factors exercised some influence on their thinking. And in the case of Russell at least, there is fairly clear evidence that he was explicitly aware of both the relevant nineteenth-century philosophical views and the twentieth-century disputes in biology. As we shall see in Chapter Three, both of these played a role in his conclusions about Darwin and evolution. For Moore and Husserl the influence is less direct. But in all three cases these factors make somewhat more plausible their negative attitudes toward the relationship between philosophy and evolution. First, then, nineteenth-century philosophy and Darwin.

Some Early Philosophical Responses to Darwin

It was inevitable that the publication of Darwin's views would bring *some* philosophical response. As John Passmore puts it, one important dimension of Darwin's impact on philosophy in Great Britain was that it "encouraged and reinforced ... such diverse philosophical tendencies as agnosticism, naturalism, and idealism, which he [Darwin] certainly did not create but nevertheless helped to shape."[28] Analogous claims could be made about the impact on philosophy in Germany.

In addition to these more diffuse philosophical reactions, there were explicit responses to the views of Darwin as such. It has been suggested that among philosophers there were several types of response: obviously there were the opponents and the supporters; among the supporters there were the "adjusters" and the "transformers."[29]* These possibilities do not capture the full range of philosophical responses, but they provide a fair enough sample.

First, the supporters. Among these, the "adjusters" were the philosophers who tried to fit Darwin's ideas into the tradition. They used his account of evolution as a new solution to old problems. Herbert Spencer was to some extent an "adjuster." Some have claimed that he used evolution as a replacement for religion.[30] Indeed, Spencer's references to the "Unknowable" have been characterized as having clear religious overtones.[31]* As an "adjuster," Spencer tried to respond to traditional questions about the meaning and purpose of existence with evolutionary answers. His views, as we shall see, were not exclusively Darwinian, incorporating as they did strong Lamarckian strains. Nonetheless, his views formed part of the background against which Moore and Russell evaluated the plausibility of an evolutionary philosophy. His efforts to incorporate evolutionary considerations into philosophy were extensive as well as influential. In late nineteenth century Britain he was indeed a force to be reckoned with. But both Moore and Russell had serious reservations about the clarity and the cogency of Spencer's views. They had little respect for his habit of making claims that remained unsupported by careful argument. For them, Spencer came to symbolize the hopeless attempt to blend evolutionary theory with philosophy. I shall have a good deal more to say about Spencer's views in Chapters Two and Three, when I discuss Moore's and Russell's responses to Evolutionism. For now, suffice it to say that Spencer's enthusiastic support for an evolutionary philosophy became one of the chief stumbling blocks for both Moore and Russell when they came to consider the role of evolution theory in the philosophy they were forging.

The "transformers," by contrast, used Darwin's views to recast many of the fundamental questions of philosophy. John Dewey and William James are good examples. In their case, one sees a distinct effort to shift philosophical inquiry from a framework of fixed categories and final truths to a framework of process and open-ended inquiry. Russell, for his part, was unable to follow their lead, at least in part because of what he took to be the untenable consequences of such a view for logic and for the theory of truth. Fluid categories, for Russell, had no place in accounts of either truth or logic. This was, in fact, one of the sources of his abiding disagreement with the Pragmatists.[32]

Of course, there were in addition to the supportive "adjusters" and "transformers," those philosophers who opposed Darwin's views. The early British Idealists like J.H. Stirling and T.H. Green were among the staunchest opponents of the naturalism of the Darwinian view. Moore and Russell, educated in the Idealist tradition, may well have inherited some of the antipathy to Naturalism that so marked Idealist thought.

But there was another kind of opponent to Darwinism. This included philosophers like Friedrich Nietzsche and Henri Bergson. While they were unwilling to accept all of Darwin's views, they were nonetheless supportive of *some* evolutionary view of things—in both cases they appear to have seen

Lamarck as closer to the truth than Darwin.[33]* So they were Evolutionist philosophers but not Darwinians.

In *The Joyful Wisdom*, originally published in 1882, Nietzsche complains that thinkers like Spinoza and Darwin, who take the instinct for self-preservation to be fundamental, have probably arisen from very poor, humble backgrounds where life was difficult.

> To seek self-preservation merely, is the expression of a state of distress, or of limitation of the true, fundamental instinct of life, which aims at the *extension of power*. . . . Over the whole of English Darwinism there hovers something of the suffocating air of over-crowded England, something of the odour of humble people in need and in straits.[34]

At the very least, for Nietzsche, the Darwinian account of evolution is an impoverished view of life and of the actual struggle to expand and to increase in power. As he will emphasize in later writings, not self-preservation but will to power is the fundamental instinct.[35]

In a striking comment on evolution theory in general, he says:

> If the doctrines of sovereign Becoming, of the liquidity of all . . . species, of the lack of any cardinal distinction between man and animal—doctrines which I consider true but deadly—are hurled into the people for another generation . . . then nobody should be surprised when . . . brotherhoods with the aim of robbery and exploitation of the non-brothers . . . will appear on the arena of the future. [36]

So Nietzsche apparently thought that some version of evolution theory was true but dangerous. If people were told about it they might descend to robbing and exploiting one another. It is remarkable that he didn't notice that they had been doing that and worse for a very long time before Darwin (or Lamarck) appeared on the scene.

Nietzsche levels a variety of other objections at what he takes to be Darwin's view. He denies that there is any progress from lower to higher, he thinks the notion of species to be grossly overrated in comparison with the truly valuable individual ego, he believes that the accidents in the struggle for existence serve the weak and ill-adapted as much as they serve the strong, and he argues that nature actually favours the mastery of the mediocre.[37]

In spite of Nietzsche's many reservations about some of Darwin's views, Russell rightly counted him among the Evolutionist philosophers, along with Pragmatists like William James.[38] What both James and Nietzsche *do* seem to share is a determination to challenge the framework of fixed categories that had been home to traditional philosophy. To Russell, with his focus on issues in the philosophy of mathematics and logic, such a challenge would not be tolerated.

While Nietzsche's positive influence on the development of analytic philosophy and phenomenology was minimal, some of his concerns about Darwinism later recur in both traditions. In particular, skepticism about the supposed progress of the evolutionary process, concern about the value of the individual human being and about the efficacy of individual human efforts, and worries about certain repugnant socio-political consequences that might follow from acceptance of natural selection—each of these concerns will surface again at the turn of the century.

Another opponent of Darwinism who was nonetheless firmly in the Evolutionist camp was Henri Bergson. He shared with Nietzsche, James and Dewey a distrust of immutable categories. He insisted on the flowing character of reality and believed that our most reliable access to it was by way of what he called "intuition." His preference for intuition over the fixed nature of intellectual classifications irritated Russell. As in the case of Nietzsche and the Pragmatists, Russell saw Bergson's views as contesting the timeless validity of logic and mathematics, and the unalterable status of truth. As a consequence, he saw Bergson's views as challenging the very possibility of both science and philosophy itself. Russell had the same general difficulty with Bergson's views that he had with Spencer's—in his judgment they suffered from a lack of clarity and supporting argument. And, as in the case of Spencer, Bergson's account of an evolutionary philosophy was taken to be a good example of why philosophy and evolution are not relevant to one another. I shall return to a more detailed account of Russell's quarrels with Bergson in Chapter Three. For now, the point is that he, like Spencer and the American Pragmatists provided some of the background against which Russell, and to some extent, Moore, judged the evolutionary issue for philosophy.

If Henri Bergson and Herbert Spencer were the villains for some in England, it is likely that Ernst Haeckel played that role in Germany. He, too, was a vigorous supporter of evolutionary views, although his views were not exclusively Darwinian. And while the vehemence of his support for evolution apparently intimidated some, it is likely that his use of it to attack religion was particularly objectionable to philosophers like Husserl. In his dismissal of evolution from philosophy, Husserl makes no mention of Haeckel or other German Evolutionists, but he can hardly have been unaware of the controversies surrounding Haeckel's attitudes. As we shall see, Husserl had far more radical reasons for his rejection of evolution theory from philosophy. Still, it is not implausible to suppose that Haeckel and others like him played some role.

John Stuart Mill, unlike the clear supporters and opponents, was ambivalent about Darwin's views. Although he was somewhat favorably impressed by Darwin's views, in the end he counts as neither a supporter nor an opponent. In spite of his thinking that Darwin might be right, he made no effort to incorporate Darwin's views into his own philosophy. In this regard perhaps, Russell and Moore followed more closely in Mill's footsteps than in those of any other nineteenth-century thinker with respect to the issue of evolution. They differed from Mill, of course, in some of the explicit reasons they offered for leaving evolution and Darwin to one side, but the outcome for philosophy was roughly the same.

In his *System of Logic*, Mill praises Darwin for opening "a path of inquiry full of promise, the results of which none can foresee."[39] In a letter to Alexander Bain, dated April 11, 1860, he says:

> I have read since my return here several things which have interested me, above all Darwin's book [*Origin of Species*]. It far surpasses my expectation. Though he cannot be said to have proved the truth of his doctrine, he does seem to have proved that it *may* be true which I take to be as great a triumph as knowledge and ingenuity could possibly achieve on such a question. Certainly nothing can be at first sight more entirely unplausible than his [Darwin's] theory, and yet after beginning by thinking it impossible, one arrives at something like an actual belief in it, and one certainly does not relapse into complete disbelief. [40]

But Mill's early optimism about the theory will weaken somewhat by the end of the decade. Sometime between 1868 and 1870, he wrote an essay entitled "Theism," in which he examines various proofs for Theism, looking for one that will stand up to the standards of scientific evidence and argument. He finds the Argument from Design to be the most promising. After considering the design exemplified in the eye, he finds a good inductive argument to support the claim that it had an intelligent designer. But he goes on to consider a parallel explanation for the eye by the theory of "survival of the fittest" and says:

> It must be acknowledged that there is something very startling, and *prima facie* improbable in this hypothetical history of Nature. [But] . . . Of this theory when pushed to this extreme point, all that can now be said is that it is not so absurd as it looks, and that the analogies which have been discovered in experience, favourable to its possibility, far exceed what anyone could have supposed beforehand. Whether it will ever be possible to say more than this, is at present uncertain. The theory if admitted would be in no way whatever inconsistent with Creation. But it must be acknowledged that it would greatly attenuate the evidence for it. [41]

Mill concludes the essay " ... in the present state of our knowledge, the adaptations in Nature afford a large balance of probability in favour of creation by intelligence. It is equally certain that this is no more than a probability; ... " By this time Mill's religious beliefs apparently prevented him from accepting Darwin's theory as unconditionally as his earlier response might have predicted. (It hardly needs to be said that Russell's reservations about evolution theory had nothing to do with a preference for the Design Argument.)

Mill's commitment to reform in society may also have contributed to his lack of enthusiasm for Darwin's views—especially as the latter were often mistakenly construed as making human beings completely subject to the vagaries of the impersonal forces in nature.[42] This concern with social and political reform will recur as a theme in the twentieth-century evaluation of Darwin, particularly in Russell's views of the matter. And since Mill was Russell's "godfather," there is some reason to think that Mill's influence on this issue was very likely direct.

And finally there were Karl Marx and Friedrich Engels. They harbored quite a different sort of ambivalence toward Darwin's theory. They clearly had none of Mill's interest in protecting the claims of religion against the scientific hypothesis. Nor were they hesitant about the validity of the hypothesis itself. Their concern centered instead on the scope of Darwin's theory. With respect to biology, Marx and Engels took Darwin's views on natural selection to be right; with respect to the social domain, however, they claimed that the materialist theory of history—with the materials and relations of production as the driving forces—was correct.[43]

In 1880 Engels wrote that Kant, with his nebular hypothesis, undid the stable universe of Newton. Hegel followed, he said, by offering a system in which "the whole world, natural, historical, intellectual, is represented as a process, i.e., as in constant motion, change, transformation, development; and the attempt is made to trace out the internal connection that makes a continuous whole of all this movement and development."[44] For Engels, Darwin has specified this developmental model for nature, and Marx has extended it to society.

There are, of course, some important similarities in the two approaches. Darwin as well as Marx and Engels offered theories based on historical development, and that development was driven by completely natural forces. Furthermore, both saw human beings as "fluid," shaped to a considerable extent by features of their environment. Both eschew the fixed types that had dominated much of western thought until the nineteenth century.

But the differences were equally important. Marx rejected the Malthusian doctrine that had apparently inspired Darwin to formulate his account of natural selection. For Marx, the struggle for existence ought not to be seen as resulting in the inevitable elimination of the weaker members of a society. Like Mill, he insisted on making a place for the *reform* of society in such a way that its weaker members, as well as its stronger ones, might survive and thrive. [45*]

There is no evidence that Moore or Husserl were impressed by any of Marx' views, and there is abundant evidence that Russell became a vehement opponent of Marxism. Nonetheless, all three philosophers in their construction of twentieth-century philosophy, sided with the view that society could be reformed in ways that might maximize the well-being of all its members. So whatever value Darwin's theory might have, its scope must not be extended beyond the realm of biology. Like Marx, the founders of analytic philosophy and phenomenology had no qualms about limiting the relevance of the biological theory of evolution.

The responses, then, of nineteenth-century philosophers to Darwin's theory were diverse. They ran a full continuum from enthusiastic approval, to ambivalence, to outright rejection. But each left its mark on the shape that twentieth-century philosophy took. Very little of it was shaped by supporters of Darwin who were "transformers." The work of William James and John Dewey did not come to dominate twentieth-century philosophy. In the English-speaking world it was the work of Moore and Russell that set the direction.[46*] And in the early years they led philosophy back to Plato, as far removed from Darwinian considerations as one might conceivably find oneself.[47*] And while the philosophy of Nietzsche surely had some impact on Continental thought, particularly Existentialism, its challenge to the fixed categories of the tradition was not assimilated into the phenomenology of Husserl. Furthermore, the influence of Existentialism on philosophical theories of perception and mind was minimal.

In fact, not much of the new philosophy was shaped even by "adjusters," like Herbert Spencer. It was molded largely by philosophers who, like Mill, proposed philosophical views that remained largely untouched by Darwin. In both Great Britain and Europe, some of the reservations about Darwinism that were expressed by earlier philosophers continued to be of concern to Moore, Russell, and Husserl. Not least among these was the fear that a Darwinian account of human beings somehow entailed the end of individual freedom and responsibility or the acceptance of repugnant sociopolitical consequences.

If the early philosophical response to Darwin had issued in clear, carefully argued, and positive proposals for integrating his views into certain aspects of philosophy, the reaction at the turn of the century might well have been different. As we shall see, however, the ambivalence of nineteenth-century philosophy toward Darwin left the door open for his exclusion by

Moore, Russell, and Husserl and consequently from a considerable amount of twentieth-century philosophy that followed.

Of course, there have been *pockets* of Darwinian philosophy through-out the twentieth century. Philosophy of biology, most notably, has con-cerned itself extensively with Darwin's views. More recently, "evolutionary epistemology" has become a center of debate.[48] And evolutionary ethics has returned to the philosophical arena.[49] But one could hardly say that Darwin has *transformed* the philosophical scene.[50]* As one writer put it as recently as 1986, "The Darwinian Revolution has only barely started to work its charm on philosophy. . . . A century and a quarter after the first appearance of *On the Origin of Species*, the time has surely come to take Darwin seriously."[51]

Biological Responses to Darwinism

I turn now to consider the second background factor that very likely exercised some influence on philosophical decisions at the turn of the century. That factor was the unsettled state of *biological* views on evolution around that time.

As philosophers surveyed the cultural scene looking for new para-digms for philosophy, one would expect that they would be drawn quite naturally to the sciences. In particular, one might expect that developments in both physics and biology would catch their attention. In 1905 Einstein published some of his most important work; in 1900 the papers of Gregor Mendel were rediscovered; in 1871 Darwin had published his *Descent of Man*, in 1859, his *Origin of Species*.

But G.E. Moore had no interest or formal training in science. So, not surprisingly, his formulation of analytic philosophy bears no stamp of either contemporary scientific method or content. Russell, by contrast, was quite familiar with developments in science, especially in physics. And it is possible that his insistence on physics, rather than biology, as the science on which philosophy could model its method, might have been motivated at least indirectly by the disarray in biology. Husserl, continuing in the tradi-tions of Descartes and Kant, was determined to establish new philosophical foundations for the sciences. One of Husserl's motivations for insisting on the need for such foundations could conceivably have been his recognition of the unsettled condition of the biological sciences.

What, then, was the state of biology and of evolution theory during the first third of the century?

After Darwin published *Origin of Species* it did not take long for large numbers of biologists to become convinced that evolution had indeed taken place. The idea of evolution had been around for a very long while. And what Darwin provided to biologists was a plausible account of the mechanism that could explain how it occurred, namely natural selection. But it also did not take long for opposition to Darwin's views to build in various quarters. Ernst Mayr notes that Nordenskiold's *History of Biology*, published in 1928, claimed that Darwinism was virtually dead, having been attacked on most if its essential claims. Mayr goes on to say that "contemporary European literature indicates that this statement reflected a widespread, if not prevailing opinion."[52] Mayr lists *five* types of evolution theories that were functioning between 1860 and 1940—Geoffroyism, orthogenesis (including original Lamarckism), saltationism (including Mutation theory), Darwinism, and neo-Darwinism. He says "most authors between 1860 and 1940 adopted a mixture of these theories." Peter Bowler adds one more, theistic evolution, where the process is directed by God.[53] So biologists were far from any consensus at the turn of the century.

Consider in a bit more detail just what some of the issues were that faced Darwin's account of evolution.

In the earliest years, theology was probably its chief opponent. Natural selection was clearly meant to replace the work of an intelligent, divine designer. And along with the work of the Creator, many other portions of the biblical history of human beings could be called into question by Darwin's account of things. Many of the clergy were troubled. But, until the fairly recent resurrection of creationism, the theological opposition gradually moved from center stage. What followed it was perhaps even more damaging to Darwin's views; there was an increasingly splintered reaction on the part of scientists themselves.

In 1868 William Thompson (Lord Kelvin) argued that the earth could not possibly be as old as Darwin's theory required it to be. His calculations were later proven wrong, but at the time he provided one reason for scientists to be cautious.

Among biologists there were a host of troubling questions. There was concern about gaps in the fossil record. These indicated a lack of evidence for the gradual transitions among species that the Darwinian theory required. There were questions about the plausibility of "blending" inheritance (where the characteristics of parents were thought to blend in their offspring) because significant variations would likely be swamped by it, making species-formation problematic.[54] There was, in addition, widespread dissatisfaction with Darwin's theory of "pangenesis."

Many biologists were also unhappy about Darwin's account of secondary sexual characteristics. It seemed clear that these provided a problem for natural selection because such characteristics (like the peacock's tail) appeared to have no utility in the struggle for existence and in fact seemed to put the organism in some danger. Darwin had provided his theory of *sexual* selection to account for them. But for some scientists it was unthinkable that the female of the species had any aesthetic sensibility such that beautiful colors in a tail or beautiful songs by a male bird could lead the female to *choose* a partner on the basis of these characteristics.[55] If the theory of sexual selection was unacceptable, and natural selection alone could not account for secondary sexual characteristics, then Darwin's account of natural selection was in jeopardy.[56*]

There was even some question about the reality and role of the struggle for existence. Vernon Kellogg suggested in 1908 that if it exists at all it must be largely over before the organism reaches maturity.[57] We will find echoes of this view in some of Russell's criticisms.

On a more global level, there were objections that Darwin's theory was not good science since it was not based on either observation or mathematics, as every good scientific theory should be.[58*]

In addition, there were systemic problems within the discipline of biology itself that contributed to an absence of consensus about the mechanisms involved in evolution. Biology was divided into a number of virtually independent sub-disciplines like paleontology, zoology, genetics, botany, embryology, cytology, and comparative physiology. In conjunction with these divisions, biologists were generally either experimentalists, like the geneticists, or field naturalists, like the paleontologists. The experimentalists concerned themselves chiefly with what Mayr calls "proximate causes," microevolutionary issues involved, for example, in genetic changes. The field naturalists, on the other hand, looked for "ultimate causes," factors in macroevolution like species formation. The methods and goals and vocabularies of each group were distinctive. Sub-disciplines each had their own journals that were rarely read by members of other sub-disciplines. As a consequence, they were not in a position to learn about and build on one another's insights.[59] Instead, each group regarded the others' work with suspicion. These factors undoubtedly contributed their share to the long delay in the development of the Evolutionary Synthesis that provided some degree of cohesion to biology by the 1940s.

But perhaps the issues that most divided the biological community centered on variation and on the role of natural selection. The first of these was a difficulty recognized by Darwin himself. His theory provided no account of the *origin* of variations. That they occurred was clear; how they occurred remained a mystery. Darwin's claim was simply that they were random, small, and continuous, and that they formed the raw material on which natural selection worked to generate new species.

One of the opposing views that developed was called *orthogenesis*. It developed in at least two forms. On one view variations were the product of an internal drive within the organism itself—a sort of *elan vital*—that directed species-formation. On the other view, variations were the product of environmental influences like climate or food supply. In either case, the development of variations was a directed, not a random process. In the absence of convincing scientific evidence for the presence of such inner drives or such a directed process, orthogenesis gradually faded as a significant competing theory. Versions of the view, however, have continued to appear through the years, perhaps most recently in the work of Teilhard de Chardin.

A second area of controversy concerned the precise connection between variations and the process of species formation. For Darwin, the process was directed by natural selection, culling small, favorable variations and eliminating unfavorable ones. One of the objections to Darwin's view on this point was that small, continuous variations could never by themselves really be favorable in the struggle for existence until they had become larger and more complex. Further, it was argued that such variations were capable of only linear, quantitative changes, and were incapable of accounting for the qualitative changes required for the formation of new species. In fact, one of Darwin's earliest and staunchest supporters, T.H. Huxley, as well as Darwin's cousin, Francis Galton, both opposed Darwin on this and supported the the view that larger, discontinuous variations were required for the formation of new species.[60]

As a response to this concern, Hugo de Vries proposed a competing theory, the *Mutation theory*.[61] It claimed that the small variations of Darwin's account played no role at all in species formation. Rather, large discontinuous mutations occurred, having no relation to utility but giving rise to new species at one stroke. Natural selection's only role in the process was to eliminate the unfit species.[62]

As things turned out, the Mutation theory contributed to one of the decisive divisions among biologists in the early decades of the century. Shortly after Darwin had published *Origin of Species*, Gregor Mendel published the results of his experiments on heredity in plants. Mendel's paper contained the seeds of the solution to the problems surrounding variation. Unfortunately, neither Darwin nor most other biologists knew anything about Mendel's work at the time. It was not rediscovered until 1900. But instead of being used to complete the lacunae in Darwin's theory, it provided the occasion for further and even more damaging divisions among biologists. The work of Francis Galton was instrumental in this.

In the 1890s Galton had proposed a view with two distinct and influential aspects. On the one hand, his view encouraged a mathematical, i.e., statistical, treatment of variations; on the other hand, it shared with T.H. Huxley the view that variations are discontinuous. Paradoxically, his views gave rise to a bitter dispute between partisans of each of its two aspects.

On one side a group of Darwinian biologists, including Karl Pearson and W.F.R. Weldon, capitalized on the *mathematical* portion of Galton's theory, calling their view "biometry." They were committed to the directive powers of natural selection, to blending inheritance, and to a statistical approach to the continuous variations proposed by Darwin's theory. A second group, supporters of *discontinuous variations* of the sort proposed by the Mutation theory, and of Mendel's views on particulate inheritance, included William Bateson and Hugo de Vries. This second group, the "Mendelians," convinced that Mendelian inheritance required discontinuous variations, claimed that Mendel's work proved that Darwin was mistaken. Part of the conflict between the Mendelians and the Darwinians centered on whether particulate (Mendelian) inheritance was consistent with Darwin's small, continuous variations. The Mendelians supposed that only large, discontinuous mutations were particulate in the required sense. Unfortunately, the biometricians agreed that Mendel's view was incompatible with Darwin's.

Theoretical disagreements were further fueled by personal antagonisms among the disputants. The conflict between the Darwinians and the Mendelians reached its pitch during the first decade of the century. But versions of the dispute continued until the Evolutionary Synthesis, begun in the 1920s, concluded by the 1940s. In the interim various pieces of research began to show that Mendelism and Darwinism were actually consistent. Ernst Mayr, R.A. Fisher, J.B.S. Haldane, and Sewall Wright were among the architects of that synthesis.[63]

One additional, longstanding competitor in the field of evolution theories was Lamarckism. Darwin himself had incorporated aspects of Lamarck's view into his own but always subordinate to natural selection. On the Lamarckian view, individual organisms developed habits in response to the exigencies of their environment. These habits were capable of altering the structure of the organism itself and could then be passed on to some of the offspring. What made this view particularly attractive to some was the fact that variations were to some considerable extent within the control of individual organisms. By their constructive responses to their environment these organisms could thereby play a role in the direction that evolution took. Such a view seemed to leave ample room for notions like biological progress, social improvement, and individual responsibility.[64] It was also able to account for some of the problems that faced natural selection, for example it could explain the degeneration of useless organs. Versions of Lamarckism persisted into the 1930s. Its one drawback was that it, like orthogenesis (with which it had much in common) and the Mutation theory, apparently had little solid scientific evidence to support it. However, a number of philosophers as well as biologists found aspects of Lamarckism appealing, Herbert Spencer and Henri Bergson among them.

Much of what I have said here about biological disputes in the English-speaking world was true also in Germany. Although evolution theory was widely accepted very early, there was considerable disagreement about its causes. Most prominent in the disputes were Ernst Haeckel and August Weismann. Haeckel accepted a combination of natural selection and Lamarckism, and his view was shared by Theodor Eimer and Paul Kammerer. Weismann, who had earlier supported some version of directed variation, became a vehement opponent of Lamarckian inheritance. It was he who distinguished "germ plasm" as the vehicle for heredity, separating it decisively from the rest of the body. Acquired characteristics could not possibly be inherited if he was right. Unfortunately, Weismann's theory was not entirely consistent with Mendelian inheritance, and its lack of experimental support left it open to much criticism in the early years.[65] Spencer, among others, opposed him.

In addition to the quarrels about Lamarckism, German biologists also entered into the controversy over de Vries' Mutation theory. As in England, the divisions continued into the 1930s. Eberhart Dennert published a book in Germany in 1903, whose title translates as *At the Deathbed of Darwinism.*[66]

This brief sketch of the status of evolutionary biology in the early decades of the century is far from complete.[67] It is meant primarily to give the reader some insight into the situation that a philosopher would confront when considering whether or not to incorporate Darwin's theory into the new philosophy that was being formed. Given the many disputes among biologists themselves about the viability of Darwin's views, it is perhaps not entirely surprising that philosophers might feel some hesitation about building them into a new philosophic framework. The biological view of evolution may have looked to philosophers far too confused to be a safe bet for incorporation into the new versions of philosophy they were constructing. And as for a new method on which philosophy ought to pattern itself, biology may have presented anything but an ideal model of coherence and reliability. Coupled with the ambivalence of nineteenth-century philosophers with respect to Darwin, the outcome was perhaps predictable.

Having looked at some of the historical and scientific backdrop against which Moore, Russell, and Husserl made their decisions about the future of philosophy, I turn now to examine the *explicit* reasons that each of them gave for the exclusion of evolution and Darwin from their respective philosophic traditions. As we shall see, the background considerations we have discussed will figure into some of the explicit reasons offered by the philosophers—especially Russell.

Chapter 2

G.E. Moore And Evolutionary Ethics

The influence of the fallacious opinion that to be 'better' means to be 'more evolved' was illustrated by an examination of Mr Herbert Spencer's Ethics; and it was pointed out that, but for the influence of this opinion, Evolution could hardly have been supposed to have any important bearing upon Ethics.
—G.E. Moore (1903)

Introduction

G. E. Moore, it is commonly agreed, was the first to set the new direction for British analytic philosophy. Readers familiar with Moore's philosophy may find odd any effort to discuss his attitude toward Darwin. Part of that oddness is attributable to the fact that Moore's approach to philosophy was for the most part as innocent of scientific influence as one could find. In a wonderfully appropriate line John Passmore says of Moore that "... neither Freud, nor Marx, nor Einstein, so far as one can judge, has affected his thinking in the least."[1] Darwin had a similar impact.

And if one looks only to Moore's epistemology, it might seem as if he largely ignored Darwin. One is tempted to take him at his word when he says that neither the world nor science ever suggested any philosophic problems to him.[2] This in turn might be attributed to his lack of formal training in science and his apparent lack of interest in it.[3] But it would strain credibility that such a significant lacuna could be traceable to nothing more than an oversight. Moore was, after all, an educated man—educated, like Darwin, at Cambridge.

The fact is that Moore did not simply ignore Darwin. To see this clearly, however, one needs to look not at his epistemology but at his ethics, most notably his *Principia Ethica*. It is there that he offers a critique of Herbert Spencer's attempt to relate evolution and ethics, and he dismisses it as a hopeless deadend for moral theory.

It might seem that a discussion of Moore's critique of what he called "evolutionistic ethics" would be a digression from our main concern. The central issue is, after all, the relation between evolution theory and theories of perception and mind. But for Moore (and for Russell, as I shall later argue), the early encounter with evolutionary ethics was a decisive factor in his failure to incorporate evolutionary insights into his emerging philosophy, including his theories of perception. If it can be shown that his reasons for excluding evolutionary ethics are open to question, then perhaps the consequences for his theories of perception can be reevaluated.

In what follows I shall not be concerned to provide a detailed account of Moore's ethics nor an extensive evaluation of it. Neither will I provide a detailed analysis and evaluation of Spencer's ethics. It is not my purpose here to argue the case for either Spencer or Moore. Both of their moral theories are, in my view, problematic. What I shall do is examine some of the broader reasons that Moore apparently had for rejecting evolution theory as irrelevant to ethics in particular and to philosophy in general.

As a start, it may be useful to make some comments about Moore's attitude toward Darwin and the theory of natural selection. In the process, one begins to get a feel for his attitude on the broader issue of the relationship between science and philosophy.

Darwin and Science

As early as 1898, in a series of lectures entitled, "Elements of Ethics," Moore makes explicit reference to Darwin's views. This reference will be repeated, almost verbatim, five years later in his *Principia Ethica*.

> Darwin formed a *strictly biological hypothesis* as to the manner in which certain forms of animal life became established, while others died out and disappeared. . . . It was very natural to suppose that evolution meant evolution from what was lower into what was higher; . . . The doctrine of evolution was then represented as an explanation of how the higher species survives the lower. . . . But please note that this forms no part of Darwin's *scientific theory*. . . . the value of the scientific theory, and it is a theory of great value, just consists in shewing what are the causes which produce certain *biological effects*. Whether these effects are good or bad it cannot pretend to judge.[4] [Italics added.]

The first thing the quote makes clear is that Moore's attitude toward the relationship between evolution and philosophy was not the result of his rejection of *Darwin's* views. His attitude was neither anti-Darwinian nor anti-evolutionary. Furthermore, there is no reason to think that he preferred Lamarckism or orthogenesis or Mutation theory. Moore's concerns apparently had no connection with the disagreements occurring in biology at the time. In fact, he gives no indication that he was even aware of them. But in the context of ethical theorizing, it would not be unreasonable to suppose that someone in Moore's position would be more favorably inclined toward a Lamarckian rather than a Darwinian view of things.

As it happened, at the time Moore was writing, Lamarckism, was still considered by some to be a satisfactory account of evolution. Recall that Darwin had himself included strains of Lamarckism in his own account. By the mid-1880s August Weismann had proposed his theory of the "germ plasm," insisting on the impossibility of the inheritance of acquired characteristics. But in spite of the fact that the viability of Lamarckism was called into question, it remained one of the competing theories into the 1930s.

What made Lamarckism particularly appealing to some moral theorists and social reformers was their reluctance to put "nature" in the driver's seat, as Darwin's account of natural selection appeared to do. Mutation theory and orthogenesis similarly put the direction of evolution outside the control of human effort. Moralists and reformers preferred an account of evolution that made room for the long-term significance of individual human *effort*. And Lamarck's account did just that. If an individual worked hard to acquire some habit or skill, she might pass that on to her offspring. On this view, change was very much under the control of human beings and was not simply a function of impersonal natural forces.

Given this scenario, one might assume that Moore, as a turn-of-the-century moral theorist, simply opted for a Lamarckian account of evolution and that Darwin fell by the wayside as a consequence of this choice. But there is fairly clear evidence that this was not the case. Moore's specific objections to evolutionary ethics are aimed at Herbert Spencer's work which incorporates clear Lamarckian strains. Spencer's moral theory, for example, extols the value of effort on the part of individuals to contribute to the progress of evolutionary change.[5] So the plausibility of Darwin's view as contrasted with Lamarck's, or with any of the other available theories of evolution, is not the issue for Moore. Notice that he says, in fact, that Darwin's is "a theory of great value."

But the quote from Moore notes that Darwin's biological theory must be strictly distinguished from moral considerations. "Whether these [biological] effects are [morally] good or bad it [the scientific theory] cannot pretend to judge." As a consequence, Darwin's valuable theory was strictly a matter for biology (as it had been for Marx). Moore's conviction that science and ethics are completely discrete domains may also help to explain why Moore was not motivated to opt for any other evolutionary view. He apparently saw no reason to think that *any* theory of evolution had consequences for our moral evaluations of human behavior. Science concerns itself with factual (e.g., biological) claims, while ethics deals with normative claims. As a consequence, ethics must be cut loose from any dependence on the natural sciences.[6]*

There is one more thing to notice about Moore's comment on Darwin. When he says that Darwin's is a strictly biological theory, that might suggest Moore did not realize that Darwin himself had proposed an evolutionary account of the moral sense and of moral values in his *Descent of Man* in 1871. Indeed, Moore makes no mention of that work and gives no indication that he was acquainted with it. But I suspect that a more plausible account of the omission is that Moore was influenced in his attitude toward Darwin's book by his former teacher at Cambridge, Henry Sidgwick. Sidgwick was familiar with Darwin's *Descent of Man* and was convinced that its claims about morality, in particular about the origin of the moral sense, were not relevant to moral philosophy.[7] Moore simply may have accepted Sidgwick's view on the matter and felt on that account there was no reason to mention the book.

Whatever his actual reasons, Moore appears to have believed that Darwin had proposed nothing more than a very valuable biological hypothesis, and one had to look to Spencer and others for any attempt to draw moral consequences from it.

The quote from Moore closes with a puzzling comment. He says that the scientific theory cannot judge whether the biological effects of natural selection are good or bad. That is surely true. But why should one suppose that an evolutionary ethics must base itself on the claim that the theory of natural selection itself provides a moral evaluation of the results of natural selection? This extraordinarily narrow reading of an ethics based on evolutionary considerations was, I believe, the result of Moore's interpretation of Spencer's views. As I shall argue later in the chapter, Darwin provided a dramatically different account of the relation between evolution and ethics—an account that has considerably greater plausibility than the one Moore rejects here.

Spencer and Ethics

The primary target of Moore's critique of efforts to link evolution and ethics is not Darwin, but Herbert Spencer. To appreciate the historical importance of Moore's critique of Spencer's ethics, consider some recent comments that have been made about that critique. Robert Richards, writing in 1987, puts the point well: "Moore is generally thought to have demonstrated the fallacy of Spencer's position, and thus to have rendered any further efforts at constructing an evolutionary ethics sterile."[8] (Richards, in fact, believes that evaluation to be mistaken.) Twenty years earlier, in 1966, Anthony Quinton noted that efforts by men like Julian Huxley and C.H. Waddington to reintroduce evolutionary considerations into ethics were largely ignored by philosophers because of the "extraordinary authority and influence of G.E. Moore's refutation of naturalism. First presented to the world in his *Principia Ethica* in 1903 it has dominated philosophical inquiry into morals in Great Britain ever since."[9]*

Given the tremendous repercussions of Moore's critique of Spencer (and Naturalism) for the future of ethics in the analytic tradition, it will be useful to look, at least briefly, at both Spencer's views on ethics and Moore's criticisms of those views.

Spencer was, in his prime, an enormously influential figure in nineteenth-century British and American thought. He published a large number of books and essays during the last half of the century, covering aspects of both the natural and the social sciences as well as philosophy. Because his influence on twentieth-century philosophy has largely evaporated, it is perhaps difficult for us to realize just how significant a force he was a century ago. One reason for his diminished stature is that later philosophers—Moore and Russell prominent among them—objected that he was not given to providing careful arguments in support of his many sweeping claims. And whatever other characteristics analytic philosophy may have, emphasis on the importance of careful argument is surely one of them.

Further, Spencer's theories came to be identified with "Social Darwinism," a view that many saw as encouraging a ruthless competitive attitude in society, culminating in the "survival of the fittest." Not surprisingly, reform-minded philosophers and social scientists were profoundly antagonistic to Social Darwinism. Spencer was the beneficiary of some of that antagonism. And while Spencer was indeed frequently guilty of making grand claims without giving them the benefit of supporting argument, it is less clear that his social views really entailed ruthless competition.[10]* There are texts that can be interpreted as supporting Social Darwinist goals, but there are others that appear to contradict that view. He says, for example,

> Goodness, standing by itself, suggests, above all other things, the conduct of one who aids the sick in re-acquiring normal vitality, assists the unfortunate to recover the means of maintaining themselves, defends those who are threatened with harm in person, property, or reputation, and aids whatever promises to improve the living of all his fellows.[11]

Statements like the foregoing surely call into question the easy identification of Spencer with the ruthless individualism generally associated with Social Darwinism.

While Moore's criticisms of Spencer's ethics do not focus explicitly on the issue of Social Darwinism, both it and Spencer's habit of omitting careful argument form part of the background of Moore's discussion.

The only one of Spencer's books to which Moore refers, both in his 1898 lectures on ethics and in his *Principia Ethica*, is *Data of Ethics* (1879).[12]* For that reason, in what follows, I too shall focus on just that one work.

I should perhaps begin by saying that Moore was somewhat ambivalent about his choice of Spencer to represent what he termed "evolutionistic ethics." There is clearly a strain of evolutionism in Spencer's *Data of Ethics*, but there is also a hedonistic aspect to his theory, and for Moore this latter dimension clouds the issue a bit. Moore proposes, in *Principia Ethica*, [PE] "to confine the term 'Evolutionistic Ethics' to the view that we need only to consider the tendency of 'evolution' in order to discover the direction in which we *ought* to go."[13]* Given Spencer's hedonism, as well as some lack of clarity in his account of his views, Moore isn't entirely sure that Spencer's is simply an evolutionary ethics. But Moore decides that Spencer's view is close enough. As he says at the conclusion of his critique in *Principia*:

> The influence of the fallacious opinion that to be 'better' means to be 'more evolved' was illustrated by an examination of Mr Herbert Spencer's Ethics; and it was pointed out that, but for the influence of this opinion, Evolution could hardly have been supposed to have any important bearing upon Ethics. (*PE*, 58)

So in the end, Spencer's account is not only judged to be a good enough representative of evolutionary ethics, it comes to serve as the paradigm case. Spencer was, in fact, the best-known of the evolutionary ethicists. And he had, coincidentally, been the subject of a series of critical lectures by Henry Sidgwick—lectures Moore attended as a student at Cambridge. So Spencer's view is selected to represent the only significant way that evolution might be thought to have any bearing on ethics.

There are three aspects of Spencer's view that are of particular relevance to Moore's critique: (i) his insistence that the notions of moral conduct and moral good should be understood as continuous with natural human conduct and natural goods; (ii) his belief in the progressive character of both biological and moral evolution; and (iii) his apparent belief that moral goodness is somehow determined by impersonal evolutionary forces in nature.

Since Spencer's views no longer form a particularly familiar portion of the history of philosophy, I shall say a bit about them in order to provide a context for Moore's objections.

A first point of dispute between Spencer and Moore centers around what counts as an adequate account of *good*.

Spencer opens *Data of Ethics* [*DE*] with a discussion of conduct, arguing that if one is to understand moral conduct one must have some understanding of conduct in general. This latter he defines as "acts adjusted to ends." (*DE*, 14) Placing this in an evolutionary context, he argues that as life forms become more complex (progressing from homogeneity to greater and greater heterogeneity), this adjustment of acts to ends also becomes more complex. So there is an evolution in conduct as well as in organic forms. Ethics, he says,

> . . . has for its subject-matter that form which universal conduct assumes during the last stages of its evolution. . . . these last stages in the evolution of conduct are those displayed by the highest type of being [human being], when he is forced, by increase of numbers, to live more and more in presence of his fellows. (*DE*, 31)

So ethics deals with evolved human conduct, and its origin lies in the needs generated by social interaction.

Spencer then looks to the notion of "good." Again he begins with the broad context, with a view to locating moral goodness within the framework of other types of goodness. Good objects or actions are those that are well adapted to achieve prescribed ends. (*DE*, 32) A primary end for living organisms is the preservation of their lives and the lives of their offspring. Good conduct, practically speaking, will be conduct that achieves that end. The goal or end of *ethical* conduct is to provide a long and pleasurable life for both self and others. Morally good conduct, then, is that which is well-adapted to achieve this end.

Here Moore thinks that Spencer commits, or comes close to committing, the naturalistic fallacy—the fallacious effort to define *the* good in terms of some natural property. He isn't entirely sure that Spencer has committed the naturalistic fallacy in the evolutionary side of his thought, but he decides that Spencer is at least "influenced" by such fallacious views.[14*] (Moore does not specify what it means to be "influenced" by a fallacy even when one has not committed that fallacy.) His hesitation about whether or not the fallacy has been committed arises from the fact that he is not sure whether Spencer means to *define* "better" as "more evolved" or merely to claim that being more evolved is a *criterion* of what is better in that it is a concomitant of it.

Moore's account of moral goodness is dramatically different from the one proposed by Spencer. In Moore's view, *moral* goodness, "the good," is a timeless object that cannot be defined in terms of any natural property. He sees a sharp division between natural goods and moral good. So one of his most basic disagreements with Spencer arises from the latter's naturalism.

On this point Moore was probably right about Spencer. Whether or not he committed the naturalistic fallacy in the evolutionary side of his ethics, there is good reason to believe that Spencer's ethics was naturalistic.

A great deal has been written on the subject of the naturalistic fallacy, and I have nothing original to contribute to that literature. But two points may be worth making. First, in later years Moore himself saw numerous difficulties with his characterization of the naturalistic fallacy, including the possibility that strictly speaking there was no *fallacy* involved. Nonetheless, he continued to argue that good was not a natural property.[15] Secondly, if it is the case that human beings have evolved through natural processes, it seems reasonable to suppose that there is a *natural* story that can be told about our moral sense and about the moral values that we have. Keeping in mind the fact that Moore did not reject Darwin's theory of evolution, one wonders why he thought that the moral sphere could be so thoroughly insulated from the accepted facts of human evolution. At any rate, if Naturalism is a mistake in ethics, then Moore was surely right in his critique of Spencer on that account.

A second concern for Moore is Spencer's progressionism. As early as 1851 Spencer wrote, "Progress, therefore, is not an accident, but a necessity."[16] And later, in one of his well-known essays, "Progress: Its Law and Cause," published in 1857, Spencer argues that the real nature of progress consists in the "change from the homogeneous to the heterogeneous."[17] The things that we commonly take to be progress—for example, an increase in the quantity or quality of things, particularly things that contribute to our happiness—are merely the accompaniments of this process. The move to complexity constitutes the substance of progress. And Spencer sees this progress as taking place at all levels of reality from the organic growth of individuals to the development of social and political institutions.

Ethical conduct, like conduct in general, evolves. And that evolution involves progress, the movement from homogeneity to heterogeneity.

> The better a man fulfills every requirement of life, alike as regards his own body and mind, as regards the bodies and minds of those dependent on him, and as regards the bodies and minds of his fellow citizens, the more varied do his activities become. The more fully he does all these things, the more heterogeneous must be his movements. (*DE*, 89)

So human beings will continue, in spite of occasional lapses, to improve in their ability to contribute to the "greatest totality of life" for both self and others. Ultimately, evolution is moving us toward an ideal condition in which society will progress from a state in which egoism prevails to one in which there is a balance of concern for self and others, from a society in which war is common to one in which industrialism will serve peacefully to satisfy the needs of all.

From Moore's point of view there are, I think, at least two problems with such a view. First, Moore says, "Spencer ... constantly uses 'more evolved' as equivalent to 'higher.' " (*PE*, 47) And on Moore's view, while it *might* be true that what is more evolved is higher or better, and that progress is assured, Spencer has not given any *reason* for thinking that this is the case. If Spencer thinks that it is obviously true in virtue of the meaning of the terms, that is, if he thinks that "more evolved" *means* "better" then he has committed the naturalistic fallacy. So Moore concludes that Spencer has either provided no argument for the progressive character of moral evolution or he has offered a type of argument that commits the naturalistic fallacy.

But Moore sees a second difficulty with the "progressionism" in Spencer's view. The "fact" from which Spencer derives ethical consequences is itself highly questionable. As Moore puts it,

> It was very natural to suppose that evolution meant evolution from what was lower into what was higher; in fact it was observed that at least one species, commonly called higher—the species man—had so survived, and among men again it was supposed that the higher races, ourselves for example, had shown a tendency to survive the lower, such as the North American Indians. We can kill them more easily than they can kill us. The doctrine of evolution was then represented as an explanation of how the higher species survives the lower. (*PE*, 47)

Moore is concerned here about at least three related claims: (a) evolution involves progress from lower to higher; (b) human beings are a more evolved and therefore "higher" species; and (c) among human beings, some "higher" races (like ourselves) survive "lower" races (like the North American Indians) because we are better at killing than they are.

Moore attributes both claims (a) and (b) to Spencer: evolution involves progress from lower to higher, and we humans are clearly among the higher species. And there is good evidence to support Moore's claims on this. In fact, for Spencer, human beings are the *highest* species. This is the sort of "fact" that Moore takes to be false, and that could not, therefore, provide the basis for a conclusion about moral progress. He argues that Darwin's theory "will explain equally well, how by an alteration in the environment ... quite a different species from man, a species which we think infinitely lower, might survive us." (*PE*, 47-48.) This is an important claim on Moore's part, for it clearly indicates that Moore did not see Darwin's theory as entailing progress.

As for the third claim, Moore does not explicitly attribute it to Spencer. But his reference to the killing of the Indians appears to be an effort to construct a sort of *reductio* argument against the progressive view of moral evolution. The survival of what we consider the higher races has been achieved by slaughtering our competitors. Moore's unasked question lies just below the surface: how could this conceivably be an example of *moral* progress?

For Moore there is no reason to believe that the facts of biological evolution entail either biological or moral progress. As he said, "It was very natural to suppose that evolution meant evolution from what was lower into what was higher.... But please note that this forms no part of Darwin's scientific theory.... "[18] How then could the facts of biological evolution entail moral consequences that are grounded on that progress? On this point Moore' objections to Spencer's progressionism are well-founded.

But there is good reason to doubt Moore when he goes on to say that the fallacy of claiming that "more evolved is better" is "constantly committed by those who profess to 'base' Ethics on Evolution." (*PE*, 49) One can acknowledge Spencer's progressionism without conceding that all evolutionary accounts of ethics are necessarily progressionist. Part of the difficulty here is that Moore does not specify the other theorists he has in mind who also "constantly" commit the fallacy of claiming that "more evolved is better." Whoever he is referring to, the general point that evolutionary ethics must commit that fallacy is surely false.

T.H. Huxley and John Dewey, both writing on evolutionary ethics in the 1890s, made no such claim. Huxley opposed basing ethics on evolutionary considerations, but neither he nor Dewey supposed that doing so entailed that more evolved is better. Freud's approach to ethics is also squarely within the evolutionary framework, with no such consequences. More recently, the views of James Rachels, Robert Richards, and numerous other theorists offer evolutionary approaches to ethics.[19]* None of these thinkers claim that "more evolved is better." None is committed to the view that morality is necessarily progressive.

So while Moore may be right in his critique of the progressionist aspect of Spencer's efforts to link evolution and ethics, the conclusion he draws is far too sweeping. His examination of one theorist, acknowledged to be not entirely representative, hardly supports the conclusion that the progressionist fallacy is constantly committed by those who profess to base ethics on evolution.

A third fundamental problem with Spencer's view, from Moore's standpoint, is that it seems to construe moral progress as the outcome of impersonal evolutionary forces in Nature. Moore characterizes 'Evolutionistic Ethics' as "the view that we ought to move in the direction of evolution simply *because* it is the direction of evolution. That the forces of Nature are working on that side is taken as a presumption that it is the right side." (*PE*, 56)

What is especially important in this quote is Moore's reference to the "forces of Nature" as the engine that is driving moral values. And there can be little doubt that Spencer does see the forces of nature as playing a large part in directing not only biological but also moral evolution. This is part of Moore's objection to the *naturalism* in evolutionary ethics. He characterizes one version of it as "a belief that Nature may be said to fix and decide what shall be good, just as she fixes and decides what shall exist." (*PE*, 42) And here he seems to mean by nature, something like the laws of nature or the general tendencies of the natural world. Within the evolutionary framework these forces of nature are easily identified with the processes involved in *natural selection*.

The difficulty with such a characterization is that it is far too narrow. One might well discredit a view like this one without thereby showing that all efforts to connect ethics and evolutionary considerations are hopeless.

There are at least two distinct ways of looking at the relationship between evolution and ethics. One—perhaps the most common, and clearly the one that Moore takes—involves assuming that the impersonal forces of evolution or natural selection themselves generate certain moral conse-quences. Spencer is generally taken as a partisan of some version of this view. But from Moore's point of view, even if Spencer is not completely guilty of holding this view, it *is* held by those who are thoroughly evolutionary in their ethics. (*PE*, 49) And this way of looking at the matter seems to have survived in some of the more recent literature on the subject. Both Anthony Flew [20*] and Anthony Quinton [21*] appear to characterize evolutionary ethics as the view that impersonal forces of evolution or its general direction are the source of moral value.

But a second way of seeing the relationship between evolution and ethics, argues that the origin of moral norms and values is not simply the impersonal forces of natural selection itself, nor the general direction of evolution, but rather *human reason*, coupled with the human desire to survive and to provide for the well-being of oneself and one's group. The context in which moral values and norms are constructed is the context of the struggle for life on the part of *intelligent, social* organisms. On this approach, no assumptions are made about the putative direction of evolution, and moral values are not seen as determined by blind and inexorable forces of nature. Darwin's view on the matter—which would surely be characterized as evolutionary—is that *human beings*, not the impersonal forces of nature, are the source of moral values.

If an intelligent, social animal hopes to survive and provide for its well-being, certain constraints on its behavior are required. Granted that reason is itself a *product* of natural selection, nonetheless it is not the single-purposed, unswerving force that natural selection is. It is a fallible tool with which human beings attempt to cope with their natural and social environments. Where the first approach takes moral norms and values to follow from impersonal, inexorable forces in nature, the second approach locates them in the consciously recognized needs of a group of fallible but rational human beings. I shall return to this second view when I discuss Darwin's account of morality. For now the point to notice is that efforts to link evolution with ethics are not limited to those mentioned by Moore. So even if Moore is justified in his criticisms of Spencer and of the type of ethics that he takes Spencer to represent, his arguments do not undermine all versions of evolutionary ethics.

For Moore, of course, the effort to locate the origin of moral value in intelligent human beings rather than impersonal forces of nature, does not constitute a significant improvement. It is just another form of Naturalism. And it is Naturalism in all its varieties that he is determined to undo. Moore sees the standard for moral goodness, *the* good, as being quite independent of all natural facts, including the decisions of human beings.

In Moore's later book, *Ethics* (1912), he omits the critique of Spencer and evolutionary ethics, but one can assume that this omission had nothing to do with a change in Moore's views about evolutionary ethics. Rather it is likely that the omission issued from a sense that evolutionary ethics was a dead issue. When Moore published a new edition of *Principia Ethica* in 1922, he said in the Preface that he was "still in agreement with its main tendency and conclusions; . . ." (*PE*, xii) In an unfinished and unpublished set of notes for a longer preface to that second edition, he finds fault with a number of his own comments about the naturalistic fallacy in the First Edition of the book, but Moore makes it clear that he continues to reject as an error any effort to define "good" in terms of *any* natural property.[22] One could reasonably assume that his negative verdict on evolutionary ethics remained unaltered. This assumption is confirmed by his claim in a 1928 lecture, that "Darwin's Theory of the Origin of Species, . . . has nothing more to do with philosophy than any other hypothesis of Natural Science. . . ."[23]

So far I have considered three of Moore's major difficulties with Spencer's account of evolutionary ethics—Spencer's progressionism, his naturalism, and his claim that the impersonal forces of nature determine moral values. If these are fair assessments of Spencer's view, and there is reason to think that they are, then Moore was justified in exposing them as problematic. As I have said, however, not all of these difficulties attend every account of evolutionary ethics.

One of the puzzling features of Moore's discussion of evolutionary ethics is his assumption that by pointing out difficulties in Spencer's views, he had effectively demolished all significant efforts to integrate the insights of evolution theory with moral theory. As Moore had put it, " . . . but for the influence of this opinion [Spencer's opinion that 'to be better' means 'to be more evolved'] Evolution could hardly have been supposed to have any important bearing upon Ethics." (*PE*, 58) Had Moore considered other accounts of the relation between evolution and ethics, he might have reached a different conclusion.[24*]

Perhaps the most troubling omission in Moore's discussion is Darwin himself, who had devoted a portion of his *Descent of Man* in 1871 to a discussion of the origin of the moral sense and of various moral values. Admittedly, Darwin does not offer a systematic *theory* of ethics. Still, he offers a number of provocative suggestions on the issue of evolution and ethics, and his approach to it was significantly different from that of Spencer. As I noted earlier, Sidgwick may have influenced Moore here. Sidgwick seems to have thought that Darwin's discussion of morality was simply irrelevant to philosophical ethics.

At any rate, it will be helpful to consider just what Darwin's views on morality were. This will afford an opportunity to see if Moore's quarrel with Spencer's views justifies his neglect of Darwin.

Darwin, Evolution, and Ethics

Darwin notes at the outset that "of all the differences between man and the lower animals, the moral sense or conscience is by far the most important."[25] He then offers an account of how the development of that moral sense might be explained within an evolutionary framework. He argues that one necessary condition for its development is the fact that we have *social instincts*.[26*] These, he says, with sympathy at their root, are the product of natural selection. Those individuals who tended to be concerned about the welfare of others in the group were themselves more likely to receive help from others when it was needed.[27*] As a consequence, such altruistic, cooperative individuals were more likely to survive and reproduce. In addition, these social instincts made humans susceptible to concern about the approval and disapproval of the other members of their group.

A second necessary condition for the development of the moral sense was the evolution of human *mental powers*. With these, human beings were better able to understand the expectations of the group, to remember those expectations, and to therefore become capable of remorse when they failed to meet them. For Darwin, this is the beginning of conscience.

Many other animals, he says, have the requisite social instincts, but they lack adequate mental powers to develop any significant sense of moral obligation. As human mental powers increased, particularly with the development of language, Darwin believes that the needs and expectations of the group could be expressed in greater detail, generating an increasingly refined awareness of what the group counted as acceptable behavior.

But the third dimension in the development of the moral sense was *community* selection.[28]* Darwin is often quoted as claiming that natural selection must always work on variations that benefit the *individual* that has them. In the *Origin* he says, for example, " . . . natural selection can act only through and for the good of each being, . . . (66) But on the very next page he also says, "In *social* animals it [natural selection] will adapt the structure of each individual for the benefit of the whole community; *if the community profits by the selected change.*" (67) [italics added].[29]*

At first glance, these two claims might be thought to be inconsistent. But careful attention to the scope of the second claim shows that they are not. A *social* animal is one whose individual well-being is inextricably bound up with the well-being of its social group. The social animal is precisely the one that cannot long survive or flourish without the direct support of its group, in the form of infant care and training, sharing of food and water, protection of the young, provision of sex partners, etc. Furthermore, each individual benefits indirectly from the overall fitness of the group. The swift, physically strong, wary, cooperative group is less vulnerable, for example, to attacks from other groups, to decimation by disease, hunger, etc. than is a slow, weak, inattentive, fragmented group. In all this, individual variations that strengthen the group have clear benefits to each individual in it as well as to the group. In social animals, individual and group welfare cannot easily be separated.

Darwin sees the development of the moral sense as a variation favored by natural selection because of its benefit to the community, and thereby to the individual. Insofar as some individuals fail to heed this moral sense, the whole community and every individual in it will to that extent be less fit than it might be.

So much for the evolution of the moral *sense*. What can be said about the *content* of our moral beliefs or the status of our moral values? Darwin remains concerned, throughout his discussion of morality, with issues of natural selection. He argues that the development of both social instincts and mental capacities were the products of natural selection. Both of these adaptations made humans better able to survive. The needs and expectations of the group likewise centered very heavily around the will to survive, so certain obligations were placed on each member of the group. Darwin notes that no human group can survive unless murder, treachery, lying, selfish and contentious behavior, and the like, are forbidden among its members. On the other hand, courage, self-sacrifice, self-command, fidelity obedience, and the like, must be required from each member of the group.

He points out that in the early development of morality, the focus was entirely on the welfare of the group or tribe—not the species and not the individual. What he calls the "self-regarding" virtues had little or no place because, he says, the intellectual powers of primitive human beings could not adequately trace the long-term consequences of actions. So they failed to understand that self-regarding virtues might ultimately be beneficial to the group. This recognition came in due course, he says.

It is also a consequence of limited intellectual powers that human beings have sometimes been mistaken about what was truly in the interest of the group. Thus practices like slavery seemed for a time to be in the interest of those who owned the slaves, but this was largely because the slaves belonged to a different tribe from their owners. And Darwin believed that as our intellectual capacity increases, so that we can recognize more and more of the consequences of our actions, the scope of our moral sense increases.

> As man advances in civilisation, and small tribes are united into larger communities, the simplest reason would tell each indiviudal that he ought to extend his social instincts and sympathies to all the members of the same nation, though personally unknown to him. This point being once reached, there is only an artificial barrier to prevent his sympathies extending to the men of all nations and races. . . . Sympathy beyond the confines of man, that is, humanity to the lower animals, seems to be one of the latest moral acquisitions.[30]

Darwin's account of the development of both the moral sense and moral values falls squarely within his account of natural selection, with a heavy emphasis on the central role played by the struggle for existence.

The issue that concerns us here is whether or not Darwin's views are susceptible to the objections Moore raised against Spencer's ethics. To the extent that Darwin's account is a form of *naturalism*, of course, Moore's objection remains.

Consider how Darwin defines *good*:

> In the case of the lower animals it seems much more appropriate to speak of their social instincts, as having been developed for the general good rather than for the general happiness of the species. The term, general good, may be defined as the rearing of the greatest number of individuals in full vigour and health, with all their faculties perfect, under the conditions to which they are subjected. As the social instincts both of man and the lower animals have no doubt been developed by nearly the same steps, it would be advisable, if found practicable, to use

the same definition in both cases, and to take as the standard of
morality, the general good or welfare of the community, rather than the
general happiness; but this definition would perhaps require some
limitation on account of political ethics.[31]

The general good is to be defined, then, not simply as happiness or pleasure
(as the Utilitarians might say) but as "the rearing of the greatest number of
individuals in full vigour and health, with all their faculties perfect, under
the conditions to which they are subjected."

Darwin's account of the general good has sometimes been interpreted
simply as "reproductive success." But it is clear from other things he says in
the same discussion that such an interpretation is far too narrow. He speaks
of *rearing* individuals, not merely of *reproducing* them. And he points out that
some individuals can do more good for the community by their teaching or
example than by leaving large numbers of offspring. "Great lawgivers, the
founders of beneficent religions, great philosophers and discoverers in
science, aid the progress of mankind in a far higher degree by their works
than by leaving a numerous progeny."[32]

The good to be achieved is not merely *survival*. Darwin also has in
mind the *well-being* of the members of the group—raising them "in full
vigour and health, with all their faculties perfect. . . ." Darwin explains his
emphasis on well-being:

> Now an animal may be led to pursue that course of action which is the
> most beneficial to the species by suffering, such as pain, hunger, thirst,
> and fear,—or by pleasure, as in eating and drinking and in the propa-
> gation of the species, etc. or by both means combined, as in the
> search for food. But pain or suffering of any kind, if long continued,
> causes depression and lessens the power of action; yet is well adapted
> to make a creature guard itself against any great or sudden evil.
> Pleasurable sensations, on the other hand, may be long continued
> without any depressing effect; on the contrary they stimulate the
> whole system to increased action. Hence it has come to pass that
> most or all sentient beings have been developed in such a manner
> through natural selection, that pleasurable sensations serve as their
> habitual guides.[33]

So human beings, along with other animals, seek not only survival but also
a sense of pleasurable well-being.[34]*

Still, with all the refinements in Darwin's view, it is clearly a form of
Naturalism. And given his definition of the general good, Moore would be
likely to convict him of committing the naturalistic fallacy. So Darwin's
views on morality suffer from at least one of the same defects that Moore
charged to Spencer's view.

What about progressionism? Spencer, I noted, appears to have urged that both biological and moral progress are necessary, albeit with an unconventional characterization of progress. Darwin, however, is not so clearly in the same camp. [35]*

There is an ongoing debate about the relationship between Darwin's theory and the necessity of progress. But for our present purposes only two issues are relevant: (i) Did *Moore* believe that Darwin's theory entailed progress? (ii) Did Darwin believe that his views entailed *moral* progress?

Consider issue (i): the answer to this question is clearly, no. He is quite explicit on the matter. On Moore's view, Darwin's theory of natural selection allows for no such progressive interpretation of evolution. As he says, the most complex forms (sometimes thought to be the most highly evolved) might well become extinct if they are unable to cope with a changing environment or are unable to compete adequately with other species. This, Moore says, would involve regression, not progress. (*PE*, 47-48)

As for issue (ii), whether Darwin believed that natural selection entailed *moral* progress, the case is more complex.[36]* But I think that Darwin's view on moral progress needs to be seen at least partly in the context of his quarrel with creationist accounts of "The Fall." Counteracting the view that humans were *created* civilized and then degenerated to barbarism (a view he attributes to Archbishop Whately, and one which readily calls to mind the story of the Fall in the Garden of Eden), Darwin argues that the reverse case is better supported by the evidence. "To believe that man was aboriginally civilised and then suffered utter degradation in so many regions, is to take a pitiably low view of human nature. It is apparently a truer and more cheerful view that progress has been much more general than retrogression; that man has risen, though by slow and interrupted steps, from a lowly condition to the highest standard as yet attained by him in knowledge, morals and religion."[37] Darwin is at pains to reassert our origins from non-human primates, and to argue that our early history is not one of retrogression from a created state of perfection, but rather of progress from minimally rational ancestors to a point at which our mental and moral capacities far exceed theirs. But there are no *guarantees* for the future.[38]*

A related dimension of progress that Darwin considers is the progress of *society*. He is quite clear about this case. Natural selection does not entail the progress of human society. Progress depends on many different factors. He says,

> Here we have the tacit assumption, so often made with respect to corporeal structures, that there is some innate tendency towards continued development in mind and body. *But development of all kinds*

depends on many concurrent favourable circumstances. Natural selection acts only in a tentative manner. Individuals and races may have acquired certain indisputable advantages, and yet have perished from failing in other characters. The Greeks may have retrograded from a want of coherence between the many small states, from the small size of their whole country, from the practice of slavery, or from extreme sensuality; . . . [39] [Italics added.]

Referring to civilization, he says, "We must remember that progress is no invariable rule."[40] There may indeed be progress of some sort. But there need not be. He says, " . . . we are apt to look at the progress as normal in human society; but history refutes this."[41]

So while there is surely some evidence that Darwin saw evolution leading to moral progress, it is less clear that he saw this progress as inevitable. He was at least concerned to counter the view that human beings were created morally perfect and have regressed since their time in the Garden of Eden. Darwin's account of evolutionary ethics is clearly a form of Naturalism, but it is less obvious that he saw it as leading to inevitable moral progress in the same sense that Spencer's view did.

Moore's third objection to Spencer's account of ethics is that it puts the source of moral values in certain impersonal forces of nature. Moore characterizes it as "the view that we ought to move in the direction of evolution simply *because* it is the direction of evolution." (*PE*, 56) Darwin's account escapes this charge. Impersonal nature (in the guise of natural selection) does not by itself generate any *oughts*. Natural selection has no investment in *our* survival or well-being. The *oughts* arise from us as intelligent social beings who decide to aim our behavior at what seems most likely to be beneficial to us in the long-run.

Our decisions about what counts as desirable and undesirable behavior can, of course, be mistaken or ambivalent. Witness our past decisions about slavery or our more recent debates about abortion. Our understanding and foresight are limited and fallible. But moral values are the product of human efforts to regulate behavior in ways most likely to be conducive to individual and collective survival and well-being.

There are, of course, some *facts* about the natural and social environment that are likely to make certain types of behavior contribute in positive ways to our goals and make other types of behavior contribute negatively. But "the direction of evolution" has nothing to do with it. And it is not the case, on Darwin's view, that whatever natural selection produces is thereby morally valuable. In short, Darwin's account of moral values does not attribute any moral authority to the impersonal forces of natural selection or its alleged direction.

Background Assumptions

In an effort to highlight some of the factors that seem to have allowed Moore to segregate evolution and ethics, I want to consider two of the important background assumptions that he brought to his discussion of ethics and of Spencer. These, I shall argue, were quite sufficient by themselves to generate the conclusions Moore reached, even without his offering any detailed critcism of Spencer. There are, I shall argue, difficulties with each of these background considerations.[42*]

My discussion concerns: (i) the formulation of the fundamental questions of ethics; and (ii) the method for answering these questions.

(i) The formulation of the fundamental questions of ethics

In the opening lines of the Preface to *Principia Ethica* Moore says: "It appears to me that in Ethics, as in all other philosophical studies, the difficulties and disagreements, of which its history is full, are mainly due to a very simple cause: namely to the attempt to answer questions, without first discovering precisely *what* question it is which you desire to answer." (*PE*, vii) Readers familiar with Moore will recognize this as a concern that pervades his philosophy.

It is instructive to observe the way in which Moore himself formulates the fundamental questions of ethics. Noticing how he frames the *questions* is important in that it makes clear just what sorts of answers could possibly be found satisfactory. He has three fundamental questions (although he occasionally collapses them into two):

1. *What is meant by good?*
   His well-known answer is that " 'good' denotes a simple and indefinable quality." (*PE*, 10) He also claims that goodness—like numbers—cannot exist in time and is not a part of nature. (*PE*, 110-111)
2. *What things are good in themselves?*
   He will list a few things, like "the pleasures of human intercourse and the enjoyment of beautiful objects." (*PE*, 188) But these are meant only as plausible examples, part of a long list of possible candidates to which each individual may append what seems to him or her to be other reasonable additions.
3. *What causal relations hold between what is best in itself and other things— so that we can maximize the goodness in the world.* (*PE*, 37)
   Here he sees room for a great many different answers. Individuals with varying dispositions and changing circumstances will need different means to achieve the end of maximizing the good. (*PE*, 22-23)

One of the striking features of Moore's formulation of these questions is the *platonism* from which they emerge. A question like "what things are good *in themselves?*"—suggests that the true answer is completely independent of context and is thus fixed and timeless. In fact, Moore makes it quite clear that what we mean by the adjective "good" belongs to the class of timeless objects. That is, it will be a value holding in all possible worlds. This assumption of the timelessness and unchanging character of goodness is undoubtedly related to Moore's desire to establish ethics on an objective basis and his decision to use a platonic framework to do it. He is quite explicit about his commitment to platonism. Moore wrote to Desmond MacCarthy in 1898: "I am pleased to believe that this is the most Platonic system of modern times."[43] This platonic system to which Moore refers continued at least through his publication of *Principia Ethica*. Its importance in relation to Moore's formulation of the questions of ethics is that it plays a limiting role in establishing the *sorts* of answers that could possibly be found acceptable. Moore, of course, would have known this better than anyone. One of his most fruitful contributions to philosophy was his emphasis on getting very clear about the meaning of the questions that were being asked before attempting to provide answers to them. And Moore's way of posing the questions of ethics is, among other things, profoundly inimical to the sorts of answers that would issue from evolutionary frameworks. The latter are permeated with time, development, and mutability.

So Moore, in spite of his apparent acceptance of evolution as a fact about human beings, argues for the complete independence of ethical values from the whole framework within which human beings evolved. He posits instead a realm of timeless, immutable goodness (and beauty and truth) and of things that ought to exist for their own sakes—for which, he acknowledges, no relevant evidence can be produced. (*PE*, viii)

Tom Regan argues persuasively that Moore's ethics in *Principia* is in many ways a replacement for the lost religion of his youth. Along with comfort, it provides the possibility of experiencing pleasure in the contemplation of what we think "most truly and perfectly good."[44]* If Regan is right, this might explain Moore's preference for his platonic framework over the time-bound evolutionary one. It is less clear that it would justify that preference.

The questions of ethics are likely to be quite different when they spring from an evolutionary context. One might ask for example: If it is the case that human beings have evolved from other organisms by way of natural processes, what explanation can be given for the development of their moral sense and for the set of moral values that they espouse? Darwin, for example, asks " . . . how within the limits of the same tribe did a large number of members first become endowed with these social and moral qualities, and how was the standard of excellence raised?"[45] Darwin's questions about human beings and the standards for their behavior are framed within a natural, historical context. For Darwin, if human beings are the product of evolution from non-human animals, then it should be possible to say something about how they have developed the moral sense and moral values they have on the basis of natural history. Questions like these (and their answers) make no assumptions about there being some timeless goodness or some set of things that are simply good-in-themselves. Of course, the evolutionist's way of asking the question also limits the sorts of answers that will be found acceptable. It does not, for example, invite a supernatural or platonic answer.

While Moore might view *some* aspects of an evolutionary ethics as being compatible with his own non-naturalist ethics, these aspects would likely be limited to particular means that might be used in attempting to achieve what is good in itself. With respect to *means*, Moore could perhaps acquiesce to a natural and developmental account.[46*] But that, of course, is not the heart of the matter in the dispute between Moore and the Evolutionists. The real issue is whether or not there is some transcendent, timeless set of moral values or things that are good-in-themselves, apart from any consideration of what human beings know or do or need.

Moore's way of formulating the questions of ethics makes it virtually certain that *any* evolutionary responses will be ruled out from the very beginning.

As I noted earlier, he called attention to the importance of "discovering precisely *what* question it is which you desire to answer." But how does one decide just what that question is? How does one choose between Moore's way of formulating the questions of ethics and the evolutionist's way? One plausible way is to start from what one thinks one already knows, and to formulate one's questions on the basis of that. If one agrees that human beings have evolved from other animals (and Moore does agree), and if morality is an issue for human beings, it seems plausible to frame one's questions about morality in a way that bears some relation to the acknowledged facts of human evolution. It seems much less plausible to insist that evolution and moral values can have no possible connection with one another.

(ii) Method of answering the questions

Moore and the Evolutionists, then, begin with very different *questions*. They likewise use importantly different methods in their efforts to answer those questions. Moore claims that good is a simple, indefinable quality. Spencer, by contrast, claims that good is a long and pleasurable life. But there is much more at stake than disputes about definitions. Spencer and Moore disagree on just *how* one is to decide what "good" means. For Moore, what is required is a timeless conceptual account of good. In asking, "What is meant by good?" he deliberately separates the question from any contextual considerations and quite explicitly divorces it from any considerations of human *conduct*.[47]

Spencer, on the other hand, begins his discussion by arguing that moral questions are precisely questions of human conduct and must be investigated within the context of that conduct. For Spencer " . . . the essential meaning of a word that is variously applied, may best be learned by comparing with one another those applications of it which diverge most widely."[48] He then goes on to examine cases in which we speak of good knives, houses, umbrellas, etc., then moves to weather, dogs, and finally to men. He concludes that things are good insofar as they are well-adapted to achieve their purposes. Moral goodness, then, is to be understood within this larger framework.

Moore, by contrast, does not begin his investigation by looking at our uses of the term in ordinary, non-moral contexts. The issue of the relationship between the goodness of knives and umbrellas, on the one hand, and moral goodness on the other hand, does not arise for him.[49]* Spencer's approach is by way of an examination of ordinary experience; Moore's is by way of attempted definition, an effort to state "what are the parts which invariably compose a certain whole. . . ."[50] Spencer concludes that moral goodness is continuous with other sorts of goodness; Moore concludes that moral goodness is a simple and indefinable property that has no parts and is not continuous with anything in the natural world. In a word, Moore and Spencer begin with quite different assumptions about what sorts of information are admissible and what sort of method is to be used in answering the questions of ethics.

This point is related to a much larger one. Moore and Spencer differed profoundly on the whole direction in which they wanted to move philosophy. Spencer's philosophy was *synthetic*—an attempt to unify all the diverse aspects of human knowledge.[51]* Moore, by contrast, was clearly headed in the direction of *analysis*—separating out, for detailed investigation, bits and pieces of knowledge. Although he did not deny the validity of attempting to provide a unified account of all knowledge, Moore never attempted such a project in his own philosophy. A synthetic philosophy would be at pains to incorporate the insights of the sciences as part of its effort to unify all knowledge. Analysis of the sort that attracted Moore treated conceptual issues in isolation from science. In Moore's version of analysis, the insights of evolutionary biology clearly fell by the wayside.

The issues that surround the debate between analytic and synthetic approaches to philosophy are complex, and I cannot hope to resolve them here. There can be no doubt that philosophical analysis serves an enormously important function in the service of clarity and precision. Unless one is clear about the *parts* and about the *questions*, one's synthesis can add to the obscurity of an issue rather than contribute to better understanding. At the same time, if one focuses entirely on defining and on separating out the parts, one can easily sever some of the connections that might shed light on those parts.

This potential difficulty for an exclusively analytic approach to philosophic issues will surface again in my later discussion of the theories of perception and mind that emerged in the analytic tradition. If we are indeed the product of natural evolutionary forces, it is highly doubtful that we shall formulate an adequate account of ourselves, either as moral agents, perceivers of our world, or minded individuals, by ignoring that fact and focusing entirely on issues of timeless conceptual analysis. If the mental powers that we have developed are the outcome of adaptive interaction with our environment, then an account that tries to isolate them from that interaction, and to understand them stripped of all context, will be significantly off the mark. More on this in Chapter Seven.

The method that Moore brought to his investigation of ethics was not only significantly different from Spencer's method, but it was virtually guaranteed to eliminate any incorporation of evolutionary considerations—Spencer's or anyone else's. Within the framework of method, Spencer was merely the occasion, not the cause, of Moore's bypassing evolution in relation to ethics.

Evolution and Philosophy

What consequences does Moore's verdict on evolutionary ethics have for other areas of philosophy—theories of perception and mind, for example?

In a lecture delivered in the late 1920s, Moore explicitly extended his views on the relationship between evolution and ethics, asserting that the theory of evolution has no relevance to philosophy in general. In a lecture entitled "What is Meant by 'Nature'?" (1928-29), he says:

> ... everybody would agree with Wittgenstein, [*Tractatus*] 4.1122, that Darwin's Theory of the Origin of Species, including man, has nothing more to do with philosophy than any other hypothesis of Natural Science: and that whatever it *may* have to do with it, it's *not* the business of philosophy to discuss whether it's true or not. [52]

On Moore's view, then, scientific theories have little or nothing to do, not only with ethics, but with philosophy in general. While he offered some

detailed arguments for his views about ethics and biology, he says little
about why he thought that he could generalize his view to include all of
philosophy. The fact that in this lecture Moore quotes Ludwig Wittgenstein,
coupled with the considerable influence that Wittgenstein exerted on
Cambridge philosophy by the late 1920's, might suggest that Moore was
simply following Wittgenstein's lead on the matter. But there is reason to
think that Moore had his own motives, even in his early work, for thinking
that philosophy in general and evolution theory had little or nothing to do
with one another. And one can make an educated guess about what some
of those motives were.

The most obvious one, already alluded to, is his acceptance of the
widely held conviction that science and philosophy were simply two profoundly distinct disciplines. British Idealism which had dominated late
nineteenth-century philosophy and in which Moore had been trained, paid
virtually no attention to science. Furthermore, many thinkers in the broader
philosophical community were especially concerned at this point in history
to distinguish sharply between philosophy, on the one hand, and the natural
and social sciences on the other; the latter disciplines having disengaged
themselves from philosophy within recent memory. Given the historical
context within which Moore was approaching philosophy, his first motive is
perhaps understandable.

Furthermore, Moore was heavily influenced by Kant in his early work.
Although by 1904 he published a paper arguing that Kantian idealism was
false,[53] Moore retained at least two remnants of the Kantian view—his
distaste for empiricism and his distinction between the realm of the time-
bound and the realm of the timeless.[54] Both of these play a significant role
in his attitude toward evolution and philosophy.

"Evolutionism"—that school of philosophy that attempted to incorporate certain insights of evolution theory into a new philosophical view—
was generally identified with empiricism. That alone would have made
Moore cautious about assimilating it into his philosophy.

And Moore's commitment to the distinction between the *time-bound*,
to which the sciences belong, and the *timeless*, to which norms, values, and
concepts belong, further motivates his decision to locate philosophical
issues well beyond the realm of natural facts. This allegiance to a timeless
realm, as well as the general popularity in the late nineteenth century, of
Hermann Lotze's neo-platonism may well have contributed to Moore's
admitted platonism in his early philosophy. It is here, perhaps, that the
anti-evolutionist stance would generalize most easily to epistemology as
well as to ethics. In both areas Moore was at pains to establish *objectivity* in
opposition to what he took to be the excessive subjectivism of British
Idealism. Goodness and truth must be what they are, independent of human

desires and human knowledge. A platonic view of goodness, beauty, truth, like the one proposed by Moore, sits uneasily with an evolutionary account of reality. While Moore made no effort to discredit Darwin's view, he apparently saw it as belonging to a realm wholly distinct from that to which philosophy belongs. He was never able to satisfactorily account for the relation between these two realms, but he may have thought that if one puts sufficient distance between one's science and one's philosophy there is no need to work out consistency relations between them.

As I suggested in connection with Moore's omission of Darwin's views on morality, it is also very likely that Moore's views on the general relationship of evolution to philosophy were influenced once again by Henry Sidgwick. The latter's views on the matter are characterized by Jerome Schneewind: "Cautious willingness to accept the hypothesis of evolution by means of natural selection as a valuable scientific theory, coupled with scepticism as to its bearing on philosophy in general and on ethics in particular, characterized Sidgwick's attitude throughout his life."[55] Moore acknowledges a large debt to Sidgwick for many of the views expressed in *Principia Ethica*. He may well have been indebted for this one as well.

One further speculation. Moore may have felt that his dismissal of evolutionary *ethics*, in the work of Herbert Spencer, took care of all the normative issues appropriate to philosophy. This may be one reason that he does not return to the question of evolution when he works at his *epistemology*. If epistemology, like ethics, is taken to be normative, then the arguments against Spencer might be thought to generalize fairly easily. Truth, after all, would have roughly the same status as goodness, especially on a platonic reading. And if epistemology is concerned primarily with truth, then one wants a non-naturalistic epistemology parallel to one's non-naturalistic ethics. Evolution is factual, ethics and epistemology are normative. Therefore, the facts of evolution have no bearing on the norms of either ethics or epistemology.

A quote from one of Russell's early papers sheds some light on this assumed parallel between ethics and epistemology. Moore had invited Russell to read a paper to the Cambridge Apostles in 1897.[56*] The paper Russell gave was "On Ethics as a Branch of Empirical Psychology,"[57*] and it begins:

> Between the foundations of ethics and the foundations of epistemology, a certain analogy may be traced. The one is a theory of the good, the other a theory of the true. Both are due, in a sense, to the existence of states of consciousness with an objective reference. In desire, as in knowledge, we have a mental state with a reference to something other than itself. The two differ in the *manner*, but agree in the *fact*, of reference. (100)

Russell then goes on to argue that the "theory of knowledge is, in its foundations, independent of empirical psychology." That is, epistemology is independent of who we are and how we happen to acquire knowledge. The focus is exclusively on the objective validity of knowledge claims.

Moore surely shared this conviction that both ethics and epistemology concerned the *objective* side of things. Truth, as well as the good, were independently valid and were not affected by the human mind. Given this profoundly important parallel, Moore may have assumed that what was the case for ethics in relation to evolution would obviously be the case, too, for epistemology. In neither case should one be concerned about the nature of the *subject*. Whether knowledge served the needs of an individual organism was simply beside the point. The philosophical issue concerned the *objective* side.[58*]

So Moore's reasons for by-passing Darwin's theory as he formulated his new approach to philosophy included not only his objections to an evolutionary account of ethics. Moore's early platonism with its commitment to the objectivity of truth and goodness, and very likely his views about the importance of distinguishing between the sciences and philosophy, coupled with his antipathy to empiricism, also played a part.

Preliminary Consequences

One apparent consequence of Moore's attack on evolutionary ethics is that when he turned to epistemology; Darwin and the theory of evolution had nothing to say on the issues. This is particularly arresting in light of the fact that Moore was intent on showing that in perception we have knowledge of the physical world. His epistemology was a calculated attack on British Idealism and as such was intended to show that (a) not all reality is mental, and (b) in perception we are capable of knowing something about the mind-independent world around us.

If Darwin was right, our sensory mechanisms had developed through random variations that had allowed us to deal with our environment in ways that were adaptive. Having some reasonable degree of access to the physical environment would surely give us an adaptive advantage. One might think that such an account of the senses would be taken to have considerable relevance to any philosophical theory committed to arguing for our perceptual access to the physical world. For Moore it had none.

I should point out that I am not suggesting that evolution theory somehow *proves* that perceptual realism is correct. Anthony O'Hear has provided compelling arguments against such a view.[59] My claim is weaker than that. It is simply that if one wants to argue that there is a world that is not purely mental and that we have some degree of access to it, a Darwinian framework surely offers some support for that position.

There is a certain irony in the fact that in the early years of British Idealism, one of its chief goals was to undo the influence of evolutionary thinking. The early proponents of Idealism in England were distressed by the apparent godlessness of evolutionary theory, and their efforts to establish an idealist philosophy were motivated in part by a desire to re-establish the primacy of the spiritual over the material.[60] It is true that the later British Idealists had given up on such a goal, and it was these later ones who had educated Moore. Still, it is a curious turn of history to see Moore repudiate the school of philosophy that had as part of its original aim the elimination of evolutionary naturalism from philosophy.

What consequences does all this have for the development of that new method in philosophy with which Moore is credited? At the very least it becomes clear that Moore's well-known method of analysis does not emerge from any effort to integrate the insights of the sciences with the new philosophy.

Earlier I quoted from one of Moore's papers to show that he did, in fact, think that evolution was irrelevant to all of philosophy and not just to ethics. But there is one more point to notice about that quote. Moore had said:

> ... whatever it [Darwin's Theory of the Origin of Species] *may* have to do with it [philosophy], it's *not* the business of philosophy to discuss whether it's true or not. [61]

There is cogency in Moore's claim that it is not the business of philosophy to discuss whether or not the theories of science are true. The enigma, however, lies in Moore's phrase " ... whatever it *may* have to do with [philosophy]. ... " He says nothing further about that issue.[62]* And his own philosophy proceeds, for all practical purposes, as if Darwin had never written *Origin of Species* or *The Descent of Man*. Whatever claims Darwin made about us—about the nature of our relations with our environment, about our mental powers and moral sense, about the accidental character of sensory apparatus—these are not the business of philosophy.

Moore does not consider the possibility that there are dimensions of science other than the truth-value of its theories that might have consequences for philosophy. The *method* of one or more of the sciences might, for example, offer some lessons for philosophy. (This was clearly the view in Russell's later work.) Or the *consequences* of a scientific theory might be worth philosophical investigation, particularly if those consequences relate to the nature and capacities of the human being as cognizer of its world. One might even find in a theory of biological evolution some motivation for accepting Moore's assumptions about the reliability of common sense beliefs. Moore, however, constructed his version of analytic philosophy as if Darwin (like Freud, Marx, and Einstein) had, for all practical purposes, never existed.

    I shall explore the consequences of all this for Moore's theorizing about perception in Chapter Four. But first I turn to examine Bertrand Russell's explicit reasons for eliminating evolution and Darwin from philosophy.

Chapter 3

Bertrand Russell and Evolutionism

What biology has rendered probable is that the diverse species arose by adaptation from a less differentiated ancestry. This fact is in itself exceedingly interesting, but it is not the kind of fact from which philosophical consequences follow.
—Bertrand Russell (1914)

Bertrand Russell's reflections on the relation between philosophy and evolution theory are considerably more extensive than those of G.E. Moore. The conclusions of the two men came to much the same thing; their reasons sometimes differed.

In their early years Russell and Moore shared a great deal in common. They were students at Trinity College, Cambridge, at roughly the same time. Both were schooled in the British Idealist tradition that was heir to Hegel and Kant. Both were members of the Cambridge Apostles. And sometime near the turn of the century both rejected British Idealism in favor of a Realism that not only accepted the mind-independent status of the physical world but also espoused a fairly robust version of platonism. In time they came, too, to share the conviction that Darwin's views on the evolution of species had no relevance to philosophy and in particular to the new philosophy that they were jointly forging. One significant difference between the two, however, is worth mentioning. Whereas Moore did not have reservations about *Darwin's* particular account of evolution, Russell apparently did. A persistent undercurrent in his writings suggests that it was certain facets of the Darwinian view that especially troubled him. This will surface most explicitly in his discussions of what he took to be some of its socio-political consequences.

Like Moore, Russell explored the evolutionary ethics of Herbert Spencer and decided against it. Unlike Moore, in the context of his deliberations on evolution theory Russell also made extensive proposals about the nature of philosophy and the method it ought to employ, about the relative merits of biology and physics in relation to philosophy, and about the status of logic in relation to evolution. And in what became for Russell, I believe, a decisive factor in his attitude toward Darwin's theory, he called attention to what he considered to be some undesirable socio-political implications of the Darwinian account of evolution. In addition, Russell offered an extensive critique of "Evolutionism," that blend of philosophy and evolution that he credited to such divergent figures as Henri Bergson, William James and the Pragmatists, Friedrich Nietzsche, and Herbert Spencer. Finally, he offered some biting criticisms of what he called "Darwinism"—a popularized version of Darwin's ideas. Russell mounted a broad but cohesive attack on any effort to link his new philosophy with the doctrines of Darwin, the Evolutionists, or the Darwinists.

Each of these facets of Russell's discussion of evolution and philosophy provides insights into the direction in which he took his version of analytic philosophy. Each of them reveals some of the underlying beliefs that left a good deal of twentieth-century philosophy isolated from the influence of Darwin's views.

Russell's arguments had such important consequences for the development of analytic philosophy that it will be instructive to look at them in some detail. If the force of his arguments can be mitigated, that should lay the groundwork for the more positive thesis that I shall argue in Chapter Seven, namely that philosophic theories of perception and mind need to incorporate certain insights from Darwin's theory of evolution.

Ethics and Evolution

A good many of Russell's earliest writings reflect his concerns about the implications of evolution.[1] Even before he went to Cambridge he explored the possible relationship between evolution and immortality, religion, and free will.[2] It seems clear from these early essays that Russell was convinced that evolution had indeed occurred. He was less sure about what difference that fact should make to his views about some of the important questions in life.

In those very early years Russell first broached the question of the relationship between evolution and ethics. In April, 1888, he asks "what idea can we form of right and wrong?" His answer is an evolutionary one, but of a peculiar sort. " . . . I think that primitive morality always originates in the idea of the preservation of the species. But is this a rule which a civilized community ought to follow? I think not. . . . And since, as I believe, conscience is merely the combined product of evolution and education, then obviously it is an absurdity to follow that rather than reason."[3] The implication seems to be that although conscience is the outcome of evolution and education, reason is not. One might be tempted to discount this view as being little more than the musings of a young man who had not yet begun his university studies. But almost ten years later, when Russell had completed his Cambridge education, he wrote an essay in which he expressed an expanded version of that same general idea.

In "Mechanical Morals," of 1896, Russell offers a developmental (one might say "evolutionary") account of morals. Morality was, he says, first "instinctive," "when 'kill in order not to be killed' was the main principle of morals." Gradually "conventional" morality arose—

> that body of common sense which we call, according to our tastes, conventional morality, virtue, true Christianity, priggery or hypocrisy. It consists essentially, on the one side, of a moral standard applied to others and honouring those qualities which are helpful in war, and on the other side, of a desire to conform to the moral standard of others, with the conscious or unconscious end of winning their approbation.[4]

Both instinctive and conventional morality had their *raison d'etre*, he believes, in the struggle for existence. But because, as Russell also believes, the struggle for existence "is rapidly becoming a thing of the past," the only plausible basis for morality is "the rational." Reasoned morality "does not defer blindly to authority, does not believe any precept because that precept is generally accepted, does not bow down before the wisdom of its ancestors; but reflects for itself on the ends of human life, and on the means for attaining those ends in its actual milieu."[5]

There are several things worth noting in these early reflections on ethics and evolution. First, Russell believes that evolution had something to do with the early stages of morality. Not only is conscience a product of evolution and education, but both instinctive and conventional morality are taken to be fruits of the struggle to survive.

Second, he believes that the struggle for survival is virtually a thing of the past. Intelligence, he claims, has made it possible for us to produce the means necessary to provide for the needs of all. Given the fruits of modern technology, a struggle to survive is no longer required.[6*]

Third, and most revealing for the direction his later views would take, he believes that we have progressed beyond the point where evolution-based morality is adequate. We require a *reasoned* morality. Implicit here is the view from the 1888 reflections—that whereas conscience is the product of evolution and education, reason is not. Reason is somehow independent of historical and biological forces. This view will come to dominate many aspects of Russell's philosophy, not just his ethics, in the early years of the century.

Russell's second claim, that the struggle for existence is rapidly becoming a thing of the past, is startling. Again, it is not simply an early aberration;

it is a claim that he will repeat a decade later, in 1908.[7] Recall, as I noted in Chapter One, that certain biologists around the turn of the century were raising questions about the reality and scope of the struggle for existence. Vernon Kellogg's 1908 book mentions just such uncertainty. So Russell's comment on the issue may have been consistent with some currents in the cultural milieu at the time. But almost a century after Russell made the claim, it still seems wildly optimistic even in relation to the "most civilized nations" as he says. We continue to struggle against diseases and rattle-snakes, tornadoes and earthquakes, muggers and drug-induced violence, nations bent on war and the threat of nuclear disaster. The suggestion that intelligence and technology have virtually eliminated all serious threat to individual or collective survival is baffling. But in the last years of the nineteenth century Russell shared the optimism and belief in progress that were characteristic of the age. By 1901, as we shall see, his optimism will begin to cool. And he will eventually level a scathing criticism against the belief in progress that he credited to the Evolutionist philosophers.

Russell's early belief that the struggle for survival is nearly over, proved to be an extremely important one because it served as one of his early motivations for isolating ethics from all evolutionary considerations. One need not base ethics on concerns about individual or collective survival, he reasoned, because survival is no longer a significant issue. In fact, there are positive dangers in basing ethics on evolutionary considerations. We must move on to "reasoned" morality in which selfish and competitive motivations have no place. "The mere art of keeping alive, formerly the precondition of all virtue, has become unimportant, and the question becomes, not how to keep alive, but how to live. Formerly the alternatives were life or death; now the alternatives are a good or a bad life."[8] Enter *reasoned* morality.

Russell's insistence that reasoned morality is independent of all evolutionary factors reveals the extreme narrowness of his view of the struggle for existence. He sees an ethics that originates in evolutionary considerations as having the maxim, "Kill in order not to be killed," progressing later to hypocrisy and priggery. His view of the struggle for existence is framed as the war of all against all. One might think that Russell simply never read Darwin's discussion of the struggle for existence in *Origin of Species* or his discussion of morality in *Descent of Man*. But Russell lists *Descent* among the books that he read in September, 1891, and *Origin* among those read in July, 1895.[9*]

In addition to misconstruing Darwin's notion of the struggle for existence, Russell also missed the role that highly developed mental powers were to play in the development of our moral sense. Darwin's version of evolutionary ethics is not simply an ethics based on *instinct*. If that were the case, non-human animals might have developed ethics. Darwin is quite clear that the social instincts must be supplemented by developing *mental* powers,[10] by what Russell calls reason and intelligence. Darwin thought that the further evolution of those powers would generate a more highly refined sense of moral obligation and would extend the scope of individuals to whom one would feel some moral obligation. Furthermore, for Darwin the development of our mental powers did not cut them off from evolution. Reason and intelligence were simply the most recent consequences of that process.

Russell does not offer any evidence for his belief that reason and reasoned morality must somehow be independent of evolution. But his grounds may well have been related to his move toward metaphysical dualism, a move motivated by his opposition to the monism of the Idealists.[11*]

However, Russell's interest in mathematics may offer the best clue to his view of reason and its relation to ethics.[12*] In 1894, Russell tried to apply the mathematical model to ethics. Mathematics, he was convinced, was beyond historical and biological conditions. Perhaps ethics, too, could be elevated to such a status. In an essay for Henry Sidgwick's course on Ethics, entitled "Ethical Axioms," Russell wrote,

> Thus some basis *must* be found for ethical judgments. And it is sufficiently obvious that such a basis cannot be sought in any proposition about what is or has been. No theory of the origin of the moral sentiments, . . . can afford even the shadow of an ultimate ethical axiom, being themselves concerned with what is and not with what ought to be.[13*]

He argued that we require ethical *axioms* "as self-evident as those of Arithmetic, . . . "

So Russell's early understanding of the role of reason in ethics was that it would parallel its function in mathematics. In both cases he thought that we can discover an axiomatic system whose truth is quite independent of any facts about what is or has been. And pure, abstract reason is our faculty for recognizing the truth in both areas. Along with Russell's emphasis on the a-historical status of reason, one begins to see the emergence of an important role for the mathematical model in philosophy. Obviously the two views are not unrelated.

The most plausible explanation for Russell's views at this time lies with his budding need for some version of platonism. His explicit commitment to platonism will not emerge until close to the turn of the century, along with his and Moore's rejection of Idealism. But Russell's efforts to establish the *objectivity* of both mathematical truth and ethical values on an a-historical foundation is surely a move toward the tradition of Plato.

Reflecting back on this period of his life, Russell later wrote

> I came to think of mathematics, not primarily as a tool for understanding and manipulating the sensible world, but as an abstract edifice subsisting in a Platonic heaven and only reaching the world of sense in an impure and degraded form. My general outlook, in the early years of this century, was profoundly ascetic. I disliked the real world and sought refuge in a timeless world, without change or decay or the will-o'-the-wisp of progress.[14]

He might plausibly have offered similar reflections on his early views of ethics.

At roughly the same time that Russell was trying to forge links between ethics and mathematics, he was also trying to pry ethics loose from biology. A second paper for Sidgwick, also in 1894, "The Ethical Bearings of Psychogony,"[15*] offers an extended critique of Herbert Spencer, and argues that nothing compels us to value life alone or survival alone. Russell's position here, almost ten years before Moore published his *Principia Ethica*, is clearly opposed to grounding ethics along Spencerian lines. And while his particular views on ethics changed somewhat during the 1890's, moving from non-naturalism to naturalism, and back again, his opposition to an evolutionary account of ethics apparently never altered.

On this particular issue, it is likely that Russell, like Moore, was heavily influenced during his years at Cambridge by Henry Sidgwick's views. In later years, the influence of Moore's *Principia* was evident. In the first footnote to his paper, "The Elements of Ethics," originally published in sections between 1908 and 1910, Russell says: "What follows is largely based on Mr G.E. Moore's *Principia Ethica*, to which the reader is referred for fuller discussions." [16*] The essay, however, was not simply a synopsis of Moore's views; it was also an expression of Russell's own views at the time.[17*]

Russell agreed with Moore on virtually every significant issue with respect to ethics. He argued that good is a simple property and therefore unanalyzable; good is objective, and is what it is independently of us and of our actions; the primary issue for ethics is not right conduct, but the nature of the good in itself; and evolutionary ethics is profoundly mistaken. The concurrence with Moore's *Principia* is clear and strong.

Russell's interpretation of evolutionary ethics is at least as narrow as Moore's. And although he makes no mention of Spencer in this essay, the views he attacks bear a transparent resemblance to those Moore condemned in Spencer. Russell attacks the alleged commitment of evolutionary ethics to inevitable future progress, its supposed identification of good with whatever the impersonal forces of nature produce, and assumptions about the ruthless selfishness implied in the struggle for existence. He rejects the idea that those most recent on the evolutionary time-scale will, in the end, be the morally "fittest." He points, as Moore did, to the covert chauvinism nested in European attitudes about who is, indeed, the fittest.

I need not repeat here my discussion of similar views expressed by Moore. However, it is in some of the details of his discussion of evolutionary ethics that a couple of Russell's differences from Moore surface. It is not that Russell disagrees with Moore; rather, he adds some considerations to the discussion, in particular his concern about certain socio-political issues, to which I shall turn in the next section.

Russell's views on many things changed dramatically over the years, but the views he expressed here on the relation between evolution and ethics apparently never did. In his later years he concluded that mathematics is nothing more than a system of tautologies,[18] that intellect is not superior to sense,[19] and ethical values are not objective.[20]* But these eventual alterations in his views did not motivate him to reconsider his early attitude toward the relation between evolution and ethics. In the Preface to the 1966 edition of *Philosophical Essays*, Russell says: "The chief change [in his opinions since he first published these essays] is that I no longer believe in objective ethical values as I did when (following Moore) I wrote the first essay in the present volume ["Elements of Ethics"]."[21] There is no suggestion that his evaluation of *evolutionary* ethics had altered in any way.

Socio-Political Concerns

One of the motivations that encouraged Russell in his opposition to an evolutionary account of ethics appears to have been his view of its broader socio-political consequences. The tone of the 1896 essay, "Mechanical Morals," suggests worries about Social Darwinism and its anti-Liberal implications. Russell says:

> It is a singular fact that the doctrines of Malthus and Darwin were discovered almost at the very moment when, as applied to human beings, they ceased to be true. . . . Where are all the pretty phrases which Darwinians taught us to lisp in the nursery? Where the virtues based on these phrases? *Where the morality which has gathered round the necessity, to you own survival, of your neighbour's starvation?*[22] [Italics added.]

Russell did not reject evolution, but he believed that its Darwinian version was ultimately dangerous to the well-being of human society. On his view, such an account rests on assumptions about the ruthless selfishness of human beings in their struggle to survive at the expense of their neighbors. Russell's interpretation of the struggle for existence suggests a view more appropriately attributed to Malthus than to Darwin. Unfortunately, Russell seemed to think that the two men had exactly the same ideas about it. There are, however, good reasons to think that there were important differences between them.[23]*

As I argued in Chapter One, Darwin's notion of the struggle for existence was a very broad one that incorporated cooperative as well as competitive behaviors. The simple identification of the Darwinian view with the image of nature "red in tooth and claw" is a mistake.[24]* Relationships of cooperation, dependency, and "mutualism" of various sorts can play as decisive a role in the struggle to survive as do predatory relationships. Russell's narrow construal of Darwin's notion of the struggle for existence was not simply an early aberration. It continued through the years to dominate his view of Darwinism in all its forms and to be one of the chief motivations for his opposition to it.

In 1901, Russell underwent what he called a "conversion" that may well have confirmed him in his anti-Darwinian views. It was apparently precipitated by an attack of angina that Evelyn Whitehead had in Russell's presence.[25]* Her acute pain and his inability to do anything to alleviate it made a deep impression on him. The incident apparently heightened Russell's awareness of individual human suffering and of the need to work to alleviate it. It also seems to have strengthened his opposition to any account of human relations that was based on the ruthless struggle of each individual against every other, a view he clearly attributed to Darwin. Referring to the incident Russell later said:

> Within five minutes I went through some such reflections as the follow-
> ing: the loneliness of the human soul is unendurable; nothing can pene-
> trate it except the highest intensity of the sort of love that religious teach-
> ers have preached; whatever does not spring from this motive is harmful,
> or at best useless; it follows that war is wrong, . . . that the use of force
> is to be deprecated, and that in human relations one should penetrate
> to the core of loneliness in each person and speak to that.[26]

It was a dramatic turning-point for Russell, altering many of his views.[27]* Among other things, he moved away from being a supporter of the Boer war toward opposition not only to the war but more generally to imperialism. He would write much later that he found that "Darwinism in its popular form tended to be bellicose and imperialistic. . . . "[28]*

One might well conclude that Russell's "conversion" of 1901 contributed its share of motivation for rejecting any efforts to incorporate the views of Spencer or Darwin into philosophy. On Russell's interpretation, both views represented attitudes and values that Russell could no longer tolerate.

In addition, Russell's family had a long history of involvement with liberal politics, and Russell himself felt a life-long commitment to work for the improvement of human society.[29]* Any view that suggested that "might makes right," or that the only possible improvement of society lay in the hands of impersonal evolutionary forces, would be anathema to him.[30]*

By the time Russell wrote "Elements of Ethics" in 1910 his objections to evolutionary ethics also contain hints of the attitude toward war that he would assume during World War I.[31]* He objects strenuously to the view that "what fights most successfully is most admirable, and that what does not help in fighting is worthless."[32] But, there are no grounds for attributing such a view to Darwin. He is far from praising war and fighting as the most admirable activities that human beings can undertake—a point that Russell would concede.

There was, however, another dimension to Russell's concerns about Darwin. It centers on the issue of *laissez-faire* economics. As late as 1948 Russell would write:

> The doctrine of evolution, . . . is now generally accepted. But the particular motive force which Darwin suggested, namely the struggle for existence and the survival of the fittest, is not nearly so popular among biologists as it was fifty years ago. Darwin's theory was an extension, to the whole of life, of *laissez-faire* economics; now that this kind of economics, and the associated kind of politics, are out of fashion, people prefer other ways of accounting for biological changes.[33]

Russell's reason for thinking that Darwin's account of evolution was not current in biology was his belief that a version of the Mutation theory had triumphed with the Mendelians. He says:

> . . . sometimes there are sports or 'mutants' which differ substantially from the parent. They occur naturally in a small proportion of cases, and they can be produced artificially by x-rays. It is these sports that give the best opportunity for evolution, i.e., for the development of new kinds of animals or plants by descent from old kinds.

And later,

> "Where such changes have already occurred in part of a given stock, the Darwinian mechanism is still allowed to explain why one side gets the victory in a contest between the mutants and the conservatives. But whereas the earlier Darwinians [e.g., Karl Pearson, whose works he had read] thought that minute changes occurred, by selection, in each generation, the modern Mendelians lay stress on comparatively large changes occurring only occasionally, . . . "[34]

What makes this claim especially puzzling is the fact that his only footnote here is to Julian Huxley's 1943 book, *Evolution: the Modern Synthesis.*

As it turns out, Russell was mistaken about what biologists thought about Darwin's views by 1948. The "evolutionary synthesis" of Mendel's theories with Darwin's had begun to take shape in biology by the 1920's, bringing Darwin back to center stage by the 1930's, with the synthesis emerging in the 1940's.[35]* The Mutation theory was by no means in a state of triumph.

But part of the concern in Russell's comments is directed toward the supposed connection between the theory of natural selection and *laissez-faire* theories in economics. Julian Huxley shared Russell's concern about economic and political competition. But Huxley did not see either as being justified by Darwin's views. He did, however, believe that the struggle for existence must give way and be replaced by human efforts toward fulfillment and progress. Eugenics must take the place of natural selection.[36]

While Russell shared some of Huxley's views about eugenics, he apparently saw *laissez-faire* economics as closely related to the Darwinian account of evolution. He is not explicit on just what the relationship between the two is supposed to be. But one can interpret the relationship in different ways, neither of which would support a rejection of the biological theory because of its association with the economic theory. One might believe that Darwin drew inspiration for his theory from *laissez-faire* ecnomics; or, one might believe that Darwin's theory provided support and encouragement to *laissez-faire* economics. First the issue of inspiration.

Darwin may well have been inspired by *laissez-faire* theories in economics when he formulated his theory of natural selection. It is difficult to be entirely sure about sources of inspiration. But that by itself has little relevance to the question of the validity of the biological theory itself. If, for example, a theory about the structure of the benzene molecule was inspired by a dream about a snake swallowing its tail, arguments to the effect that snakes do not swallow their tails are quite irrelevant to the issue of whether or not the benzene molecule has a particular structure. So if the source of Darwin's inspiration for his theory is the issue, there is reason to believe that it is quite irrelevant to any judgment about the validity of the biological theory itself.

At the same time, as Russell knew, *laissez-faire* economics of the sort that Adam Smith advocated, was not simply supposed to be a system of "survival of the fittest."[37]* But even if Smith was mistaken, and *laissez-faire* economics is a completely selfish, competitive system in which only the ruthless prosper economically, it is not clear why that in itself should entail a rejection of Darwin's view. Again, whatever the validity or desirability of *laissez-faire* principles in economics, a biological version of similar principles might still be true.

On the other hand, if Russell was concerned that Darwin's theory somehow lent support to *laissez-faire* economics, it should be noted that Darwin was used as well to support various aspects of socialism and Marxism. The use to which Darwinian ideas were put seemed to depend on the particular portion of Darwin's theory that was isolated and emphasized.[38]* Of course, in later years Russell would have objected as strenuously to any support that Darwin's views might have given to Marxism as he did to its supposed links with *laissez-faire* systems.

Many years later when Russell published his *Human Knowledge: Its Scope and Limits*, he made some limited concessions to Darwin and natural selection. But these concessions did little to alter the character of Russell's own philosophy or much of subsequent analytic philosophy. In fact, shortly after conceding some degree of probability to aspects of natural selection, Russell says: "There is no reason to suppose living matter subject to any laws other than those to which inanimate matter is subject, and considerable reason to think that everything in the behavior of living matter is theoretically explicable in terms of *physics and chemistry*." [39] Not all that much had changed. Biological considerations continued to remain outside the pale.

At the very least, the basic idea that evolutionary ideas provide an inadequate basis for morality as well as for politics is one that Russell held to the end of his life. And it is one that deeply influenced his attitudes about the relationship between philosophy and evolution. Ironically, he will eventually place ethics as well as politics outside the scope of philosophy, urging that philosophy take its inspiration from science. The relevant science will not, however, be biology.[40]*

Evolution and Philosophy

Russell, unlike Moore, did not just tacitly generalize his views on ethics and evolution to cover the whole of philosophy. Instead, Russell approached the issue quite explicitly from a variety of viewpoints. And each approach led him to conclude that evolution had no consequences for philosophy in general.

Russell argued not only against Darwin's account of evolution, but in numerous of his works he argued against the relevance of *any* evolution theory to any portion of philosophy. A Lamarckian account, then, would be equally excluded from philosophy. In later years Russell explicitly rejects Lamarckism: "The Lamarckian mechanism of evolution cannot ... be accepted." [41] He makes no explicit reference to orthogenesis, but one can reasonably assume that his verdict on its relevance to philosophy would have been the same. Even his defense of the Mutation theory in the late 1940s does not involve its incorporation into his philosophy in any significant way.

It is perhaps worth noting that, unlike Moore, Russell was familiar with many of the discussions about evolution theory that were carried on within the scientific community around the turn of the century. During the mid-1890s he read not only Darwin's *Origin of Species* (he had read *Descent of Man* four years earlier), but also Francis Galton's works, *Hereditary Genius* and *Natural Inheritance* and so was familiar with Galton's criticism of Darwin's views on continuous variation. During that same period he read Karl Pearson's *Chances of Death, Grammar of Science,* Book 3 of *Ethic of Freethought* and four of his papers on *Mathematical Theory of Evolution.* Russell's initial interest in Pearson may have been motivated by mathematics, but he could hardly have failed to be aware of developments in biometry in relation to Darwin and Mendelism. In addition, he read Lord Kelvin's papers on heat, and so was acquainted with the questions that had been raised in physics about the age of the earth. At about the same time he read Malthus' *Essay on Population* as well as a number of books on Darwinism—Haycraft's *Darwinism and Race Progress,* Geddes and Thompson's *The Evolution of Sex,* Ritchie's *Darwinism and Politics,* and a number of books by Walter Bagehot including *Physics and Politics* which included influential discussions of evolutionary issues.[42]* Russell was also familiar with George Bernard Shaw's work, including his scathing criticism of Darwinism.[43]

In sum, given Russell's reading, there is reason to think that his views on Darwin and evolution were considerably better informed than were those of Moore. But his reading may also have left him with the impression that evolution theory was an area of science that was in significant disarray. In light of this it is perhaps not surprising that he would decline to incorporate evolution theory into his new philosophy. He may have seen it in much the same way that some current philosophers see sociobiology. What is surprising, however, is that Russell never gave the scientific disputes about the theory as one of his reasons for excluding it from philosophy. Still, it can hardly be doubted that it exercised some influence on his thinking.

One other notable person on the biological scene figures in Russell's life. It was Julian Huxley, with whom he was good friends. The two corresponded at least from 1915 until 1969,[44] and their correspondence suggests that they met with some frequency. There is, however, virtually no mention of biology or evolution in the extant letters and cards. One letter from Huxley, dated in 1963, contains a suggestion that the mind-body problem "must be approached from an evolutionary angle." Unfortunately, there is no copy of a response from Russell indicating what prompted the comment or what Russell thought about it. So we are left with no direct evidence that Huxley influenced Russell's views on biology or evolution. Nonetheless, it is surely plausible to assume that Russell was aware of many of Huxley's views on evolution. Still, there may be good reasons to think that Russell would have resisted any influence from Huxley on evolutionary matters. On Huxley's view, intellectual matters were best approached from a *synthetic* viewpoint—an attitude Russell could hardly have shared.[45] More problematic still, Huxley's 1912 book, *The Individual in the Animal Kingdom*, spoke explicitly of the influence of Henri Bergson.[46] As we shall see, Russell's opinion of Bergson was low indeed. So however close their friendship, Russell would have strenuously opposed aspects of Huxley's views on evolution. What the two did share, however, were political concerns connected with reform. They apparently had some common interests in eugenics as a method for improving society.

When Russell provides his detailed arguments against including evolutionary considerations in philosophy, he makes no mention of what the biologists themselves are saying. As we shall see, this fact is quite consistent with part of his argument, namely, that biology as a whole is simply not relevant to philosophy.

Russell's most extensive discussion of the relation between philosophy and evolution can be found in his Lowell lectures delivered at Harvard in 1914, later published as *Our Knowledge of the External World as a Field for Scientific Method in Philosophy*.[47]* The book is an extended explanation, defense, and application of Russell's "logico-analytic" method for philosophy. And he uses the occasion to show why that method is to be preferred to other candidates that were popular at the turn of the century, including Evolutionism. Before beginning a consideration of his criticism of alternative philosophical views, it may be useful to say a bit about Russell's preferred approach to philosophy.

Russell had several motivations for developing his *analytic* method for philosophy. Perhaps the best known of these is his opposition to the holism of Idealist philosophy, with its doctrine of internal relations. On the Idealist view, things are defined by *all* of their relations, and any effort to define things in isolation from one another generates distortion and some degree of falsehood. Russell argued that this view is mistaken and that analysis leads to neither distortion nor falsification. In one of his better-known comments on the subject Russell says: "Hegel had maintained that all separateness is illusory and that the universe is more like a pot of treacle than a heap of shot. I therefore said, 'the universe is exactly like a heap of shot.' Each separate shot, according to the creed I then held, had hard and precise boundaries and was as absolute as Hegel's Absolute."[48]

But at this point in time an equally important target for Russell's insistence on analysis was Henri Bergson's view that reality is continuous and flowing, that the intellect's efforts to cut it into conceptual bits involves distortion in spite of its practical utility. Like Hegel, Bergson had opted for the pot of treacle. In Russell's chapters on Continuity and Infinity, in *Our Knowledge of the External World*, he argues that both the Idealists (especially Bradley)[49*] and the Evolutionists (especially Bergson) are mistaken in their accounts of a seamless reality. An adequate understanding of modern mathematics, he argues, reveals that reality can indeed be seen atomistically without either contradiction or distortion. Russell's method of analysis flows directly from his conclusions about the mistaken metaphysics of *both* of these schools of thought.

It is likely, too, that Russell's work on Leibniz at the turn of the century encouraged him in the view that the method of analysis was not only legitimate but also necessary if one was to arrive at a clear understanding of things. In addition, Russell's conviction that three of the most fruitful disciplines in modern thought—mathematics, logic, and physics—had achieved their successes largely by an analytic approach to problems was undoubtedly another factor that encouraged him to adopt a similar method for philosophy.

Russell's own version of analysis clearly differs from the method that Moore was developing.[50*] Among other things, it relies far more heavily on logic than Moore did. Unlike Moore, Russell is concerned primarily with the *formal structure* of the claims he analyzes. But there are important similarities between the two methods of analysis too. Both are concerned with clarity, both analyze ordinary sentences of English to see how they are to be properly understood.

However, again unlike Moore, Russell takes a broad look at the philosophic panorama and makes an explicit proposal about the direction twentieth-century philosophy should take—both in method and content. In the process, he strikes a vigorous blow at evolutionary philosophy.

In the opening chapter of *Our Knowledge of the External World* Russell distinguishes three types of philosophy that were current at the time,[51*]—classical philosophy, Evolutionism, and logical atomism (what he also terms the logico-analytic approach). His purpose is to examine and reject the first two types and to propose that twentieth-century philosophy identify itself exclusively with logico-analytic philosophy.

The first type, the classical tradition, Russell identifies with the work of the "great constructive philosophers" from Plato through Kant and Hegel and their followers. (14) British Idealism, an heir to the philosophies of Kant and Hegel, is included in this category of classical philosophy and is the main target of his criticism of that tradition.

British Idealism

Extensive accounts of Russell's rejection of British Idealism are already in print.[52] I shall not repeat much of what they have to say. My concern, rather, is to suggest some of the similarities and differences in Russell's treatment of Idealism and his treatment of Evolutionism.

In addition to its emphasis on holism and the doctrine of internal relations, the Idealist approach to philosophy is rejected largely on the grounds that it operates with *a priori* reasoning, whereas for Russell philosophy requires a "scientific attitude." (16) He makes it abundantly clear that philosophy should, on his view, be genuinely *scientific*. He argues that the Idealist believed that he could reveal truths about the universe by using purely deductive arguments while entirely ignoring empirical evidence. This reliance on logic, Russell argues, was particularly debilitating because it was Aristotelian logic that was used—a logic that Russell and others had already shown to be not only limited in scope, but profoundly mistaken in its basic assumptions.

In addition to the use of an inadequate logic the Idealists ignored the data of concrete experience. They used logic to construct an account of the world that differs dramatically from common sense accounts, by showing all the common sense alternatives to be impossible because self-contradictory. Russell criticizes Bradley for using logic in a "constructive" way—that is, using it to draw substantive conclusions about the nature of reality. Russell, by contrast, sees the role of his new logic to be *analytic*.

So his critique of Idealism rests, to some extent, on his view of the nature and role of logic in philosophy. But while the Idealists use an outmoded logic, and use it in the wrong way, they at least have the merit of seeing that logic is important to philosophy. Part of his quarrel with the Evolutionists will center on the claim that their views either ignore logic altogether or assume that the laws of logic can change over time.

For our purposes, what is significant about Russell's critique here is his claim that philosophy must take modern logic, science and mathematics very seriously indeed. He would not agree with Moore that the hypotheses of science have nothing to do with philosophy. Both science and mathematics provide grist for the philosophic mill. Philosophy focuses on the *logical form* of the facts, eliminating their particular content, and proceeds "towards the simple and abstract by means of *analysis*." (189)

The conclusion of Russell's discussion of Idealism is that, of the three types of philosophy current in 1914, the Idealist option is ruled out as inadequate on virtually all grounds.

Evolution and Evolutionism

"Evolutionism" is the second type of philosophy Russell considers. He cites Nietzsche,[53]* Pragmatism (especially William James), Herbert Spencer,[54]* and Henri Bergson as its chief proponents, although his extended criticisms of the view focus almost exclusively on the work of Bergson. Russell's reasons for rejecting the philosophical significance of evolution move in two quite different directions, one having to do with the *biological* theory of evolution and the other dealing with the *philosophical* view, "Evolutionism."

The Biological Theory

Consider first Russell's views on the scientific theory. He does not dismiss the theory of evolution as philosophically irrelevant because he thinks that it is mistaken—a move that had been made by some of the early British Idealists. On the contrary, even as early as 1888 he had noted that it carried a high degree of probability.[55]

Nor does he exclude it on the grounds on which Moore had rejected it, namely that the hypotheses of the natural sciences are irrelevant to philosophy. As our earlier discussion makes clear, one of the faults he finds with Idealism is that it fails to take science seriously. Indeed, as one commentator puts it, "Russell's philosophy, ... moves in an atmosphere thick with science." [56] Unlike Moore, Russell was well-informed about science and quickly saw its importance for the new understanding of philosophy. But for Russell, the only relevant science was *mathematical physics.*

There are several reasons for Russell's preferences here. His own profound and lasting interest in mathematics undoubtedly played some role in his choice. Furthermore, he was much impressed by important developments that were taking place in physics.[57]* In addition, Russell's overarching conviction that philosophy should be concerned with the *formal structure* of facts would clearly make physics the plausible candidate for the science that should be of interest to philosophy. In fact, he takes physics to be the paradigm for science. " . . . [B]iology is neither the only science, nor yet the model to which all other sciences must adapt themselves." (22)[58]* Physics, on his view, was the only relevant science for philosophy primarily because of its generality and the mathematical method that it employed. Add to these considerations the fact that Russell was apparently well aware of many of the disputes that were current among biologists, and one can see some plausibility in his decision that physics was to be taken as the paradigm science.

But Russell's own stated reasons for preferring physics to biology don't mention the unsettled state of biology. Russell explains his attitude toward the biological theory of evolution as follows:

> What biology has rendered probable is that the diverse species arose by adaptation from a less differentiated ancestry. This fact is in itself exceedingly interesting, but it is not the kind of fact from which philosophical consequences follow. Philosophy is general, and takes an impartial interest in all that exists. The changes suffered by minute portions of matter on the earth's surface are very important to us as active sentient beings; but to us as philosophers they have no greater interest than other changes in portions of matter elsewhere. (26)

One of Russell's difficulties, then, with biology and with the biological theory of evolution in particular is that they are not sufficiently *general* to merit philosophical consideration. Note that this is an objection to making *any* biological theory relevant to philosophy. It is not directed specifically at Darwin or natural selection. The point seems to be that philosophy by its very nature concerns itself only with theories that govern everything that exists. Biological theories clearly do not; therefore, they are not relevant to philosophy. The only natural science that is sufficiently general to have philosophical relevance is *physics*.

There is some reason to believe that Russell saw the question about biology and physics as an either/or question—either biology or physics should be relevant to philosophy. He says in a 1914 lecture that a pre-Copernican world, because of its geocentric frame of reference, also develops an *anthropocentric* view of the universe. Modern physics has clearly shaken the foundations of the pre-Copernican world but, unaccountably, the anthropocentric viewpoint has continued.[59] Apparently for Russell, efforts to take biology seriously in philosophy were little more than misguided efforts to maintain the anthropocentrism of a pre-Copernican age. There are numerous texts that suggest that for Russell (and perhaps also for some of the Evolutionists) a philosophy of evolution would require that *everything* be treated exclusively from the point of view of human interests. There is, however, reason to think that a philosophy that takes evolution seriously need do no such thing. Since evolution theory locates human beings as part of the whole natural network of interdependent parts, a philosophy that assimilates evolutionary insights ought to be far from anthropocentric. The focus on exclusively human interests ought to be considerably less in an evolutionary context than is found in some traditional philosophy.

Still, for Russell, the choice is thought to be between a pre-Copernican, anthropocentric philosophy that takes account of biology, and a post-Copernican, non-anthropocentric philosophy based on modern physics. He seems not to have considered at this point that both sciences might have relevance to philosophy, and that there need be no conflict between them. While incorporation of biological insights need not return us to a naively anthropocentric view, their exclusion could lead us, as I shall argue, to a skewed account of human mental powers.

There is an irony in Russell's position, in that it excludes from consideration a full account of the philosopher himself.[60]* Russell notes that evolution is very important and relevant to us "as active sentient beings; but to us as philosophers . . . " it is of no particular interest. The implication seems to be that we, *as philosophers* are somehow other than active sentient beings. Russell assumes that theories about the nature and origin of the cognitive capacities of the active sentient human being have no consequences for how the philosopher knows what he or she knows. He further assumes that *what is known* is unaffected by the fact that human *knowers* are active, sentient beings.

This attitude is very likely a consequence of several views that Russell developed much earlier—his belief that reason is somehow separate from and independent of history and biology, his focus on mathematics and logic, and his commitment to a version of platonism. And finally, there was his determination to distance himself from Idealism with its emphasis on the importance of the contributions that Subjectivity makes to knowledge. For Russell, as for Moore, the rejection of Idealism included a rejection of any significant role for Subjectivity in the generating of knowledge. The active, sentient being that was the focus of evolution theory may have been too close to the active, constructive mind of Idealism. The focus of the new philosophy would be entirely on the *objective* side of the knowledge relation. The philosopher, then, is to be concerned primarily with the *known*, not with the *knower*.[61]*

In addition, for Russell, the philosopher is not to be concerned with the practical problems associated with living in the everyday world, the sorts of problems that face an active, sentient being. Rather, the philosopher is to be concerned with purely theoretical matters, and these are governed by eternal laws and eternal truths. Our active sentient nature will be of little assistance in discovering these.

In light of Russell's enduring concern with problems of knowledge, his views on all these issues have far-reaching consequences for his philosophy, consequences which become particularly problematic when he deals with perception. The perceiver is inescapably an active, sentient being. And the interests of the ordinary perceiver are more often practical than theoretical. Some of these practical interests have to do with the survival and well-being of the perceiver. Unfortunately, all of this is lost in the formation of his new logico-analytic method for philosophy. Unhappily, his relative indifference to the living organism in the knowledge-gathering process echoes through much of twentieth-century analytic epistemology. (I shall return to this point in Chapter Four.)

Russell further specifies his objection to considering biology as relevant to philosophy.

> . . . a philosophical proposition must be applicable to everything that exists or may exist. . . . it [philosophy] is concerned with those general statements which can be made concerning everything without mentioning any one thing or predicate or relation, such for example as 'if *x* is a member of the class a, and every member of *a* is a member of *B*, then *x* is a member of the class *B*, whatever *x*, *a*, and *B* may be.[62]

Given this way of understanding philosophy, it seems to follow that the concrete peculiarities attaching to biological organisms would be irrelevant. They are indeed particular instantiations of the general philosophical propositions, but genuinely philosophical investigations have no commerce with particular instantiations. The latter belong to the special sciences.

Russell does not offer any explicit defense here for his claim that philosophy must be general in the sense of taking an impartial interest in everything that exists. One might argue that he was simply assuming a widely accepted view without giving it much thought.[63]* His own account of philosophy requires that it ignore the *content* of facts and focus exclusively on their *formal structure*. If one is to consider only the formal structure of facts, and ignore their concrete content, then one will as a consequence be interested in *all* facts. Biology is obviously not concerned with the formal structure of everything that exists. Physics is. So biology is out, and physics is in.

But *why* should philosophy be concerned exclusively with the structure of facts and not with their content? Because, on Russell's view, *logic* is the essence of philosophy, and logic deals only with structure, not with particular content. And why is logic the essence of philosophy?

It is difficult to be sure just what the proper answer to that question is. Perhaps because logic was clear, and rule-governed, and generated some reasonably certain conclusions—like mathematics (for which it provided the foundations). Perhaps because it could mimic some of the best features of the sciences, particularly their disinterestedness, while still carving out for itself its own distinctive niche. Perhaps because it was able to shed light on some of the traditional puzzles in philosophy, like the problems associated with continuity and infinity, and thus held out some promise of making progress in resolving perennial philosophical difficulties. All of these considerations undoubtedly contributed to Russell's decision to redefine philosophy in this remarkably narrow way.

In later years he would come to soften his position on the role of logic.[64]* But he never softened it to the point where evolution theory would influence his philosophy in any significant way. When he loosened methodological constraints on the scope of philosophy, socio-political worries continued to bar the way for any reasonable bond between philosophy and evolution.

So the biological theory of evolution is irrelevant to philosophy because it is not sufficiently *general* in that it does not take an impartial interest in all that exists, it is not applicable to everything that exists.

But there is another aspect to the generality that Russell requires for philosophy. And this too, evolution theory fails to satisfy. Philosophical propositions must be true in all possible worlds. Russell says that philosophy, like mathematics, is

> ... general and *a priori*. Neither of them asserts propositions which, like those of history and geography, depend upon the actual concrete facts being just what they are.... In all the many possible worlds, philosophy and mathematics will be the same; the differences [in those worlds] will only be in respect of those particular facts which are chronicled by the descriptive sciences. Any quality, therefore, by which our actual world is distinguished from other abstractly possible worlds, must be ignored by mathematics and philosophy alike. (190)

In addition, then, to taking an impartial interest in all that exists, philosophy is general in that it is concerned with propositions that are universally valid, true in all possible worlds. Evolution, driven as it is by historical contingencies, clearly fails to meet Russell's second dimension of generality.[65]*

Russell's first objections, then, have to do with the strategy of assimilating the insights of any biological theory into the new philosophy. Evolution theory is dismissed because it belongs to the partial, the contingent, and as such is simply irrelevant to philosophy.

The Philosophy of Evolutionism

Russell's second set of objections deals with specific attempts that were made by philosophers to incorporate some of the insights of evolution theory into philosophy. These efforts are lumped together under the general name "Evolutionism." One account of the view describes it in the following way:

> Evolution, a biological hypothesis, was transformed in the minds of many liberals into Evolutionism, a cosmic doctrine. When thus extended in its application, Evolutionism became the dominant factor in the interpretation of any organic change. By a still greater extension, it was used as a basis for the interpretation of human history and the history of human ideas. [66]

A second commentator suggests that Evolutionism "viewed all things as part of a process of upward development."[67] Given these sorts of characterizations it is not surprising that Russell took Evolutionism as one of his targets. While these characterizations of Evolutionism may not be apt descriptions of the views of all the Evolutionists, they are not entirely innappropriate for the views of Spencer and Bergson, Russell's chief quarries.[68]*

Russell notes that when Darwin's theory swept away the fixed categories of the biological world "human conceit was staggered for a moment." The philosophy of Evolutionism came to the rescue and helped human conceit reassert itself. (23) This theme, that Evolutionism is largely an effort to comfort people, will be repeated by Russell in a variety of ways. Russell claims that the Evolutionists saw the development toward man as *progress*, and they interpreted the scientific theory of change as "a law of development towards good in the universe." (23) The parallels with Moore's discussion of Spencer are evident. Russell's arguments, however, focus heavily on Bergson's views.[69]*

Unfortunately, Bergson, like Spencer, is not the most convincing proponent of Evolutionism. In addition, Bergson was an opponent of a Darwinian account of evolution, an account that he viewed as too mechanistic. Still, Russell's criticisms are instructive. They tell us not only what may be wrong with Bergson's views, but they also highlight some of the motivations that led Russell to take early analytic philosophy in the direction he did.

Russell's summary criticism of Evolutionism is that it "is not a truly scientific philosophy, either in its method or in the problems which it considers." (22) Russell offers two specific criticisms:

(i) its truth does not follow from what science has rendered probable concerning the facts of evolution;

and

(ii) the motives and interests which inspire it are so exclusively practical, and the problems it deals with are so special, that it can hardly be regarded as really touching any of the questions that to my mind consititute genuine philosophy. (25-6)

Russell's discussion of each of these objections can be divided into a number of distinct points.

(i) *The truth of Evolutionism does not follow from what science has rendered probable concerning the facts of evolution.* Russell's first criticism has three elements:

(a) The first part includes Russell's claims, discussed earlier, that biological theories are irrelevant to philosophy because they lack the requisite generality. The function of these claims in the longer argument about Evolutionism is to show that Evolutionism could not possibly follow from the biological theory of evolution because *no* biological theory is sufficiently general to have any relevance for a genuine philosophy. By extension, the biological theory of evolution can have no philosophical consequences. Thus, no philosophical theory could *follow* from the truth of the biological theory.

(b) The second part of the criticism argues that in spite of the fact that as we look at changes from the past to the present, they appear to us to involve progress, "that gives no ground for believing that progress is a general law of the universe." (26) Such a conclusion would be a "crude generalization" from a tiny selection of facts.[70]* So again, Evolutionism's belief in future progress does not follow from what the biological theory has shown to be the case with respect to the past. On this point Russell seems to be on firm ground. There is evidence that at least some of the Evolutionist philosophers did indeed believe that progress was an inevitable consequence of evolution. [71]*

Russell's worry about a claim that progress is a general law of the universe is particularly understandable when one recalls that he is writing in 1914. The future of the world at the start of the first World War looked anything but promising.

In spite of the views of Spencer, Bergson, and even Russell on the future progress of mankind, there is good reason to believe that a philosophy that takes evolution theory seriously need not make any commitment to inevitable progress, either biological or moral.

Consider the case of biological progress. There are two distinct issues here. First, what did Darwin himself think about the relationship between evolution and biological progress? And second, what does the theory of natural selection entail with respect to such progress?

As for Darwin's *beliefs* on the matter, the evidence suggests that he was ambivalent, at times favoring a progressive view, and at other times carefully distancing himself from it. It is not difficult to find quotes from his letters and from various editions of *Origin* that support his holding views on both sides of the matter. In a letter to Charles Lyell, dated March 1863, Darwin complains:

> . . . you refer repeatedly [in his book, *Antiquity of Man*] to my view as a modification of Lamarck's doctrine of development and progression. If this is your deliberate opinion there is nothing to be said, but it does not

seem so to me. . . . I believe this way of putting the case is very injurious
to its acceptance, as it implies necessary progression . . . [72]

But he also says, near the end of *Origin*, "And as natural selection works
solely by and for the good of each being, all corporeal and mental endow-
ments will tend to progress toward perfection."[73] By itself this sounds like
an unequivocal endorsement of progressionism. But there is at least one
factor that might attenuate such a conclusion. The context of the statement
suggests that Darwin may have been concerned to soften his evolutionary
view for those readers who are impressed by arguments for the grand design
of the universe. In the Sixth Edition of *Origin of Species*, Darwin begins his
concluding section with the statement, "I see no good reason why the views
given in this volume should shock the religious feelings of any one."[74] And
he concludes it with, "There is grandeur in this view of life, with its several
powers, having been originally breathed by the Creator into a few forms or
into one; and that, whilst this planet has gone cycling on according to the
fixed law of gravity, from so simple a beginning endless forms most beautiful
and most wonderful have been, and are being evolved."[75]* So the larger
context suggests that Darwin wants to emphasize that his theory *need* not
cancel out the view that there is a creator with a grand design for the ultimate
perfection of the creation.

Late in his life Darwin appears to weaken his claim that there is even
a *tendency* to progress. In a letter he wrote to Hyatt (an American paleontolo-
gist at Harvard) he says, "After long reflection I cannot avoid the conclusion
that no inherent tendency to progressive development exists."[76] Whatever
Spencer or Bergson may have thought about the necessary progress of
evolution, there is little evidence that Darwin would have given them
unqualified support. Darwin expressed hopes for human progress in the
future. But then so did Russell.[77]*

The second issue is whether or not Darwin's theory of natural selection
itself somehow entails biological progress. Scholars are divided in their
response to this question.[78]* One difficulty with providing a satisfactory
answer to this question is that there is not some widely accepted definition
of "progress."[79] As a start, one needs to distinguish between what Francisco
Ayala calls "uniform" and "net" progress.[80] In the former case, every later
member of an evolutionary line is better than every earlier with respect to
some feature. In the latter case later members need only be better on
average. There seems to be widespread agreement that evolution, if it
involves any progress at all, does not involve uniform progress. At best,
progress would be net.

But if one is to talk meaningfully about progress, one needs to specify which characteristics of organisms should be used as a measure of biological progress. A number of possibilities have been proposed: the ability to gather and process information about the environment; the ability to reproduce successfully over long periods of time; an increasing ability to store genetic information; increasing dominance; control over the environment; increasing morphological complexity; adaptive flexibility; etc.[81] Depending on which one of these characteristics one specifies, one can provide some account of progress. That account is likely to differ, however, with the choice of different characteristics. And there is no agreement about which of the proposed characteristics is the best. Serious questions can also be raised not only about the proper characteristic to be used in measuring progress but also about whether or not the notion of progress is even an appropriately scientific concept. It normally has clear evaluative overtones.

One might argue that there are obvious grounds for thinking that evolution entails progress. After all, only the fittest are selected, and they pass on their "fit" characteristics to their offspring. The less fit die out, and so organisms must be improving over time.

The difficulty with such an interpretation of natural selection is that it assumes some absolute sense of fitness. Over time, organisms would simply become more and more "fit" and there would consequently be, progress. There is no one feature whose increase demonstrates progress in fitness. On Darwin's view, fitness appears to mean nothing more than being able to cope with some particular environment better than one's competitors can. The dinosaurs were fit for a time; then something happened that made them unfit for the environment in which they lived. That is, the notion of fitness is always relative to a particular environment, including the competitors that happen to share that environment. There appears to be no fixed standard against which to measure the fitness appropriate to one environment against the fitness appropriate to a different environment. It might be the case that a particular environment is not especially demanding, or one's competitors might be very poorly equipped, or one might be part of a cooperative network that complements one's own weaknesses in the relevant ways. Or again, it might be that all that is required for adaptation to a particular environment is some small quirk that would be quite useless or even harmful in a different environment. One may indeed survive while one's competitors die out, and thereby be the "fittest," but the idea that the adaptation involved here necessarily entails progress oversimplifies the case.[82]

Rather, the raw material with which natural selection works is two-fold: *random* variations in individuals and an environmental "niche" for which that random variation could turn out to be useful (or not). The value of a variation will be relative to its adaptiveness for a given environment.

There is no reason to assume that either the environment or the variation alone, or their combination, is an improvement on the previous state of things. All that can be assumed, if the organism survives and reproduces, is that the fit between that organism and its current environmental niche is better than that of any of the actual, competing alternatives. This is an extremely modest claim.

It appears that the most that can be said is that some group of organisms has progressed beyond some other group or beyond its own progenitors *with respect to some particular feature*. They may also have re-gressed in relation to those others with respect to other significant features. My own view is that there is no independent way to determine which feature is *the one* that determines overall biological progress. As a consequence, it strikes me as problematic to claim that natural selection entails progress. Such a claim is at best equivocal.

So on this issue perhaps Russell was right to fault Evolutionism for its commitment to the necessity of progress. But more to the point, per-haps neither Russell nor the Evolutionists were quite clear about what such a claim really amounted to. However, the suggestion that issues from Russell's (and Moore's) readings of the relevant texts is that Evolutionist claims about progress were really about the move from non-human forms to human beings, and from all other human beings to western Europe-ans. On that understanding of progress, I take it that Moore and Russell were both justified in raising objections to the chauvinism implied in such claims.

But Russell's concerns about progressionism were not limited to *biological* progress. And many years later he softened his objections to claims about the probability of future progress.

> The future of mankind more and more absorbs my thoughts. I grew up in the full flood of Victorian optimism, and although the easy cheerful-ness of that time is no longer possible, something remains with me of the hopefulness that then was easy. It is now no longer easy. It demands a certain fortitude and a certain capacity to look beyond the moment to a more distant future. But I remain convinced, whatever dark times may lie before us, that mankind will emerge, that the habit of mutual forbearance, which now seems lost will be recovered, and that the reign of brutal violence will not last forever. . . . But by whatever arduous road, I am convinced that the new wisdom which the new world requires will be learned sooner or later, and that the best part of human history lies in the future, not in the past.[83]

Still, in 1914, he had dark views about any philosophy committed to a progressive view of history. And when he relented in later years on the issue of progress, he gave no evidence of softening his critique of Spencer or of Bergson. Perhaps their optimism was too easy and the expected progress too inevitable.

(c) In the third part of Russell's objection—that the truth of Evolutionism does not follow from science—he concedes to Bergson that we need a better understanding of the notions of change and continuity than we currently have. (The issues of change and continuity were favorite themes in Bergson's *Creative Evolution*.) And Russell also concedes that modern *science* shows us that a clear understanding of these notions is crucial. But on Russell's view an adequate *analysis* of change and continuity cannot be provided by science—either biology or physics. The analysis of such notions is the subject matter of *philosophy*. To this extent, he thinks, Evolutionism has put its finger on a genuine philosophical problem. But it has offered a solution to that problem that is neither scientific nor philosophical. By dogmatically assuming its own understanding of change and continuity, it ceases to be scientific. (26) And by its "dogmatic rejection of all attempts at analysis" it ceases to be genuinely philosophical. (28)

So for Russell, one proper business of philosophy is to provide an analysis of some of the concepts that function in the sciences. And not only is science itself not able to provide such an analysis, but one cannot appeal to the facts of the sciences in order to evaluate that analysis. (26) Nothing about the analysis of concepts follows from scientific facts. So once again the conclusion is that the truth of Evolutionism does not follow from what science has rendered probable concerning the facts of evolution.

It may be useful to pause here, before moving on to Russell's second general objection to Evolutionism, and consider some of the details of his objection to a Bergsonian treatment of continuity. This will make it possible to highlight two important facets of Russell's dismissal of Evolutionism and his subsequent characterization of analytic philosophy. He will argue, against Bergson's Evolutionism, that reality is not seamless (and so analysis and atomism are justifiable) and that philosophy is theoretical, not practical. Both of these points will play a major role in the logico-analytic method that Russell will propose in the book.

Bergson drew a sharp distinction between *intuition* and *intellect*. The former, he claimed, put us into immediate contact with the flowing and continuous character of reality. The latter, by contrast, artificially "sliced" reality into conceptual bits. While sometimes useful, this function of intellect distorted the actual seamless character of reality. Russell disagreed. Where Bergson's Evolutionism emphasized the importance of intuition, genuine philosophy must, on Russell's view, rely on intellect. And in place of a seamless account of reality proposed by Bergson, philosophy must insist on rigidly distinct categories that can assure timeless truth in areas like logic.

At the heart of Russell's concern is Bergson's characterization of intellect.[84]* The latter sees it as essentially *practical*. It is a guide to action. It is not capable of giving an adequate theoretical account of continuous reality because the intellect must artificially stop the flow, momentarily freezing and isolating some portion of it.

For Russell the danger of Bergson's view of the intellect is that it effectively sweeps away the very possibility of science. Science requires, on Russell's view, that we be capable of formulating a reasonably accurate conceptual description of reality. And note that the issue is not whether a given set of concepts is adequate to reality. Rather, the question is whether, on Bergson's view, *any* set of concepts could ever be adequate. And for Russell, not only science but also philosophy requires a plausible conceptual account of reality. Any view like Bergson's that dogmatically assumes the primacy of continuity and the deficiency of intellect must be rejected as inimical to the very possibility of both science and philosophy as reasoned systems. Furthermore, Russell's own emerging atomism is completely at odds with a philosophy like Bergson's that sees life as "a continuous stream in which all divisions are artificial and unreal." (25)

Russell is quick to point out, too, that "it is only through intellect that we know of the struggle for survival and of the biological ancestry of man: if the intellect is misleading, the whole of this merely inferred history is presumably untrue." (33-34) There is more than a little irony in the fact that Russell uses Darwin against Bergson in his claims about intellect. Russell argues that "If, . . . , we agree with M. Bergson in thinking that evolution took place as Darwin believed, then it is not only intellect, but all our faculties [i.e., intuition too], that have been developed under the stress of practical utility." (34) The truth is that Bergson, like Russell, disagreed with Darwin's account of evolution. Bergson's view was a version of orthogenesis, with the *elan vital* as the internal driving force of evolution. On such a view, our faculties have not developed because of their utility. They are simply the products of an innate inner drive.

In addition to Russell's misunderstanding of Bergson's view on this point, it is also puzzling that Russell uses Darwin to argue against Bergson that intellect and intuition have both developed because they are *useful*. The practical utility of intellect—its capacity to function on behalf of the individual organism—is not a theme that Russell pursues, either here or in his subsequent philosophy. In fact, he quickly distances himself from the notion, pointing out that intellect has developed, on some occasions, "beyond the point where it is useful to the individual."(34) And he gives as an example philosophy, which as a product of the intellect, is not of practical importance to most men.

Whether or not philosophy is of practical importance to most men, there is every reason to think that intellect, as well as intuition, *is* of practical importance to most people. It not only functions in theoretical contexts, but it also plays a major role in solving many sorts of practical problems. There is good reason to think that philosophical accounts of intellect should be concerned to take this issue seriously in their theories of knowledge and of our interactions with the world. But Russell here loosens the connection between intellect and practical life and leaves intuition to its evolutionary origins. Unlike intuition, which "bring[s] out our kinship with remote generations of animal and semi-human ancestors, . . . philosophy is not one of the pursuits which illustrate our affinity with the past." (36)

For the present, I mean to call attention to the fact that Russell insisted, against Bergson, that reality is not seamless and that philosophy is theoretical not practical. The first point will contribute to his later atomistic approach to philosophical issues. I shall return to the issue of the relationship between philosophy and practical considerations in the discussion of Russell's second general objection to Evolutionism.

But there is another very important dimension to Russell's objection to a Bergsonian account of continuity. If life is a "continuous stream in which all divisions are artificial and unreal," then not only science but also *logic* must be dismissed as no more than a convenient fiction. Russell states the objection this way:

> . . . with the influence of biology, the 'tender-minded' . . . [sweep aside] the whole apparently immutable apparatus of logic, with its fixed concepts, its general principles, and its reasonings which seem able to compel even the most unwilling assent. (23)

There are two distinct issues here, the question of whether or not logic has any validity at all, and the question of whether it has a validity that is immutable. The first involves the Bergsonian view that "all divisions are artificial and unreal." If Bergson's account of reality were right, it seems that logic would indeed be a "convenient fiction." The second issue is whether or not the theory of evolution itself entails that logic is subject to change along with everything else. Russell was troubled by both.

With respect to the first issue, Russell later in the book offers a detailed account of continuity, based on Cantor's theory of infinite series, that attempts to preserve both the notions of continuity and atomicity. That is, he denies Bergson's claim that all divisions are artificial and unreal. In the process, he reaffirms the legitimacy of logic.

The second, larger issue, involves the relationship between evolution and logic. Many years earlier, Gottlob Frege had addressed it.

In these times when the theory of evolution is marching triumphantly through the sciences and the method of interpreting everything histori- cally threatens to exceed its proper bounds, we must be prepared to face some strange and disconcerting questions. If man, like all other living creatures, has undergone a continuous process of evolution, have the laws of his thinking always been valid and will they always retain their validity? Will an inference that is valid now still be valid after thousands of years and was it already valid thousands of years ago? Clearly, the laws of how men do in fact think are being confounded here with the laws of valid inference.[85]

If logic is identified with the laws of human thought, and if the laws of human thought can evolve, then perhaps logic evolves. If so, it would not be immutable and universally valid. The crucial step is to show that logic is *not* to be identified with the laws of human thought. For Frege as for Russell (at this time) logical truth is objective and immutable; psychological fact is subjective and changeable. Both Frege and Russell subscribe to some version of platonism in an effort to secure the requisite objectivity and immutability for logic. There were, of course, important differences be- tween their views, even in their respective accounts of this objectivity.[86*] Nonetheless, they shared the same underlying motivation with respect to preserving the independent status of logical truth. And both of them thought that evolutionary thinking was sometimes used to undermine that status and to imply that the truths of logic were reducible to contingent psychological facts and, as such, were subject to development and change. Both Frege and Russell found such a view incoherent. (And, as we shall see in Chapter 5, Edmund Husserl agreed.) It is perhaps worth noting that Frege and Ernst Haeckel, one of the more controversial and speculative of the evolutionary biologists, were together on the faculty of the University of Jena for a number of years, Frege from 1879 until 1918, and Haeckel from 1862 until 1909.

One of the most telling objections to an evolutionary account of logic was that the very formulation of the theory of evolution itself required that the laws of logic be more than contingent facts of human psychology. If the laws of logic were not objectively valid, then the theories which they helped to structure would similarly lack objective validity. The conclusion seemed to be that if the theory of evolution were to be taken as objectively true, then the laws of logic must be objectively valid and therefore independent of human psychology. As such, they will not be subject to the same laws of develop- ment as the laws of human thinking would be in an evolutionary framework.

But the larger conclusion that both Frege and Russell (and Husserl) will draw is that the theory of evolution is irrelevant to the truths of logic. For Russell this is an especially important conclusion since he will go on, in the subsequent chapter of *Our Knowledge of the External World*, to argue that logic is the essence of philosophy. If logic is indeed the essence of philosophy, and if logic is independent of evolution, then philosophy is independent of evolution.

Russell may have been right in his view that logic must be independent of evolution. But the conclusions he draws for philosophy in 1914 are more vulnerable. Notice that he makes at least two crucial moves: first, he subscribes to some version of platonic realism (a view that will give logic an objectivity that is independent of evolution), and then he identifies logic as the essence of philosophy (a view that will enable him to establish philosophy as independent of evolution, thus undoing any effort to formulate an "Evolutionism"). In later years Russell rejected both his platonism and his identification of logic as the essence of philosophy. One would expect that once Russell had undercut two important steps in his own efforts to establish the independence of *philosophy* with respect to the theory of evolution, he would reconsider his judgment on the plausibility of some version of evolutionary philosophy. He does not.

Russell's turn toward atomism, his representation of philosophy as theoretical rather than practical, and his claim that the essence of philosophy is logic, may all have been motivated at least to some extent by his repudiation of Bergson's version of Evolutionism.

Russell concludes his first broad criticism of Evolutionism by saying that:

> Evolutionism thus consists of two parts: one not philosophical, but only a hasty generalization of the kind which the special sciences might hereafter confirm or confute [presumably referring to the issue of *progress*]; the other not scientific, but a mere unsupported dogma [about the nature of change and continuity], belonging to philosophy by its subject-matter, but in no way deducible from the facts upon which evolutionism relies. (27)

Therefore, Evolutionism is neither genuinely scientific nor genuinely philosophical.

Russell's second broad objection to Evolutionism is that its concerns are too practical.

(ii) *The motives and interests which inspire it are so exclusively practical, and the problems it deals with are so special, that it can hardly be regarded as really touching any of the questions that to my mind consititute genuine philosophy.* (25-6)

This second general objection is not unrelated to his concern to protect the traditional role of intellect against Bergson's preference for intuition. The objection is that the concerns of Evolutionism are too *practical* to touch the completely general, theoretical questions that constitute genuine philosophy. Evolutionism is more interested in "questions of human destiny," morality, and happiness than in knowledge for its own sake. Genuine scientific philosophy requires *disinterested* intellectual curiosity.

> . . . if philosophy is to become scientific—and it is our object to discover how this can be achieved—it is necessary first and foremost that philosophers should acquire the disinterested intellectual curiosity which characterizes the genuine man of science. (27)

and later, he notes that, by contrast

> [evolutionism is] . . . inspired by interests which are practical rather than theoretical. (28)

Russell regards *proper* philosophy as having as its aim the theoretical understanding of the world rather than the resolution of practical problems (36, 40); it is to be constructed on the model of disinterested science.

He offers no explicit argument to support this claim, but if one recalls his claims that philosophy is like mathematics in that both are *a priori* and are not dependent upon contingent facts, one can see this rejection of practical matters as a natural outcome of Russell's particular way of characterizing philosophy.

But an additional motivation for Russell's view is undoubtedly to be found in the fact that he is about to propose, against both classical philosophy (especially British Idealism) and Evolutionism, his third alternative for philosophy, his logico-analytic method. The logician is disinterested in the appropriate sense and his goals are general and theoretical. Unquestionably, too, Russell here sets the stage not only for his own logical atomism but also for a good deal of the classical analytic philosophy that followed. Work in formal logic and conceptual analysis (both of them theoretical, general and disinterested in the relevant senses) became models for careful philosophy in the analytic tradition.

Given the importance of Russell's claims here about the exclusively theoretical nature of philosophy and about its need for a method that will mimic the disinterested quality of scientific investigation, one would hope to find careful supporting reasons. Few explicit reasons are offered. Some motivation can surely be found in the fact that the scientific method had considerable success in extending understanding of the world. And it was undoubtedly the case that Russell was impatient with a view of philosophy, like Bergson's, that allied it more closely with mysticism and edification than with genuine understanding. A mystical attitude, he says, generally despises logic, has strong convictions not based on evidence, seeks hidden realities behind mundane facts, and appeals to "insight." In contrast to this, the scientific attitude observes cooly, analyzes without emotion, and accepts without question the equal reality of the trivial and the important. (31)

Most philosophers would probably agree that whatever philosophy is, it ought not to despise logic or develop strong convictions without evidence, etc. Truth rather than mindless comfort is a desirable goal for philosophy. That much is surely reasonable. But it does not follow from that, that philosophy ought not to concern itself with any practical matters. Even if one grants that Bergson had overstated the case on behalf of intuition, one is left with the suspicion that Russell has responded by overstating the case for the theoretical intellect.

One startling consequence of Russell's insistence on the primacy of theoretical understanding, a consequence that he states quite explicitly, is that "the ethical interests which have often inspired philosophers must remain in the background: some kind of ethical interest may inspire the whole study, but none must obtrude in the detail or be expected in the special results which are sought." (37) [87*]

Perhaps one of the things that makes his claim here so startling is the fact that Russell himself was so committed to various "ethical interests." Any number of his published works deal with ethical issues. Nonetheless, he would defend his claim by saying simply that none of those ethical interests constituted a part of genuine philosophy. This is precisely what he did say, many years later, of his own political and economic writings.

One of the obvious reasons for Russell's decision to disengage ethics from genuine philosophy lies with his claims that philosophy must be general and *a priori*. That is, it must deal impartially with everything that exists, and its propositions—dealing as they do with purely formal structures—must be true in all possible worlds. And while some of his early work, as I noted earlier, looks for ethics to have the same *a priori* character as his mathematics, by the time he wrote *Our Knowledge of the External World* his views on ethics had changed dramatically. After 1912, in light of some of the criticisms of his views on ethics, particularly in Santayana's *Winds of Doctrine*, Russell gave up his views on the objectivity of moral values. Increasingly, he came to identify ethical concerns with the objects of human *desire*. As such, they had no place in investigations of *a priori* truth. Propositions about them lacked the kind of generality that Russell required for philosophical propositions. He came to believe that " ... good and bad ... are the reflections of our own emotions on other things, not part of the substance of things as they are in themselves. And therefore an impartial contemplation, freed from all preoccupation with Self, will not judge things good or bad. . . . " [88] Philosophy, seen as "impartial contemplation," will incorporate no ethical content. To do so would be little more than to theorize about the emotional states of individuals. Whatever philosophy was to be, it wasn't that. And it was precisely this sort of view, centered on nothing more than human desires, that Russell attributed to the Evolutionists.

It is unfortunate that Russell selected philosophers like Spencer and Bergson as the only plausible representatives of a philosophy that incorporates evolutionary considerations. After all, Spencer takes evolutionary considerations well beyond Darwin's theory. Darwin himself was ambivalent about Spencer. Although he speaks of him as one of the great philosophers of the age,[89] Darwin also says in his letters that he neither understood nor was convinced by much of Spencer's view.[90]*

Bergson, on the other hand, rejected Darwin's mechanistic account of evolution and, as Passmore points out, he rejected the very idea that science could give an adequate account of living organisms.[91] So there was substantial distance between the views of Darwin on the one hand, and those of Spencer or Bergson on the other.

But, as I argued earlier, Russell also discounted Darwin's own views, particularly as they affected issues in ethics, on the basis of an unfortunately narrow reading of Darwin's notion of the struggle for existence. He does not, however, explore Darwin's views to see what consequences they might have for epistemology or for a philosophy of mind. The reason for this is undoubtedly Russell's conviction that all biological theories were irrelevant to genuine philosophy, including epistemology and philosophy of mind. So Darwin was not a genuine alternative to Spencer or Bergson as far as Russell was concerned.

Still, if Russell's real concern here was with the *philosophy* of Evolutionism, it is surprising that he took Spencer and Bergson to be the only Evolutionists worth considering. There were, in fact, other versions of Evolutionism which Russell does not discuss here. The Evolutionism of William James or John Dewey might have made a more worthwhile target for Russell's attack. Russell mentions James among the Evolutionists, but the specific criticisms of Evolutionism that he offers here are not directed to the details of James' views.

Russell's most explicit attacks on both James and Dewey are aimed at their Pragmatic Theory of Truth. And although he does not offer his objections to that theory in the context of this extended critique of Evolutionism, there is good reason to think that his objections both to the Pragmatic Theory of Truth and to Evolutionism were motivated by some of the same concerns. As Russell makes clear in his essays, "Pragmatism" and "The Philosophy of William James," he thinks that the Pragmatists have allowed their commitment to evolution to convince them to soften the boundaries that separate categories of all sorts, including the boundaries that separate truth from falsehood. They, like Bergson, prefer continua to fixed, distinct categories. This has at least two fatal consequences as far as Russell is concerned: it jeopardizes the stability of the sciences, and it allows one to suppose that religion can be "true" when it promotes happiness or virtue.[92] It is difficult to be sure about which of these two consequences Russell would find more objectionable.

Dewey and James, unlike Bergson, were not only Evolutionists, they were Darwinian Evolutionists in many crucial respects. And there is reason to believe that their philosophies were considerably more congenial to Russell than were the philosophies of Bergson and Spencer. Russell, in fact, incorporated a number of James' insights into his later philosophy, including his Neutral Monism, his rejection of Subjectivity, and his views on the "specious present." Russell unfortunately thought that his critiques of Bergson and Spencer adequately discredited all the significant variations of Evolutionism.

I have argued that Russell's version of analytic philosophy (as well as Moore's) was shaped by his rejection of Evolutionism as truly as it was by his rejection of Idealism. One might wonder why, if Evolutionism was a notable influence, Russell did not mention it later in life when he was reflecting on his philosophical development.[93*] I think that the reason for his omission has to do with his very low estimation of Evolutionist philosophers. With the exception of William James, Russell seems to have had little more than disdain for the Evolutionists. His remarks on Herbert Spencer are perhaps indicative. In 1962, Russell replied to a letter-writer who had asked why he did not "mention Herbert Spencer as an important figure of the nineteenth century . . . " Russell's response: " . . . I have not written about Herbert Spencer because I do not believe him to be of any importance. What he thought and wrote were Darwin, misapplied to areas in which the work had no relevance."[94] Incidentally, Russell's copy of Spencer's *Principles of Ethics*, (in the Russell Archives at McMaster University), has a number of marginal comments in the first part of Vol.I, most notable, perhaps, "rubbish" (79). The pages in the last parts of both Vol.I and Vol.II remain uncut.

Bergson fares no better. Russell appears to have had a profound personal dislike for Bergson. He says in a letter to Lady Ottoline Morrell, "I don't really dislike Schiller. . . . I don't feel venomous about him as I do about Bergson."[95] And later, "I do not feel with him [Bergson], as I did with James, that he is a man of first-rate ability whom I happen to disagree with—there is something fundamentally rhetorical and false about his writing—it never has the simplicity of real thought. Without the style it would be nothing."[96] In Russell's copy of Bergson's *Creative Evolution* (again, in the Russell Archives), next to a line of Bergson's text which reads: "It is as if a vague and formless being, whom we may call, as we will, man or superman ... " Russell has pencilled in the margin "or Bergson." (281) Russell's most frequent marginal comment in the book is "ROT."

The Idealists were philosophically respectable but mistaken. They were worthy opponents who deserved mention as contributors to one's philosophical development. The Evolutionists, by contrast, were for Russell not sufficiently good philosophers to merit any further attention.

Darwinism

I have described Russell's attitudes toward Darwin's biological theory of natural selection and his criticisms of Bergson's and Spencer's Evolutionism. There remains one other related target of Russell's criticism, what he calls "Darwinism." He is generally careful to distinguish it from Darwin's *scientific* theory. And it appears to be a more diffuse view than philosophical Evolutionism; he sometimes refers to it as "popular" Darwinism. Russell says that it "as it appears in the writings of its founder [presumably Darwin], and still more in those of Herbert Spencer, is the completion of Philosophical Radicalism."[97]

One of Russell's most fundamental objections to Darwinism was the stress it placed on the importance of *heredity*. He does not offer any detailed arguments against taking heredity seriously, but he makes claims that suggest a sort of *reductio* argument. He says, for example, ". . . it [Darwinism] has lessened men's belief in the omnipotence of education, and has substituted the conviction that some races are inherently superior to others. This, in turn, has led to an emphasis upon nationalism. And the recognition of war as a means of competition has dissolved the marriage of competition with pacifism. . . . " But the chain of inferences does not stop there.

> It was, of course, easy to adapt Darwinism to nationalism. The Jews, or the Nordics, or the Ecuadorians, are pronounced to be the best stock, and it is inferred that everything ought to be done to make them rich—although statistics prove that the rich have fewer descendants than the poor. In this way, also, Darwinism afforded a transition from the cosmopolitan outlook of the Philosophical Radicals to the racial bigotry of the Hiterlites.[98]

So by a remarkable series of suggested connections, Russell makes it seem that there is something in the writings of Darwin that could lead to the views of the Hitlerites. He offers no arguments to support the alleged connection nor does he evaluate the inferences in the chain. One is left with the impression that if one accepts the starting point in Darwin, the transition to

Hitler is easy and plausible. From the recognition of heredity, to a de-emphasis on education, to convictions about racial superiority, to nationalism, to bigotry and war, and finally to the Hitlerites. Russell, unfortunately, was not the only person to suggest a link between Darwinism and Nazism,[99]* but few associations could have been more damaging to Darwinism than these in 1934, when they were originally published.[100]*

His comments on heredity are particularly arresting, given the fact that he could in 1929, support eugenics.[101]

Russell assures the reader that he is not suggesting "that popular Darwinism, in drawing these inferences, has been scientifically justified."[102] But it is clear that he thinks these views do have their roots in Darwin's writings.[103]* So one might conclude that whatever he thought about the specific inferences that were made, the root problems were to be found in the original writings out of which they emerged.

Russell apparently overlooked Darwin's numerous comments in *Descent of Man* on the enormous importance of education. He also missed Darwin's view on nationalism:

> As man advances in civilization, and small tribes are united into larger communities, the simplest reason would tell each individual that he ought to extend his social instincts and sympathies to all the members of the same nation, though personally unknown to him. This point being once reached, there is only an artificial barrier to prevent his sympathies extending to the men of all nations and races. If, indeed, such men are separated from him by great differences in appearance or habits, experience unfortunately shews us how long it is before we look at them as our fellow-creatures. Sympathy beyond the confines of man, that is humanity to the lower animals, seems to be one of the latest moral acquisitions. [104]

People who are ignorant of Darwin's views and have never read his works might misconstrue his ideas and develop a "popular" but misguided view called "Darwinism" that could lead perhaps to Hitler and fascism. But it is less easy to understand how Russell, who had read Darwin, could agree that such views as the ones he describes have their origin in Darwin's writings.

Preliminary Conclusions

Russell's negative verdict on the relationship between philosophy and evolution has its roots in at least three sources: his apparent misconstrual of certain elements in Darwin's account of evolution, particularly the notion of the struggle for existence; Russell's proposal for an extraordinarily narrow account of what philosophy ought to be;[105]* and the choice of Spencer and Bergson as the most promising representatives of a philosophy that would incorporate evolutionary insights.[106]*

The Evolutionism that Russell discusses is not, however, the only candidate for a philosophy that incorporates evolutionary views. And while some of his objections are indeed valid, a plausible Evolutionism could have been constructed that would have avoided them. In order to do that, however, one has to be quite clear about what *Darwinian* claims about evolution by natural selection really entail. Most importantly, one needs to recognize that they do *not* entail a morality based on brute force, the abandonment of laws of logic, a socio-political framework in which only the rugged individualist has any value, the rejection of science with its stable conceptual frameworks, nor bigotry, war, and Hitlerites. It entails no comprehensive commitment to some global sense of inevitable future progress, nor does it promise comfort or edification.

It has been suggested that Russell's most influential contributions to the development of analytic philosophy were made by the 1920s. By his own admission, he began at the onset of World War I to devote his energies to non-philosophical work that focused heavily on politics and war. And although he wrote at least two important books in the 1920s—*Analysis of Mind* and *Analysis of Matter*—his influence in the philosophical community had begun to wane. There was some disapproval of his opposition to World War I. But perhaps more important than that was the fact that Ludwig Wittgenstein was beginning his ascent.[107]* And as the emphasis on *language* gradually overshadowed virtually all other concerns in philosophy, Russell's insistence on the inclusion of pre-linguistic and non-linguistic states further marginalized his influence.

The rising influence of Wittgenstein, however, did little to change the attitude toward philosophy's relationship to evolution theory. A friend of Wittgenstein, M. Drury, recalls a conversation he had with him in 1949:

> One day walking in the Zoological Gardens we admired the immense variety of flowers, shrubs, trees, and the similar multiplicity of birds, reptiles, animals.
>
> WITTGENSTEIN: 'I have always thought that Darwin was wrong: his theory doesn't account for all this variety of species. It hasn't the necessary multiplicity.' [108]

Wittgenstein's comment is, of course, consistent with his views on language, as expressed in his *Philosophical Investigations*. One must pay attention to the particular and stop looking for overarching commonalities. Suffice it to say,

Wittgenstein's philosophy did no more than Moore's and Russell's to incorporate Darwinian insights into twentieth-century philosophy. In fact, his taking philosophy in the direction of "therapy," and away from Russell's "scientific" philosophy may have increased the distance between analytic philosophy and evolutionary considerations.[109]*

For better or worse, Russell had helped to start analytic philosophy on a course that would emphasize logic, language, and analysis, while virtually excluding the evolutionary dimension of human *knowers* as living organisms that continue to struggle to survive and to provide for their well-being.

I turn now to consider some of the practical consequences of this for analytic theories of perception and mind that developed with Moore, Russell, and much of the subsequent tradition.

Chapter 4

Perception and Mind in the Analytic Tradition

. . . we view the world from the point of view of the here and now, not with that large impartiality which theists attribute to the Deity. To achieve such impartiality is impossible for us, but we can travel a certain distance towards it. To show the road to this end is the supreme duty of the philosopher.
—Bertrand Russell (1948)

There is, then, considerable evidence that the founders of twentieth-century analytic philosophy were explicit in their refusal to incorporate any insights from Evolutionism or the theory of evolution into their philosophy. I have tried to show that their reasons for refusing to do so are open to question. The consequences of their decision are, I think, far-reaching. But in order to get the full story, it will be necessary to broaden the picture a bit. I hope to show that the character of analytic philosophy was shaped by its attitude toward evolution and Evolutionism as truly as it was by its rejection of Idealism.

Philosophical Options

There were in England around the turn of the century several important possibilities for providing the framework within which philosophy would be done. Idealism and Evolutionism were the most obvious of these. The two had little in common. In fact, the early British Idealists were fierce opponents of Naturalism, particularly in its Darwinian/evolutionary form. James Hutchison Stirling's *The Secret of Hegel*, published in 1865, became one important element in the struggle against evolutionary Naturalism.[1]* Indeed, it has been suggested that one of the earliest motivations for the introduction of German Idealism into Great Britain in the latter half of the nineteenth century was the determination to combat the materialism, agnosticism, and Naturalism that seemed to flourish among the Darwinians.[2]

So when Moore and Russell repudiated Idealism near the turn of the century, Evolutionism would have provided a natural alternative for them.

It is true that by the early 1900s Evolutionism in Britain had been significantly discredited by the Idealists.[3]* Nonetheless, it was still of sufficiently recent vintage that it might have been considered by Moore and Russell as a credible alternative to Idealism. Moore and Russell did not, of course, opt for this alternative.

A third alternative that was available, but was not immediately selected, was the long-standing tradition of British Empiricism, most recently championed by John Stuart Mill. This might have been the most obvious choice, especially for Russell, given his close personal connection with Mill, his "lay god-father." But there is little evidence that Mill's Empiricism had much influence in the early years when Russell was looking for alternatives to Idealism. There may be several reasons for this. Both Moore and Russell were familiar with the harsh criticisms that Idealists like T.H. Green had leveled against Empiricism.[4]* They may have assumed that these criticisms were decisive.

But it is also likely that their determination to undercut the heavy subjectivism of Idealism led them to an extreme form of objectivism that was profoundly inimical to the assimilation of any psychological considerations in philosophy. Russell, particularly in the early years, was virulently anti-psychologistic. Mill, of course, following Hume, put a great deal of stock in psychological considerations. This fact alone would have made Empiricism an unlikely choice. Add to this the fact that Moore (and later, Russell) saw serious difficulties in Mill's version of utilitarian ethics.

For Russell there was an additional reason to reject Mill's philosophy. He found problematic Mill's account of logic and mathematics,[5] and he may have felt compelled to bypass the whole of the philosophic method associated with it. As he later put it, "In spite of strong bias towards empiricism, I could not believe that 'two plus two equals four' is an inductive generalisation from experience."[6]

It is worth pointing out, too, that Darwin, Huxley, Spencer, and other supporters of evolutionary thinking, were commonly classed among "the empiricists." Objections to evolutionary ways of thinking and objections to empiricist ways of thinking may have had telling overlap around the turn of the century.

So at least at the beginning of the revolt against Idealism, neither Moore nor Russell took classical Empiricism to be a viable alternative. There were, nonetheless, aspects of their philosophies that bore the clear mark of Empiricism. For example, in their concern to ground their theories in something unquestionable, something obviously "given," both Moore and Russell turn to sense data, some versions of which bore a close resemblance to Hume's impressions of sense. Their accounts differed, of course, from Hume's in that, in the early years at least, sense data were thought to be physical.[7] But in spite of some commonalities, at the outset, they did not return to this traditional framework for British philosophy.

The direction in which they both turned was toward Platonic Realism. Where the Idealists had argued against the reality of time, space, and matter, Russell says that he reacted at first by accepting the reality of anything that couldn't be *disproved*, including Platonic universals.[8] In time, both Moore's and Russell's commitment to platonism subsided, but at the start Plato's realm of timeless and immutable entities provided their mind-independent antidote to Idealism. In particular, it provided the kind of objectivity that they both sought for ethics and that Russell also required for logic and mathematics.

By 1910, however, Russell says that he began to be a bit more cautious in his ontological commitments. And later, under the influence of Wittgenstein, he came to the conclusion that logical truths were essentially linguistic in character and no longer required a platonic ontology.[9]* Still, he never quite deserted one of his basic motivations for embracing platonism—namely, his quest for *objectivity*, for the possibility of grounding knowledge in something more than the time-bound and fallible human mind.

In what follows it will be apparent that the theories of perception and mind that developed with Russell and Moore were shaped by their attitudes toward each of these four philosophic frameworks. And while I shall have something to say in connection with each of them, the influence of three— Idealism, Empiricism, and platonism—has already been well-documented by other commentators. So my comments on these three will be less central than what I have to say about the role played by evolution and Evolutionism.

My claim is that some of the significant features of early analytic philosophy owe their development to the rejection of evolutionary insights, whether of Darwin or the Evolutionists, as well as to the rejection of Idealism.

The Anti-Idealist Legacy

I want to highlight briefly a couple of features of the reaction against Idealism that are of particular interest in connection with the resulting analytic approaches to perception and mind. I have in mind especially two pairs of related notions: realism and objectivism, and analysis and atomism.

Realism and Objectivity

Both Moore and Russell devoted an extensive part of their work to providing an epistemology (and metaphysics) that would contest in detail the major tenets of Idealism and would replace them with Realist alternatives. Establishing robust claims for *objectivity* was, as I said, one motive for their move to platonism. It provided Russell with an avenue for knowledge of an external world, by way of acquaintance with the universals that would play a role in our knowledge (by description) of physical objects. Platonism was one avenue of exit from Idealism, and access to mind-independent objects was a central desideratum for both Moore and Russell. As part of their efforts to establish some version of realism, they were intent on undoing what they took to be the excessive *subjectivism* of Idealism.

Analysis and Atomism

Furthermore, Russell in particular made a concerted effort to undo the holism that was associated with Idealism by instituting an *analytic*, and eventually an *atomistic*, approach to philosophic issues. He attacked the Idealist doctrine of internal relations, substituting for it the view that entities can be defined independently of their relations. Things could, he argued, be understood in isolation from one another.

In addition to challenging the holism of the Idealists, the method of analysis had a further benefit. Some philosophers felt that many of the claims of Idealism were buried in a welter of unclear statements and unsubstantiated generalizations. The remedy proposed by the analysts was to focus on clarity and on detailed argument. To this end, they concentrated on very specific, limited problems rather than attempting to synthesize large systems of thought. The analytic method, with its various permutations, emerged.

The reaction against Idealism issued, then, in a heavy emphasis on realism and objectivity, with a correlative depreciation of the role of Subjectivity in the knowledge relation. It also generated an analytic, sometimes atomistic, treatment of philosophic issues. This, in turn, often led to an investigation of things in total abstraction from their context. Each of these features was reinforced by the antipathy, especially on Russell's part, to Evolutionism.

The Anti-Evolutionist Legacy

The anti-evolutionist move made by Moore and Russell shares some common features with their repudiation of Idealism: the emphasis on the method of analysis, with its occasional atomism, and the virtual elimination of Subjectivity. But there are also some additional features: the preference for timeless analyses, the segregation of cognitive from non-cognitive states, and the almost complete neglect of the relation between knowledge and the living organism. All of these characteristics of the philosophies of Moore and Russell are attributable (at least in part) to their early attitudes toward evolution and Evolutionism. Such attitudes continued to infect many subsequent theories of both perception and mind in the analytic tradition.

Analysis and Atomism

While Russell's method of analysis and his atomism were surely motivated by his rejection of Idealism, there is good reason to believe that both were also motivated by his rejection of Evolutionism. He objected strenuously to the views of men like Bergson who claimed that reality was continuous, seamless. "Life, in this philosophy [Evolutionism], is a continuous stream, in which all divisions are artificial and unreal. Separate things, beginnings and endings, are mere convenient fictions: there is only smooth unbroken transition."[10] Although the details of this view differed from those characterizing the British Idealist's holism, the consequence for Russell was the same: insist on the distinctness of things and on the importance of isolating them for analysis and thereby for understanding.

Russell's response to both Idealism and Evolutionism is, in this instance, an unfortunate one. He counters extreme forms of holism—in which nothing could be understood when detached from the larger whole to which it belonged—with an extreme form of atomism—in which everything could be understood in complete isolation from everything else.[11]* An intermediate position, claiming that *some* things are best understood by taking account of *some* of their relations, offers a reasonable compromise between these two extremes. And it is a position that is able to take account of the Darwinian insight that relations between a living organism and its environment are crucial for understanding that organism. Still, it does not require, as the doctrine of internal relations seemed to do, that every relation be equally authoritative.

Timelessness

The platonism that Moore and Russell adopted at the turn of the century provided them not only with objective knowledge and values, but it also spoke to their preference for the timeless and the unchanging. Even after Russell had abandoned his commitment to objective ethical values in 1912, his predilection for the timeless remained strong. In 1914, he could write:

> The [Idealist] contention that time is unreal and that the world of sense is illusory must, I think, be regarded as based upon fallacious reasoning. Nevertheless, there is some sense—easier to feel than to state—in which time is an unimportant and superficial characteristic of reality. Past and future must be acknowledged to be as real as the present, and a certain emancipation from slavery to time is essential to philosophic thought. The importance of time is rather practical than theoretical, rather in relation to our desires than in relation to truth. A truer image of the world, I think, is obtained by picturing things as entering into the stream of time from an eternal world outside, than from a view which regards time as the devouring tyrant of all that is. Both in thought and in feeling, to realize the unimportance of time is the gate of wisdom.[12]*

On Russell's view, then, time is important for the realm of the practical rather than the theoretical; it relates more to our desires than to truth. Recall that Russell's objections to Evolutionism included the claim that it was too concerned with practical issues, with human desires. The devaluation of time was one way of eliminating what he took to be the Evolutionists' inappropriate concern with the practical dimensions of life.

Note, too, the claim that one can obtain a "truer image of the world, . . . by picturing things as entering into the stream of time from an eternal world outside, ..." This is surely not an endorsement of an evolutionary account of the world.

In "Mysticism and Logic," he was even more explicit. "Evolutionism, in spite of its appeals to particular scientific facts, fails to be a truly scientific philosophy because of its slavery to time, its ethical preoccupations, and its predominant interest in our mundane concerns."[13] Genuine philosophy, by contrast, was to be theoretical and concerned with issues of timeless truth. This attitude was not a momentary aberration in Russell's early thought. As he put it several years later, "The occurrence of tense in verbs is an exceedingly annoying vulgarity due to our preoccupation with practical affairs."[14]

References to temporal considerations were not simply lost in the shuffle, an accidental casualty to other interests. For Russell, the genuinely philosophic point of view was the *timeless* point of view. This preference for timelessness was, of course, closely connected with his interest in mathematics and logic. But one might argue for a timeless treatment of these two areas without insisting that "time is an unimportant and superficial characteristic of reality." Clearly, Russell's attitude toward the philosophical insignificance of time and temporal considerations extended well beyond his concerns about mathematics and logic. Although Moore is less explicit about it, no one familiar with Moore's work can doubt that the same sort of timelessness attends his method of analysis.

This preference for the timeless was undoubtedly also motivated to some extent by their negative attitude toward Hegel's philosophy, with its emphasis on a historically developing reality. But notice that Hegel's emphasis on temporal development is not integral to his *Idealism*. It is, however, clearly integral to Evolutionist views. And Russell counts Hegel among the early Evolutionists as well as among the Idealists: "There are two kinds of evolutionist philosophy, of which both Hegel and Spencer represent the older and less radical kind, while Pragmatism and Bergson represent the more modern and revolutionary variety."[15] So the repudiation of Hegelian philosophy encompassed the Evolutionist dimension with its emphasis on the importance of temporal development, as well as its Idealist dimensions.

There were other considerations, related to the Evolutionists, that may well have motivated the dismissal of temporal considerations as philosophically unimportant. Russell was intensely critical of Bergson's insistence on the temporal flow of things and his consequent opposition to timeless, fixed categories. While Russell surely had stronger reasons for preferring those very timeless, fixed categories, the fact that they were under attack by Bergson would have provided him with additional motivation to champion them.

I do not mean to suggest that Moore and Russell had no investment at all in the importance of either time or history. Moore, for example, wrote on time.[16] But his interest centered primarily on issues relating to the reality of time and to the distinction between things that "exist" and those that are "real," based on whether or not they have temporal properties. His interests were in the static, rather than the dynamic, aspects of time.

Russell was, of course, greatly interested in history—particularly political history. In addition to his well-known *History of Western Philosophy*, he wrote other works with historical focus, like *Freedom versus Organization, 1814-1914*. But he did not consider these to be the same sort of thing as the doing of philosophy. History was one thing, philosophy was quite another. And his philosophy was done in a way that minimized the temporal and historical aspects not only of experience, but also of reality.

In his strictly philosophical work Russell did offer some accounts of time and temporal notions. But these were generally in relation to issues in physics, where he was concerned to offer some elucidation of certain temporal *concepts*.[17*] Both his earlier and later analyses remained at a static conceptual level, effectively skirting issues relating to temporal development.

In some of his later work Russell pays some attention to time in connection with his efforts to distinguish between living organisms and non-living matter. The former, but not the latter, are subject to what he calls "mnemic causation." That is to say, living organisms can be altered by their past experiences. But this notion never becomes central to his account of either perception or of mind (and he will eventually drop it). It is part of an effort to say something about how persons might differ from photographic plates. In one instance Russell defines a person as a series of experiences, where the experiences are related by some unspecified relation, R, (he later gives memory as an example of such an "empirically given relation"). His reason for defining a person as a series (rather than simply as a timeless class) of experiences is that "you want to know which is the beginning of a man's life and which is the end."[18] That is all. Once again, the developmental aspect of time is not an issue. And as we shall see when we discuss his theory of mind in greater detail, even his reliance on mnemic causation to distinguish minds from non-living things will eventually erode.

Obviously I do not want to suggest that there is something wrong with the project of getting clear about concepts related to time. But that sort of analysis ought not to simply replace or disallow developmental questions. Nonetheless, as analytic philosophy emerged under the leadership of Moore and Russell, it displayed a near complete disregard for temporal, developmental considerations. As Peter Hylton put it, " . . . analytic philosophy seems to think of itself as taking place within a single timeless moment."[19] This, as we shall see, will have consequences for theories of both perception and mind.

So the virtually a-temporal character that Moore and Russell bequeathed to analytic philosophy was to a considerable extent a consequence of their attitude toward Evolutionist philosophy. One need only recall that some of the Idealists had argued for the *unreality* of time. Had Russell's and Moore's reaction been shaped simply by their rejection of Idealism, one might expect them, as part of their protest, to emphasize the *importance* of time and temporal considerations. Their primary target in this case was, however, the Evolutionists. Platonism was able to play a dual role here. It provided objectivity, against Idealism, and timelessness, against the Evolutionists.

Empiricism played a role here, too. As I noted earlier, Russell had found Mill's psychologistic account of mathematics unacceptable. He argued that all the philosophers of arithmetic before Frege had been mistaken in thinking that numbers resulted from counting.[20] In both cases, Russell is troubled by the claim that the truths of mathematics (and logic) depend in some way on what happens in the time-bound world of human experience.[21]* (Some Idealist accounts of mathematics, notably Kant's, were also seen by Russell as psychologistic.[22]*) His alternative to Empiricist accounts of logic and mathematics is to appeal to the realm of timeless platonic entities. The Empiricists, like the Evolutionists, were not hospitable to appeals to timeless, immutable objects.

Cognition and Emotion

Another consequence of the dismissal of Evolutionism was the sharp separation that was maintained, by Russell in particular, between cognitive states and non-cognitive states like emotions and moods. As he says in his 1913 manuscript, "But as we are concerned with the theory of *knowledge*, we will ignore the non-cognitive part of the problem, and consider only what is relevant to knowledge."[23*]

I have already noted that Russell frequently accused the Evolutionists of being more concerned with human happiness and human desires than with the truth. Happiness and desires, he said, have to do with the practical side of things; philosophy, by contrast, is concerned with theoretical matters. And non-cognitive states like emotions are, for him, bound up with desires, happiness, and the practical concerns of life. As a consequence, apparently in an effort to avoid making the same mistake that he took the Evolutionists to be making, he almost always avoids any discussion of the role of feelings, moods, desires, or any other practical considerations, in his treatment of knowledge. It is, on his view, an independent phenomenon that can be effectively isolated from the taint of any practical or non-cognitive influence. And while he never argues that *all* knowledge must be theoretical, he clearly takes theoretical knowledge to be the paradigm case and argues explicitly that it is the only type of knowledge which belongs on the philosophical agenda.

In some of Russell's later works, particularly under the influence of behaviorism, he occasionally appears to soften his stance on the purely theoretical character of knowledge within the philosophical framework.[24*] But if there was indeed any momentary relaxation on the question of the philosophical importance of the practical dimensions of knowledge, it did not have a significant influence on the development of either Russell's own philosophy or that of many of his early analytic heirs.

This isolation of the cognitive from all non-cognitive contamination is made possible by Russell's method of analysis and his emerging "atomism." His method generally leads him to isolate items under investigation and to treat them as if they remain substantially unaffected by the severance of all their normal relations. He analyzes things as if each were independent and self-contained, much like Leibnizian monads. It is true that he speaks favorably about *synthesis* as well, but the most extensive type of synthesis that he carries out takes the form of "logical construction" in which he argues that complex things like physical objects and minds are best understood as constructions from simpler "atoms" like sensory data. He does not attempt the kind of synthesis that might show the interdependence of cognitive states, emotions, and desires.

Synthesis and integration are clearly not to play a significant part in Russell's philosophical program. "Speaking generally," he says, "scientific progress has been made by analysis and artificial isolation."[25] His view of philosophical progress precisely parallels his views about its scientific counterpart.

Knowledge and the Living Organism

Yet another consequence of the reaction against Evolutionism, closely related to the previous one, was Moore's and Russell's disregard for the role that cognition plays on behalf of the individual living organism. The theories of knowledge that they formulate offer primarily "spectator" accounts of the knowledge relation, and take its function to be almost exclusively that of attempts at truth-gathering. Russell, in particular, often cites contemplation as a paradigm case of knowledge.

By contrast, the philosophers who took evolution seriously in formulating their theories of knowledge—John Dewey is a good example—make explicit reference to the connection between knowledge, action, and the needs of the organism. Capacity for knowledge, and its link with bodily action, were seen by evolutionary thinkers as adaptations that assist the organism in its struggle for survival and well-being. All of this, for Russell, lies outside the scope of philosophy.

In a telling passage in one of his later works, Russell argues against the view that the notion of "organism" is fundamental for understanding the behavior of an animal. His objections stem partly from a suspicion that reliance on "organism" implies a species of holism of the sort that he rejected with the Idealism of Hegel. Although he does not mention internal relations, his way of characterizing the view is revealing: " . . . the logical essence of the theory . . . holds that the body of an animal or plant is a unity, in the sense that the laws governing the behavior of the parts can only be stated by considering the place of the parts in the whole."[26] One might expect that he would find no difficulties with a milder rendering of the claim, namely, that the notion "organism" should play *some* significant role in theories about behavior. More particularly, if one softened the holistic tone of the claim and reformulated it in such a way as to assert that at least some of the functions of an organism need to be understood in relation to the environment of the organism or in relation to the well-being of the organism as a whole, one would expect no objection. So for example, a claim that perception ought to be understood in relation to the needs and interests of the perceiving organism, might seem unproblematic. But Russell's rejection of practical considerations in philosophy, as well as his atomism, apparently made such a consideration unacceptable.

Russell has a second objection that blocks this milder assertion, namely his increasing commitment to a reductionistic account of biology.[27]* On his view, the behavior of an organism will eventually be fully explicable in terms of physics and chemistry, neither of which makes reference to the organism as such. This reductionistic view of biology adds further weight to his refusal to assimilate any of the insights of evolutionary biology into philosophy. If biology is, in principle, reducible to physics and chemistry, then one needs only the theories of the latter. They will incorporate everything essential from the reduced science.

The living organism, its needs and interests, are explicitly excluded from any significant role in the theories of knowledge that will emerge from early analytic philosophy. Partly as a consequence of this, Subjectivity will also be submerged and eventually discarded as an unnecessary factor in the knowledge relation.

In sum, Russell's reaction against Evolutionism reinforced his commitment to a method of analysis and eventually to atomism. It also added a timeless, static framework to his philosophy and sanctioned his isolation of cognitive states from their relations both with non-cognitive states and the needs and interests of the living organism.

To understand, then, the theories of perception and of mind that emerged under the leadership of Moore and Russell, one needs to understand their rejection of both Idealism and Evolutionism. It was this combination of reactions that forged a new philosophy that was objectivist, atomistic, largely a-temporal, cognitivist, and quite detached from the practical considerations that touch living organisms. I shall discuss each of these characteristics as it appears in the early analytic accounts of perception and of mind.

In my discussion, I shall focus primarily on Russell's theories for two reasons. First, he had a good deal more to say about Darwin and Evolutionism than did Moore. And secondly, whereas Russell often changed his views on various topics, he nonetheless argued for very specific positions at different times in his life. Moore, by contrast, spent a great deal of energy exploring the possibilities in connection with problems in philosophy, trying to clarify the issues rather than to argue for the adequacy of one particular solution. His views often amount to tendencies in the direction of a position, rather than carefully argued conclusions. And while Moore occasionally approached a definite theory of perception, he himself acknowledges that he never found one that satisfied him. He was even further from proposing a complete theory of mind. As a consequence, when I speak of Moore and Russell as, for example, minimizing the role of Subjectivity in perception, my claim is that Russell argues explicitly for an account of Subjectivity that makes it quite passive and eventually deleterious. Moore, by contrast, does not argue for any particular account of the perceiving subject. He simply has a tendency to let the notion of Subjectivity slip into oblivion in his accounts of perception.[28] So while my claims are about Moore and Russell, the strength of the claims as they relate to each should be understood with the foregoing caveat in mind.

I should perhaps add that although many of my comments on Moore's and Russell's views of perception and mind will be negative, I do not mean to minimize in any way their many valuable contributions to other areas of philosophy.

Theories of Perception

A great deal has been written about the details of both Moore's and Russell's accounts of perception. I shall not repeat much of that here. But I want to call attention to some common features of their theories that have received less explicit attention.

In spite of differences in their particular approaches, Moore and Russell provided us with theories of perception that were similar in several significant respects. And the similarities on which I shall focus attention are particular instances of the ones that I discussed in the previous section—they are characteristics that resulted to a very large extent from their repudiation of Evolutionism and of any insights issuing from the theory of evolution.

Realism, Objectivism, and Justification

In his book, *A Hundred Years of British Philosophy*, Rudolf Metz characterizes the philosophy that emerged with Moore and Russell as "New Realism." He says, "Above all, it is the problem of perception, . . . that has been attacked afresh; . . . ."[29] Their efforts on behalf of perceptual realism have been well-documented. My concern is to show that even in the context of establishing realism, their particular approaches further undercut the possibility of taking evolutionary considerations into account.

In their papers on perception, discussions of the nature of the perceived object proliferate. Sense-data, sensibilia, percepts, and the like, figure prominently. The original significance of these discussions is best understood against the background of the quarrel with Idealism. They are part of an effort to re-establish the legitimacy of our claims to know something about non-mental reality—a claim with which evolution theory need have no quarrel.

Nonetheless, one consequence of the emphasis that Moore and Russell placed on issues surrounding perceptual realism was the exclusion of other considerations that would indeed have been of interest to a theory of perception influenced by evolutionary considerations. Selective attention, for example, assists an organism to gather information relevant to its own survival and well-being. But theories that concentrate almost exclusively on the nature of the perceived object standardly overlook issues like selective attention because it relates primarily to a function of the perceiving subject.

Consider Moore's approach to perception. A primary goal in much of his theorizing about perception is to show how it is possible that we have knowledge of a physical, external world. As he says in some of his later work, we are certain that many of our common sense beliefs about the external world are true. What is needed is an adequate *analysis* of the propositions that express those beliefs—an analysis that will make clear the grounds for our certainty.[30] Whatever changes in emphasis his views underwent over the years, they never deviated far from this primary goal. From his early paper, "Refutation of Idealism" (1903), through his numerous subsequent papers on sense-data, Moore is at pains to establish some form of epistemological realism. He approaches it from two angles.

In his early work he focuses on distinguishing between the acts of consciousness and their objects, with a view to establishing the mind-independent character of those objects. Part of this effort involves minimizing the role of an active perceiver to such an extent that it is virtually eliminated from consideration. One way to establish a robust sense of objectivity, and thereby of perceptual realism, is to undercut any constructive role for Subjectivity.[31]* So while conscious *acts* play a role in Moore's early work, their primary function is to allow him to highlight the distinction between such acts and their objects. The latter are the genuine focus of concern.

Later, Moore's attention shifts more explicitly to an analysis of the nature of sense-data, his preferred candidate for the perceived object. He explores various ways of interpreting them, including the possibility that they are parts of the surfaces of physical objects or that they are at least caused by physical objects. By his own admission, he never arrived at a completely satisfactory account of them.

In spite of the shift in focus, Moore's target remained unaltered: the formulation of a plausible theory to account for the claim that the objects of perception are not a product of the perceiving mind. Realism took the form of an objectivism that lost sight of the role of an active, interested perceiving subject.

Russell, although much of his early work was concerned with issues in the philosophy of mathematics and logic, notes that between 1910 and 1914 he had begun to give serious attention to perception.[32] His interest took a slightly different turn from Moore's. He was not only anxious to provide a Realist account of perception, but he also wanted to clarify the relationship between perception and science. The relevant science was, of course, not biology but physics. This interest gradually came to dominate Russell's attention in his theorizing about perception. The apparent discrepancy between the objects described by physics and the objects of our ordinary experience posed a continuing problem for him. Russell came to believe that one of philosophy's principal tasks was to offer an interpretation of the claims of ordinary perception that would show how they provide evidence for the truth of the basic claims of physics.

Russell's account of perception in *Problems of Philosophy* (1912), is not yet dominated by the concern to explain and justify the relationship between perception and physics. But he has by then laid the ground for such a justification, with his distinction between knowledge by acquaintance and knowledge by description.[33]* So at the outset Russell has built a bridge that will justify our claims to have knowledge of a mind-independent world of physical objects.

By 1913, the problems posed by the claims of physics have begun to assert themselves: " . . . 'matter,' which in Descartes' time was supposed to be an obvious datum, has now, under the influence of scientific hypotheses, become a remote super-sensuous construction, connected, no doubt, with sense, but only through a long chain of intermediate inferences."[34] And by 1914, his paper, "The Relation of Sense-Data to Physics," is devoted completely to an explanation of the relationship between the claims of physics and the data of ordinary perception.[35]* By 1927, he states his overriding concern with the relationship between perception and science quite explicitly:

> It will be understood that my purpose is epistemological: I am considering perception because it is involved in the premises of empirical sciences, not because it is interesting as a mental process. It is of course necessary to consider its intrinsic character, but we do not do this for its own sake, we do it for the sake of the light that it may throw upon the character and extent of our knowledge.[36]

So his interest in perception is prompted primarily by his concerns about its relation to the premises of science. Other aspects are secondary at best.

Russell's views on the relation between sense-data and the objects of empirical science change over the years. In 1912, he argues for a causal account of the relation. By 1913, he has been converted, apparently by Whitehead, to the view that "the world of physics [is] a construction rather than an inference."[37]* During the next decade he will argue that both matter and mind are best understood as logical constructions from simpler elements, generally sensory data.[38]* And then in 1927, Russell reverted to his earlier causal theory.[39]*

The details of these accounts, and Russell's reasons for moving from one to another of them, are less important for our purposes than is the general motivation for the theories. What remains constant through their alterations is the determination to provide a theory of perception that will not only undermine Idealism[40]* but will also explain and justify the relationship between perception and physical science.

Like Moore, Russell was preoccupied with providing an objectivist account of perception; unlike Moore, he was also intent on providing a justification for the claims of science.

This preoccupation with the relation between perception and physics not only leads Russell to emphasize issues of truth and justification, it also explains to some extent his exclusive attention to the objective and the cognitive aspects of perception while excluding its subjective and non-cognitive dimensions.[41]* The former, but not the latter, are taken to be relevant to justification.

While a project that would explain how we are able to have perceptual knowledge of the physical world is an enormously important one, this is not the only significant project to be undertaken by philosophical theories of perception. And truth-gathering, even in the interest of science, is only one of the many functions of perception. The latter is also an adaptive capacity that assists living organisms to deal with their environments in ways that serve their individual interests and needs. And it can serve those interests and needs not only by generating true beliefs but sometimes even with false ones. The person who jumps back to the curb when he hears something that sounds like a car approaching from his left, will be well-served by that false perceptual belief if there is in fact a truck approaching from his right. Similarly, an individual might mistake Coke® for Pepsi®, or a hot dog for bratwurst, and still have its bodily needs satisfied. Obviously, it is not the case that one has *no* concern for truth in these cases. Mistaking toadstools for mushrooms could be fatal. But the point is that a perceptual system that delivers to an organism information that is relevant to its needs and interests, even if that information is not infallibly correct, is crucial to the survival and well-being of that organism. That fact must surely be relevant to an adequate account of perception.[42]*

So while the truth of perceptual beliefs is undoubtedly important, it constitutes only one part of a full account of perception. Similarly, the justification of the general, impersonal claims of science is important too, but gathering data that is relevant to the needs and interests of the individual perceiving organism is an equally important aspect of perception.

Non-cognitive States

The emphasis on objectivity, with its attendant focus on the justificatory dimension of perception, is related to a second commonality in the theories of perception proposed by Moore and Russell. Their theories make little allowance for the role of non-cognitive states like emotions and moods. Perception is treated as if non-cognitive states were utterly unrelated to it. In theories of perception whose exclusive goal is to justify claims about our knowledge of an external world, consideration of perceivers' emotions and moods might do little more than muddy the waters. However, an additional goal for an adequate theory of perception is to account for the fact that individuals regularly perceive aspects of their environments not merely as green, large, or square, but also as frightening, attractive, or annoying.

In addition, various of our non-cognitive states play a controlling role in our perceptions. They can, for example, direct our perceptions by activating selective attention; they can motivate us to *look for* things and *listen for* things that we love, fear, or are angry about. A frightened person who is walking alone on a dark street at night is likely to select for attention objects that might pose a threat—a dark alley, the figure of a person in the shadows, the sound of footsteps. Similarly, a person who is jealous will be likely to look for any indications of infidelity on the part of his partner. Notice that such examples assume that perception is not a purely passive affair. In important ways it can be guided by the perceiving subject and by non-cognitive states of that subject.

Non-cognitive states can also contribute to the way sensory data is conceptualized. A human figure emerging from a dark alley could be seen as a "mugger" or a "neighbor," as a "threat" or a "passer-by," depending on whether the perceiver is frightened or calmly confident.

In addition to emotions, an evolutionary account of perception will incorporate other non-cognitive states such as hunger and sexual attraction. These, too, can both guide selective attention and contribute to the conceptualization of sensory information. An integration of such states into theories of perception is required if we are to understand how perception functions effectively on behalf of the well-being of the organism.

To see just how the issue of *justification* contributed to the compartmentalization of cognitive and non-cognitive states, consider Russell's project in broad outline. Russell begins with some complex, unclear bit of ordinary experience and analyzes it into elements—sense-data, percepts, and the like—that can provide the simplest, most certain bits of data from which more complex, less certain objects and beliefs can be generated.[43] His general goal is to isolate the "minimum assumptions that will justify such beliefs [as our belief in other people, cats, tables, etc.]."[44]

His goal of teasing out the *order* in epistemology is accomplished by eliminating from consideration anything that is not required for *justificatory* purposes. It is clear that a goal of this sort virtually assures the elimination of all the non-cognitive aspects of perception.

An additional reason for isolating perception from non-cognitive states arises directly from Russell's attitude toward Evolutionism. The Evolutionists, he argued, placed too much emphasis on practical issues relating to human desires and human happiness. Non-cognitive states like emotions and moods are most plausibly identified with practical concerns and with human desires. A philosophy that concerns itself with purely theoretical matters has no particular interest in the function of non-cognitive states.

The Living Organism

Closely related to this purely cognitive approach to perception is the tacit assumption on the part of both Moore and Russell that perception's ties to an active, living body are philosophically unimportant. The perceiver is treated more like a *res cogitans* than like a living organism. When the body figures at all in these theories (and that is rare) its status is primarily that of a collection of sensory systems that provide data for perception. It is little more than a vehicle for the transmission of information. There is virtually no consideration of perception's function on behalf of the body itself, no thought given to the fact that perception plays a pivotal role in the efforts of the organism to find food, to avoid dangers to itself, and to select sexual partners. On Moore's and Russell's approach to perception, perceivers are treated as impersonal cognitive systems, with nothing peculiar to them as living organisms. The perceiving subject is most often treated simply as a pair of mental eyes that might belong to any system. Among the later analytic philosophers this treatment of the perceiver culminates in its complete formalization. Statements about perception come to be framed as "x appears . . . to S," or "It is true that S perceives M if and only if. . . . "

By contrast, when a Darwinian account of us is taken seriously, it becomes clear that the capacity of the individual organism to relate sensory data to its own needs and interests assists that organism in its efforts to survive and provide for its well-being. Impersonal, generic information about the world can't do the required job.

As I noted in Chapter One, a fairly predictable objection to the claims I have made so far is that these impersonal, purely cognitive issues are all that epistemology or a *philosophical* theory of perception *ought* to be concerned with. These are, after all, normative theories that are concerned precisely with issues of truth and justification.

The objection is important, and the response to it is fundamentally important to my goals in the book. So it may not be amiss to repeat my response to it. The objection assumes one particular way of defining epistemology and perception. And efforts to settle the issue by appealing to this or some different definition are likely to beg the question and end in a standoff. But one can approach the objection without appealing to a particular definition of perception. One can ask whether the approach taken by Moore and Russell (and subsequent analytic epistemology) has omitted anything of significance from its accounts of perception. And one can ask if such omissions generate problematic consequences.

The answer to the first question is, as I have argued, clearly affirmative, and I have catalogued some of the significant omissions. Even if it is possible that some perceptions are totally unaffected by the emotions, moods, and bodily needs of an organism—and I am not sure that even this minimal case is plausible—the fact remains that a good deal of human perception *is* affected by these non-cognitive states. An adequate theory of perception should take account of this fact.

My objector, however, is not likely to accept this portion of a response as satisfactory. It is precisely this claim, that things are being omitted, that the objection challenges. But the omissions generate some problematic consequences, most notably that one is left with a distorted view about how mental states relate to one another and to the needs of the organism. When one treats perception as a purely cognitive affair, one easily goes on to construct models of the *mind* which leave cognitive and non-cognitive states wholly independent of one another. This in turn encourages the belief that a purely cognitive system like a computer provides an adequate model for human psychological processes.

I have no quarrel with efforts to program computers to function as if they were carrying out certain isolated mental functions. My concern is with the view that such computer programs provide an adequate model for the formulation of psychological theories that explain human mental function as well as they explain computer function. It is here that excessively narrow theories of perception, like those of Moore, Russell, and their followers, have misled our research programs.

I shall return to the issue of the computer model in Chapter Seven. The point I want to stress here is that, however one chooses to define epistemology, perception needs to be seen as more than a virtually disembodied, purely cognitive, truth-gathering process, if one is to have an adequate account of human mental states and their relations to one another.

Theories of the sort proposed by Moore and Russell would perhaps be better called theories of *sensory justification*. If epistemology is indeed

concerned exclusively with issues of justification, then perhaps it should
include theories of sensory justification, leaving theories of *perception* to
some broader region of philosophy. Whether or not Russell's and Moore's
accounts are adequate as theories of sensory justification, they are at best
misleading if meant to provide adequate theories of perception.

Unfortunately, giving an account of perception exclusively as a process
of truth-gathering is largely where twentieth-century analytic theories of
perception stalled. Those theories have been standardly constructed from
three or four elements: sensory bits, concepts, perceptual beliefs, and
sometimes inference. All of the elements are purely cognitive and impersonal. This way of approaching perception is, of course, the standard one,
and it has a long philosophic tradition behind it. From the time of Descartes
at least, the goal of most theories of perception has been the justification of
truth-claims about the world, and often the truth-claims of the sciences.
Other aspects of perception were discarded as irrelevant. Russell and his
philosophic heirs have been loyal to this tradition.

Even in later years when Russell expands his account of perception,
particularly in *Analysis of Mind*, the items that he adds are still purely
cognitive—things like memories, expectations (he notes that these are
really *beliefs*), and "theories." What is unfortunate is the fact that after the
arguments for realism had virtually demolished British Idealism, and Evolutionism was no longer a significant rival, attention to the relation between
perception and realism, and the treatment of perception as a purely cognitive and virtually disembodied affair, continued unabated.

Passivity and Selective Attention

Still another commonality in Moore's and Russell's approaches to perception appears in their views of sense-data. Their primary appeal was their
certainty, their immediacy as objects of "acquaintance." While Russell and
Moore differed at times in their accounts of sense-data, they agreed that
sense-data were, as their name suggests, simply *given* in perception. So when
Subjectivity plays any role at all it is fundamentally a passive role. Assumptions about the *givenness* of sensory data are often closely related to a
commitment to perceptual realism. If sense-data are not to be mind-dependent, then it is thought that they should be understood as *presented* to
the mind.[45]* The difficulty with the approach taken by Moore and Russell
is that there is virtually nothing but givenness. The perceiver becomes little
more than a passive spectator of its world.

A revealing example of this bias toward passivity surfaces in Moore's
uses of the term "look." In ordinary usage the term has at least two meanings: it is a verb that suggests an actively attentive gaze or even an active

searching for something ("He looked at her." or "He looked everywhere for his keys."); a second use is as a noun (or its cognate verbs) meaning the appearance of something ("It had the look of something dead." or "It looked blue."). Moore uses the term often, but not in its first and active sense. He always uses it in the sense of *an appearance*, something given to the perceiver.

The perceiver can, of course, react to the sense-data, but neither Moore nor Russell give much consideration to the fact that a perceiver often actively *selects* from among available sensory information. For them the data of sense are simply presented, much as sense impressions were for Hume. If the perceiver does respond to them, it is generally by simply being aware of them, or alert, and then the perceiver is said to be "attentive." That is to say, the notion of attention is limited for the most part to the state of alert awareness of what is presented in the perceptual field.

This minimal characterization of attention is one that persists in most of the analytic literature on perception. It is rare for these theories to make significant use of the notion of *selective attention*, a much more active phenomenon than mere attentive awareness. In cases of selective attention the perceiver selects for particular, focused attention some subset of the available sensory information. These data generally carry information relating to the interests or needs of the individual perceiver. So, if a person is *looking for* her red car, then red objects of a certain size are likely to be selected from the visual field for attention. Again, if a person is expecting an important phone call, he actively *listens for* the sound of the phone, allowing other noises to slip into the background.

Needless to say, neither Moore nor Russell *denies* that selective attention occurs. But Moore, for example, in his occasional references to the notion of attention is always concerned with the sense of *paying* attention, concentrating.[46*] His focus is on issues relating to our capacity to acquire accurate knowledge of external objects. Individual interests and needs have nothing to do with it.

Russell, on the other hand, discusses both attention and selective attention. But his interest in them has little to do with exploring their role in perceptual experience. In one case, for example, he explores the relationship between selective attention and analysis:

> Mere selective attention, which makes us aware of what is in fact part of a previously given complex, without making us aware of its being a part, is not analysis. . . . All that is necessary is that the area of attention should be narrowed, not that we should realize, as analysis requires, the relation of the new partial objects to the old total one.[47*]

The contrast that Russell suggests here between selective attention and analysis might explain why he omitted the former in his subsequent accounts of perception. His primary concern was *analysis*, and he may have been anxious not to have it confused with anything that might partially resemble it.

In the same manuscript, but in a somewhat different context, he discusses the role of attention in picking out *logical forms*.

> Attention, as a psychical occurrence, is governed by biological considerations: particulars may be good to eat or likely to kill us, and therefore it is useful to pay attention to them; but logical forms are not edible or hostile, and attention to them is not a cause of longevity. This sufficiently explains why it is only a few eccentric persons, unusually relieved from the struggle for existence, whose attention wanders to such unimportant objects.[48]

Given these comments about the connection between biological needs and attention, one would expect that Russell would have taken selective attention to be very important for *perception*. But he says little about it in that context. As he says, the struggle for existence requires it. But the struggle for existence, he argues that same year, has no relevance to philosophical theories of perception or anything else. And some, presumably he includes himself, "are unusually relieved from the struggle for existence," and can thus focus their attention on logical forms.

There is one context in which Russell argues for the importance of some version of selective attention. It also occurs in the 1913 manuscript. One overriding goal of that work is to argue against the Neutral Monism of William James. On James' view, the mental and the physical are constructed from the same neutral material, "pure experience," and the distinction between the two is a matter of the types of relations they enter into.

In arguing against James' view, one tactic that Russell uses to defend his view that the mental and the physical are really distinct is the phenomenon of selective attention. The "objects" that such attention picks out are what Russell calls the "emphatic particulars." He says, ". . . to me it seems obvious that such 'emphatic particulars' as 'this' and 'I' and 'now' would be impossible without the selectiveness of mind."[49]* Undoubtedly there is some suggestion here of activity on the part of attentive consciousness. But it appears to be the minimal sort of activity that will allow Russell to explain our capacity to isolate one object from among others, particularly one of the emphatic particulars. Its function is not to act on behalf of the individual subject. Rather, it is to provide justification for our supposed knowledge of individual objects. And as he makes clear many years later, this ability to attend to one object is important as a preliminary to *abstraction*.[50] Again, it has little to do with individual interests or needs.

There are two points to be made about Russell's claims in this context. First, in spite of his protestations about the importance of selectiveness and emphatic particulars, Russell does not make any significant use of either notion in his theories of perception. Secondly, when in 1919 Russell embraces Neutral Monism himself, he says nothing more about the crucial importance of selective activity on the part of the mind. This attitude of relative indifference toward selective attention was undoubtedly influenced by his anti-Idealist commitment to minimizing any active role for Subjectivity. And selectiveness, on Russell's own account, requires an active subject. But his indifference was also influenced, I believe, by Russell's determination to eliminate from philosophy all the Evolutionists' practical considerations that relate to human desires and human happiness. A theory of perception that takes the phenomenon of selective attention seriously needs some account of a *subject* that has interests and needs and is capable of selecting from among the available data those that might be relevant to her interests or needs. The selective attention that a particular individual exercises on her own behalf has virtually no role to play in the theoretical philosophy that Russell advocated. Selective attention is worlds away from the "godlike impartiality" that he so values.

> ... we cannot escape from perception with all its personal limitations. How far the information which we obtain from this tainted source can be purified in the filter of scientific method, and emerge resplendently godlike in its impartiality, is a difficult question, with which we shall be much concerned.[51]

Subjectivity

It may be useful here to consider more carefully Russell's views on Subjectivity. They go through a number of different stages. At its best, Subjectivity is construed as a purely passive recipient of sense-data. Gradually Russell comes to see it as a logical fiction that is as applicable to lifeless things as to human beings. And eventually he takes it to be little more than a source of distortion and error.

In his earlier work Russell thinks that it is probable, though not indubitable, that we are acquainted with something that could be called the self or the "I," the one who is aware of sense-data. He is cautious to point out that this self need not be one unified, enduring self. Although he does not rule out that possibility.[52*]

In the 1913 manuscript on Theory of Knowledge he defines the *subject* as "any entity which is acquainted with something ... "[53] Elsewhere he characterizes "acquaintance," " ... to say that S [a Subject] has acquaintance with O is essentially the same thing as to say that O is presented to S."[54] So a subject is little more than a bare second term required for the dyadic relation of acquaintance. By 1917 he is more explicit about this: "What the mind adds to *sensibilia*,[55]* in fact is *merely* awareness: everything else is physical or physiological."[56] Presumably, when he refers to "mind" here he means either the subject or at the very least, the locus of the subject. So even in those cases where Russell argues for the inclusion of some notion of subject in his theories of perception, his view does not include a role for an *active, bodily* subject. [57]* In these early papers the subject is the locus of awareness, that-to-which presentations can be given.

After 1919, Russell no longer thought of sense-data as being *given*.[58] But this did not lead him to devise a more active role for the perceiver. On the contrary, his reason for thinking that sense-data were not *given* was that such a view seemed to entail that there had to be a subject receiving them. By this time he has discarded Subjectivity. His 1919 essay, "On Propositions: What They Are and How They Mean" marks the complete elimination of any consideration of a positive role for a subject.

In his *Analysis of Mind* in 1921 Russell says that he considers the subject to be a logical fiction. It is linguistically convenient, but we have no evidence that it exists. He then characterizes Subjectivity in terms of "perspectives," spatial points of view, noting that it is exhibited equally by photographic plates. It does not involve consciousness, experience, or memory.[59]* The parallel between perception in a living organism and the sensitivity of photographic plates is a continuing theme in Russell's work. He states the case forcefully in his *Analysis of Matter* in 1927:

> In fact, it may be said that the essential characteristic of a sense-organ is sensitiveness to one sort of stimulus, which, in the case of the eye or the ear, must be a periodic movement. In this the sense-organs do not differ from lifeless instruments, such as photographic plates and gramophones. Such instruments have something closely analogous to perception, when we leave out of account the mental consequences which we observe in ourselves as a result of perception. And in a certain extended sense we may say that every body which behaves in a characteristic manner when a certain stimulus is present, and only then, has a 'perception' of that stimulus.[60]

Subjectivity that acts on behalf of a living, bodily organism has no role to play.

By the time he writes *The Analysis of Matter*, Russell has come to view Subjectivity as little more than a source of distortion in experience. He distinguishes three sources of Subjectivity: physical, physiological (or sensory), and cerebral (or psychological). Physical Subjectivity includes all distortions caused by physical objects intervening between the body of the percipient and the "centre of the group to which the percept belongs." A photograph and a gramaphone record share this type of Subjectivity. Physiological or sensory Subjectivity arises from defects in the sensory organs or afferent nerves. Cerebral or psychological Subjectivity arises as a result of past experience; it leads to correlations not contained in the present situation. (He uses the amputated limb as an example.) "All these sources of error have to be guarded against if perception is not to mislead us."[61] The same year he says,

> The subjectivity of percepts is a matter of degree. They are more subjective when people are drunk or asleep than when they are sober or awake. They are more subjective in regard to distant objects than in regard to such as are near. They may acquire various peculiar kinds of subjectivity through injuries to the brain or to the nerves. When I speak of a percept as 'subjective' I mean that the physiological inferences to which it gives rise are mistaken or vague.[62]

Subjectivity has become little more than a problem to be minimized or neutralized as much as possible.

By 1935 he could say, "Now we can only say that we react to stimuli, and so do stones, though the stimuli to which they react are fewer. So far, therefore, as external 'perception' is concerned, the difference between us and a stone is only one of degree." [63] So perception as well as Subjectivity is properly attributed to non-living as well as to living entities. This makes it extraordinarily clear that Russell sees no connection between perception and the needs or interests of a living organism. Perception is seen entirely in connection with the impersonal reception of stimuli.[64*]

The decline in the fortunes of the perceiving subject began with a concern to establish a Realist (or at least a non-Idealist) account of perception. It was further encouraged by Russell's determination to eliminate from philosophy what he took to be the Evolutionists' preoccupation with practical matters, in particular to exclude any consideration of the desires or happiness of individuals. The complete elimination of the subject followed upon Russell's gradual embracing of Neutral Monism.

The analytic tradition, following in Russell's footsteps, continued to minimize the notion of Subjectivity in perception. The motives often differed from Russell's, in particular they had little to do with his Neutral Monism. But the result was much the same. And in those cases where Subjectivity was taken into account at all, it was often as a *formal* notion: "*S* sees that *p*." There is little trace, in analytic theories of perception, of a perceiver as an active, living organism, on the lookout for its own well-being or survival.

Atomism

Another characteristic of Russell's treatment of sense-data is its atomism. Russell treats sense-data as independent bits of data that do not enhance or cancel one another; they do not alter one another in any way.[65]*Furthermore, they remain unaffected by a perceiver's expectations, mood, or preferences. They are self-contained bits of data whose only function is to provide us with information about a mind-independent world. They can fit together to form a coherent picture, somewhat like the independent pieces of a jigsaw puzzle, but they maintain their individual integrity. Recall Russell's statement, "Hegel had maintained that all separateness is illusory and that the universe is more like a pot of treacle than a heap of shot. I therefore said, 'the universe is exactly like a heap of shot.' Each separate shot, according to the creed I then held, had hard and precise boundaries and was as absolute as Hegel's Absolute." He continues a few pages later: "I still think that, on the whole, this view is right."[66] So from his very early rejection of Idealism right through this statement in 1951, Russell's adherence to atomism was self-conscious and unwavering.

And although he does not say so explicitly, there is good reason to believe that on his view each of the bits of shot, each of the sensory atoms, "weighed" exactly the same as all the others. Theoretically they all have the same importance because their value is to provide information. And each bit does exactly that. So there is no basis for any significant hierarchy. In the absence of an active Subject with interests and preferences and needs, each sense-datum is an equally important item of data with every other one.

Russell means to put together his heap of shot in such a way that one gets significant wholes while maintaining the separability of the bits. But the atomism apparently works its way up to each level that one "constructs." Each object in turn can be isolated and analyzed on its own independent terms. Context and relations are treated as if they make no difference to our philosophical understanding of the items in our world.

Timelessness

Moore's and Russell's philosophies were, as I have said, for all practical purposes a-temporal. Not surprisingly, their theories have very little to say about the temporal factors that function in perception. But in Russell's *Analysis of Mind* in 1921, his account of things begins to make reference to some temporal considerations. He says, for example,

> Adhering, for the moment, to the standpoint of physics, we may define a 'perception' of an object as the appearance of the object from a place where there is a brain (or, in lower animals, some suitable nervous

structure), with sense-organs and nerves forming part of the intervening medium. Such appearances of objects are distinguished from appearances in other places by certain peculiarities, namely: (1) They give rise to mnemic phenomena; (2) They are themselves affected by mnemic phenomena.

That is to say, they may be remembered and associated or influence our habits, or give rise to images, etc., and they are themselves different from what they would have been if our past experience had been different—.... It is these two characteristics, both connected with mnemic phenomena, that distinguish perceptions from the appearances of objects in places where there is no living being.[67]

Russell's claim, that in perception the appearance of things can actually be altered for a particular living organism because of its past experiences, is a significant move away from his earlier a-temporal theorizing. It also appears to diminish the force of his atomism.

But the *mnemic* phenomena, the various versions of memory, that he adds are treated as exclusively cognitive. And one's hopes or expectations for the future get no mention. Watson's Behaviorism has convinced Russell that the response of a living organism to a stimulus can be altered by conditioning. So he now believes that the *past* counts in perception. But Russell goes a bit further:

If we confine ourselves to facts which have been actually observed, we must say that past occurrences, in addition to the present stimulus and the present ascertainable condition of the organism, enter into the causation of the response. . . . In the case of living organisms, practically everything that is distinctive both of their physical and of their mental behaviour is bound up with this persistent influence of the past. Further, speaking broadly, the change in response is usually of a kind that is biologically advantageous to the organism.[68]

In addition to past experiences, then, he also believes that the present condition of the organism also contributes to the response of that organism. It would seem that Russell has begun to take temporal factors in the perceiver seriously. In addition, he notes the relevance of considering *biological advantage* in certain responses of an organism.

These concessions in 1921 appear to go a long way toward addressing what I have claimed are some of the shortcomings of his earlier accounts of perception. But the alterations he makes here will turn out to be neither as sweeping nor as significant for future theorizing as they first appear to be.

As early as 1927 Russell begins to take back many of his earlier concessions on the importance of past experience to a theory of perception.

"Perception must include those elements which are irreducibly physiological, but it need not on that account include those elements which come, or can be made to come, within the sphere of conscious inference. . . . I should therefore say that a great deal of the interpretation that usually accompanies a perception can be made conscious by mere attention,and that this part ought not to be included in the perception."[69] Interpretation in perception will depend, of course, on past experience. The presence of such interpretation is acknowledged, but Russell decides that a great deal of it simply does not belong to perception. So whatever concessions were made to the importance of temporal factors in perceptual experience, particularly to the role of past experience, these were largely excised by 1927.

And by 1935, he makes it clear that his recognition of the role of past experience does not really alter the essential atomism of his views. The various psychological states, like perceiving and remembering, may be *causally* related, but each remains completely self-contained and apparently unaltered by its causal relations:

> I am thinking of the actual quality of the subjective experience: seeing is one thing, recollecting is another; hearing is one thing, expecting is another. The relations of the present to the past and the future, in psychology as elsewhere, are causal relations, not relations of interpenetration.[70]

The causal relations among these various states are taken to be of the same sort as the causal relations that exist among the proverbial billiard balls. Each can start something else going, but it is incapable of changing the character of that thing in any way. Memories, perceptions, expectations, and emotions, retain their character as bits of shot.

By 1959, Russell's yearning for the timeless is again in full flower: " . . . we view the world from the point of view of the *here* and *now*, not with that large impartiality which theists attribute to the Deity. To achieve such impartiality is impossible for us, but we can travel a certain distance towards it. To show the road to this end is the supreme duty of the philosopher."[71]

However far Russell may have moved toward a richer, more integrated account of perception in 1921, he not only retreated from it in later years, but his 1921 view had little impact on the future of analytic theories. This latter point may be partly a consequence of the fact that the Neutral Monism that characterized a good deal of Russell's thought from *Analysis of Mind* onward was not absorbed into the analytic tradition. His discussion of perception within that context may have been bypassed to some extent because of that.

Summary

Theories of perception in the analytic tradition were undoubtedly shaped to a very great extent by the attack that Moore and Russell launched against British Idealism. For philosophers coming after them, the overriding question about perception was whether or not it was capable of generating justified beliefs about the world. A dominant issue in the discussions remained, as it had been for Moore and Russell, the nature of the perceived object. For decades the debate centered almost exclusively on the plausibility of realism of one sort or another. The literature is filled with debates about phenomenalism, critical realism, representational realism, and their various linguistic counterparts. Obviously, all of this has had its value. The unfortunate aspect of the debate between realism and Idealism is that many other considerations disappeared from view.

But, as I have tried to show, the disappearance of these other considerations was not simply a matter of oversight, at least in the early years. Russell in particular was quite deliberate in his exclusion of temporal considerations, of an active Subjectivity, and of non-cognitive states. All this was, to a considerable extent, attributable to his repudiation of Evolutionism. And his insistence that physics, not biology, was relevant to philosophy, promoted the further elimination of any considerations that might arise from the biological theory of evolution.

Long after Moore and Russell had dismissed Evolutionism, analytic theories of perception continued to be purely cognitive, essentially a-temporal, and largely objectivist. Philosophers talked for decades about the perception of green patches and red after images, or debated the meaning of "S sees that p." A perceiver that is an active living organism, with a unique past, a set of bodily needs and individual interests, and a cluster of emotions that can alter its perception of its environment—these were not factors in the theories of perception that emerged. Those theories took account of only certain cognitive states of essentially anonymous, timeless information-gathering systems.

In sum, a very substantial portion of twentieth-century theorizing about perception in the analytic tradition has been carried on within the anti-Idealist and anti-Evolutionist framework that Moore and Russell erected.

Theories of Mind

Not surprisingly, there are some significant parallels between Russell's approach to perception, and his approach to the mind. (Unlike Russell,

Moore does not propose a fully developed theory of the mind. And while I shall make occasional reference to some of his relevant views, my primary focus will again be on Russell.) However, before considering the parallels between Russell's accounts of perception and mind, I want to begin by looking at the broader context within which Russell approaches his philosophy of mind. A number of his concerns continue to reverberate in analytic philosophy of mind, and some of the consequences of his anti-Evolutionism are still with us.

Genesis of Russell's Views on the Mental

Russell's early account of the mind also appears to be heavily influenced by his opposition to Idealism. He was a dualist, arguing that the mental is distinct from the physical in that the mental involves consciousness.[72]* As late as 1915 he writes, "Common sense is accustomed to the division of the world into mind and matter.... This simple faith [that the distinction between the two is clear] survives in Descartes. . . . It is my intention in this article to defend this dualism; . . . ."[73]

A defender of dualism today is generally pressed to justify his belief in *non-physical* items. But given Russell's opposition to the Idealists, he is most concerned in the early years to defend the physical side of the duality. The mental had been ably defended, after all, by the Idealists.

But by 1919, Russell was beginning to " . . . like behaviorism and neutral monism, and to search for reasons in their favor."[74] His interest in the behaviorism of Watson is one of the few contexts in which evolutionary thinking makes some impression on his views. He says in 1918 that although Behaviorism is not adequate as a complete theory of knowledge, one reason for going a long way with it is that, "The evolutionary continuity of men and animals makes it imperative to find explanations of mental phenomena which are not too unlike what we may suppose to occur in animals."[75]

By the time he wrote his major work on mind, *The Analysis of Mind*, in 1921, Russell not only incorporated aspects of Behaviorism into his theory of mind (as well as a touch of Freud), but he had also converted to a version of William James' Neutral Monism. As he put it in 1918, his earlier concern to distinguish act from object was part of his attack on Idealism, but he now thinks that he can rescue the mental, too, from Idealism via Neutral Monism.[76]*

For Russell, as for James, the mental and the physical were constructed out of "neutral" stuff, and were to be distinguished solely on the basis on the sorts of relations into which they entered. On Russell's account, the physical was governed by causal laws of physics; the mental by causal laws of psychology. And some things, like sensations, enter into both sorts of relations, while others like images enter exclusively into the relations governing mental things.

This issue of the relationship between the mental and the physical came to dominate a great deal of philosophy of mind in the analytic tradition for its first half century. Neutral Monism, it is true, was not a serious contender in most of the debates. But there have been behavioral theories, identity theories, and reductive theories, and eliminative theories, etc., as well as various linguistic counterparts to some of these.

Concern with the link between the physical and the mental is obviously of great philosophical importance. Again, it is telling that virtually all of the debates about it proceeded without any reference to evolution or Darwin. There had been, around the turn of the century, a substantial literature dealing with the issue of the evolution of mind. But that literature was not picked up and elaborated by the analytic tradition, largely I suspect, because of Russell's influence.

C.D. Broad's *The Mind and Its Place in Nature* (1925) might appear to be an exception. But Broad's work was often classed with that of the "emergent evolutionists." Furthermore, Russell published a highly critical review of Broad's book in *Mind* in 1926, a review that can hardly have failed to dampen the impact of Broad's evolutionary views. And Russell took the discussion of mind in a quite different direction. One aspect of the course that he set for analytic philosophy had to do, as I have said, with the mind-body problem. The other concerned the analysis of various types of mental phenomena.

Russell's most extensive account of both of these aspects appears in 1921 in his *Analysis of Mind*.

Structure vs. Function

One striking feature of Russell's approach in that book is that it is heavily weighted toward a *structural*,[77]* as contrasted with what psychologists called a *functional*, account of the mental. E.G. Boring describes the contrast between functionalist and structuralist approaches in the following way: "Functional psychology is the psychology of the *Is-for*, structural psychology the psychology of the *Is*."[78] Russell's philosophy of mind was primarily about the *Is* and only incidentally and rarely about the *Is-for*. Given Russell's early insistence that philosophy must concern itself with formal structures, perhaps this way of approaching the mind should not be surprising.

The distinction between structural and functional theories is familiar in psychology; it has had less currency in philosophy. Recent Functionalist theories in philosophy of mind share a family resemblance with their earlier counterpart in psychology, but there is at least one important difference of relevance to our purposes here. Psychological Functionalism, as exemplified in the work of men like William James and John Dewey, takes as a primary focus the function of mental phenomena on behalf of the living organism. By contrast, recent philosophical work in Functionalism, particularly in Machine Functionalism, explicitly bypasses any substantive reference to the living organism. Part of the goal in this type of Functionalism is to construct psychological theories that are sufficiently general to apply to mental states not only in living organisms but also in non-living systems like the computer. Clearly there is no concern for how such mental states might serve the computer itself. The obvious reason is that such states do not operate on behalf of the computer. There is, then, a crucial difference between the Psychological Functionalism of James and Dewey, on the one hand, and the more recent Machine Functionalism in philosophy of mind, on the other. On at least one account, the James-Dewey version of Functionalism had a good deal to do with their positive views toward Darwin and evolution theory:

> It [America in the late nineteenth century] still had the pioneers' spirit, the readiness to accept change, the lack of veneration for the old, the belief that usefulness is the chief good. In a new country with free land it is the fittest who survive, those strong enough to wrest a living from nature. Of course Darwin's theory was destined for enthusiastic reception in such an atmosphere. And the result of this theory was that American psychology went *functional, assessing mind and mental activity in terms of use and survival value.* William James was the first to see psychology in this way. John Dewey supported him. Together they brought functional gospel into philosophy as pragmatism.[79] [Italics added.]

Whether or not Boring is right about the reasons for America's enthusiasm for Darwin, it does seem to be the case that both James and Dewey gave considerable importance to the *function* of mental phenomena on behalf of the living organism in its dealings with its environment. Much of twentieth-century analytic philosophy of mind, including Machine Functionalism, has bypassed this concern.

Russell's philosophy of mind contributed in some degree to this omission. It was, I suggested, largely structuralist rather than functionalist in the psychological sense of the terms. As such, his theory was not especially concerned with an investigation of how mental states work on behalf of the living organism that has them. His interest lay, rather, with the elements that are constitutive of each type of mental state. One gets the structuralist flavor of his project in statements like the following:

> As against the view that introspection reveals a mental world radically
> different from sensations, I propose to argue that thoughts, beliefs,
> desires, pleasures, pains and emotions are all built up out of sensations
> and images alone, and that there is reason to think that images do not
> differ from sensations in their intrinsic character. We thus effect a
> mutual *rapprochement* of mind and matter, and reduce the ultimate data
> of introspection . . . to images alone.[80]

The emphasis here is clearly on the constitution of mental phenomena, not
on their function in relation to the organism that has them. All mental states,
he argues, are *composed of* sensations and images. This is the central thesis
of the book.

Russell's way of characterizing *mind* is equally focused on what it *is*
rather than what it *does*:

> We spoke earlier of two ways of classifying particulars. One way col-
> lects together the appearances commonly regarded as a given object
> from different places; this is, . . . the way of physics. . . . The other
> way collects together the appearances of different objects from a
> given place, the result being what we call a perspective. In the particu-
> lar case where the place concerned is a human brain, the perspec-
> tive belonging to the place consists of all the perceptions of a certain
> man at a given time. Thus classification by perspectives is relevant
> to psychology, and is essential in defining what we mean by one
> mind.[81]

So the mind is to be defined by a set of "perspectives," a collection of
appearances of different objects belonging to a place which is a brain. As in
the case of mental phenomena, so also with the mind itself, Russell's project
is structural, or as he might call it, constructionist. He aims to show how both
mental states and the mind itself are *logical constructions* from sensations and
images. His constructionism is a philosophical counterpart to structuralist
psychology.

Structuralist concerns about mind and mental phenomena are undoubtedly important. Once again, however, the difficulty with Russell's
approach is that he focuses on these concerns to the virtual exclusion of
functional considerations. Although he occasionally indicates some concern
for how certain mental phenomena function in relation to the environment,
this is clearly not his primary interest. And that fact has to do, I suggest, with
his attitude toward Evolutionism.

Russell's insistence, against the Evolutionists, that philosophy deals
with theoretical rather than practical matters, influenced his preference for
structuralist models of theorizing. Functionalist considerations of the sort

that interested James and Dewey undoubtedly came too close to practical issues to be relevant to Russell's conception of philosophy. Although he was eventually converted to James' Neutral Monism, Russell never gave in to James' emphasis on the practical—either in his pragmatism or in his pragmatic account of truth. Usefulness was not a notion in Russell's philosophical lexicon.

It is true that Russell occasionally makes reference to the functional aspects of mental phenomena. He says, for example,

> We may regard a human being as an instrument, which makes various responses to various stimuli. If we observe these responses from outside, we shall regard them as showing knowledge when they display two characteristics, *accuracy* and *appropriateness*. These two are quite distinct, and even sometimes incompatible. If I am being pursued by a tiger, accuracy is furthered by turning round to look at him, but appropriateness by running away without making any search for further knowledge of the beast. I shall return to the question of appropriateness later; for the present it is accuracy that I wish to consider.[82]

In fact, he says very little else about appropriateness; the rest of the chapter is taken up with issues of accuracy. A bit later in the book, he raises a question about why we show a preference for true beliefs over false beliefs. His response: "This preference is only explicable by taking account of the causal efficacy of beliefs, and of the greater appropriateness of the responses resulting from true beliefs. But appropriateness depends upon purpose, and purpose thus becomes a vital part of theory of knowledge."[83] Unfortunately, he leaves the matter there.

On the rare occasions where Russell does take notice of the relations between an organism and its environment, this is motivated largely by his interest in Behaviorism.[84] Nonetheless, his preferred philosophic approach to mind and mental phenomena is unquestionably atomistic, and as such it minimizes the importance of relations. In this case, the relations that are short-changed are especially those that might obtain among the mental states of an organism and between those mental states and its dealings with its surroundings. I shall return to his atomism shortly.

If one looks through the literature on philosophy of mind in the English-speaking world for the subsequent thirty or forty years, one is hard-pressed to find discussions of mind or mental phenomena that make reference to their function on behalf of the living organism. Russell's approach, not that of James and Dewey, clearly came to dominate the debates.

Parallels with Perception

Russell's theory of mind grew out of much the same soil as his theory of perception. Consider some of the parallels between the two sets of theories.

Cognitive Atomism. Russell's method of analysis led him to formulate theories of perception in terms of cognitive bits of sensory data. It undoubtedly also contributed to his partiality toward a structuralist approach to mental phenomena. His analytic method begins with something familiar, complex, and not very clear and breaks it down into its simplest essential elements, its "atoms." His psychic atoms are sensations and images. After the atoms have been isolated, then one can show how more complex phenomena are logical *constructions* out of these atoms.

There is little assessment of the use or survival value of either the atoms or the logical constructions. Russell, did not set aside the useful functions of mental states in the interest of pursuing another, admittedly partial, aspect of philosophy of mind. Had that been the case, one might simply note that his theory was *incomplete.* But Russell's view was much stronger than that. He did not believe that the functions mental states might perform for the benefit of the organism were the business of philosophy. He did not simply leave them aside in the interest of a different issue; he excluded them from philosophy altogether because they belong to *practical* considerations.

Consider first the strength and pervasiveness of Russell's atomism. Over the years he proposed a series of views that might be characterized as "sensory atomism," "logical atomism," and "psychical atomism," as part of his effort to provide an analysis of physical objects, facts and propositions, and mental phenomena. In all cases, the "atoms" were sensory data. In his "Philosophy of Logical Atomism" he referred to these atoms as "particulars" and characterized them is this way:

> Particulars have this peculiarity . . . that each of them stands entirely alone and is completely self-subsistent. . . . That is to say, each particular that there is in the world does not in any way logically depend upon any other particular. Each one might happen to be the whole universe; it is merely an empirical fact that this is not the case.[85]

Russell's insistence on the logical independence of particulars is part of his rejection of the Idealist theory of internal relations and part of his rejection of Bergson's Evolutionism. He was so concerned to avoid theories that insisted on the primacy of unity and continuity that he seems to have gone to the opposite extreme, making the atoms of his theories entirely self-subsistent.

Many years later he restates the view in even stronger language: "... I have retained a very large part of the logical beliefs that I had fifty-five years ago. I am persuaded that the world is made up of an immense number of bits, and that, so far as logic can show, each bit might be exactly as it is even if other bits did not exist."[86] This commitment to the logical independence of the bits that make up the physical and mental world encourages the view that things can be studied in complete isolation from their context.

On Russell's view things are, of course, *causally* related. But his account of those causal relations is, as I noted earlier, quasi-*mechanical* on the model of billiard balls moving one another. He sees the relations among perceptions, memories, expectations, etc., as causal, but he is explicit in his claim that such relations are *not relations of interpenetration.* The implication seems to be that causal relations leave both cause and effect intrinsically unaltered. Once again this view appears to have its roots in his opposition to the Idealist theory of internal relations. All relations, including causal relations, must remain extrinsic. Relations must never reduce to properties of objects such that the objects are defined by them.

But consider a case involving mental phenomena. Imagine a person seeing something frightening—perhaps a coiled rattlesnake on the ground nearby. It is difficult to suppose that the seeing remains independent of the fear. Under the influence of fear one's seeing fails to note much of the detail about the designs on the snake's skin, and it probably also ignores most of the surrounding context. One's seeing is selectively attentive to items like the coiled shape and its distance from oneself. The causal relations between seeing and fear do not involve a cool, cognitive state of seeing, followed by a completely independent non-cognitive state of fear.[87*] The seeing is penetrated with fear, which affects the seeing by motivating and directing its focus. The fear, in turn, is intensified by the seeing. The content and psychological quality of each of the two states is constituted at least partially by the other state.

To see that this is so, consider by contrast a situation in which one sees the same coiled rattlesnake from outside a glass-enclosed cage. In the latter case, one's seeing of the snake can include coolly taking in the designs on its back, its length, the rocks and tree branches around it. What one sees and how one sees it are dramatically different from the situation in which the seeing is penetrated with fear.[88*]

Some causal relations may indeed function on the billiard ball model, but there are numerous examples of causal relations that involve interpenetration. Russell's atomism, with its assumptions about the "completely self-subsistent" character of mental states, may well have encouraged the view, still prevalent in more recent analytic philosophies of mind, that cognitive states can be investigated in complete isolation from non-cognitive states like emotions and moods. Each is treated as if it might cause the onset of the other but as if its own character and that of the other remains qualitatively unaltered by the relation. As we saw earlier, the theories of perception of both Russell and subsequent analytic philosophers have also been formulated with this assumption firmly in place.

It is true that on a great many subjects Russell changed his views over the years. And his view of the relation between cognition and emotion might appear to be no exception. For example, in his *Outline of Philosophy* (1927) he says, "The separation of an emotional element in our integral reaction to a situation is more or less artificial." And a bit later, "We cannot, in our integral reaction to a situation, separate out one event as knowledge and another as desire; both knowledge and desire are features which characterise the reaction, but do not exist in isolation . . ."[89] But Russell prefaced this particular section of his investigation by saying:

> Hitherto, in our investigation of man from within, we have considered only the cognitive aspect, which is, in fact, the most important to philosophy. But now we must turn our attention to the other sides of human nature. If we treat them more briefly than the cognitive side, it is not because they are less important, but because *their main importance is practical and our task is theoretical.* Let us begin with the emotions.[90] [Italics added.]

So although Russell notes in passing that efforts to separate the cognitive and the emotive in an experience are artificial, he nonetheless believes that emotions belong to the practical side of things. And philosophy, being concerned exclusively with theoretical matters, can plausibly put emotions aside after a brief treatment and can focus its attention wholly on the cognitive side of experience. This approach ignores the possibility that the cognitive states that are artificially isolated from the emotions and that, together with them, comprise the "integral reaction to a situation" might each be distorted by such isolation.

Emotions. In spite of his emphasis on cognition, over the years Russell expresses a number of different views on non-cognitive states. In one of his very early essays (1894) Russell discusses the passions, and his approach to these non-cognitive states is functional rather than structural. (At this time he distinguishes emotions from passions, but his distinction is not one that he later retains and it is not of any particular interest for our purposes.[91]*) He says:

> . . . a passion cannot be valuable for its own sake, though an emotion may. For the essence of passion is desire, and desire is consciousness

of imperfection, of contrast between the ideal and the actual. . . . it is a means, not an end. But as a means it can hardly be valued too highly— the passions for knowledge, for beauty, for love are the very conditions for all development, of all that is good—if the Good is that which satisfies, the desire is essential to the struggle after it, . . .[92]

For the early Russell, then, the passions are a source of energy and drive. As he puts it, " . . .nothing can be accomplished without powerful passions— the most efficient men are the men wholly in the grip of some great passion which carries them over difficulties and obstacles and makes them neglect all but what conduces to their end. . . . "[93]

Much later, in a 1912 letter to Lady Ottoline Morrell, Russell writes, concerning his work on *Principia Mathematica*, " . . . What makes it vital, what makes it fruitful, is the absolute unbridled Titanic passion that I have put into it. *It is passion that has made my intellect clear*, passion that has made me never stop to ask myself if the work was worth doing. . . . "[94] [Italics added.]

So for him, passion was indeed a source of energy and motivation— even, on occasion, of intellectual clarity. But when he comes to write his extended defense of his new logico-analytical philosophy in 1914, there is no mention of the passions as a positive force. He does not deny their great power and importance; rather, he excludes them along with all other prac- tical concerns. Again his reason arises from his rejection of Evolutionism.

One other significant aspect of Russell's early discussion of the pas- sions deserves mention. He gets it from Spinoza. One passion, he says, can only be overcome by a stronger passion. What is important here is that Russell takes seriously the differences in *intensity* among passions. Whether or not the particular Spinozistic claim is true, it does seem to be the case that the causal roles of psychological states are affected by their intensity. And this appears to be the case for more than just the passions or emotions. A stronger belief can neutralize a weaker one, a stronger desire can neutralize a weaker one, etc. One's belief that rulers are reliable instruments for measuring can undo one's perceptual belief that one line in a particular drawing is longer than another. One's desire to lose weight can overrule one's desire for a second helping at dinner. While it may be difficult to give a precise measurement for different intensities among mental states, it can hardly be denied that they are "weighted" in such a way that not every belief or desire or emotion will have an equal effect on our behavior at any given time. Unfortunately, Russell's attention to the important role played by differing intensities among passions was later lost.

In his *Analysis of Mind*, the most obvious place to look for a complete account of his mature theory of emotions, one finds six pages (out of more than 300) devoted to a discussion of emotions and the will together. And he prefaces this discussion by noting that he has nothing original to say about them and is "treating them only in order to complete the discussion of my main thesis, namely that all psychic phenomena are built up out of sensations and images alone." His purpose, he says, is to provide an analysis that will show whether or not an emotion, which is "essentially complex, . . . ever contains any non-physiological material not reducible to sensations and images and their relations." (279)

An analysis of emotion, he says, shows it to be a process that includes sensations, images, and bodily movements (whatever the order of their occurrence). And any desires, pleasures, or pains there may be are properties of the process and not separate elements "in the stuff of which the emotion is composed."(284)

His interest by this time has clearly shifted from functional considerations, like the energy and drive that they can provide to an organism, to purely structural ones.

By 1928, he appears to believe that from a philosophical point of view emotions are a hindrance to cognition. So presumably, one has a better account of cognition under its ideal conditions if one isolates it from emotions.

> The emotions are what makes life interesting, and what makes us feel it important. From this point of view, they are the most valuable element in human existence. But when, as in philosophy, we are trying to understand the world, they appear rather as a hindrance. They generate irrational opinions, since emotional associations seldom correspond with collocations in the external world. They cause us to view the universe in the mirror of our moods, as now bright, now dim, according to the state of the mirror. With the sole exception of curiosity, the emotions are on the whole a hindrance to the intellectual life, . . . If I say little about the emotions in this book, it is not from underestimating their human importance, but solely because the task upon which we are engaged is theoretical rather than practical: to understand the world, not to change it.[95]*

When he wrote *Outline of Philosophy* in 1927, Russell had noted important connections between cognition and emotion, but that recognition turns out to have had no bearing on his philosophy. While he acknowledges the integration of the two in experience, he also believes that philosophy ought to isolate the cognitive dimension because it alone has theoretical importance, and it should leave the emotions to those concerned with practical matters. One year later he will acknowledge that "the line between emotion and reason is not so sharp as some people think."[96] But once again, this assessment has virtually no consequences either for his own philosophy or for a great deal of what followed him in the analytic tradition. Theorists about emotions have given much consideration to the possibility that emotions have cognitive components, but theorists of cognition have given virtually no attention to the possibility that emotions play any role in cognition.

Moore, like Russell, never denies the importance of non-cognitive states like emotions. In fact, in the final chapter of *Principia Ethica* Moore has high praise for certain emotions. He is discussing " . . . the most valuable things which we know or can imagine . . . , " (188) and he includes among them the enjoyment of beautiful objects. He says,

> . . . in those instances of aesthetic appreciation, which we think most valuable, there is included, not merely a bare cognition of what is beautiful in the object, but also some kind of feeling or emotion. It is not sufficient that a man should merely see the beautiful qualities in a picture and know that they are beautiful, in order that we may give his state of mind the highest praise. We require that he should also *appreciate* the beauty of that which he sees and which he knows to be beautiful—that he should feel and see *its beauty*.[97]

Moore is concerned here not with perception as such, but with what he takes to be morally valuable types of experience. And he does not argue explicitly that in these experiences the perception and the feeling are integrated with one another. It appears that their happening together would be sufficient. He nowhere suggests that perception itself might be imbued with emotion. In fact, in a paper he presented to the Aristotelian Society in 1920, "The Character of Cognitive Acts," Moore takes cases of perception as paradigm cases of cognitive acts. His whole analysis of perception in that paper is in terms of sense data and their qualities.[98]

Both Moore and Russell acknowledge the importance of emotions in human experience. But neither man takes them to have any significant bearing on our theories of cognition. And Russell's only interest in emotions when he writes his *Analysis of Mind* is to show that they, too, can fit into his structuralist reduction of mental states to sensations and images (plus some physiology).

Timeless Mental States. So far, I have noted several parallels between Russell's accounts of perception and of mind. Both were atomistic. In both cases, as a consequence of his rejection of Evolutionism, practical considerations were excluded in favor of purely theoretical ones, leading to an isolation of cognitive states from non-cognitive states like emotions. There is one other parallel with the perceptual case that seems to be a consequence of Russell's repudiation of Evolutionism, and his subsequent emphasis on structuralist aspects of mind. His account of mental states is largely a-temporal, *static*.

In 1918, Russell says, "It is quite clear that a highly educated person sees, hears, feels, does everything in a very different way from a young child or animal, and that this whole manner of experiencing the world and of thinking about the world is very much more analytic than that of a more primitive experience."[99]

If Russell had carried this perfectly plausible view to its logical conclusion, he might have noted that temporal factors are important to an adequate account of mental phenomena. If accumulating experience through time alters the way one experiences the world, and if particular types of experience (like learning) alter the way different adults experience the world, it is reasonable to conclude that *any* experience might be capable of altering the way an individual experiences her world.

But by 1922, responding to F.C.S. Schiller's review of his *Analysis of Mind*, Russell notes that Schiller objected that his

> method is not historical or evolutionary. I have, it is true, discussed the process of learning somewhat fully, but I am equally interested in processes which are not progressive. I think the interest in development which came in with evolution is a barrier to the elementary understanding of the simpler facts upon which any solid science must be built. . . . There will be no beginning of a genuine science of psychology so long as people are obsessed by such complex facts as growth and progress.[100]

There are a couple of revealing things about this response to Schiller. First, Russell does not defend his lack of attention to temporal considerations on the grounds that they are the business of psychology, and he is doing philosophy of mind. His claim is that *psychology* can only get started if it bypasses questions of growth and progress.

Secondly, Russell's use of the terms "growth and *progress*" is instructive. (Schiller speaks of "development.") For Russell, the notion of progress is, as we have seen, closely associated with Evolutionism. Could it be that because he sees evidence that progress is not a necessary law of the universe, he dismisses the suggestion that mental "progress" (*development*) needs to be taken seriously in an adequate account of the mind? Yet as I noted above, he himself acknowledged just a few years earlier that there is such development. And he apparently saw it as a development toward a more "analytic" manner of thinking—surely on Russell's view that would represent progress.

But the relevant issue here is Russell's treatment of temporal factors. His emphasis on the undesirability of making progress an issue for philosophy, and his claim that evolutionary thinking is a barrier to understanding, suggest again that his minimal attention to the temporal aspects of experience was motivated by his determination to reject Evolutionism and all its concerns.

When I speak of the importance of temporal considerations in accounts of the mental, I am not concerned primarily with the importance of learning, and still less of progress. I am rather urging that the content and relative intensity of the mental states that develop in individuals will be shaped and colored by their unique *past* (a point that Russell willingly concedes) and also by their *current* emotions, bodily needs, interests, mood, and their expectations and hopes for the *future*.

There are places in Russell's writings where he allows for the importance of temporal concerns. But by 1935, he appears to eliminate them as having no relevance to an account of human experience. Speaking of "personality" he says,

> It is thought, by those who believe in it [personality], that everything in the mind of John Smith has a John-Smithy quality which makes it impossible for anything quite similar to be in anyone else's mind. If you are trying to give a scientific account of John Smith's mind, you must not be content with general rules, such as can be given for all pieces of matter indiscriminately; you must remember that the events concerned are happening to that particular man, and are what they are because of his whole history and character.
>
> There is something attractive about this view, but I see no reason to regard it as true. It is, of course, obvious that two men in the same situation may react differently because of differences in their past histories, but the same is true of two bits of iron of which one has been magnetized and the other not. [101]

Russell's quarrel with the notion of "personality" is not really the issue here. The issue is more subtle than that. On the one hand, Russell acknowledges that past history can affect present responses to stimuli. But he argues that fact does not distinguish living organisms from bits of metal. Recall that on his view biology will be eventually reducible to chemistry and physics. So all aspects of living organisms, including such apparently mysterious things as "personality" will ultimately be reducible to facts of chemistry and physics. And temporal considerations will presumably not make John Smith's case unique.

Consider first the issue of reducibility. On Russell's account, what happens to a piece of metal when it is magnetized is precisely paralleled by what happens to a person when she is influenced by her past memories. In both cases something happened in the past, and it affects the responses to present stimuli. For Russell there is nothing special about the psychological case that singles it out for a different sort of theorizing.

But there are at least two crucial differences between the two cases.

The first difference is that at least some of the past events that have affected the person have been selected for attention by that person. From all the stimuli impinging on a human being at any given time, only some small number will leave an imprint that will show up in memory. Other stimuli that could in principle have generated a response, will be ignored. And the bits that are selected for attention can differ from one person to another and from one time to another. It is not the case that one sort of stimulus will always, and necessarily, be the one that elicits attention and a predictable response.

Pieces of metal, I take it, are not capable of being selective in this way from among the stimuli that can affect them. Magnetism cannot normally be ignored; a brightly colored butterfly cannot normally be "selected" by the piece of metal (unless, of course, the butterfly is magnetized).

The point is that for John Smith, his past is to some extent constructed by him through his selection of at least some of the stimuli that will impinge on him sufficiently to leave traces in the memory bank. The role that temporal factors play in his interpretation of events is, to this extent at least, dramatically different from the role played by the past of a piece of metal.

My point is not to suggest that there is no scientific account that can be given for the memories a person has collected. We may not have such an account now, but there is no reason in principle why we could never have one. The issue is not science versus mystery. Rather, it is a question of how those past events are selected. For non-living entities the process is fairly generic. For living systems, the process is highly variable. As a consequence, the way that past events will affect the response to present stimuli is likely to be far more complex and far less predictable in the case of John Smith than it is in the case of a piece of metal.

This is the second crucial difference between the two cases. Living organisms like John Smith can be, and usually are, selective from among available stimuli with a view to their own survival and well-being. Pieces of metal are not. And even if the concern for survival and well-being is eventually explained by physics alone, the relevant factors would not be applicable to bits of metal. Taking a cue from Russell's comments in a different context, one can say that although we have no incontrovertible evidence that bits of metal are *not* concerned with their own survival and well-being, there isn't the slightest reason to think that they *are*. So on that ground at least, there are good reasons to think that the case of John Smith and the case of the magnetized bit of metal are not parallel.

As for worries about mystery, when one argues for the importance of individual differences in perception and other experiences, a common objection is that such a view obviates the possibility of a *general* account of knowledge. It is thought that such a view calls for a theory of Janet Brown and another theory for John Smith, etc. But such an objection misses the point, I believe. On the one hand, one can have general laws that govern things like bits of metal. Generally, they are relatively simple and straightforward. Virtually every ordinary piece of iron, for example, will respond in the same way to magnetism. On the other hand, one can have other general laws that include—as part of the law—variables that can each be filled in a number of different ways. As the value of the variables changes, the outcome of a given interaction can be altered. On such a model, temporal considerations can be essential. If the variables can alter from time to time, changing the outcome as they do, then one needs to take account of temporal factors. But this does not entail mystery; it merely means that the laws applicable to living organisms will be considerably more complex than those applicable to bits of metal.

Changes in mental (and physical) states over time must figure in the account we give of the mind. As Russell himself acknowledges, a given stimulus will elicit different responses in an adult and a child. But the differences are even more individual than that. The jealous wife, the adoring child, and a new acquaintance, are each likely to view John Smith differently as he converses animatedly with an attractive female colleague. And some days later, with changed attitudes—now the reassured wife, the angry child, and the envious acquaintance—the ways of seeing Smith and his companion in conversation are likely to have changed as well. The peculiar concatenation of mental states *at any given time* will affect how the stimulus is taken and what response is forthcoming.

In 1951, Russell reaffirms his belief that the capacity to be affected by past experience is not a defining property of the living organism. He begins, as he had done years earlier, by distinguishing *intelligent* life by its capacity to be affected by the principle of the conditioned reflex—to have its current experience altered by its past. He takes this to be "the most essential characteristic of mind." But he then goes on to say that a dry river bed, cut out in the past by water, will affect the flow of future water. To this extent, the new river water is affected by the past and is therefore, on his view, *thinking*, "though its thinking is somewhat rudimentary."[102]

Whatever the merits of the examples, they confirm one's suspicion that Russell's view of the mind is that it is essentially receptive—to present data and to past influence. Furthermore, there is nothing about the mind that distinguishes it in any essential way from various non-living systems. He clearly does not see it as an adaptation that actively assists living organisms.

My contention is that the number of variables that can affect an organism's response to stimuli is not only quite large but it also changes frequently over time. The relevant variables include not only memories but also emotions, moods, interests, needs, bodily states like hunger, illness, or fatigue, hopes, and values of all sorts. The content of any and all of these states is in flux. As a consequence, the particular response of an individual will depend on the particular configuration of these states, which in turn must be indexed to a particular time.

One can, then, formulate general laws that govern what goes on in perception or other mental states, but one cannot assume that those laws will be such that they can specify the type of response to be expected from every organism in the presence of some given stimulus. The response will be, to a very large extent, a function of the mental and physical state of the individual organism at a specific time. A timeless approach to mind won't do.

There can be little doubt that one strong motivation for Russell's static approach to mind was his virulent opposition to Bergson's theory of intuition, with its emphasis on the flowing character of reality. As I argued in connection with perception, Russell was so concerned about the consequences of such a view for science that he moved to the opposite extreme, insisting on the importance of intellect with its capacity to isolate and "freeze" aspects of the experienced world. The results for his theory of mind were unfortunate. Mental states are treated like "bits of shot," each one virtually timeless and independent. Temporal development and the possibility of interpenetration are lost from sight, and one is left with an account of mental states that bears little resemblance to what experience suggests. More importantly, one has an account that ignores one crucial function of mental states—their service on behalf of the organism that has them.

Subjectivity. One final parallel between Russell's accounts of perception and mind remains. In my discussion of perception I have already said a good deal about Russell's and Moore's playing down the role of the subject. Before adding to that, I should point out that for both Moore and Russell, the notions of *self* and *subject* (as well as, occasionally, *act of consciousness* [103]*) were not always clearly distinguished. As Russell puts it,

> . . . the question as to what is to be reckoned part of the Self and what is not, is a very difficult one. Among many other things which we may mean by the Self, two may be selected as specially important, namely (1) the bare subject which thinks and is aware of objects, (2) the whole assemblage of things that would necessarily cease to exist if our lives came to an end.[104]*

When I refer to the subject or to Subjectivity, I use the term in the first of these senses, the "bare subject." In Moore and Russell, it is sometimes difficult to be sure which of these two notions, or perhaps some third, is at stake.

For Russell the subject began as a requirement for his theory of knowledge by acquaintance. When he embraced Neutral Monism, he followed James in abandoning the notion of the subject. Russell argues that it is not empirically discoverable and must therefore be regarded as a construct, much like the points and instants of physics. He does not, it is true, deny that there is a subject. But, as he himself points out the "practical effect of this is the same as if we assumed that they [Subjects and acts of consciousness] did not exist, ..."[105] Russell reaffirms his abandonment of Subjectivity many years later: "I was glad when I realised that abandonment of the 'subject' made it possible to accept this simplification [Neutral Monism] and to regard the traditional problem of the relation of mind and matter as definitively solved." [106]

As he puts it in 1927, " . . . when we say, 'I think first this and then that,' we ought not to mean that there is a single entity 'I' which 'has' two successive thoughts. We ought to mean only that there are two successive thoughts which have causal relations of the kind that makes us call them parts of one biography, in the same sort of way in which successive notes maybe parts of one tune."[107] But Russell's analogy between successive thoughts and the notes in a tune is not illuminating. It is not clear that the successive notes in a tune are *causally* related, as he claims that successive thoughts are. And more importantly, while tunes generally have a unity given to them by their composers, one wonders what is supposed to compose the analogous unity of the biography. Causal relations by themselves need not confer any particular unity on the things they relate. This would be particularly apparent if one sees causality on the billiard ball model, as Russell often does.

When William James wrote his well-known paper, "Does Consciousness Exist?" he was concerned to deny the necessity of any *entity* of the traditional Cartesian sort that would underwrite psychological phenomena. Russell, too, wanted to distance himself from the need for such an entity. He saw the notion of the subject as a descendant of the earlier notions of soul and mental substance.[108] His bias toward empiricism made him suspicious of entities like these for which one could gather no direct evidence. Ockham's razor eliminated them. In his later theories Subjectivity reappears, but he redefines it in such away that it becomes an umbrella term for distortion and error in perception.

I have no quarrel with the move that both James and Russell made to eliminate reliance on an enduring mental entity called a self or a subject. But one requires some "locus" of concern in the mental life of living organisms—concern for the survival and well-being of the organism itself. Anonymous mental states are unable to account for these enduring concerns. And this drive for survival and well-being will provide the kinds of causal connections that the notes in Russell's tune lack. More on this in Chapter Seven.

The Analytic Legacy

At the beginning of this chapter I suggested that the particular character that Moore and Russell gave to analytic philosophy was conditioned by their rejection of Evolutionism as truly as it was by their rejection of Idealism. Let me summarize the consequences of that fact for their theories of perception and mind.

In the case of perception we are left with theories that take as their primary focus the cluster of issues connected largely with a defense of realism. Questions about the nature of the perceived object, about the justification of perceptual beliefs, and about the relationship between the claims of perception and of physics, dominated the theories of perception. These issues in turn led to a concern with objectivity that virtually eliminated all consideration of the role of a subject in perception. Where a subject does appear in the early work, it is little more than a passive spectator of the world.

In reaction both to the Idealist doctrine of internal relations and to the belief of some Evolutionists in the continuous character of reality, early analytic approaches to perception were atomistic to such an extent that contextual considerations were eliminated. Against the Evolutionists, Russell ruled practical concerns out of court, with the result that the role of perception on behalf of the needs and goals of the living organism was put aside as not philosophically relevant. Russell's theoretical and atomistic approach also excluded all consideration of the interplay of cognitive and non-cognitive states in perception. Finally, the rejection of Evolutionism, with its framework of historical development, led to a timeless and static account of perception.

Parallels in the treatment of mind are apparent. Russell treats mental states as timeless "bits of shot" that retain their independent character through all causal interactions. As in the case of perception, so in the case of the mind, cognitive states are treated in complete isolation from non-cognitive states of all sorts. They are subjectless bearers of data. Mental states, having purely theoretical importance, are treated structurally, in complete abstraction from their practical function on behalf of the organism.

Many of these features continue to characterize philosophical theories of the mind in the analytic tradition. Cognitive states are standardly treated in isolation from non-cognitive states like emotions. Some Functionalist theories of mind, in an effort to construct accounts of psychological states that will apply to the computer as well as to living systems, quite deliberately abstract mental states from their function on behalf of the living organism, and omit any significant consideration of both non-cognitive states and Subjectivity.

This analytic, and sometimes atomistic, approach that Moore and Russell bequeathed to their followers is nicely summarized by John Passmore:

> Moore . . . is arguing that the *essence* of a thing is always distinct from its relations. Nothing,therefore, can be 'constituted by the nature of the system to which it belongs'—this is the main point which Moore and Russell urge against Bradley's monism. To be at all is to be independent.[109]

Things, on their view, could be adequately characterized by reference to their *properties*, leaving their relations "external" to them. However, their movement toward analysis may have encouraged too robust a sense of the separateness and independence of things.

One of the lessons of biology, and of Darwin's theory of natural selection in particular, is the tremendous importance of the functional interaction between an organism and its environment. On a Darwinian view, living things are most adequately investigated and understood, not in terms of a set of timeless essential properties, but in terms of their changing functional relationships within a given environmental niche.

If Darwin's account of us is right, our mental capacities are not simply logical, rational gatherers of truths. Their most basic function is not theoretical but practical. They are adaptations that assist us in our interaction with our environment. We are, most fundamentally, living organisms that must provide for our survival and well-being. We need to be able to see things in our environment as threatening, delectable, or sexually attractive just as surely as we need to be able to see them as red or triangular. Everything else we do is built on that foundation. Whatever theory of knowledge or mind we construct, it ought not overlook that most basic fact about us.

Obviously, Moore and Russell were not the first to treat perception and mind in isolation from the rest of their context. There is a long philosophical tradition behind them. The point is that a view like Darwin's should have made a difference to the way that philosophical tradition was revised at the turn of the century. In the case of Moore and Russell (and much of subsequent analytic philosophy) it did not.

Chapter 5

Edmund Husserl, Phenomenology, and Evolution

The natural sciences have not in a single instance unraveled for us actual reality, the reality in which we live, move, and are. The general belief that it is their function to accomplish this and that they are merely not yet far enough advanced, . . . has revealed itself to those with more profound insight as a superstition. The necessary separation between natural science and philosophy . . . is in process of being established and clarified.

Edmund Husserl (1910) [1]

At roughly the same time that Moore and Russell were piecing together analytic philosophy, Edmund Husserl was formulating his phenomenology. Like Moore and Russell, he was reacting against certain contemporary philosophic trends; unlike them, he did not single out metaphysical Idealism for special criticism. He did, however, share with the early analysts a concern about the place of evolution theory in philosophy.

To understand Husserl's attitude toward evolution and its relationship to philosophy, one needs to have a clear sense of his overall view of philosophy. Whereas Moore and Russell argued against particular aspects of Darwin's, Spencer's, or Bergson's views, Husserl's objections arise at a much more fundamental level. And since his phenomenology is perhaps less familiar to English-speaking philosophers than is analytic philosophy, it may be helpful to spend some time getting an overview of classical phenomenology and its goals. It should become clear that there were fundamental currents in Husserl's philosophy that made it inimical to incorporation of evolutionary insights. After elucidating those currents, I shall argue that each of them is open to objection.

As Husserl formulated his phenomenology, he was intent on undermining the very sort of *objectivity* that Moore and Russell were trying to establish. Recall that the interest in objectivity that characterized the founders of analytic philosophy was spurred by their opposition to Idealism. And since, on their view, one of the errors of Idealism had been its emphasis on the active, constructive role of Subjectivity, the remedy for this error seemed to lie in minimizing the role of the subject.

Husserl, by contrast, was convinced that one of the enduring mistakes in the history of philosophy was the assumption that one could make objective claims about the world without any reference to the interpretive role of the Subject. This insistence on the importance of the subjective dimension in knowledge-claims figures prominently in all of the phases of Husserl's phenomenology. In order to see just why this is so, consider how his view emerges from and builds on those of some of the major figures in classical modern philosophy, particularly Descartes, Hume, and Kant. When viewed as an amendment to a good deal in these philosophies, his phenomenology loses much of its opaqueness.

Phenomenology and Classical Modern Philosophy

Descartes

Husserl's phenomenology begins in the Cartesian tradition. "All modern philosophy originates in the Cartesian *Meditations*."[2] One of his later works was, in fact, a radical re-working of Descartes' view and was titled, *Cartesian Meditations*. Husserl agreed with Descartes on a number of key points. Both believed that philosophy can and should be built on a foundation of *certainty*. Related to this, they were committed to the accessibility of a class of self-evident ("clear and distinct") truths. Foremost among these is the *cogito* (I am thinking). And for both philosophers the notion of "thinking" was to be understood in a very broad sense. Both agreed that the *cogito* was to be *foundational* for all human knowledge, including the natural and social sciences. In turn, this meant that knowledge was to have its grounding in Subjectivity.

But Husserl also disagreed with Descartes on several crucial issues. Unlike Descartes, Husserl was not willing simply to add to the bare *cogito* the notion of a mental substance that was doing the thinking. On Husserl's view, if one was looking for absolutely certain foundations for knowledge, one had to be extremely careful not to smuggle into the *cogito* any naive assumptions arising from a substance metaphysics. On the same grounds he was unwilling to assume at the outset the validity of *causal laws*. Descartes had used these laws in his proofs for the existence of God, and thereby the external world. Husserl even rejected the use of Descartes' *deductive* method, claiming that logic, like mathematics, was a special, positive science in need of philosophical grounding and could not be circularly assumed in that task.

Rather than simply assume the validity of the method of logic and mathematics, Husserl argued that a genuine "first philosophy" must proceed by an unmediated intuition of self-evident truths. His phenomenological method, therefore, involved the careful *description* of the intuited data that presented themselves clearly and distinctly to reflection. Husserl's appeal to intuition is not meant to invoke some unusual state of consciousness. He sees intuition on the model of perception—the direct awareness of something present to consciousness. The elements that present themselves in intuition will provide the self-evident truths on which phenomenology will build. Descartes' notions of substance, causality, etc., may surface again at a later stage of the investigation, but then they should be understood as *meanings* that can be given on the basis of evidence that is weaker than the self-evidence required at the start of philosophical inquiry.

Husserl thus trimmed the Cartesian *cogito* to those elements that he took to be self-evident. But then he added one element that, he argued, appeared as self-evident as the original *cogito*. It was nothing that Descartes had denied, it was simply an element on which Descartes had failed to capitalize. "If I am certain that I am thinking," Husserl argued, "I am equally certain that I am thinking *about something*."[3] This something is the experienced object.

The obvious problem, of course, is that the things I think about don't always exist. I can imagine a unicorn or believe in Santa Claus, and my mere thinking about them does not bestow existence on them. So the *cogito* does not, by itself, give one warranted certainty about the existential status of the things one thinks about. Nonetheless, if there is to be any access to reality, it is here in the objects-thought-about that reality will appear.

This emphasis on the fact that thinking is directed toward some sort of object, real or fictional, Husserl calls the *intentionality* of consciousness, capitalizing on an insight from Franz Brentano, with whom he had studied. Brentano had argued that one can distinguish between physical and psychological phenomena on the grounds that only the latter have an *intentional* structure. That is to say, only psychological states have "reference to a content . . . directedness toward an object." Physical objects, on the other hand, do not have this characteristic.[4] Unlike Brentano, however, Husserl does not use intentionality as a means of making the traditional metaphysical distinction between the mental and the physical. He explores intentionality only as an essential structure of conscious experience. All metaphysical claims must have their grounding in this experience.

One other profound difference between Descartes and Husserl lies in their understanding of science. For Descartes, the physical sciences dealt with a transcendent reality whose existence required proof. Transcendent reality lay on the far side of an epistemological chasm. The existence of a subject could be known clearly and distinctly; the existence of the physical world, by contrast, was knowable only through fallible sensory experience. One needed a "bridge" to guarantee the veracity of our access to the physical world. Descartes built that bridge by appealing to the existence of a non-deceiving God.

Husserl, on the other hand, refused at the outset to accept any epistemological gulf between consciousness and its experienced objects. The notion of transcendent reality, he argued, needed fresh understanding. The objects that appear in experience carry varying degrees of evidence regarding their existential status. On the basis of the evidence that they carry with them, consciousness assigns to them their most likely existential status. One crucial piece of evidence for transcendence is that the object appears only partially. Its temporal and spatial aspects never appear in their entirety. Such objects are assigned the meaning "transcendent." Transcendence is no longer seen to be on the far side of an epistemological divide; rather, it is among the meanings assigned to some experienced objects. Husserl is not claiming, of course, that consciousness gives existence to physical reality. His concern is with the *meaning* that one gives to some aspects of one's experience. "Transcendent" is one such meaning. Again, the issue is not metaphysics, it is experience and meaning.

This fresh way of looking at transcendence carries with it a new understanding of science. The latter, Husserl argues, is not simply a description of the laws governing objective reality, as it appeared to be for Descartes. Husserl sees science as an intersubjectively constructed system of meanings, an interpretation of aspects of the experienced world.

Acknowledging that at this point all he has is his *cogito*—i.e., *acts* of consciousness—and the *objects* of consciousness (he calls them *cogitata*), which may or may not actually exist, Husserl introduces his "phenomenological reduction" (or "epoche"). This reduction is in the spirit of Descartes' methodic doubt. The motivation for it is the belief that one cannot make assumptions about the existential status of experienced objects; one needs clear evidence to support such claims. To highlight the dubitability of our judgments about the existential status of objects, Descartes had appealed to the possibility of doubt; Husserl, with his reduction, appeals to neutrality. The phenomenological reduction is a maneuver that is intended to put aside any unexamined *assumptions* about the existential status of objects that appear in experience.

There is at least one clear parallel between Husserl's reduction and the appeal that Moore and Russell made to sense-data. In both cases, there is an effort to cut one's assumptions to a minimum and to begin with only what is indisputably *given* in experience. A pivotal difference in the two positions, however, is that Moore and Russell attend exclusively to the *objects* that are given, noting the importance of distinguishing those objects from acts of consciousness, but paying small attention to how the acts and the objects relate to one another. For Husserl, the acts of consciousness as well as their relation to objects are as important a matter for investigation as are the objects themselves.

There is another point on which Husserl's reduction puts him at odds at least with Moore, and that concerns the status to be accorded to common sense beliefs. Both Moore and Husserl were concerned about minimizing skepticism, but their respective solutions were quite different. Moore assumes that common sense beliefs about the mind-independent world are largely true, and he attempts to provide an analysis of them that will make clear the grounds for our certainty about them. Husserl, on the other hand, sees most of our common sense beliefs as being infected with the fallacy of "objectivism," assuming that one can know objects in abstraction from their relation to consciousness. In contrast, he argues that we are never in a position to know anything about mind-independent objects *alone*. Whatever we know about them is always known in the context of our *experience* of them.

From Husserl's point of view, a naive acceptance of common sense beliefs about our knowledge of the physical world was the source of a great many of philosophy's missteps. His approach to an analysis of those beliefs was far more radical than was Moore's.

> Accepting only what is evident to me, I, as an autonomous ego, must pursue to its ultimate grounds what others, following the tradition, regard as scientifically grounded. These ultimate grounds must be immediately and apodictically evident. Only in that way can I account for and justify my thought absolutely. There is no prejudice, therefore, however obvious it might be, which I can allow to pass unquestioned and ungrounded. [5]

When Husserl says he is looking for apodictic evidence, he means that he requires evidence of the sort whereby it is *inconceivable* that it could be mistaken. "An *apodictic* evidence, however, is not merely certainty of the affairs or affair-complexes (states-of-affairs) evident in it; rather it discloses itself, to a critical reflection, as having the signal peculiarity of being *at the same time the absolute unimaginableness* (inconceivability) of their *non-being. . . .*"[6] Where Moore and Russell were satisfied to begin their philosophical investigations with some reasonable degree of psychological certainty, Husserl demands a far more exacting starting-point.

Kant

So Husserl's first debt to Descartes is his insistence on grounding philosophy in the absolute certainty of the *cogito*. But his supplement to Descartes, his adding of the intended object to the act of thinking, brings him to a version of Kant: subject and object become inextricably linked. Husserl preserves the most general aspect of the Kantian tradition in that he insists on giving serious consideration to the contributions of both subject and object in experience. The abiding importance for Husserl of the Kantian point cannot be overestimated: any effort to understand objects *requires* that one take into consideration the subjective state in which they are experienced. Understanding what the subjective state is will shed light on the possible existential status of its object. So, for example, if I have evidence that the subjective state I am in is *imagining*, then I have evidence that the object I am experiencing is probably not actual. Reciprocally, if I have evidence that the object of my awareness does not exist, then I have evidence that I am probably imagining rather than perceiving.

Husserl is not naive about the degree of certainty that one can have about the existential status of the objects of one's experience. Like every other philosopher who takes seriously our fallibility, he believes that we can achieve varying degrees of *probability* about whether the experienced object is actual or fictional. What he offers are explicit indications about how to look for relevant evidence. More on that in a moment.

An "objectivist" view sees consciousness, to use the phrase made famous by Richard Rorty, as no more than "a mirror of nature." Husserl, by contrast, was just enough of a Kantian to insist that perceptual experience (an important basis for natural science) is not purely receptive. As he puts it, " . . . nothing exists for me otherwise than by virtue of the *actual and potential performance of my own consciousness.*"[7] Phenomenology becomes the philosophical investigation of meanings.[8]*

But in highlighting Husserl's debt to Kant it is important to point out that Husserl was not simply a Kantian. Most importantly, he denied Kant's distinction between phenomena and noumena.[9] While phenomena include fictional objects of various sorts, for Husserl they also include aspects of reality. Husserl replaces the distinction between phenomena and noumena with a distinction between part and whole. When actual physical objects appear in experience they always appear partially, but they are nonetheless aspects of *reality*.

It becomes clear, then, that Husserl's view was not a version of the Idealism that Moore and Russell were busy rejecting. Husserl never doubted the existence of mind-independent reality.

> Now, to be sure, external Objects too are originally there for us only in
> our subjective experiencing. But they present themselves in it as
> Objects already factually existent beforehand . . . and only entering into
> our experiencing. They are not there for us, like thought-formations
> (judgments, proofs, and so forth), as coming from our own thinking
> activity and fashioned by it purely. . . . In other words: Physical things
> are given beforehand to active living as objects originally other than the
> Ego's own; they are given from outside.[10]

While he thought that the existence of the physical world could never be
proved, he also believed that arguments intended to call it into question
were inescapably flawed.[11]* The issue for Husserl was not between realism and metaphysical Idealism. His phenomenology was intended as a third
alternative that simply bypassed the traditional quarrel between the
two.[12]* Each of these latter views was, he thought, misconceived. Each, in
a sense, emphasized one aspect of experience to the exclusion of the
other. Thus, naive realism claimed access to an objective, uninterpreted
world, while Idealism reduced the world to the subjective, to utter mind-
dependency.

For Husserl, the truth lay somewhere between these two extremes.
He indeed accepted the existence of a world that was not the product of the
mind, but he argued that *access* to that world would always be conditioned
by the consciousness that experienced it. Any science that we construct, as
well as any metaphysics, must always understand itself as an *interpretation*
of reality by conscious subjects—neither a simple mirroring, nor a pure
construction of that reality.

So one profound difference between Husserl's phenomenology, and
the analytic tradition of Moore and Russell, is that Husserl reinstates
Subjectivity into the heart of philosophy.

Husserl's claims about the importance of recognizing the role of
Subjectivity and interpretation in experience might suggest that he was
advocating a view about the theory-ladenness of observation. But that is not
the case. N.R. Hanson argued, in *Patterns of Discovery*, that one's observa-
tions are shaped by what one knows, by one's background information.[13]*
Husserl's claims are more fundamental than that, focusing as they do on
structures that are universally shared by all subjects, rather than on the
particular background knowledge of individual observers. So, for example,
in the case of physical objects, he argues that all perceivers will experience
them *partially*, they will experience temporal and spatial "perspectives"
(i.e., portions of the objects), but never the entire objects themselves.
Husserl highlights these sorts of universal structures governing experience,

to indicate one essential portion of the subjective conditions that shape our experience.

This early phase in Husserl's philosophy came to be known as his "static" phenomenology because it paid so little attention to developmental aspects of knowledge. One might expect that a more developmental framework for his theory of knowledge would bring Husserl closer to Hanson's point. And in one small way it does. In later years, especially in his *Formal and Transcendental Logic* and his *Cartesian Meditations*, Husserl spells out a "genetic" phenomenology, one that pays attention to the development (the "sedimentation") of meanings in experience. But even in its genetic phase, with its emphasis on development in knowledge structures, Husserl's phenomenology does not concern itself primarily with the role of individual differences in background knowledge. Rather, he focuses on the laws that govern what *types* of experiences must precede other types, and on the laws that govern the development of habitual or dispositional states.[14] The emphasis continues to be on essential structures governing any consciousness; the difference between the static and genetic accounts is that the latter takes seriously the temporal relations among those types of structures. From the early phase through the later one, this much of Kant remains: the focus is on *a priori* structures of experience, not on empirical differences among subjects.

The one small concession to a view like Hanson's is the claim that each subject is indeed changed by its experiences. Each develops dispositions, "habitualities," and convictions, that come to define the subject.[15] One consequence of this is, of course, that each subject will bring a somewhat different framework to experience. But Husserl does not go on to argue that visual perception is therefore "theory-laden." The contents that define the Subject may develop and change, but Husserl believes that one can still perceive an object as it is itself (albeit, partially). His theory of intuition, as we shall see, depends on this.

Hume

How does one put together a Cartesian quest for certainty and a Kantian insistence on the pervasive role of Subjectivity? This is where Husserl revises a bit of Hume. Husserl was as committed as Hume to the necessity of grounding one's philosophical claims in experience. But he was strenuously opposed to Hume's skepticism. His remedy was to argue that if one looks closely at experience, one will discover that it is not filled with random bits of data ("impressions" or "ideas") that somehow gravitate toward one another by associative mechanisms. Rather, on close investigation one discovers that experience is filled with essentially distinct *types* of things.[16]

And these types, their characteristics, and the relations among them, are law-governed and predictable. Even Hume's claim about the distinction between "impressions" and "ideas" is based on a recognition of two different types of experience. On Husserl's view, there are many more than two types, but Hume's acknowledgement of the two types is enough to give Husserl the leverage he needs.

Husserl's view can be elaborated in the following way: If I can distinguish between impressions and ideas, I do so on the basis of certain qualities of the two (vividness, etc.). Once that distinction is made, I can go on to distinguish among the kinds of psychological states in which those objects appear. If the object appears vivid, etc., I take myself to be perceiving, if it is faded, etc., I take myself to be remembering or imagining. In other words, there are law-governed relationships between the types of objects I experience and the types of psychological states in which I experience them. Framed in Humean language, when I take myself to be experiencing an *impression*, that counts as some evidence that I am *perceiving*. When I take myself to be experiencing an *idea*, that counts as some evidence that I am remembering or imagining. So the correlations between the characteristics of the data and the type of experience one takes oneself to be having are not random; they are law-governed and predictable. This is the sort of Humean assumption that Husserl makes explicit and capitalizes on. As he did with Descartes, so Husserl does with Hume—he ferrets out an unexploited assumption and puts it to work.

One's recognition of these *types* and their law-governed relationships is what Husserl calls, in an unfortunate choice of expressions, the "intuition of essences." Recall that by "intuition" he merely means the seeing of something, even partially, as it is. And it is this capacity to see, to intuit, law-governed types in my experience that, on Husserl's view, disarms skepticism. Granted that I never have *certainty* about the existential status of the object. I can, after all, take an object to be physical when it is an hallucination. Any philosophy needs to recognize this possibility. Nonetheless, I can have some degree of certainty about the *types* of experiences that I have, about the *types* of objects that appear in them, and about the laws or rules that govern the two.

Notice an important distinction here. The certainty that Husserl claims for us is not certainty that I am, for example, now perceiving. Rather, it is certainty about what would have to be the case if I were perceiving. When I take myself to be perceiving a chair, I do so because I believe (perhaps mistakenly) that a particular set of conditions has been met. For example, I believe that if I were to walk around the object it would continue to appear as a three-dimensional object, that if I were to see it at a later time it would still appear as a chair, etc. That is, my *experience* (not just objects pure and simple) is a structured set of law-governed types. To that extent, one is capable of some degree of knowledge about experience. One may misread the data, but one still has some knowledge of what the *rules* are that govern the proper assignment of *meaning* to both acts and objects in experience.

So this is where the Cartesian quest for certainty and the Kantian commitment to the pervasiveness of subjective interpretation come together. By carefully examining experience, one can discover with some degree of certainty the laws that govern the subjective assignments of meaning. But one can also assume with some degree of certainty, Husserl believes, that every possible consciousness is governed by the same set of laws. As Husserl put it,

> . . . it is evident that whenever something like numbers, mathematical multiplicities, propositions, theories, etc., are to become subjectively given, become objects of consciousness in subjective lived experiences, the lived experiences which are needed for that to happen must have their essentially necessary and everywhere identical structure. In other words, whether we take us men as thinking subjects, or whether we imagine angels or devils or gods, etc., any sort of beings which count, compute, do mathematics—the counting, mathematising internal doing and living is, if the logical-mathematical is to result from it, in a priori necessity everywhere essentially the same. . . .
>
> The same holds for all investigations of psychic correlations referring to objects of every region and category, . . . [17]

Husserl begins his claim by making it in relation to mathematics and logic, but he explicitly extends it to cover the correlations between every type of psychic act and its object. And his claims about the essential structures of conscious experience are not simply empirical claims about human psychology. They cover every conceivable type of thinking being, apparently from gods to humans.[18]* That is, for Husserl an insistence on the role of subjective interpretation does not entail simple subjectivism or even species-relativism. Absolutely universal, a priori laws of conscious experience are supposed to be at work.

Husserl's phenomenology, then, has a Cartesian starting-point in what he takes to be the absolute certainty of the *cogito*. He pares down the *cogito* to eliminate any appeal to substance, causality, or deductive logic, and expands the act, *cogito*, to include an intentional object. The intentional (act-object) structure of experience is taken to be law-governed in the types of meanings that are assigned to acts and their correlated objects. And all of this is taken to entail the view that objects alone are never available to philosophical theorizing; they can only be treated as *experienced* objects—

objects that have been given meaning of some sort. The existential status of these experienced objects cannot be assumed at the outset; one applies the "phenomenological reduction" and then looks for evidence in the characteristics of the phenomena that will point, with some degree of probability, to their existential status.

So once again, the kind of objectivity that Moore and Russell sought—that is achieved by minimizing or eliminating Subjectivity—is not only not a goal for Husserl, it is ruled impossible to achieve. And while, for the later Russell, Subjectivity reappeared in his epistemology, it was seen only as a source of distortion and error. Husserl, by contrast, acknowledges the possibility of subjective error but argues that conscious Subjects are the source not only of possible error, but also of all *meaning*.

Method in Phenomenology

Husserl's insistence on the importance of the subjective element in the knowledge relation leads quite naturally to his distinctive phenomenological *method*. It has several steps, and I shall make some artificial distinctions in those steps in an effort to lay out the elements clearly.

(1) The starting point for Husserl's method is dramatically different not only from that of Moore and Russell, but also from most of the classical tradition in philosophy. These latter normally take as their focus some object—either a bit of the world or of language, or perhaps a concept or some sensory data. Husserl, in contrast to this, begins by explicitly moving to an attitude of *reflection*. Rather than focus attention "outward," toward objects of whatever sort, he turns his attention to his conscious-awareness-of-objects, that is, to the whole of the intentional structure. The traditional, non-reflective philosophical attitude (Husserl calls it the "natural attitude") allows consciousness to be "transparent." That is, it effectively ignores consciousness and trains its attention exclusively on some object. And even in those moments when philosophers take mental states as their object of investigation, Husserl would claim that they allow the investigating consciousness to remain "transparent." In addition, they artificially isolate the states of consciousness being investigated from their *objects*. As I noted earlier, what is crucial for him is that *both* conscious acts and their objects must always be seen as requiring each other.

Husserl calls this move to reflective awareness of both consciousness and its objects, the "phenomenological attitude." Unless one keeps in mind that Husserl's phenomenology always operates from this reflective stance, with attention to the whole intentional structure of consciousness, act-and-object, one can easily misconstrue what his claims amount to.

(2) Within this reflective attitude, one then suspends judgment on the existential status of all the elements under investigation. This is Husserl's *phenomenological reduction*. Since one makes no assumptions about existential status, everything can be treated at least as a *phenomenon*. To understand this particular move it is useful to recall that Husserl has no interest in proving the truth of either realism or Idealism. His goal here is to put aside as many assumptions as possible and to look for *evidence* that would motivate belief in the existential status of objects of various sorts.

(3) Given the move to reflection and to the phenomenological reduction, the next step consists in careful attention to the data, with a detailed *description* of what appears to reflecting consciousness. The idea at this point is to put aside traditional philosophical methods, including deduction, and to simply pay attention to what is given, what presents itself to the investigating consciousness. This step is closely related to what Husserl calls his "principle of all principles:" "I . . . must neither make nor go on accepting any judgment as scientific [he uses the term in its most general sense of 'well-grounded cognition]' *that I have not derived from evidence*, from 'experiences' in which the affairs in question are present to me as *'they themselves'*."[19] (One can hardly fail to notice the significant parallel here with Russell's early insistence on the fundamental role of Knowledge by Acquaintance.)

It is perhaps worth noting that when philosophers complain that Husserl does not *argue* for his claims, they sometimes fail to make a distinction between two quite different contexts. When he is "outside" the phenomenological attitude, Husserl often argues carefully and at length for his view. The Prolegomena to his *Logical Investigations*, where he argues against psychologism, is a particularly good example of this. But when he moves to phenomenology proper, he has put aside the methods of deductive and inductive inference and has moved to detailed *description*. Whether his claims are compelling or moot, he has not accidentally overlooked the need for careful supporting argument. He believes that anyone who looks at the data revealed in reflection will simply *see*, as he does, that the descriptions of the data are accurate. This is where intuition, rather than argument, is crucial for him.

In relation to the descriptive portion of this step Husserl says that what is given must then be described in unambiguous language.[20] (This latter requirement may have encouraged the introduction of neologisms and unfamiliar terminology that can be daunting to new readers of phenomenology.)

(4) With the descriptive data available, Husserl insists that one further "reduction" is needed. He calls it the "eidetic reduction" (from the Greek *eidos*, generally interpreted as idea, form, or essence). This terminology sounds decidedly platonic, but Husserl argues that no such framework is

assumed. Recall that his phenomenological reduction neutralized all ontological commitments. So whatever echoes of platonism reverberate here (he
sometimes even uses the metaphor of "participation"),[21] Husserl tries to
avoid any assumptions about a realm of Platonic *Being*.[22] What he has in
mind with this reduction is the elimination of all the data that do not have
an essential role in determining the character of the phenomenon in question.

One important caveat: when Husserl speaks of an essence, he does
not mean the collection of properties that a physical object must have in
order to belong to a particular class. Recalling that for Husserl one is always
dealing, not with objects alone, but with consciousness-of-objects, and
therefore with meaningful objects, his "essences" are perhaps best understood as the necessary conditions for proper meaning assignments. That is,
their status is primarily epistemological.

The process of winnowing the essential from the non-essential
Husserl calls "free variation."[23] That is to say, one varies portions of the data
to see which variations alter the fundamental character of the phenomenon.
Those portions of the data that cannot be altered without modifying the
basic character of the phenomenon are taken to constitute a portion of its
"essence."

To take an apparently simple example, in the case of reflecting on a
memory-of-something, any attempt to vary the temporal quality of the
phenomenon, say from past to future, would destroy its character as a
memory. On the other hand, one can vary certain other aspects of the
remembered object without necessarily distorting the character of the
experience as a memory. One would conclude, then, that pastness is one of
the essential characteristics of remembered objects, contributing one of the
necessary conditions for assigning the meaning *memory* to the experience.
On Husserl's view, one can simply *see* that some aspects of a phenomenon
are essential while others are not. That is, one can *intuit* essences. He calls
this "eidetic intuition."[24]*

There is one additional aspect of Husserl's "reductions" that should
be mentioned. Husserl sometimes refers to a reduction that uncovers the
transcendental ego. And although his terminology is not always consistent, I
shall call this the "transcendental reduction." The transcendental ego that
is to be uncovered is most plausibly interpreted, I believe, as the *meaning-
giver* in experience. But here, as in the case of acts and objects of consciousness, Husserl's goal is to uncover essences. He is concerned, that is, with
universal and necessary structures, and not with empirical facts. In the case
of the transcendental ego Husserl's phenomenology has no interest in the
peculiar factual aspects of human Subjectivity or human mental states. As
we shall see, this exclusive emphasis on essences, and the elimination of all

consideration of factual and contingent material, will figure in Husserl's attitude toward the relevance of insights from the theory of evolution.

So a primary goal of Husserl's phenomenology is to discover the essential conditions that govern meaning-assignments for all acts and objects of consciousness.

It is this final portion of his method, the intuition of essences, that is of primary importance to Husserl.

> ... pure or transcendental phenomenology will be established not as a science of facts, but as a science of essential being (as 'eidetic' Science); a science which aims exclusively at establishing 'knowledge of essences' and absolutely no 'facts.' [25]

Darwin And Phenomenology

Given this sketch of Husserl's phenomenology and its method, one can begin to see a number of fundamental reasons for Husserl's refusal to incorporate into his new philosophy any insights from evolution. While some of these are treated explicitly in his work, most of them are implicit in Husserl's view of what constitutes genuine philosophy. I shall explore four of the reasons I believe motivated his attitude toward the relationship between philosophy and evolution theory: (i) Husserl's anti-objectivism; (ii) his belief that consciousness is not reducible to nature; (iii) his emphasis on timeless, immutable truths; and (iv) his view of philosophy as providing the foundation for all the sciences, including biology.

(i) Anti-Objectivism

Husserl's argument against objectivism rests on his claims about the essential correlation between subjective and objective elements in knowledge. His point was, as I have noted, that the role of the knowing *subject* had been systematically overlooked or at least underestimated in both science and philosophy. All experience, on the Husserlian view, involves a reciprocity between subject and object.

In the sciences, then, one is never dealing simply with nature; one always has nature-as-experienced-by-a-subject (or subjects). A theory in biology, then, is not a straightforward description of nature; rather, it is a complex meaning-structure. While natural scientists have no interest in the subjective contribution to scientific investigation, and focus their attention exclusively on objects in nature, they do so, on Husserl's view, by abstracting those objects from the full context in which they actually appear.[26] There may well be practical reasons for the natural scientist to do this. But philosophers, he argues, must always take explicit account of the complete intentional context. This will, he believes, both clarify and provide an ultimate justification for what the scientist is actually doing. So while natural scientists may legitimately pursue their investigations in an objectivist way, philosophy must not.

One part of philosophy's task is to lay out the laws that govern the subjective contribution to all meaning-structures, including those of natural science. A biological theory, given its purely objectivist bent, will of necessity be irrelevant to this philosophical task.

Husserl's critique of philosophical *Naturalism* in all its forms—"psychologism," "anthropologism," "biologism"[27]*—makes his position on this quite explicit. On his view, one of the problems of Naturalism in any of its forms is that it takes naively objectivist science as its basis. Since science, as an interpretation of nature, must be understood as at least partly a product of Subjectivity, Husserl concludes that Subjectivity, and not science, must therefore be the starting point for philosophy.[28]

Husserl's claim that scientific theories are *interpretations* of nature by conscious subjects is surely plausible. However, it does not necessarily follow from that, that philosophy must begin with an account of Subjectivity and must refuse to incorporate any insights from the sciences.

If Darwin is right, conscious subjects are a relatively recent product of completely contingent natural processes. While science is indeed dependent on Subjectivity in that all theorizing is a product of conscious subjects, nonetheless, Subjectivity itself is a product of events in the natural world, events about which science has much to tell us. On such a view, it is futile to insist that Subjectivity *or* natural science is the only possible starting point for inquiry. Each of them (and other things as well) has something to contribute to our understanding of ourselves and of our world. Rather than insisting on either science or Subjectivity as the absolutely certain foundation for all knowledge, we may need to simply dispense altogether with the need for absolute priority.

Russell, in his paper, "On the Relation of Sense-Data to Physics," made just such a move.[29] He assumed the basic reliability of both experience and science, and then tried to provide an analysis of both that would reveal their mutual consistency.

Husserl's likely response to the objection that Subjectivity itself has a natural source and history, is that he is not talking about factual, empirical Subjectivity. His concern is with Transcendental Subjectivity. Such a response, however, simply leaves the quarrel between Husserl and naturalistic philosophy at an impasse. The naturalist wants to know the origin of such non-empirical Subjectivity, and wonders how any factual science could be the product of anything but factual Subjectivity. Part of Husserl's defense here relies on his insistence on the role of the *essential* rather than the factual in his phenomenology. And I shall consider that point in a moment. But there remains a question about the subject that functions in the construction of scientific theories.

One difficulty with Husserl's view here is that it seems to preclude the possibility of asking questions about the nature and origin of Subjectivity itself. One might grant Husserl his claim that objectivism is mistaken. But it would not follow that the subject, as meaning-giver, must be assumed to be outside the biological context. Husserl's eidetic reduction has so removed the subject from all factual considerations that one is left with a virtually disembodied, impersonal meaning-giver. The theory that emerges is meant to be as true of gods as it is of human beings. Although one can obviously hypothesize such an abstract version of Subjectivity, it is difficult to see that it will have great value when one is constructing a theory of knowledge that has relevance to *human* experience. Perhaps it will establish some outer limits within which human Subjectivity should be understood, but it will leave one far removed from a theory about how human subjects give meaning to their world. The human subject as a living organism, as an organism struggling to survive in a given environment, and as preeminently interested in its own well-being—all these ways of understanding human Subjectivity are relevant to its function as meaning-giver. The sort of meaning that such a subject generates will differ in important ways from the sort of meaning that a disembodied, disinterested subject might be expected to generate.

In other words, if Husserl is right in thinking that the subject plays a crucial role in knowledge and must, therefore, count in the philosophical theory of knowledge, then he is not entitled to disregard whatever insights we may have concerning the nature of the human subjects that are involved in knowledge relations with that world. Issues of survival and well-being are intimately bound up with the function of human Subjectivity at least, and probably with the subjective dimension of most of the more highly developed animals.

In his later work, especially in his *Phenomenological Psychology* and *The Crisis of European Sciences*, Husserl does begin to speak of an embodied subject—one capable of bodily activities. But the recognition of the importance of this aspect of Subjectivity does not motivate him to consider how that bodily subject's concern for its own survival and well-being might affect its role as meaning-giver, or should affect the theory of knowledge—in particular, of perception—that philosophy constructs for it.

One of the later phenomenologists, Maurice Merleau-Ponty, argues in great detail for the embodied character of human Subjectivity, above all in perception. But even Merleau-Ponty, for all his insights into the "lived body" as it functions in perception, does not re-open the question of evolution theory, and its possible relevance to human experience and a philosophical theory of human knowledge.[30]

For later phenomenology as for later analytic philosophy, the great bulk of theorizing was done without looking back to reconsider the verdict that was issued by Russell, Moore, and Husserl early in the century on the relevance of evolution and Darwin.

Husserl's earlier position on the completely non-biological character of Transcendental Subjectivity is closely related to his view that consciousness is not reducible to some aspect of the natural world. I turn now to consider that view.

(ii) Consciousness and Nature

Another facet of Husserl's philosophy, that motivates him to exclude evolutionary considerations was his insistence that consciousness cannot be naturalized, cannot be treated as part of the natural world. In his extended critique of naturalistic philosophy, Husserl makes clear his opposition to a naturalistic account of consciousness.

> Characteristic of all forms of extreme and consistent naturalism . . . is on the one hand the naturalizing of consciousness . . . and on the other the naturalizing of ideas and consequently of all absolute ideals and norms.
> From the latter point of view, . . . naturalism refutes itself.[31]

Naturalism is mistaken both in its naturalizing of consciousness and ideas.

In his 1925 lectures Husserl offers a much more detailed account of his views on the relationship between consciousness and nature. Recall his comment there that he is concerned with any possible consciousness, "angels or devils or gods. . . . " It is clear, then, that Husserl does not see consciousness as reducible to nature, let alone as an evolved adaptation of biological organisms. " . . . [W]e give voice to the most fundamental and pivotal difference between ways of being, that between *Consciousness* and *Reality*."[32]

But what is one to say about *human* consciousness? Might that be naturalized? Not completely. While Husserl speaks of the close connection between psychic acts and the body in humans and other animals,[33] he is also careful to say that physical nature and mentality "each can nevertheless be pursued purely on its own as a self-enclosed nexus."[34] One might well argue that he is here speaking only of the two different *methods* that should be used in investigating the mental and the physical. And indeed Husserl agrees with Dilthey that the methods of the natural and social sciences must be kept quite distinct. To that extent, the mental won't be simply reducible to the physical.

But there is evidence that Husserl's view of the distinction was more than methodological. He argues (in a way partially reminiscent of Gilbert Ryle) that "Cartesian dualism requires the parallelization of *mens* and *corpus*, together with the naturalization of psychic being implied in this parallelization, and hence also requires the parallelization of the required methods."[35] This, from Husserl's point of view, is a mistake that has plagued philosophy for centuries. His alternative is not, however, Rylean. He goes on to say,

> In any case, we can already say in advance, on the basis of insight, that the psychic, considered purely in terms of its own essence, has no [physical] nature, has no conceivable in-itself in the natural sense, no spatiotemporally causal, no idealizable and mathematizable in-itself, no laws after the fashion of natural laws; here there are no theories with the same relatedness back to the intuitive life-world, no observations or experiments with a function for theorizing similar to natural science. . . . Our task is critically to make transparent . . . the naturalistic—or, more exactly, physicalistic—prejudice of the whole of modern psychology.[36]

Husserl's view that consciousness cannot be naturalized may not rely on a Cartesian dualism as traditionally understood. Still, there is more at stake than simple differences of method. The methodological considerations arise from different "ways of being."[37]* These two ways of being are not to be understood simply as having distinct but parallel sets of properties. A naturalistic psychology that mimics natural science is, he believes, completely misguided.

Given this view of the psychic or mental, it is not surprising that Husserl would see evolution theory as completely irrelevant to his science of the intentional structures of consciousness. To take evolution theory to be relevant would be to treat the mental within the framework of natural causality; it would be to naturalize consciousness.

There are two ways one might understand Husserl's claims about the non-natural character of consciousness. On one account, he is saying nothing more than that physical reality and consciousness are *experienced* as being quite different—that is, one could take his claim to be phenomenological. And I shall argue in Chapter Six, that this is indeed the most promising interpretation of his view—namely that mind and body, *as experienced*, belong to two different systems of *meanings*, neither of which is reducible to the other.

On the second way of understanding his account, he is making a claim about two different kinds of *realities*—that is, his claim is a metaphysical one.

Although I believe that Husserl means for his phenomenological account to undergird the metaphysical account, that way of construing things is not without its problems. For example, Husserl elsewhere makes comments that suggest that the stronger, metaphysical position may motivate some of his phenomenological claims. He notes that the doctrine of immortality would require that "the natural consideration of the world . . . need not and perhaps must not have the last word."[38]* He does not pursue the issue, but the context suggests that he views such a doctrine as one that should be taken into account in any complete theory of the mental.

In addition to his concerns about immortality, I believe that Husserl had at least two reasons for claiming that the psychic (or mental) dimension has a special way of being. The first was that psychic acts "animate" the body; the second was the intentionality of consciousness.

With respect to its animating function, Husserl sees the psychic as contributing something quite unique to a body. Without it, the body is incapable of its animate functions, including sensory perception. Such a claim is plausible. But such an animating function can be explained in at least two ways: the psychic might be a distinct way of being that can be "added" to a body and that is amenable only to a non-natural science; or it might be a natural property or set of properties belonging to certain bodies at certain times and be fully accessible to natural science.

Husserl appears to favor the first option. And his motivation seems to be that the psychic has certain unusual characteristics. But the fact that the psychic appears to have some properties that are different from the properties we ascribe to ordinary material objects is not, by itself, a decisive objection to the claim that it is natural. Neutrinos, for example, are natural—i.e., subject to the laws of physics—although they lack most of the properties that we normally attribute to material objects (e.g., mass), and they possess some properties that such objects normally lack (e.g., they can pass directly through ordinary material objects). Photons, too, are natural, although quantum physics tells us that they do not appear to be subject to the ordinary laws of individuation, or even of causality, that govern the middle-sized objects of common experience. So having unusual properties that are not had by all other natural objects does not seem to provide an adequate reason for characterizing the psychic as non-natural. The capacity of the psychic or mental to animate some bodies might, then, require an extended understanding of the possible characteristics of the natural realm rather than the postulation of a distinct way of being that has its own unique essence, laws, and science.

Husserl's other reason for treating the mental as non-natural was undoubtedly its intentional structure. Intentionality carries with it two characteristics: intentional states have content, are directed toward something; and the object to which they are directed need not exist. Recall that Husserl's teacher, Brentano, had used intentionality to distinguish the mental from the physical. And Husserl takes intentionality to be the distinguishing and non-natural characteristic of consciousness. But it is not obvious that intentionality necessarily qualifies as a property of *non*-natural systems. If there is such a thing as a physically instantiated "language of thought," then one can account for the intentionality of systems within a natural framework.[39]* Physical tokens of "Mentalese" could account for the content of psychological states relating to objects that may or may not exist. Such an account leaves consciousness both intentional and natural.

If, as Husserl suggests, consciousness cannot be naturalized, is not a "mere causal appendage to nature," then it would remain untouched by theories of nature, including the theory of evolution. And furthermore, if philosophy is the science of the *essential* structures of non-natural consciousness, then perhaps philosophy need have nothing to do with theories of evolution. Although Husserl does not explicitly state such an argument, reasoning something like this surely contributed to the attitude he took toward the relationship between phenomenology and the theory of evolution. But Husserl does not offer the kind of evidence or argument that would show his claim to be beyond dispute. The consciousness of which Husserl speaks (and in particular, Transcendental Subjectivity) becomes for all practical purposes a disembodied, disinterested, and impersonal one. Whatever one takes its metaphysical status to be, one surely ought to ask about the role that such a Subjectivity can play on behalf of the needs of the particular living body with which it is associated.

(iii) Timeless Truths

A third consideration that likely motivated Husserl to eliminate evolution theory from philosophy was his concern with timeless truths. His insistence on our capacity to intuit timeless objects (e.g., truths of logic, mathematics, and essences) bears some resemblance to Russell's preference for the timeless, and his early claim that universals are among the objects of Knowledge by Acquaintance. There are some important differences in their views, to be sure, but there was a common source for their interest in timeless truth—their early training and continuing interest in mathematics and logic. For both men mathematics and logic provided a model for genuine knowledge that is available to human beings but in no way dependent on them for its validity. These preferences for timeless truth played significant roles in shaping their respective philosophies and in encouraging the elimination of evolutionary considerations.

In Husserl's *Phenomenological Psychology*, he gives a lucid account of how his concern with issues in the cognition of logic and mathematics led him to his phenomenology. He notes that his *Logical Investigations*, published at the turn of the century, was an effort to articulate the structure of experiences which are correlated with timeless logical and mathematical objects. "This designates the proper theme of the *Logical Investigations* and, in corresponding amplification, of all phenomenology."[40] The "amplification" to which he refers involved extending his investigation to include not only the psychic acts that allow us to know mathematics and logic, but also every psychic act in which we come to know *anything*. "I must however add that a broadening of the problem area had to thrust itself to the fore at once. Plainly, the same problems which had arisen here starting with the logical and mathematical idealities had to be posed for all objectivities, even for real [i.e., time-bound] objects of knowledge."[41] The knowledge of logic and mathematics is to provide the framework within which a comprehensive theory of experience must be formulated.

From logic and mathematics to phenomenology. This development explains, I think, Husserl's emphasis on the importance of the universal, the a priori, the necessary, and the timeless in philosophy. This appears most clearly in the role he assigns to essences, including the essential structures of consciousness, *ideal* (i.e., timeless) objects that were not subject to the conditions of the factual world. Husserl characterized his phenomenology as the "science of essences," of pure possibilities. When Husserl expands his investigation from logic and mathematics to include all experience, his emphasis rests heavily on our capacity to intuit essences as surely as we intuit truths in logic and mathematics. One is reminded yet again of Russell's position in *Our Knowledge of the External World*: genuine philosophy ought not concern itself with time-bound affairs.

Clearly, if one's philosophy has as its goal the intuition of timeless, essential truths, then the theory of biological evolution, with its emphasis on development and change, will be excluded.

One of the familiar difficulties with Husserl's view here is the fact that he assumes that our intuition of essences is independent of all linguistic and cultural influence; they are absolutely universal and immune to change. He offers no argument to support any of these assumptions—each of which could be challenged by work in anthropology, psychology, and linguistics.[42*] But Husserl cannot offer arguments here because his claim is that one can, if one looks properly, simply *see* these essences. The ultimate appeal is to the power of intuition. If one cannot see the essences, or if one sees something different or variable, there is for Husserl no court of appeal. This is not a highly desirable situation for a philosophy that claims to eliminate all questionable assumptions and establish knowledge on absolutely certain foundations.

There was one additional aspect of timelessness that motivated Husserl to exclude evolution. He shared with Russell and Frege a concern to defend the immutable status of logic against any possible threat from evolution theory. In *The Idea of Phenomenology* Husserl put the matter this way:

> We are reminded of the modern theory of evolution, according to which man has evolved in the struggle for existence and by natural selection, and with him his intellect too has evolved naturally and along with his intellect all of its characteristic forms, particularly the logical forms. Accordingly, is it not the case that the logical forms and laws express the accidental peculiarity of the human species, which would have been different and which will be different in the course of future evolution? Cognition is, after all, only *human cognition*, bound up with *human intellectual forms*, and unfit to reach the very nature of things, to reach the things in themselves.
>
> But at once another piece of absurdity arises. Can the cognitions by which such a view operates and the possibilities which it ponders make any sense themselves if the laws of logic are given over to such relativism? Does not the truth that there is this and that possibility implicitly presuppose the absolute validity of the principle of non-contradiction, according to which any given truth excludes its contradictory?[43]

Recall that both Frege and Russell also expressed concern about the relationship between logic and evolution. Frege had argued that evolution has no bearing on *laws* of any kind, including the laws of logic. " '2 times 2 is 4' is true and will continue to be true even if, as a result of Darwinian evolution, human beings were to come to assert that 2 times 2 is five."[44] Russell expanded on this, in 1914, and identified philosophy with logic, thereby making philosophy itself independent of evolution.

Husserl's viewpoint differs from both. He appears to believe that the "modern theory of evolution" itself claims that the laws of logic evolve. He characterizes the theory as claiming that not only have humans and their intellects evolved naturally, but so also have all the "characteristic forms [of the intellect] particularly the logical forms." Husserl does not specify whose version of the theory of evolution he is critiquing. But the reference here to natural selection makes it clear that he has some version of the Darwinian view in mind. However, Darwin's theory makes no claims about the evolution of any sort of laws. His is a theory about biological organisms. And unless one assumes that the fortunes of logic are tied to the processes that govern such organisms, there is no reason to suppose that evolution theory must threaten logic.

But there is some reason to think that Husserl may have had Herbert

Spencer's views in mind here. As early as 1900 Husserl had mounted a detailed attack on "empiricist" treatments of logic. His primary targets were John Stuart Mill and Herbert Spencer.[45]* Husserl shares with Russell an unwillingness to accept their psychologistic interpretation of logic.

Once again, it seems that Herbert Spencer, rather than Darwin, may have been taken as the reliable spokesman for the theory of evolution and its implications.

Whatever its source, Husserl apparently thought that some version of Darwinism included a commitment to the mutability of the laws of logic. He argued that if the truths of logic can be relativized to a time on the evolutionary scale, then all genuine knowledge, including knowledge of evolution itself, becomes impossible. If one is to make any sense of either truth or meaning, then one must be able to count something like the Law of Contradiction as fixed and absolutely certain. But if Darwin's theory itself does not *entail* psychologism or the evolution of the laws of logic, then Husserl's concern about the possibility of genuine knowledge with a Darwinian framework never gets off the ground.

Husserl's emphasis on timeless and immutable validity was partially in reaction against historicism—a view prevalent in nineteenth-century Germany, that everything had to be understood in the context of historical development.[46] Husserl's opposition to historicism, as well as to Naturalism, was more than the purely theoretical concern with the laws of logic and with essences. Like the early Moore and Russell, he was also defending another group of ideal objects, timeless *ethical* values.

When one reads Husserl's published philosophical works, one might suppose that his interests and goals were purely theoretical, and almost exclusively epistemological. But one commentator has argued persuasively that "the fundamental impetus of Husserl's work was profoundly . . . moral, an urgent quest for a renewed moral orientation in a time of disintegrating values."[47] In support of this claim, he points to a letter Husserl wrote to one of his former students, responding to a manuscript that the student had sent him. Husserl's daughter had read portions of the manuscript to him, and Husserl replies:

> . . . we understood the radical determination to keep life from degenerating into a commercial enterprise viewed in terms of 'Debit' and 'Credit' sides of a ledger in which the debit is never more than a demand on credit. We understood the determination which is radically opposed to all 'Capitalism' which values possession—and thus its senseless accumulation—above all else, a dedication which corrects even all egotistic personal values, whether honor, fame, or pride—yes, even the pride of reforming insights, goals, and tasks. . . . I, too, can point to such determination as the final fruition of the unfolding of my own . . . life.

. . . I can only think that you have sensed some of the sustaining ethos through the laconic sobriety and strict concentration on the matters at hand in my writings. [Italics added.] [48]

In this final line Husserl surely acknowledges that, underneath the theoretical focus of his published work there lies a "sustaining ethos" that shares much in common with the work of this former student—primarily, marked by a concern with moral values. He writes that he agrees with his student's critical examination of " . . . naturalism of every form and type . . . " Most significantly, he also agrees with the way the student points out "how every anthropologism, *biologism*, and positivism metamorphoses into an anti-ethical egoism, which is ethically without foundation because it is devoid of ideals, . . . "[49] [Italics added.] Admittedly there is still no explicit mention of Darwin, but Darwinism would surely count among the "biologisms" to which Husserl refers. On this point, Husserl's attitude to the relationship between biology and ethics is quite close to that of Moore's *Principia Ethica* and Russell's "Elements of Ethics." For all three philosophers in the early years of the century, ethical values must be safeguarded against any claims of their having a natural origin or historical development.

Husserl's references here to the undesirable goals of capitalism also calls to mind some of Russell's concerns with *laissez-faire* economics.

So in spite of Husserl's explicit emphasis on theoretical epistemological issues in his philosophy, concerns about the status of ethics and values appear to have motivated him as forcefully as did his concerns about the status of logic. Like logic, the realm of values was to be given an immutable status, a status not dependent on the doings of human beings.

Further evidence for Husserl's attitude on value-oriented issues appears in a brief manuscript which he wrote in praise of George Bernard Shaw. Shaw was, of course, a vehement opponent of Darwinism. His introductory essay for *Back to Methuselah* offers a scathing critique of Darwinism and a defense of Lamarckism. What is at issue for Shaw is human freedom to work toward a better world. He sees Darwinism as condemning human beings to be blindly subject to the forces of natural selection. Lamarckism, on the other hand, makes much of the importance of individual human effort, allowing the human person to make a significant difference to how things turn out. Husserl was deeply sympathetic to the Shavian view. Speaking of Shaw, he says:

> In his hands art becomes a power of life itself working toward the social-ethical and religious renewal of life. . . . No one matches Shaw's ability to arouse our social conscience and instill the belief that no world existing for us simply is, but that any world is what we make it or let it

become through strength or weakness, through unmitigated selfishness or the power of our true freedom. In a word, Shaw the artist is Europe's most effective preacher at present . . . [50]

Husserl does not mention any of Shaw's specific works in this essay, so it is difficult to know if he has *Back to Methuselah* in mind. But it is not difficult to see that Husserl is supporting the general sort of point that Shaw made in that work. He champions, along with Shaw, the value of individual striving and the power of human beings to make the world better. Husserl says later in the essay, " . . . he [Shaw] and I are comrades in pursuit of the same goal. . . . "[51]

Whether Husserl meant to support Shaw's Lamarckism, against Darwin, is not entirely clear. But given what has been said about Husserl's views on the relationship between philosophy and science, this much *is* clear: his exclusion of Darwinian views from philosophy was not simply part of an effort to make room for Lamarckism. *No* theory of evolution could be relevant to Husserl's philosophy, since no scientific theory is relevant.

Husserl's worries about logic are not so different, then, from his less publicized worries about moral values.[52] In both cases he believes that one needs a "foundation," one that is independent of any time-bound facts about human beings, about their biology or their psychology. And as I said in my discussion of Moore and the early Russell, a commitment to the centrality of a realm of a-temporal, immutable objects (of whatever sort) makes a philosophy generally inhospitable to incorporating evolution theory.

Furthermore, if one is at pains to discover timeless structures for every possible consciousness, evolutionary views again present difficulties. Darwin's theory includes the evolution of mental powers. No provision is made for some a-temporal paradigm that must govern such evolution. On the contrary, even our mental powers are thought to arise from *accidental* variations that proved adaptive (or at least not maladaptive) in the past. There is little reason to suppose that there cannot, in principle, be additional variations that could further alter our mental powers. On this count at least, Husserl was right to think that evolutionary considerations pose a difficulty for his phenomenology.

A framework of timeless, essential truths may function for mathematics. There is little evidence that such a framework transfers easily or well to the realm of all human experience.

(iv) Philosophy as the foundation of science

This fourth motivation for Husserl's attitude toward evolution theory was perhaps the most fundamental of all of them. Husserl's approach to the relationship between science and philosophy differed from that of both Russell and Moore. Unlike Moore, he did not ignore science; unlike Russell, he did not see in the methods of the natural sciences a model for a genuine philosophy. For Husserl, philosophy is the "science of all sciences," in the tradition of Descartes. He says,

> Merely empirical, descriptive classificatory (inductive) knowledge is not yet science in the full sense of the word. It merely furnishes relative truth, tied to specific situations. Philosophy, genuine science, aims at absolute, ultimately valid truths which transcend all relativity. Such truth defines what exists, as it exists in itself."[53]

So Husserl's position treats philosophy as absolutely foundational for science. As a consequence of this, philosophy cannot assume the validity of the method or the content of any of the sciences. On Husserl's view, the claims of the sciences need more than to be shown consistent with and dependent on the claims of perception (as Russell had thought). Rather, every claim made by any of the sciences gets its clarification and validation from the theory of knowledge provided by philosophy. Obviously, then, none of the insights of evolution theory can have any place at all in philosophy, on pain of circularity.

In a series of lectures formulated in 1907 and later published as *The Idea of Phenomenology*, Husserl says:

> ... the theory of knowledge qualifies as the critique of cognition, more exactly, as *the critique of natural cognition* in all the sciences of a natural sort. It puts us, in other words, in a position to interpret in an accurate and definitive way the teachings of these sciences about what exists. . . .

And a bit later he adds:

> ... *pure* philosophy, within the whole of the critique of cognition . . . , must disregard, and must refrain from using, the intellectual achievements of the sciences of a natural sort. . . .[54]

Philosophy, then, must begin with a critique of knowledge, and it must make no use of the sciences in its critique. On Husserl's view, what such a critique reveals is that knowledge is, among other things, structured *hierarchically*. At the base lies a foundation, presumably the *cogito*, followed by intuitions of essences—followed by perceptual intuitions, then beliefs and theories and interpretations of all sorts. The order is justificational, not temporal. The knowledge at the base is that on which every other piece of knowledge is systematically built. The sciences appear at the more highly developed end of the system and depend for their validity on the lower, foundational strata on which they rest.

Although Husserl's position is foundationalist, he differs from other foundationalists like the phenomenalists in that he does not argue for a privileged sort of *object* of knowledge, like sense-data. Rather, his claim is that the validity of all knowledge rests ultimately on a particular sort of *act of consciousness*—namely, intuition. The sort of intuition he has in mind is not some unusual or elusive state of consciousness. It has little in common, for instance, with Bergson's notion of intuition. Husserl means simply the *seeing*, in a *non-inferential* way, of what is the case. He gives as examples sensory perception and the recognition of universals. His notion of intuition bears significant resemblance to Russell's Knowledge by Acquaintance.

To evaluate Husserl's claims about the foundational character of genuine philosophy, one needs to consider the claims he makes on behalf of intuition. Since this, rather than sense-data, is to be the basis for the primacy of philosophy, his foundational reading of philosophy is intimately connected with the validity of his claims about the role of intuition.

Husserl emphasizes the primacy of intuition in his method when he enunciates his "Principle of All Principles:"

> . . . *that every primordial dator Intuition is a source of authority for knowledge,* that *whatever presents itself in "intuition" in primordial form* (as it were in its bodily reality), *is simply to be accepted as it gives itself out to be*, though *only within the limits in which it then presents itself.* [55]

For the moment, let us give the view its strongest possible case. Recall the claim of Locke, for example, in connection with demonstrative arguments—that in order to understand a demonstration, one must *see* the connection between the premises and the conclusion of the argument. That connection cannot itself require a demonstration. Although Husserl's notion of intuition is a bit more complex than this, at its base it is this straightforward sense of intuition that he has in mind. And there is some sense in which we do rely at times on insight or intuition.

Still, the apparent lucidity of Husserl's notion of intuition is deceptive. On the one hand, theoretically it seems entirely reasonable to suppose that there are some situations in which we need to *see* that something is so, if we are to be able to make knowledge-claims. On the other hand, in practice it is notoriously difficult to specify the conditions under which one can be certain (a) that one *has*, in fact, intuited something, and (b) that one can truly express the content of what one has intuited. Note that Husserl's notion of intuition will be useless as an absolutely certain foundation for knowledge, including science, unless one can know for certain when it occurs and can articulate clearly and accurately the content of the intuition.

A further difficulty arises from Husserl's claim about the care that must be taken to fit the insight into the proper language.[56] His assumption here—well-known and hotly debated—is that language itself does not shape the original intuition in any way. Language is simply a vehicle for the expression of the content of the intuition, a vehicle that can be made unambiguous. I won't pursue that particular difficulty here. Rather, I want to suggest a slightly different one.

To begin with, grant the theoretical possibility of genuine intuition on the very sort of grounds that Locke urges. Still, our capacity to have conflicting "intuitions" in relation to the same situation surely makes plausible the claim that intuitions are not simply self-certifying. In a case of perceptual intuition, I might see an object as perfectly rectilinear while you see it as slightly oblique. Both of our experiences cannot count as intuitions in the relevant sense if science is to have absolutely certain foundations. We need to look to some court of appeal to decide the case, something *other* than our apparent intuitions—for example, data drawn from other contexts, including the *sciences*, that might suggest a defect in your visual system. Husserl acknowledges the "imperfection" of empirical intuitions of this sort and focuses rather on essential intuition.[57] Examples include our intuiting of mathematical and logical truths and our intuiting of the essential structures of our own mental processes.

But a similar "imperfection" occurs at this level of intuition. There was a time, for example, when we could "see" that there could be only one line parallel to a given line through a given external point—and then we discovered non-euclidean geometries. There was a time when we could "see" that remembering was simply a *re*-presenting of some past experience. Then we uncovered strong evidence that memory is probably quite different from that, involving perhaps "scripts" or "schemas," and sometimes including "confabulation" (i.e., reorganizing and embellishing the material to make it more coherent).[58]

As in the case of empirical or perceptual intuition, so in the case of "essential" intuition, we need to be able to cross-reference our apparent intuitions with *other* sources of information. That is to say, we are rarely in a position to be certain that a genuine intuition has occurred. What we generally do is to operate on a *provisional* basis—i.e., we operate with our apparent intuitions until some discrepant data emerges. This is to say, we put our apparent intuitions on equally revisable footing with other forms of cognition like inference and theory construction.

In defense of Husserl's view, one might object that he acknowledged that genuine intuition is difficult to achieve. Further, in cases like the one involving parallel lines, one might say that it is not that we failed to intuit the data but rather that they were merely partial (a possibility that Husserl freely acknowledges). According to such an objection, our genuine but partial intuitions have been clarified now and placed in the larger context which includes non-euclidean as well as euclidean geometries.

Such an objection surely carries some warrant. The difficulty is that it overlooks the way in which we clarify and amplify our purported intuitions. We do not simply intuit a new and larger context. Rather, we proceed by largely inferential and constructive processes. The development of new theories generally involves attempts to put apparently recalcitrant data into coherent form. We use the newly constructed framework to re-evaluate our earlier "intuitions" about parallel lines and such. That is to say, our intuitions do not stand by themselves as an absolute self-certifying base for all knowledge. They are tested and revised in the light of complex systems of knowledge. More simply, they are not foundational in any strong and workable sense at all. If this is right it calls into question Husserl's insistence that philosophy, with its method of intuition, provides the absolutely certain foundation for all other knowledge claims, including those of the sciences.[59]

There is another difficulty with Husserl's appeal to intuition. I suggested earlier that even if we grant the possibility of intuition, we have no clear criteria by which to be certain in most cases that it has actually occurred. Husserl seems to have thought that there was one sure way to know that intuition has occurred. Although he makes no explicit claim to this effect, it can reasonably be inferred from what he does say.

> Every intellectual process and indeed every mental process whatever, while being enacted, *can be made the object of a pure "seeing" and understanding, and is something absolutely given in this "seeing."* [60]

It seems that Husserl effectively claims that we are capable of second-order intuitions that simply show the nature of our first-order acts. Presumably this second-order intuition should reveal, in a given case, the presence of a first-order intuition. Such a claim, however, leads to an infinite regress. We can hardly say that we know intuition has occurred because we can intuit it in reflection. One then wants to know how we know that the act of reflection itself is a case of genuine intuition.

More generally, Husserl nowhere offers evidence or argument to support this crucial claim as it applies to *every* mental process. That may be because it poses a peculiar dilemma for him. If he says that one can simply *intuit* (by a third-order act of intuition?) the truth of the claim that every mental process can be made the object of a genuine intuition, he could surely be accused of begging the question. On the other hand, if he calls on any other type of evidence, i.e., non-intuitive evidence, he will be making his ultimate appeal to something other than intuition. Nonetheless, the claim that we can intuit every one of our mental processes as absolutely given requires *some* kind of argument because it is far from self-evident.

If the views of thinkers like Freud have any plausibility at all, it is legitimate to call into question our alleged capacity to intuit and understand our own mental processes. Add to this the current attacks on Folk Psychology, which claim that the "geography" of mental states that we, the folk, have mapped out for ourselves bears little relation to what actually goes on. One of Husserl's crucial assumptions here is that consciousness and its structures are transparently clear to our reflective gaze. But there is increasing evidence that such a view is highly doubtful. Again, if this is right, it poses a fundamental problem for Husserl's claims about the foundational role of phenomenological philosophy, with its method of intuiting essences.

But even if one is willing to grant intuition any sort of role in human knowledge, one still needs to ask about the nature and source of our capacity for intuition; one needs to ask what its scope and limitations are. An adequate answer to such questions ought to lead one to give some consideration to evolutionary biology. If a capacity for intuition is indeed the product of natural selection acting on random variations, one ought at least to feel some concern about whether such a process can be relied on to produce the kind of unquestionable foundation that one's philosophy requires it to be.[61*]

Husserl excludes evolution theory from his newly-formed phenomenology, then, because of his anti-objectivism, his conviction that consciousness cannot be naturalized, his emphasis on timeless truth, and his foundational view of philosophy. I have argued that each of these factors is open to serious objection.

There was, however, one additional factor that may have motivated Husserl's attitude toward evolution theory. In Germany, as elsewhere, biologists were divided in their reactions to Darwin's theory. Instead of simply deciding to bypass a theory that had not yet achieved a consensus in the scientific community, Husserl might have seen the situation as reinforcing his own conviction that the sciences were in need of new philosophical foundations. With the proper epistemological foundation, scientists might then be in a position to decide in a more reasoned way among competing theories. Since Husserl himself does not explicitly state this as one of his motivations, my comments are little more than conjecture. But Husserl did join the faculty at the University at Freiburg in 1916. August Weismann, an outspoken and controversial Darwinian, had been Professor of Zoology there until 1912. Husserl could hardly have been unaware of the disputes that had centered on Weismann's work. So there is some possibility that the debates among biologists in Germany around the turn of the century would have affected his thinking about science and about its relationship to philosophy. His first book had, in fact, been an effort to provide philosophical foundations for mathematics.

I turn now to a consideration of Husserl's views on perception and mind. Given his views on the nature and method of philosophy, one might expect that the theories of perception and mind that he proposed would be as profoundly inhospitable to Darwinian insights as were the theories of Moore and Russell. In fact, they were not.

Chapter 6

Husserl on
Perception and Mind

The carefulness with which we are pursuing the subjective element which the natural scientist excludes by his method in order to attain to pure nature freed from each and every 'merely subjective element' has of course a double purpose for us. On the one hand, to bring the idea of these natural scientists to clarity and to recognize it as a mere product of abstraction; on the other hand, to survey gradually the entire subjective field in all its experiential forms.

Edmund Husserl (1925)[1]

The last chapter set out some of the main goals and methods in Husserl's phenomenology. Given those goals and methods, I suggested that it was not surprising that Husserl declined to incorporate any insights from Darwin into his new philosophy.

In excluding Darwin, Husserl shared with the early analysts a desire to preserve timeless ideal objects, in particular, logical truths and moral values, from the supposed corroding influence of temporal development. He differed from Moore and Russell, however, in the precise relationship he saw between natural science and philosophy. Still, the final verdict for evolution theory was the same: in both traditions it was excluded.

But while there were significant points of agreement between early analytic philosophy and phenomenology, their respective approaches to both perception and mind were dramatically different. The most obvious and pervasive contrast arises from the fact that Moore and Russell explored perception and mind from an "objectivist" viewpoint, while Husserl, insisting on the importance of the subject, addressed both areas from the posture of reflection. As he says in the opening quote to this chapter, one of his purposes is to "survey . . . the entire subjective field in all its experiential forms." Both perception and mind will be surveyed as part of that subjective field.

In what follows, I shall explore some of the ways in which Husserl's theories of mind and perception contrast sharply with those of the early analysts as a consequence of their differing methods. And in spite of the difficulties I have mentioned in connection with Husserl's phenomenological method,

I hope to show that he offers some useful insights particularly on perception. One need not see these insights as timelessly true or as generated by infallible intuitions in order to recognize that they suggest a rich, contextual approach to perception that is wholly in keeping with a Darwinian framework—and perhaps more in keeping than Husserl himself might have wished.

Perception

Most English-speaking philosophers are familiar with the general character of the accounts of perception put together by Moore, Russell, and their philosophical heirs. Talk of sense-data, phenomenalism, causal theories of perception, etc., is standard in the literature. Husserl's account of perception develops a quite different vocabulary. Like Russell, he owes a significant debt to William James—particularly to his *Principles of Psychology*—but the portions of James that Husserl borrowed were quite different from the ones that Russell took. It is perhaps a mark of the richness of James' thought that two such different philosophical traditions could both draw on it.

Some Contrasts

Perhaps the first thing to notice about Husserl's approach to perception, in contrast with work in the analytic tradition, is that he is not primarily exercised by the question of whether the perceived object is physical or mental—a pivotal issue for the anti-Idealism of Moore and Russell. For him, the opening question for an investigation of perception is not, "Is the perceived object a sense-datum or a mental representation or a physical object?" Rather, the opening phenomenological question asks what data present themselves clearly and evidently when one takes oneself to be perceiving. More precisely, the questions that Husserl asks about perception are: what role in perception does the *perceiver* play? what distinguishes an act of perception from other acts of consciousness? and what are the defining characteristics of an object experienced as perceived? So, from the start, the reflective framework within which Husserl investigates perception differs substantially from that of Moore and Russell. Unlike them, Husserl is as concerned with the subject and the act of perceiving as he is with the character of perceived objects.

Moore and Russell had assumed a passive spectator perceiving its world. Sensory material was *given*, and the passivity of the perceiver was so marked that there was virtually no role for a perceiver to play. And eventually the notion of a perceiving subject was largely dropped from consideration.

For Husserl, on the other hand, while he would agree that perception involves the reception of sensory material, he claims that the perceiver is not simply passive to it. Sense-data are received and these data generally appear with characteristics that one is not free to alter. To this extent, there is some degree of receptivity in the early phase of perception. But Husserl makes much of the fact that a perceiver can actively turn his attention toward the data or ignore it, can "lift" it away from its background, focus on it, and give it meaning. Focusing attention on the data and giving meaning to it are primary examples of the active role that Husserl assigns to the perceiving subject. But even in the reception of the sense-data, Husserl sees an aspect of activity.

> This phenomenologically necessary concept of receptivity is in no way exclusively opposed to that of the *activity of the ego*. . . . On the contrary, receptivity must be regarded as the lowest level of activity. The ego consents to what is coming and takes it in.[2]

Perception, then, includes an active as well as a receptive stage. And even in the receiving of the data, the perceiver actively "consents to what is coming and takes it in." So, on Husserl's account, the perceiving subject retains a pivotal role. With respect to the *act* of perceiving, Moore like Husserl did pay some attention to it. But Moore's concern was primarily to distinguish the act from the object of perception with a view to giving the object a mind-independent status. Since Husserl's primary opponent was not Idealism, but all varieties of objectivism and Naturalism, he felt no particular need to attack the view that all *experienced* reality is mind-dependent. His attention to the act of perceiving was rather intended to uncover the character of such acts and to show how they differ from other acts of consciousness like imagining and remembering.

And even when Husserl focuses on the *object* of perception his approach differs from that of Moore or Russell. He takes it as given (i.e., as shown clearly by reflection on the properties of perceived objects) that we perceive objects that are not the product of mind. And he speaks of sense-data, but they are the *means by which* one perceives. They are not themselves the immediate objects of perception. One can become aware of them, but only by abstracting them from the original perceptual experience.[3]

The questions that guide Husserl's investigation of perception are, then, notably different from those that guided the analysts. Furthermore, the method that he uses in answering those questions is also far removed from that used by Moore and Russell. Recall that the approach Husserl takes is by way of *describing* the data that appear clearly in reflection. He does not use deductive inference, conceptual analysis, or data from the natural sciences. He claims to be merely looking carefully and describing what appears as evident.

Another contrast arises between the atomistic analyses, particularly of Russell, and Husserl's *contextual* approach to perception. Russell treated sense-data as independent, self-contained bits of sensory information. Husserl, on the other hand, sees the objects of perception in such a way as to emphasize their dependence on more than what is explicitly given. Husserl's contextualism is perhaps most apparent in his description of "horizons," a notion modeled on William James' description of the "fringe" in experience. As Husserl says, "What is actually perceived, and what is more or less clearly co-present and determinate (to some extent at least) is partly pervaded, partly girt about with a *dimly apprehended depth or fringe of indeterminate reality*."[4] He goes on to note that the indeterminate portion can be made at least partially determinate when we turn our attention to it.[5]

In spite of the acknowledged relationship of his horizons to James' "fringe," Husserl put a good deal more structure and predictability into the notion than James had. In James, the fringe suggests the relatedness of experiences; the latter are not discrete and independent, but are portions of a "stream" of experiences in which each portion is "fringed" with other portions that are related to it. When Husserl picks up on the notion, he emphasizes the aspect of relatedness, of the interdependence of experiences. He even uses the "stream" metaphor. But he systematizes the idea of the fringe in ways that James did not. For Husserl, horizons are *law-governed* sets of possibilities for further experiences, that are implicit in, or suggested by, actual experiences.

So, for example, part of the meaning that a perceptual experience carries with it is that certain further, related experiences of the perceived object are possible. The horizons point to the directions in which these further experiences would have to develop, and Husserl describes several different sorts of horizons that an experience of perception has.

> Every experience has its own horizon; . . . This implies that every experience refers to the possibility—and it is a question here of the capacity of the ego—not only of explicating, step by step, the thing which has been given in a first view . . . but also of obtaining, little by little as experience continues, new determinations of the same thing.[6]

Husserl describes a number of different horizons that appear in perception. Some attend the *act* of perceiving, others attend the perceived *object*.

Each *act* of perception, then, has its own horizon of possibilities. That is to say, when I perceive something, I am aware that I can carry out further acts in relation to that thing; this act of perceiving can be supplemented with other acts of perceiving or with related acts like remembering the same object. In other words, an act of perception is not isolated or independent. It is part of a larger network of related acts, and it is experienced as belonging to that larger network. Even if I do not pursue further perceptions of the object or other acts of consciousness in relation to it, I know that these are possible and that they are related to the original experience, perhaps as extensions or reproductions of it at a later time. On Husserl's view, this is part of the *meaning* that an act of perception carries with it.

One of the fairly obvious horizons that Husserl attributes to a perceived *object* is external to it and is *spatial*. What this amounts to is the claim that one visually perceives most objects as having a horizon, a background, of other perceived and perceivable objects. More simply, things are normally perceived in a spatial *context*.[7] The importance of this apparently uncontroversial point is that, on Husserl's view, the spatial horizon or context often contributes to the meaning one gives to objects.[8] Seen out of context, things can seem puzzling or even unfamiliar. And at the very least, Husserl says, this external horizon of other spatio-temporal objects contributes to one's belief that the experienced object is real.[9] Thus, when one perceives a house in the context of other apparently normal spatial objects, that fact usually contributes at least implicitly, to one's taking the experienced object to be real. If, on the other hand, one were to see a house floating by itself, with no other spatial objects around it, one is inclined to suspect that one is dreaming or hallucinating. So the external, spatial horizon is a significant factor for Husserl, not only because it normally appears as the background in relation to which things are interpreted, but also because it can play a part in determining the existential status assigned to objects.

A second horizon he mentions in connection with a perceived object is also *spatial*, but this one is "internal." It consists of the other aspects of the object itself that are not currently visible but that could be made visible if, for example, one rotated the object or entered it.

> The house stands there in bodily actuality and yet at the same time in such a way that it, this house, enters into particular perceptions only according to a part of its determinations. But I can expand the circle of experience; I can step closer, go around, enter the house, and thereby exercise continually new particular views.[10]

Like the external spatial horizon, this horizon also contributes to the meaning I give to an object. To perceive something *as a house* is to experience it as having a back, sides, an inside, etc., that normally belong to houses—even though none of these items appears explicitly in the immediate perception.

Each of these is a portion of the internal horizon of the perceived house. Each contributes to my interpretation of the object as a house and also as an actually existing object. If one follows out the horizons and is surprised in some way, or one's expectations are disappointed in certain ways (e.g., one discovers that the apparent house has no back or no insides) then one needs to revise one's beliefs about the character of that object. Perhaps it now needs to be interpreted as a stage prop or a dream image.

Russell's notion of *sensibilia* bears a faint resemblance to these horizons of Husserl's. Perhaps the most significant difference lies in the fact that Husserl specifies precisely how these potential perspectives on an object are related to what actually appears. These are not *mere* possibilities; they are law-governed and predictable possibilities that help to define the perceived object. The data that appear get their significance in relation to the data that have not yet appeared but are expected. For Husserl, a theory about perceived objects can never be constructed simply from isolated sense-data.

Yet another horizon is *temporal*. Objects are perceived as having a certain sort of past and future.[11] One might expect, for example, that the temporal horizon of a rock would differ from that of a rainbow, or perhaps most obviously the temporal horizon of a perceived object will differ from that of an imagined or remembered object. As a rule, perceived objects are experienced as having a relatively enduring past and future (unlike imagined objects), and their temporal horizons are experienced as extending through the present toward the future (unlike remembered objects). So, for example, when I perceive a cup, I perceive it as something that has endured for some period of time and that will continue to endure after I perceive it. An object in a daydream, by contrast, does not have that sort of duration as part of its meaning. The temporal horizon need not be, and usually isn't, a part of our *explicit* awareness of things. But were an apparently perceived object suddenly to be without any duration, we would surely suspect that we were not perceiving it at all. Certain assumptions about the temporal character of an object are an implicit part of its meaning for us.

One other dimension of temporal context bears noting. While Husserl does not treat it as part of his account of horizons, the similarity between the two is clear. Husserl says that the perception of most things requires that they be synthesized over some portion of time into a meaningful whole. He uses the example of perceiving a melody.[12] In order to perceive sounds *as a melody*, and not simply as a series of independent notes, the perceiver has to synthesize the notes into a whole. But for Husserl the example can be generalized. One does not give meaning to any of one's normal perceptions in isolated split-second bits. One always needs what William James called the "specious present." That is, one needs to be able to hold on to the bit of data that is just fading into the past (Husserl calls this "retention") and to anticipate something of what is about to become present (he calls this "protention"). Giving a perceived object meaning requires that one put together an expanded moment's worth of data into an experienced whole. Unlike Moore and Russell, Husserl stresses the importance of the duration of a perception through some period of time. In spite of his overriding concern with essences, he did not, like Russell, think that time was philosophically unimportant. In fact, he took temporal structures to be part of the *essential* structures of perception (though the essential structures themselves were not time-bound).

Husserl's extended discussions of various types of horizons that attend both the acts and the objects of perception provide a *contextual* approach to perception. This points to a profound difference from Russell's atomistic approach to the objects of perception. For the analysts, and in particular for Russell's atomism, things are best understood by isolating them. For Husserl, things are best understood in relation to the spatial and temporal contexts in which they appear and function.

> We can also draw from our reflexions the eidetically valid and self-evident proposition, that *no concrete experience* can pass *as independent in the full sense of the term*. Each 'stands in need of completion' in respect of some connected whole, which in form and in kind is not something we are free to choose, but are rather bound to accept."[13]

Husserl's *anti-atomism* is one of the factors that distinguishes his phenomenology from phenomenalism. Sensory objects, for Husserl, point to law-governed and predictable ways in which further experiences of those objects should proceed.

So, to experience an object as a perceived house is to: see it in the context of grass, trees, other houses, or people (its external horizon); to see it as having sides, a back, and an inside that may not now be showing but could be seen (its internal spatial horizon); to see it as having existed before this act of perception and as likely to endure beyond it (its temporal horizon); and as an object in relation to which I can carry out other conscious acts like other perceptions or recollections.

Husserl is not arguing here for the kind of holism that the British Idealists proposed. He is saying, rather, that our perception of things is always partial, and to understand the *thing* (rather than just the partial aspect that is perceived) one needs to supplement the given data with further data available in the horizons of the act and its object.

In the preceding chapter I said that Husserl claimed there was much more order and predictability in experience than Hume had noticed. The various types of horizons he describes are additional examples of that order and predictability. They provide clues to the perceiver about the character of the object being experienced, and when the clues are followed, one's beliefs about the object are either confirmed or defeated. Horizons, for example, point to ways of gathering evidence in support of our beliefs about the existential status of the objects in our experiences. When assumptions about existential status were bracketed or neutralized by the pheno-menological reduction at the outset of the investigation, it was with a view to looking for evidence to support the assignment of existential status. The horizons attending both act and object, when examined carefully, provide a significant measure of that evidence.

Implicit in this talk about the horizons of perceived objects is Husserl's claim that such objects are always experienced *partially*. The horizons, after all, indicate further spatial or temporal aspects of the object that can become available to experience although they are not explicitly present in it now. Husserl takes this to be one of the essential characteristics of perceivable objects: they are not totally present in any one moment of perception.

This, in turn, leads to a further contrast with the analysts. Russell (at least until his Neutral Monism emerged) and Moore rely on the traditional notion of a transcendent object, namely, an object that is mind-independent. So for them the problem for a theory of perception is to account for our access to mind-independent objects. Husserl, in contrast, redefines the notion of a *transcendent* object. For him, it is not something that is independent of consciousness.[14] Rather, it is related to consciousness (actually or poten-tially), but is always *experienced partially*, as having temporal and spatial horizons that are not yet explicitly present. There is always more that could be perceived. Thus, a defining characteristic of transcendent objects is that they are experienced partially, and any further experiences of them will normally be rule-governed and predictable.

Part of the significance of all this is that Husserl's account of perception does not begin with the assumption that our experience of the world is in doubt. As a consequence, he does not view a philosophical theory of perception as having as its only task the justification of empirical beliefs. While justification and evidence are among the issues that Husserl treats, he considerably broadens the scope of theories of perception. He places a good deal of emphasis on the *description* of what goes on in perception, and not all of that description relates directly to issues of justification.

There are, then, several significant ways in which Husserl's theory of perception contrasts with those of Moore and Russell: it does not make realism the central issue of perception; it makes much of the active role of the perceiving subject; it treats both the act and the object of perceiving contextually rather than atomistically, where context includes temporal as well as spatial factors; it redefines the notion of a transcendent object; and its descriptive method expands the content of the theory of perception so that it includes more than issues of empirical justification.

Three of these features of Husserl's view are particularly relevant to a Darwinian approach to perception: namely, the active role of the subject, the importance of contextual considerations, and the use of a descriptive method in constructing a theory of perception. In spite of Husserl's views on the irrelevance of Darwinian insights, his account of perception is hospitable to those very insights in ways that I believe an adequate account of perception should be.

Darwinian Possibilities

Let me begin with the most general of the three positive facets of Husserl's view, his descriptive method. There are, as I suggested in the previous chapter, fundamental difficulties with Husserl's phenomenological project, but his decision to use a descriptive approach to experience has one over-riding virtue. It allows for consideration of any aspect of perception that appears in reflection. An exclusively justificational approach sets excessively narrow limits on what counts as relevant. Within the context of Darwinian considerations, the truth of our perceptual beliefs is only one among several important issues relating to perception.

There can be little doubt that the move toward description will generate disagreements about the descriptive content of perceptual experience. But if one abandons the quest for absolute certainty, those disagreements can be a healthy incentive for further investigations. At any rate, several of the elements that surface within a descriptive framework seem to be reasonably uncontroversial, although they have been omitted or minimized in most other theories of perception. They include the other two positive features of Husserl's view that I mentioned: the active role played by perceivers (and here I shall focus particularly on *selective attention*); and the importance of *context* in the interpretation of perceived things. I shall add one other feature that seems clearly to occur in perception which Husserl's account allows for but does not emphasize, and that is the *variability of individual interpretations* in perception. This factor, like selective attention, is a function of *active* Subjectivity.

Selective attention and variable interpretation are, I think, undisputed factors in perception. Neither Moore, Russell nor any theorists in the analytic tradition have, to my knowledge, made any effort to deny them. These features were simply ignored because, I suspect, they were considered irrelevant to issues of justification. The same may hold true for the role of contextual factors. Russell explicitly denies the importance of context *for purposes of philosophical analysis*, but he does not deny that contextual factors function in ordinary cases of perception.

How are each of these three—selective attention, context, and variable interpretations—specifically related to Darwin's account of us?

Selective attention indicates that the organism is scanning the perceptual field and is selecting from among the available data whatever has particular interest or relevance to that organism. The most basic factors determining this interest or relevance are the needs of the organism. These needs, in turn, are heavily dominated by concerns for the survival and well-being (broadly construed) both of the organism itself and, in the case of social animals like ourselves, for the survival and well-being of others related by biological or social ties.

There are undoubtedly other factors that influence selective attention, but these are surely the most basic and the most pervasive. The Darwinian theme is evident. An organism that is incapable of selective attention, that is simply passive to its environment, would be seriously disadvantaged in its efforts to avoid dangers and to provide for its own particular needs. So Husserl's emphasis on the active role of a perceiving Subject, on its ability to consent to or to ignore incoming sensory data and to focus on some of that data to the exclusion of the rest, lends itself nicely to a Darwinian approach to perception.

Context is another important consideration for a Darwinian framework. Husserl's discussions of the various horizons that function in perception highlight the important role that context plays in our interpretation of experience. Each of the horizons of perceived objects very likely aids a perceiver in interpreting her environment in ways that are relevant to her well-being. But perhaps the most obvious example, from a Darwinian point of view, is the external spatial horizon of a perceived object. It can provide information, for example, about how dangerous a perceived animal is, by indicating any restraints that may hinder its approach to oneself or by showing various means of assistance available to one in dealing with it. The rattlesnake in a glass cage has quite a different meaning for one's well-being than does one that is free and unhindered in its approach. The presence of a nearby car, when one sees a bear approaching, is vitally important data in the perceptual field. More commonly, the spatial context within which another person is perceived likewise makes some contribution to our interpretation of that person as a likely sexual partner or a threat to life and limb. So the spatial horizon of perceived objects provides information that is highly relevant to Darwinian concerns about survival and well-being.

But Husserlian horizons attend the acts of perception as well as its objects. And while I do not deny the importance of what one might term the "generic" horizon that Husserl mentions in connection with acts of perception (i.e., one is aware of the other acts of consciousness that could be carried out in connection with the current act of perception), I want to expand the notion well beyond what Husserl had in mind. Since his concerns were primarily with the *essence* of various experiences, he said very little about the individual peculiarities that might attend such experiences. It is just these individual peculiarities that I want to call attention to.

The context that concerns me is the other psychological states that are current in a given perceiver at the time of the perception. There is, I believe, a context of other psychological states—both occurrent and dispositional—within which perception occurs. And just as the spatial context of other objects affects our interpretation of the object on which we focus, so too the context of our other psychological states affects that interpretation as well. For example, one sees a figure approaching. The "generic" horizon of the act of perceiving involves the possibility that I (or any conscious subject) could carry out further acts of perception in relation to it, etc. And the "generic" interpretation of the object, for example as "a person," is a function of the spatial and temporal horizons attending that figure. But our perceptual interpretations are rarely this minimal. The added meaning that is given to the approaching figure is often much richer than simply "person." The figure is seen and interpreted in the context of other concurrent psychological states of the perceiver. So, a perceiver recalling an earlier unpleasant incident with this person, and feeling intimidated by her, per-haps sees the approaching person as a threatening competitor. A perceiver who is expecting good news may see the same person as a welcome friend who is bringing that news.

The examples are simple and, I believe, commonplace. Many actual cases of perception probably involve more complex sets of psychological states and therefore more complex interpretations than these suggest. But the point is that one's interpretation is colored not only by general concepts, spatial context, and temporal horizon. It is also affected by the psychological context in which the experience occurs—the personal memories, expecta-tions, mood, desires, awareness of bodily needs, dispositions of all sorts, etc., that one brings to the perception. Notice that the relevant psychological states that may contribute to one's interpretation include non-cognitive as well as cognitive states.

Things are perceived, then, not only as green or square, or as having this or that spatial and temporal context. They are also perceived as having this or that relation to oneself. What this suggests is that the interpretation one gives to perceived objects or events, while it usually has a common dimension (e.g., "approaching person"), it also has a highly individual dimension that is a function of the bodily and psychological states that each particular perceiver brings to a perception. There is, in a word, considerable variability in individual interpretation in perception.

This variability has one further dimension, and it is related to an aspect of context that Husserl emphasizes in his later philosophy, namely, temporal development. However, there is a dimension to the role of temporal development in experience which Husserl does not fully exploit and which strikes me as enormously important.[15*] It concerns the variability over time, of the interpretations that an individual gives to perceived objects and events. That variability is a function of changes that occur in the bodily and psychological context within which things are perceived. As one's needs, capabilities, and psychological states alter—which they do continually—one's interpretation of one's environment and its relation to oneself will change in corresponding ways. An adequate account of these interpretations will need to recognize the significance of this temporal development in individual perceivers. A timeless or static account of perception fails to do this.

The variability of individual interpretations of perceived objects and events also has a Darwinian impetus. If organisms and groups are going to survive and thrive, they need to be able to take account not only of the environment, but also of their own current needs and current capacity to deal with each of the first two. It is the latter two requirements that generate the necessity for variable individual interpretations. In the face of identical environmental factors, two different organisms may have differing bodily or psychological needs at that particular time, as well as differing capacities to deal with that environment or those needs. Stereotypical interpretations of the perceived situation would be hopelessly inadequate. Their respective interpretations of the situation need to be tailored to their individual situations.

What is seen as desirable food by a hungry organism may look like unappealing clutter to one who has just overeaten. What is perceived as a challenging competitor for one organism may be perceived as a dangerous threat by a weaker or less experienced organism. What is perceived by one person as a stimulating conversation may be perceived by an envious competitor as a threat.

The context, then, within which things are perceived includes the spatial and temporal context of the object or event, as Husserl pointed out, but also the changing context of an organism's bodily needs and capacities, and the fluctuating psychological context of the organism's cognitive and non-cognitive states (both occurrent and dispositional). Because the context is multi-dimensional, I shall argue in the next chapter that perception involves the formation of an interpretation that draws on all of these dimensions. Picking up on a notion from Husserl, I call this interpretation a *perceptual meaning*.

In some passages Husserl appears to come close to such a multi-dimensional view of perceived objects:

> Therefore this world is not there for me as a mere *world of facts and affairs*, but, with the same immediacy, as a *world of values, a world of goods, a practical world*. Without further effort on my part I find the things before me furnished not only with the qualities that befit their positive nature, but with value-characters such as beautiful or ugly, agreeable or disagreeable, pleasant or unpleasant, and so forth. Things in their immediacy stand there as objects to be used, the 'table' with its 'books,' the 'glass to drink from,' the 'vase,' the 'piano,' and so forth. These values and practicalities, they too belong to *the constitution of the 'actually present' objects as such*. . . . The same considerations apply of course just as well to the men and beasts in my surroundings as to 'mere things.' They are my 'friends' or my 'foes,' my 'servants' or superiors,' 'strangers' or 'relatives,' and so forth.[16]

These values and practicalities are just what one should expect when meaning is understood within a Darwinian framework. In a number of ways, then, Husserl's account of perception is hospitable to the addition of certain significant Darwinian considerations.

Some Limitations

For my purposes, however, there are aspects of Husserl's view that do not go quite far enough toward accommodating evolutionary notions. And one of the limitations of Husserl's account is that it fails to integrate perception fully with other acts of consciousness that can be related to it—for example, with non-cognitive states like emotions. While Husserl allows for some coordination of cognitive and non-cognitive elements in meanings, his model is not one that does full justice to the interaction that I believe exists among these elements. He uses a "stratified" model.

Following an extended discussion of perception and its meaning (noema, pl. noemata), Husserl says:

> Analogous considerations apply then, as one may easily convince oneself, to the spheres of sentiment and will, to experiences of pleasure and displeasure, to valuation in every sense, to wish, decision, and practical action; these are all experiences which contain many and often varied intentional stratifications, . . .
>
> Moreover, the stratifications, speaking generally, are so ordered that the uppermost strata of the phenomenon as a whole can fall away without the residue ceasing to be a concrete complete intentional experience, . . .

> When a perceiving, fancying, judging, and the like lies in this way at the base of a stratum of valuation that completely covers it, we have, in *the stratified block as a whole*, called, after its highest stratum a concrete experience of valuation, *different noemata, different meanings*. The perceived as such belongs as meaning specifically to the perceiving, but enters into the meaning of the concrete valuing, providing this meaning with a basis.[17]

At the base, providing the ground for any other "stratified layers" of meaning, is perceiving. That act of perceiving has its own integrity, it maintains its own identity through the various "layers" that might be added or subtracted. So, for example, one perceives a blossoming tree. The meaning of that perceived tree will remain the same while one may add to it a "layer" of valuing or a layer of pleasure, etc. The meaning of the perceived tree will "enter into" the meaning of the pleasant perceived tree, but there is no suggestion that the two will fully integrate, allowing for reciprocal relations between them. While the perception and its meaning can contribute to the valuing and its meaning, Husserl says nothing about the possibility that the valuing will do anything to alter the perception and *its* meaning.

Two things seem clear. First, Husserl's account allows for the possibility that feelings and valuings, etc., can have a close connection with perception. And second, that connection is the fairly traditional one in which perceptions can give rise to feelings. He says nothing about the possible influence of feelings and valuings on perception, and in fact treats perception as the independent portion of the experience.

In Husserl, then, we have the beginnings of a theory of *meaning* in perception, a theory that includes more than simply the conceptual sorting of isolated bits of sensory data. But while his account of perceptual meaning flirts with its possible relationship to non-cognitive states, in the end it seems that he wants to preserve the integrity of perceptual meaning from any incursions by other mental states. Perceptual meaning remains what it was initially, unchanged by any additional layers of meaning that might arise on its basis. In my discussion of Husserl's view of the mind I shall return to this issue and shall expand on some comments I made in connection with Moore's and Russell's views on the matter.

A second limitation attending Husserl's treatment of perception is his abstraction of the notion of Subjectivity from real world concerns. In most of his writings, even into the 1930's, he was determined to investigate the structures of "any consciousness, without exception. . . ."[18] This led him to undervalue the distinctive character of the Subjectivity belonging to human beings and non-human animals. He is formulating a science of

Subjectivity that differs completely from that offered by natural or social (i.e., "objective") science.

> . . . among the Objective sciences there is indeed a science of subjectivity: but it is precisely the science of Objective subjectivity; the subjectivity of men and other animals, a subjectivity that is part of the world. Now, however, we are envisaging a science that is, so to speak, absolutely subjective, whose thematic object [i.e., subjectivity] exists whether or not the world exists.[19]

So the structures of Transcendental Subjectivity that Husserl seeks are far removed from the needs that attend the actual existence of a living organism. They belong to any conceivable Subjectivity, and they would remain what they are even if the actual world did not exist.

Recall that part of Husserl's quarrel with the philosophical tradition was its undervaluing of Subjectivity in the interests of objective knowledge. But Husserl's remedy for "objectivism" is problematic. He postulates a version of Subjectivity that has been so abstracted from its relations with the actual world that its functions need have nothing to do with a subject's efforts to cope with that world.

Perhaps there are some things that can be said meaningfully about an abstract Subjectivity of this sort, things that would have to be true even if no world existed. It is difficult to be sure. But what does seem clear is that there are vital aspects of *human* Subjectivity that have everything to do with the bodily existence of individuals in a world that offers them nourishment and companionship as well as dangers and challenges. Unlike gods, devils, and robots, human subjects are continually enmeshed in efforts to cope with that world.

If our knowledge of the objective world requires Subjective interpretation, so too, our knowledge of human subjects requires acknowledgement of their practical connections with their actual world. I take it that the existential turn in later phenomenology had just such a point in mind.

In spite of its limitations, however, the Husserlian approach to perception answers to several Darwinian requirements—it makes use of a descriptive method that should allow for the inclusion of any data that appears in our experience of perception, it includes an active perceiving subject, and it takes into consideration various contextual factors that function in perception. Although Husserl himself does not construct a fully satisfactory account of perception from an evolutionary viewpoint, he nonetheless provides a framework within which such an account can be constructed.

Mind And Consciousness

Husserl does not propose a theory of mind in a traditional sense. He does not provide a metaphysical account of its nature or a systematic account of its relation to brain and behavior. Part of this is a function of his *epistemological* goals. Part of it is probably also to be explained by the fact that he is providing a description of the structures of *experience*, and mind is not easily abstracted from that context and given an independent theory of its own. Nonetheless, Husserl's *Phenomenological Psychology*, offers a particularly illuminating glimpse of his views on the *mental* (or as he often calls it, the "psychic"). The lectures are, for the most part, set outside the framework of phenomenological *philosophy*. Nonetheless, Husserl uses the occasion to explain how his philosophy relates to empirical psychology as well as to what he terms "a priori psychology."

Empirical psychology deals with the factual aspects of the psychic; a priori psychology cuts itself loose from everything empirical or factual and focuses entirely on what is essential to every conceivable mind, thereby providing a foundation for empirical psychology. It is clear that this a priori approach to psychology is *very* close to Husserl's phenomenology; what phenomenology adds to it is the foundation of a "critique of knowledge." That is to say, phenomenological philosophy provides a priori psychology with its subjective underpinnings, just as it does for a priori logic and mathematics.[20]

Husserl's "geography" of this theoretical domain makes it clear that phenomenology is a philosophy in which psychological or mental states have been divorced from all their connections with empirical fact. (This, of course, was precisely the point of his eidetic reduction—and it is not far removed from the aspirations of some versions of functionalism that emerged thirty years later.) That consideration alone sets enormously important constraints upon anything that Husserl will have to say about the mental, reinforcing among other things his decision not to take an evolutionary approach to it.

A further consequence of his positioning phenomenology close to *a priori* psychology is that Husserl does not involve himself in the standard twentieth-century mind-body debates. One finds no discussion of such things as the pros and cons of identity theories. Recall that his concern lies with any *possible* consciousness. Nonetheless, while it is true that Husserl does not enter the mind-body debate, there are strong undercurrents of a mind-body dualism in his writings. His dualism is not quite the same as the traditional metaphysical dualism of someone like Descartes.[21]* Claims for that sort of dualism arise out of the "objectivist" posture that Husserl has disparaged.

" . . . we do not construe anything metaphysically, . . . rather, we do and must do nothing further than to disclose the *sense* of the experiential objectivities which is itself included in the natural experience of the world, and with it the *sense* of the psyches which appear in it as animating bodies."[22] [Italics added.]

What is at stake in his phenomenology is the *sense* of the objects in the natural world and the *sense* of the psychic. Metaphysical claims must come at a later stage of investigation. Husserl's reflections on experience lead him to conclude that the sense of consciousness and extensional reality incorporate importantly different characteristics in spite of the fact that the two are "intertwined" in experience.[23]

As I noted in Chapter Five, he distinguishes the "way of being" of consciousness from that of the natural world. And he is at pains to argue that consciousness cannot be "naturalized" and treated as an object of study for the natural sciences. This attempt to isolate consciousness from nature is partly methodological; consciousness cannot be treated adequately, he believes, by using the same quantitative methods that are so successful in the natural sciences.[24]

But there is more than a methodological worry here. Although Husserl allows that consciousness can be spatialized by its relation to a living body, he claims that its essence is not truly spatial. "The psychic comes into the spatial world only through a species of annexation; it is not extensional in itself, but acquires secondary participation in extensionality and locality only by a physical body."[25] And again, "But if one is serious about describing the mental in its own essentiality, then one must soon become aware that the psychic . . . is a self-contained unity which is subordinated to totally unique essential concepts."[26]

On first reading, these quotes may sound simply like an expression of a Cartesian dualism. But if one keeps Husserl's method clearly in focus, one can see that he begins with the way things appear in our *experience* of them. So his claim here is that our experience of the psychic shows it to have its own form of unity and its own set of concepts that govern the meanings we give it. While it can be experienced as integrated with the body, it can also be seen as having a conceptual realm of its own. The temporal structures that govern the mental, for example, differ from those that govern the physical. And for Husserl, "psychic causality" (the causality of mental motivation) "is something totally different from inductive causality [the causality we attribute to physical things on the basis of our accumulating experience of their relations with one another]."[27]

So there is indeed a mind-body dualism in Husserl's phenomenology, but it is a dualism of *meanings* rather than a metaphysical dualism. I suggested in Chapter Five that those dual meanings may ground a stronger metaphysical claim, especially when one recalls Husserl's remarks about the kind of theory of mind needed to support the doctrine of immortality. But within the context of his phenomenology proper, he makes every effort to restrict his claims to experience and its meanings.[28]* And when he reflects on experience, using his descriptive method, what sort of an account of the mental does he provide?

Consider his account of Subjectivity. In my discussion of Moore and Russell, I noted that they sometimes speak as if there is no distinction to be made between the self and the subject or between the subject and the acts of consciousness. In Husserl there is a sense in which those distinctions might seem to be blurred even further. On occasion he speaks of phenomenology as an "egology," that is, a science of the ego. But what he means to include in that notion of the ego is all of experience—all the acts of consciousness, all the meanings, and all the intended objects. He sometimes refers to this as the "concrete ego." That, of course, has motivated some commentators to interpret his phenomenology as a good old fashioned Idealism. But in fact, his view is much closer to that of the American Pragmatists; he thinks that one cannot speak meaningfully of anything that lies outside actual and possible experience. And experience, on his view, is always given its "shape," i.e., is "constituted," by a subject, an ego. So for him, the science of experience will be the science of the ego that has it and shapes it.

Within his discussion of this "egology," he makes a number of significant distinctions that suggest contrasts between notions like subject and self. There is the "transcendental ego," which I have suggested is best understood as the giver of all meaning in experience. There is the "ego pole" of experience, which seems to be a fairly formal theoretical notion that allows Husserl to distinguish one "pole" in experience from the other, the "object pole." It may come closest to the notion of a bare subject of experience. Then there is the ego as "substrate of habitualities." This probably comes closest to a notion of self; it is what underlies, and maintains, habits and dispositions. It carries some sense of an enduring self, and although it bears some of the marks of a substance, Husserl is careful not to commit himself explicitly to a substantial self.

If one were still looking for the place of *Mind* in all this, it is not entirely clear just what should be isolated. At the very least, one would expect subject, self, act, and meaning to be aspects of the traditional notion of mind. But given Husserl's theory of intentionality, according to which act and object of consciousness require each other, it is likely that the notion of the Intended Object should be included as well.

In order to make this last claim more plausible, recall that in his extension of Descartes' *cogito*, Husserl argued that if one is thinking, then one is thinking *about something*. Husserl takes the import of that claim to be much more radical than the simple requirement that consciousness is directed toward something. He argues that neither an act of consciousness nor an intentional object can be understood *without reference to one another*. So, one does not understand what remembering is, unless one also understands its relationship to objects of a certain sort (e.g., objects from some past experience). One has no insight into perception unless one also has insight into the sorts of objects that appear in perception. Analogously, one cannot understand the meanings that are given to intentional objects unless one also has insight into the sort of acts in which those meanings are given. For Husserl, the correlations between types conscious acts, types of meanings, and types of intentional objects are not contingent. One cannot truly understand any one of them without understanding its relations to the others. So, if one is to construct a theory of consciousness, on Husserl's view, one must include all of the elements that function in conscious experience: the ego (in its various descriptions), the acts of consciousness, the meanings and the intended objects.

Given the inclusive character of Husserl's view of conscious experience, it is perhaps not surprising that he did not offer a theory of mind in the traditional sense. He would have counted such a theory as an abstraction. One knows nothing about mind unless one understands how all the pieces of experience fit together.

In fact, Husserl rarely speaks of *the mind*. His phenomenology is first of all a theory about the nature of conscious experience. In this connection, his most fundamental claim about consciousness is its intentional structure. And while an intentional theory of consciousness relieves the latter of its traditional characterization as a "container of ideas," and emphasizes its directedness toward objects, Husserl's view hardly qualifies as a "functional" rather than "structural" approach to the mental. In fact, he shows very little interest in the question of what consciousness is *for*. Like Russell, his attention is very much on the *structure* of mind. His characterization of that structure is somewhat different from Russell's. He makes no effort to reduce the mental to a few psychic atoms, like sensations and images. Quite the contrary. He specifies one *relational* structure that defines *all* mental states. There is in each mental state an ego, an act, and an intentional object. No one element is reducible to the others; none is independent of the others. Perhaps the most important aspect of the structure is that it is essentially relational. As in the case of perception, so in the case of the mental, Husserl's position is anti-atomistic.

So while Husserl's precise account of the structure of consciousness is not like Russell's account of mind, there is one significant commonality.

Both men concern themselves primarily with the structure of mental states, not with their function. The absence of functional considerations weakens Husserl's account of the mental in much the same way that it did for Russell. But Husserl's failure to include a functional dimension in his account is perhaps more surprising than it was in the case of Russell.

Given Husserl's theoretical framework, permeated as it is with relations of all sorts, one might expect that the functional role of mental states would have appeared to him as obviously important. For example, one would expect that he would make much of the relations between consciousness and the body, on the one hand, and between cognitive and non-cognitive states on the other. He does, in fact, give some attention to both sets of relations, but in both cases he takes account of only one half of the set. And it is the other half that is crucial for a full understanding of the functional role that mental states can play on behalf of an organism.

Consider first Husserl's treatment of the relation between mental states and the body. In his early philosophy, when he first gives shape to his phenomenology, Husserl pays virtually no attention to the body. The human body seems to be put into the same ontological limbo that the ordinary objects of consciousness enter, with the phenomenological reduction. As a consequence, the early phenomenology has the tone of a Cartesian philosophy that treats consciousness largely in abstraction from its connection to a living organism. The paradigm case of knowing something is "seeing" it, where seeing is understood primarily as having an intellectual intuition of it.

In his later work, including the 1925 lectures, Husserl begins to give some attention to the body in its relation to consciousness. He discusses the actions of the body, its "kinesthesis," in relation to a subject's knowledge of its surrounding "life-world." Knowledge is expanded from its character as a virtually disembodied activity, to a context in which one can come to know things by moving around them, handling them, etc., as truly as one does by simply seeing them. So at least half of the relation between cognition and body begins to make its appearance: the body can be of assistance in our coming to know the world. As it was for Russell and Moore, the body for Husserl functions as a vehicle for transmitting information to the mind. It provides a system of sensory organs, a pair of feet that can gather more data by walking around an object, etc.

Unfortunately, the other half of the relation remains unmentioned: how does cognition of the world function on behalf of the body? It is here, of course, that more pronounced evolutionary considerations emerge. It is here that one begins to consider the mental capacities of the individual as having developed in a way that is advantageous to that individual in its efforts to survive and to provide for its well-being. It is here that one begins to consider the possibility that theories about the mental need to take account of all the functions of mental states, rather than attending almost exclusively to their truth-gathering functions.

For Husserl, as well as for Moore and Russell, this failure to consider the function of mental states on behalf of the body may be part of the platonic legacy that each of them assumed at the turn of the century. Even when their commitment to platonism was dropped, their privileging of the mental over the physical did not diminish. In one of its forms, this privileging fostered attention to the ways in which a body might serve mental acts, but ignored the ways in which those mental acts might serve the interests and needs of the body.[29*]

An analogous one-sidedness attends Husserl's treatment of the relation between cognitive and non-cognitive states. He does not say a great deal more about non-cognitive states ("sentiments" and "valuings" and the like) than Moore and Russell did. The one difference, however, is that he is explicit in claiming that there is a relation between certain cognitive and non-cognitive states. And that relation is not merely causal. Perceptual meanings can, for example, enter into the meanings that we characterize as feelings or valuings. The perception provides the basis on which these latter are built, and this aspect of the relation could surely be seen on a causal model. But the meaning generated in perception becomes part of the meaning of the feeling or the valuing. So, for example, when one sees a blossoming tree as beautiful, the meaning of the *perceived* tree is taken up into the meaning of the beautiful, perceived tree. There is some *integration* of cognitive and non-cognitive meanings.

This goes well beyond Moore's and Russell's accounts of non-cognitive states. For Moore, in aesthetic experiences, cognitive and non-cognitive states may accompany one another; there is no discussion of integration. For Russell the relation is at most causal, and consistent with his atomism, the two types of states remain quite independent of one another. With Husserl, one begins to see an attempt to account for some integration of the two.

But here, as in the case of the relation between mental states and the body, Husserl accounts for only one portion of the relation. Certain cognitive states like perception can affect and "ground" non-cognitive states, but there is no mention of the reciprocal relation in which non-cognitive states affect cognition.

One obvious reason for Russell's failure to be interested in these cases is that they play little, if any, role in our scientific knowledge of the world. For Husserl, such cases have individual rather than universal truths in view. Still, if one is to have a complete account of mental states, it will not do to limit one's treatment of them to a partial set of the relations into which they enter. An adequate theory of mind ought to account for all the types of relations into which mental states enter, both with one another and with states of the body. Even an essentialist approach should be able to accommodate these types of relations.

As in the case of perception, so in Husserl's approach to the mental, his framework can accommodate at least some Darwinian concerns. His treatment of mind in the context of a broad set of experiential relations, rather than atomistically, offers the possibility of extending those relations to include an organism's relations with its environment. His eventual regard for notions like kinesthesis and the "lived world" invite careful attention to the role of the body in conscious experience. His hints about possible relations between cognitive and non-cognitive states suggest further connections that might be forged. And his insistence on taking seriously the role of an active subject in conscious experience makes some room for the place of an organism actively looking out for its own needs and interests. To be sure, Husserl's account is not Darwinian. But it holds more promise for incorporating Darwinian concerns than do the theories of mind proposed by his analytic contemporaries.

I turn now from a rather long historical excursion to a sketch of some positive proposals about how one might approach both perception and mind within a Darwinian framework. The view I shall propose does not pretend to be a comprehensive theory of either mind or perception. But it elaborates on some suggestions I have already made about factors that have been omitted from both analytic and phenomenological theories and that I believe ought to be incorporated into an adequate post-Darwinian philosophy of perception and mind.

Chapter 7

Perception and Mind: A Darwinian Approach

Nothing is easier than to admit in words the truth of the universal struggle for life, or more difficult—at least I have found it so—than constantly to bear this conclusion in mind. Yet unless it be thoroughly engrained in the mind, I am convinced that the whole economy of nature, . . . will be dimly seen or quite misunderstood.

— Charles Darwin (1859)

Analytic philosophy and phenomenology were founded by philosophers explicitly committed to the view that none of Darwin's views were relevant to philosophy. I have argued that this was an unfortunate move for both philosophic traditions, and that it infected their respective theories of both perception and mind. My purpose now is to sketch some views on perception and mind that begin to integrate several Darwinian insights.[1]*

Darwin had argued that one of the most basic facts about living organisms is that they are engaged in a struggle for existence. That struggle is to be taken in a "large and metaphorical" sense, so that it includes all of the efforts, cooperative as well as selfish, that an organism makes on behalf of its life and well-being. Darwin urged an explanation of both the origin and the particular character of living organisms in terms of their relations with the environment in which that struggle takes place. On his view, living organisms are the outcome of a series of accidental variations in interaction with particular surroundings. Most significant for our purposes, Darwin saw the mental powers of some organisms as being among the variations that are, on balance, clearly beneficial.

Using this Darwinian framework, I shall argue that certain mental powers of human beings—and here I include perception, cognitive states like beliefs and desires, and non-cognitive states like some emotions—are best understood in the context of an organism's struggle to cope with its environment in ways that contribute to its life and well-being.

I shall argue that *perception* must be considered, not simply in relation to justified empirical beliefs, but also in the context of the services that it provides to an individual perceiving organism. This in turn will lead to the view that perceiving is neither a passive nor an impersonal process; it involves an active subject and is essentially "indexical"—a notion I shall elaborate shortly. Furthermore, I shall argue that when perception is seen as functioning on behalf of the organism, there is good reason to believe that it involves considerable involvement with certain non-cognitive states, like emotions and bodily needs. If this is right, then an adequate account of *mind* must make allowance for the interaction between perception and these non-cognitive states. I shall argue that mind, like perception, must be understood in the context of the service it provides to the living organism, and that such service often (perhaps always) involves the interaction of cognitive, affective, and bodily states.

One consequence of my view is that an adequate theory of the human mind cannot be abstracted from its function on behalf of the living body, as some Functionalist accounts of mind have attempted to do. That is to say, I shall argue against the view that one can provide a psychological theory that is equally applicable to non-living systems like computers and to living systems like human beings.

Perception

From the time of Descartes at least, and through most of the twentieth century, philosophical theories of perception have treated it almost exclusively in terms of sensory information and concepts. We have seen this clearly in the case of Moore and Russell. Husserl's theory was unusual in that it incorporated other considerations as well (and I shall capitalize on some of these), but his views did not come to dominate the century's theorizing about perception, at least not in the English-speaking world. Nonetheless, what seems to be common to virtually all three theories is the assumption that perception is purely cognitive and is largely a matter of the impersonal processing of data.

One might object that none of these philosophers was offering a *comprehensive* theory of perception. Each philosopher, it might be argued, was merely dealing with one aspect of perception that particularly interested him, and he ought not be criticized for failing to mention all of the other factors that might also enter into perception.[2*] There are at least two difficulties with such an objection.

First, even if it were the case that each of the three philosophers we have considered did indeed take his account of perception to be only a small piece of a comprehensive theory—and none of the three says that this was the case—still, the small piece that each provides is not simply partial, it is, I believe, inaccurate. If one treats perception as completely passive, when there is reason to believe that it involves some active selection of data, then the theory is worse than partial. If one treats perception as if non-cognitive states have no role to play in the selection of its content or in the way that content is conceptualized, then one has a distorted account of perception.

Second, the impersonal, passive, and purely cognitive accounts of perception that were offered by some of the theorists I have considered, lent support to views that portray the mind as impersonal and passive, views that see no difficulty in formulating theories that systematically isolate cognitive states from non-cognitive states.

So, however limited the goals of Moore, Russell, and Husserl *might* have been, my claim is that important aspects of their views are problematic and have encouraged subsequent theories of both perception and mind that are worse than simply partial.

The view of perception I shall propose does not deny that it involves conceptual sorting of sensory material. But it differs from most traditional theories by adding four further dimensions. I shall argue that:

(a) active, individual Subjectivity regularly plays a crucial role in perception;
(b) perception involves the production of a complex psychological[3]* entity that I shall call "perceptual meaning;"
(c) perceptual meanings are essentially indexical; and
(d) perceptual meanings regularly incorporate non-cognitive as well as cognitive elements.

(a) Subjectivity in Perception

In my discussion of Moore's and Russell's accounts of perception, I argued that they were mistaken in treating it as a passive affair in which sensory data were simply *given* and the notion of Subjectivity could be either eliminated or ignored. Perception, I argued, requires an active subject at least for such phenomena as selective attention.

Traditional ways of thinking about Subjectivity have been rejected in a number of quarters in twentieth-century philosophy. For some philosophers, the notions of *Subjectivity* and *self* are sometimes used as if they were interchangeable, both thought to be ways of referring to whatever is captured by the term "I." Difficulties in providing a satisfactory account of an enduring self that can ground personal identity may have motivated philosophers to dismiss the notion of Subjectivity along with that of the self. For some theorists the problem may be that both notions appear to carry with them all the metaphysical baggage that attached to the notion of *mental substance*, and both were dismissed along with that. For others, the notion of

Subjectivity is thought to be a final and undesirable hold-out against the objectivity of science.

For a number of different reasons, then, philosophers have objected to the continued reliance on the notion of Subjectivity as it relates to human consciousness. In what follows, I shall suggest an account of Subjectivity that I believe disarms these objections and yet retains a reasonably useful account of how an organism is capable of acting on its own behalf. As a start, I shall distinguish Subjectivity from self and shall make no appeal to mental substance. Subjectivity, I shall claim, can be accounted for on a much narrower base than either "self" or "personal identity," but it provides the footing on which the two latter notions might be constructed. The nucleus of the view comes from William James' *Principles of Psychology*; the additions to it are largely darwinian[4]* in spirit.

I shall focus on just one aspect of James's view of the self, namely his account of what he calls "the pure ego," and I shall expand on that account by making explicit a darwinian dimension that James did not fully exploit. I can't claim that James would accept the view I propose; in fact, I suspect that he would have some reservations about it. And it is not a view that Darwin explicity articulated; it nonetheless capitalizes on important darwinian insights.

I begin by considering James's view of the self as it is recounted in his *Principles of Psychology*. He divides his discussion of the self into two parts: the self as *object* ("me") and the self as *subject* ("I"). His treatment of the self as object is distinctively pragmatic. There are, he suggests, a number of different ways of looking at the notion of *me*—one can consider it from the material point of view, the social, or the spiritual. Much depends on the context and the purposes of the inquiry. The discussion here is vintage James—rich, provocative, and full of insight into many dimensions of human experience.

His treatment of the self as subject, the "pure ego" as he sometimes calls it, is equally provocative. In distinguishing it from the objective self he says:

> This me is an empirical aggregate of things objectively known. The *I* which knows them cannot itself be an aggregate; neither for psychological purposes need it be considered to be an unchanging metaphysical entity like the Soul, or a principle like the pure Ego, viewed as 'out of time.' It is a *Thought*, at each moment different from that of the last moment, but *appropriative* of the latter, together with all that the latter called its own.[5]

More briefly, he says, "The passing Thought then seems to be the Thinker. . . ."[6]

The subject, then, is to be understood as the passing moment of thought in the stream of consciousness. On first reading the claim seems paradoxical. How could anything so ephemeral as a passing moment of thought be identified with human Subjectivity? James, however, has given this momentary thought at least two distinguishable functions. First, it constitutes awareness of the present moment. And second, the present thought "appropriates" to itself some past thoughts and their objects. Its first function puts it in touch with what is currently going on in or around the organism; its second function provides it with some degree of continuity.

But how does James account for this second function? What, exactly, is this notion of one thought "appropriating" another? In explaining the relation, James reverts to metaphor.

> . . . we shall assimilate them ['distant selves'] to each other and to the warm and intimate self we now feel within us as we think, and separate them as a collection from whatever selves have not this mark, much as out of a herd of cattle let loose for the winter on some wide Western prairie the owner picks out and sorts together, when the time for the round-up comes in the spring, all the beasts on which he finds his own particular brand.
>
> The various members of the collection thus set apart are felt to belong with each other whenever they are thought at all.[7]

James goes on to characterize the present thought as the "herdsman" that appropriates past thoughts. "The 'owner' symbolizes here that 'section' of consciousness, or pulse of thought, which we have all along represented as the vehicle of the judgment of identity; and the 'brand' symbolizes the characters of warmth and continuity, by reason of which the judgment is made. . . . They are not his because they are branded; they are branded because they are his."[8]

As is often the case with James, his account here is predominately descriptive. Explanation or argument, when it appears at all, takes the form of suggestive metaphors. Here he likens past thoughts to herds of cattle being rounded up by the present thought (the "I") that has inherited the title of herdsman. The issue for our purposes is whether or not such a metaphor can be replaced by a more careful account of this second function of Subjectivity and whether or not such an account can be *justified*.

A subject that is a passing momentary thought would, if it is adequate, eliminate the need for one enduring substantial self—a notion that James repudiates even more explicitly in his later work. So the view has a *prima facie* appeal for those who prefer to be cautious in their ontological commitments.

Still, one wonders if there is any stronger reason to accept such a slender view of Subjectivity, apart from its metaphysical convenience. After all, the view itself is not without problems. Why, for example, does the subject have the two particular functions that James claims for it? And how are those two functions related to one another? If they are unified in one momentary subject, what is it that unifies the function of present awareness with the function of appropriating past moments of awareness? James offers no answers to questions like these. So, on the one hand, one might be pleased with the thinner ontology that his view offers us. On the other hand, questions remain about just how it all works, or why we should think that it works in just the way that he suggests. I think that this is where darwinian insights can offer some help.

Recall that one of Darwin's most fundamental claims about living organisms is that they *struggle for existence*. For us humans at least, that struggle broadens into continuing efforts to deal with our environment, with other species, and with other individuals of our own species, in ways that seem most likely to contribute to our well-being. These efforts frequently (not always) involve some of our conscious states—states that on Darwin's view are an evolutionary advantage that compensate for our relative lack of strength and speed.

These considerations are relevant to James' momentary thought that is said to be the locus of human Subjectivity. Using a Darwinian framework, one can see that an organism needs at least five related capacities if it is going to have any chance of success in its struggle for existence:

(i) it needs to be able to pick up relevant information about its current environment;

(ii) it needs to be able to relate that information to other information it has previously gathered so that it can recognize what it is perceiving;

(iii) as part of this recognition, it needs to be able to anticipate possible behaviors of what is recognized;[9*]

(iv) it needs to be able to relate the data from these first three capacities to *its own* occurrent and dispositional needs, desires, fears, capabilities, bodily states, etc.; and,

(v) the organism must be able to bring all of this information about its environment and about its own states to bear on a possible course of action.

It is clear that James's account of the subject provides for the first of these darwinian requirements. His subject, as the present thought, is surely capable of being aware of its present environment. But notice that the information it can pick up is *relevant*. That is, the subject won't be simply passive to its perceptual field but will be capable of selective attention.

The second darwinian requirement—that the subject be able to appropriate some of its past experience so that recognition is possible—can also be accommodated on the Jamesian model. It should be noted, however, that James's concern with the subject's access to some of its past is intended to provide for the subject's own continuity so that some sense of personal identity can be grounded. On the darwinian model that I am suggesting, James's concern with personal identity is not eliminated; rather, its natural foundation is highlighted. This second capacity provides for the subject's need for a "data bank" that will allow it to make sense of its present experience in the light of its past. In the absence of such a capacity, an organism's survival would be quite brief. Lacking access to its past experience would either leave the organism "hard-wired" to respond in exactly the same way to a given stimulus regardless of any past failures, or leave it facing each stimulus as if it were entirely novel. The flexibility afforded by access to its own past is clearly an evolutionary advantage.

It is this role on behalf of the organism's survival that best explains the subject's ability to "appropriate" some of its past; it is this role that provides some justification for James' claim that this is one of the functions of the passing thought, the subject. On a darwinian view, it is a variation that has proved adaptive. Any ensuing sense of continuity or personal identity are, I think, a by-product of that *need* to appropriate one's past. And while it is highly probable that the ability to call upon information from past experience is crucial to the survival of most (perhaps all) conscious organisms, it is likely that a sense of personal identity will develop only in some cases and is not an *essential* by-product of memory in all of those organisms.

So the two functions that James ascribes to the pure ego can be given a natural, indeed a darwinian, justification. Furthermore, the unity of these two functions in the present thought is entirely plausible on darwinian grounds. Either function in the absence of the other one would be far less effective for survival purposes. However, these two functions that James specifies are not, I think, the whole story. At least three more are needed.

Closely related to the capacity to recognize, is the ability to anticipate, on the basis of that recognition, possible future behaviors of the recognized items. Without that ability, recognition would be fruitless. While we distinguish easily between the past and the future, a notion like recognition really points in both directions. We draw on past experience in order to be able to anticipate future possibilities.

The fourth darwinian requirement is the one that is most commonly overlooked in accounts of Subjectivity.[10*] This is the requirement that the organism be able to relate what it is currently experiencing and recognizing, to *its own* desires, bodily needs and abilities, fears, etc. The simple recognition of something as a piece of food, as a possible sexual partner, or as an oncoming truck is not sufficient to motivate the kind of active response that would be required in order to provide for the organism's well-being. The organism needs to see the food as related to its own hunger, the possible partner as related to its own sexual interest, and the oncoming truck as related to its own desire to avoid being hit. It is this *reflexive* capacity that provides the context in which *meaning for the organism* can emerge.

Pragmatists like James and Dewey are rightly praised for their insistence that knowledge and action are intimately related. It is, I think, this fourth darwinian requirement that best explains that connection. Unless an organism can relate what it knows about its environment to what it needs, fears, or can do, it is in no position to behave in ways appropriate to its situation.

And this fourth capacity then makes it possible for an organism to meet the fifth requirement, namely that it be able to bring all of its data to bear on some useful course of action. It is because the process of experiencing our environment incorporates the process of relating it to our own current needs and interests that we are in a position to act on our own behalf in response to that environment.

In the account that I have given so far, one crucially important dimension has been left implicit. In the darwinian context (and, of course, for James himself) one is not speaking of a disembodied thought. Both Darwin and James take it for granted that what is at stake is a living bodily organism that has developed mental capacities as part of its evolutionary advantage. Each of the five darwinian requirements must be understood as functioning on behalf of the living body. The survival value of the present thought depends on its connection with the needs of that body.

So the subject, understood as a present state of consciousness that can be aware of its environment, access its past, integrate incoming information with its other states, and stimulate appropriate responses—this sort of subject is required if conscious organisms are to survive. The subject is not a problematic residue of speculative metaphysics; it is a requirement for survival.

What we have, then, is an account of Subjectivity as a unified series of *functions*. And what unifies them is the living body on whose behalf they function. This type of account is, of course, what James had in mind—a functional replacement for the traditional substantial self. What I have argued is that the most compelling motivation for such an account arises from the context of Darwin's views on living organisms' struggle for life. The

apparent continuity that seems to be a necessary condition for any significant notion of the *self* is a continuity of functions on behalf of the living
organism.

While my account of Subjectivity relies on the capacity of the organism
to be conscious, there is no requirement that these four functions be all or
always *accessible* to consciousness. In fact, there is increasing evidence that
some portions of the data, both present and past, as well as some of the
processes that manipulate it, are handled at a subconscious or unconscious
level. Our Subjectivity is not totally transparent to ourselves.

There is one obvious objection to the view of Subjectivity that I have
offered so far. It might be posed by John Dewey or George Herbert Mead.
I refer to the role of the social environment in helping to shape the self. It
is widely agreed, of course, that the self as *object*, what James calls the "me,"
has a clear social dimension. But the issue here concerns the "I," the *subject*.
And while Mead and Dewey are surely right in arguing for the importance
of society's influence on the development of self, even as *subject*, I want to
suggest that societal influence cannot be taken as the whole story; it cannot
even be where the story begins. Any account of the social shaping of the
human subject needs to explain how the influence of a society is "absorbed"
or "integrated" by an individual organism. In the case of a severely retarded
child, for example, it seems clear that social influence is profoundly limited.
One reason is that the child is unable to take information from its environment and relate it meaningfully to its own earlier experiences or to its own
needs and interests. More generally, in order for society to help in shaping
the individual subject—which it surely does—the individual must be capable of picking up information from its environment, social or otherwise, and
must be able to relate it to its own bodily and psychological states.

One consequence of this is that the basic capacities that I have
discussed must be innate. Put another way, Subjectivity has a biological
basis. Richer notions like *self* or *personal identity* seem to require considerable
social construction beyond that innate biological basis.

What social environment *does contribute* is some of the *content* on which
the five capacities are exercised, as well as some variations in the way those
capacities develop. Thus, society can teach us what sorts of things are
important to notice in our present environment, or what sorts of interests
and fears are valued by the group. To that extent, it contributes in crucial
ways to the development of the subject. But it does not generate the
functional capacities that constitute that subject.

I said that I would present an account of Subjectivity that could disarm
some of the recent objections that have been leveled against it. One of these
concerned tacit commitments that accounts of Subjectivity might make to

suspect metaphysical notions like mental substance. It should be clear from my reliance on James's basic view that there is no requirement here for a mental substance.

The second objection to Subjectivity arises in response to views like the one proposed by Thomas Nagel. He worries that Subjectivity is an undesirable holdout against the encompassing objective viewpoint of the sciences. If objectivity requires a "view from nowhere," then perhaps my account is in trouble. On the other hand, if Subjectivity is problematic because it requires a "view from somewhere," then (taking a page from Russell) cameras ought to present a similar problem for the objectivity of science. If, however, scientific objectivity merely requires that all phenomena remain in principle amenable to third-person description, then the account I suggest is neutral on the issue. It is not the case at this point in time that we can offer a third-person description of an individual's viewpoint on its environment, the appropriated portions of its past, or its own perceived needs and interests, etc. But often we can't give a full description of all of this even from the first-person perspective—some of it occurring below the level of awareness.

Nonetheless, nothing in the account makes it impossible in principle that such descriptions, both first- and third-person, might someday become available to us. These are, after all, the products of functional capacities in a physical organism. There may eventually be empirical reasons why a third-person account of them won't be possible—it might simply require quantities of micro-level information that we can't conveniently handle in chunks. But I see no *a priori* reason for it to be in principle inaccessible.

The third objection originates with Russell and echoes through some of the contemporary views on artificial intelligence. It says that Subjectivity is nothing more than having a "perspective," and that a perspective is as available to cameras as it is to computers. So it can be disengaged from consciousness altogether. The view I have suggested is clearly not so generous as that. It is just chauvinist enough to insist that, although it shares with cameras the ability of having a view from somewhere, the sort of Subjectivity that is of interest to philosophy of perception or mind is properly attributed to conscious living organisms and not to cameras or computers. The point is not that it is impossible to expand the notion of Subjectivity in such a way as to give it a new extension. Rather, such an expansion *excludes* something of the original meaning of Subjectivity. While it may be possible for certain mechanisms to mimic some of the features of Subjectivity—like having a particular spatial perspective on an environment, or appropriating certain data from a memory bank, or even bringing both of these to bear on a course of action—they standardly lack the function of relating all the above to *their own* interests and needs. And that, for the simple reason that they *have* no interests or needs of their own. Living organisms have *intrinsic* interests and needs that issue from their struggle for existence.

But even if it were possible to program a computer, for example, to have all five capacities, the functional role of its apparent Subjectivity would differ dramatically from that of living subjects. For living organisms a functioning Subjectivity is *indispensable* to their survival and well-being. Cameras and computers, on the other hand, get along just fine in its absence. For them, it would be an entirely gratuitous appendage.

One final objection might be raised. It could be suggested that the account of Subjectivity I have offered is as applicable to non-human organisms as it is to humans.[11]* And that is true. But an important distinction needs to be made. My purpose has been to provide an account of the Subjectivity of the *conscious* living organism. My starting point, with James, is the present moment of consciousness. Nonetheless, my account still allows for the attribution of Subjectivity to non-human conscious organisms—probably chimps, dogs, and the like. And I see no problem with supposing that these organisms *do* have Subjectivity, construed as I have described it. One important way in which it will differ from human Subjectivity is in the types of *content* with which it will deal. The types of things that are attended to or remembered, the types of needs or fears as well as the possible courses of action, will vary dramatically among different species. But I see no problem in thinking that the *functions* of Subjectivity will remain fundamentally the same.

Whether or not they will provide a foundation for the development of a self or a sense of personal identity in non-human species, I do not know. For human beings, however, I take this expanded account of a Jamesian subject to provide the necessary foundation on which any adequate account of self or personal identity would be built. By itself, it is unable to do all the work that these robust notions are called upon to do. Numerous other items need to be added to it, but Subjectivity is its ineliminable core. [12]*

Given this understanding of Subjectivity, I take it that its role in perception clearly involves at least the first four of its functions: awareness of aspects of the present environment, relating this information to relevant past experience and future possibilities and to the organism's own interests, needs, and capabilities. A plan of action may also be included, but it need not be required in every case.

It is important to stress that the relations among these functions is not simply linear, starting with the first and concluding with the fourth or fifth function. Perceptions are virtually continuous and very often built on one another. One should expect feedback loops among the functions.

Subjectivity in perception, then, should be understood as a set of functions by which an organism coordinates its interactions with its current environment in light of the needs and interests of that organism. Normally, the most fundamental needs and interests are life and well-being.

(b) Meaning in Perception

My second claim is that perception involves the generation of a complex psychological entity that I call "perceptual meaning." It is generated by the perceiving subject and is the outcome of the five "Darwinian" functions I sketched in the last section. Before looking at its content in greater detail, a broader question should perhaps be answered: "Why introduce *meaning* into perception?"

It has been a century since Frege introduced his distinction between the *sense* and the *reference* of a linguistic expression. The distinction has become familiar in the philosophy of language. One of my contentions is that some analogue of it deserves an equally important role in philosophical theories of perception. Perceiving an object or an event is more than bare awareness of its sensible presence. It regularly includes as well, taking a viewpoint on that object or event, seeing it in relation to one's needs or expectations or values, etc. So, for example, perceiving an approaching car includes the conceptualization of certain sensory information, but it can also include seeing it as the arrival of an expected ride, or as an annoying obstacle to one's crossing the street, or as an attractive model one might buy.

This viewpoint on a perceived object or event is what I call *perceptual meaning*. As the perceived object parallels the linguistic referent, so perceptual meaning[13*] parallels linguistic sense. To be sure, there are disanalogies between linguistic sense and perceptual meaning, some of which will become apparent in what follows. But one general motivation for making the distinction in the linguistic context also carries weight in the perceptual context: there is in both cases a difference between what is picked out (the referent or the perceived object), and the particular viewpoint that is taken on it (the sense or the perceptual meaning). It is the content of this viewpoint, this perceptual meaning, that enables a perceiver to relate information about her environment to information about her own interests and needs, thereby putting perception in the service of the individual perceiver. The darwinian implications are fairly obvious. I shall detail some of them shortly.

This claim, that there is such a thing as perceptual meaning, originated with Husserl's phenomenology. More recently, other philosophers including Dagfinn Follesdal, David Smith, Ronald McIntyre, Robert Solomon, et. al., have elaborated on Husserl's claim.[14*] These recent discussions have, however, treated perceptual meaning as a close analogue of Frege's linguistic sense. In particular, they argue that both the perceptual and the linguistic cases involve timeless, abstract, conceptual meanings. Their view is, I think, consonant with tacit assumptions that have regularly been made about meaning in perception (although the term "meaning" has rarely been used). The idea seems to be that whatever meaning there is in perception, it is purely conceptual. I, on the other hand, shall argue that in spite of the similarities between them, perceptual meaning differs in important respects from Fregean sense: it regularly incorporates non-cognitive elements, and it is not timeless but has an "essentially indexical" character (that is, it is indexed to a particular perceiver at a particular time and place).

As a start toward clarifying the notion of perceptual meaning, let me offer some brief considerations about meaning in general. It arises, I think, in at least *two* ways. The first of these hardly needs an introduction, since it is the focus of most of the current philosophical literature on meaning. It has its roots in Charles Peirce's theory of signs, and is the sort of meaning that arises when one thing is taken to mean another (either by laws of nature or by social convention). Thus, smoke means (or is a sign of) fire, and certain well-formed linguistic expressions can mean something other than themselves. All of this is commonplace. In the spirit of Peirce, I shall refer to this type of meaning as *signitive* meaning. Virtually all of the recent theorizing about meaning has focused almost exclusively on signitive meaning.[15*]

A second way in which meaning arises I call *network* meaning. For present purposes, I want to distinguish it from "holistic" theories of linguistic meaning. The function of the network in the two contexts is, I believe, quite different.

Both signitive and network meaning share some common ground. In both cases for something (a sign or anything else) to be meaningful, it must play some role in a broader framework, in some system of relations. For signitive meaning, this involves playing an indicating role, being in the relation of "standing for," etc. In network meaning of the sort that concerns me, on the other hand, the relations are more numerous and varied. They may include associative relations of all sorts—e.g., similarity, relations of fulfilling expectations, reminding relations—as well as causal relations and perhaps inferential relations, etc. What needs to be shown is that there are some systems of meaning relations that do not reduce to signitive relations alone.

A clear example of network meaning is to be found, I think, in perception. It is evident that the meaning that attaches to a perceived object or event is not simply a function of that object or event being taken as a sign for something else. Obviously, a perceived object or event *can* function as a sign for something else, but the meaning that arises in connection with the object itself is not primarily signitive meaning. The object *itself* is meaningful, and is not simply an indicator of something else.[16*] Consider an example.

You and I are walking along a train platform, talking, and we hear a train whistle. We both take the sound of the whistle to mean that the train is approaching. That is its signitive meaning. But the perception of the sound generally includes a good deal more than that. I may hear the sound as abrasive, familiar, or farther away than I expected. You, on the other hand, may hear it as pleasing, intrusive, or unlike train whistles at home. The list could be extended indefinitely. The point is that the train whistle is meaningful to us in all sorts of ways that do not involve signitive relations. It is not that the whistle signifies or stands for abrasiveness, familiarity, or dissimilar whistles. Rather, our perception of it involves our "locating" it in relation to a whole network of values, feelings, memories, concepts, expectations, beliefs, etc.—that is, giving it a "place" on our individual psychological maps. This I take to be the defining characteristic of perceptual meaning, and it is one of the things that distinguishes it from most standard accounts of linguistic meaning.

Psychologists like Gordon Bower[17] have proposed network theories of memory and affect. On such a view memory is represented as a rich associative network of encoded events, beliefs, emotions, autonomic patterns, etc. The kind of network I have in mind is of this general sort. While there are some important differences between Bower's model and the one that I am proposing, the significant points of similarity are that both types of networks incorporate cognitive and non-cognitive components and both types of networks involve associative links.

It is difficult to give a precise characterization of everything that might be included in such a network. In addition to all the obvious sorts of psychological states (beliefs, memories, mood, expectations, desires, interests, emotions, and values) there are states of awareness of my own body. None of these states, psychological or bodily, is at the focus of my attention since the perceived object is what I am attending to. But these states form the background against which that object becomes meaningful. Recall my comments in relation to Husserl, on the importance of *psychological* contexts, or "horizons." Note, too, how far removed this account is from an atomistic, passive account of the sort offered by Russell and others who followed in his lead.

The subset of these states that is actually brought into relation with the perceived object will provide its meaning. Some of these states may be caused directly by perceiving the object (e.g., a series of beliefs about the object, fear of it, desires in relation to it); other states may be already present in the perceiver coincidentally (e.g., a depressed mood, a hope of seeing something exciting, attention to sounds); still other states may be caused by associative links (e.g., memories of similar situations); and some may appear apparently fortuitously, unrelated to the perceived object (e.g., remembering that one left the keys in the car). Each of these states, whatever its origin, may contribute to the meaning generated by the perception. Those caused by the perception itself are obvious candidates here. But I may also see the object, a bear for example, as a welcome bit of novelty to lift me out of my depression, a quieter animal than I expected, strangely like my dog, an unexpected distraction that keeps me from retrieving my car keys, etc.

It is important to notice that the relevant states do not necessarily occur in *linear* sequence—many may be simultaneous—and they may all *jointly* contribute to my ensuing behavior.

Given that very general characterization of the network, two additional things need to be said about it: first, it is not an "anonymous" network that is roughly the same from one perceiver to another (this will lead me into my discussion of indexicality); and second, the elements in the network are not purely cognitive. These two characteristics of the network are closely related.

(c) Indexicality

To say that my psychological network is not anonymous, not simply interchangeable with yours or with that of the milkman, is really just to say that the psychological states that are current elements in that network, are uniquely mine. While you and I undoubtedly share some beliefs and some interests, our total networks of psychological states are unlikely ever to be identical. Further, my own network of psychological states will not remain the same from one time to another. As a consequence, the meaning that a psychological network will provide to a perceived object or event will be dependent on the particular perceiver and the particular time at which the meaning is generated.

Notice that his notion of the psychological network of the perceiver answers to the fourth darwinian requirement that I suggested that an adequate notion of Subjectivity wants. The subject needs to be able to relate the present incoming data to its own interests and needs. It is the network of current psychological states of the organism that provides the relevant material. So the notion of individualized perceptual meaning is not simply a gratuitous add-on to standard theories of perception. Rather, it is part of what is essential if an organism is to be able to respond to sensory data in ways that are relevant to its own interests and needs.

An indexical item is one whose meaning[18*] is dependent in some way on the context in which it is found. Indexical *terms* in language include words like "I," "here," "now." *Actions*, too, like pointing, are indexical. As Peirce puts it, indexicals have "real, dynamical" ties to the actual context in which they are used. My use of the term "indexical" has this same sense, and like Peirce I mean to pick up more than linguistic expressions as indexicals. Nonetheless, my use of the notion of indexicality differs in a couple of respects from the way it is standardly understood.

First, indexicality has been most commonly associated with *signs*. I mean to extend it from the context of signitive meaning to that of network meaning. The appropriate domain for indexical considerations is not with signs as such, but with meaning. Indexicality plays its role by contributing to the full understanding of the meaning of something, whether that thing is a sign or a psychological network.

Second, indexical expressions are generally taken to have a fixed general *meaning* but a variable *reference*, the latter being a function of the temporal and spatial context in which the expression is used. So, "here" means something like "in this place" on all the occasions of its use, while the place to which it refers can vary. In the case of perception, however, my claim is that the *meaning*, too, is indexical in the sense that it (and not merely the perceptual referent) varies with the time, place, and individual perceiver. What this comes to is that perception carries with it a *double indexicality*. On the one hand, it involves a meaning that attaches to some object or event perceived here and now. To that extent, it shares in the kind of indexicality associated with *demonstratives* like "this." This is its referential dimension, and been explained and defended in detail by others, notably David Smith.[19]

On the other hand, perception involves a meaning *for* a particular perceiver. This is its second dimension of indexicality. If, as I have suggested, perceived objects are given meaning by associations within a network of psychological states, and if that network has actual ties to a particular person at a particular time, then the network and the meaning that arises with it are a function of, and must be indexed to, that person and that time. To put the point a different way, I perceive objects and events as present to me now. This "now" is not simply a particular chronological moment, it is a particular *psychological* moment in my experience—a point at which I have certain memories but not yet others, certain feelings and no longer other feelings, certain expectations and not others. The perceptual meanings that are generated are indexical, not in the sense that the indexical concept "now" must function as part of the meaning (although it *may*), but in the sense that the meaning has temporally variable content.

There is, in addition, a *spatial* indexicality involved in perceptual meaning. This is a consequence of the fact that my perception of things is a bodily affair. That means, most obviously, that I perceive things with bodily senses, but it also means that I perceive them in relation to my body (unlike the case in which I think about a mathematical formula). By this I don't simply mean that the sensory information received from them is affected by their spatial relation to me, although this is true. What I especially have in mind is that my perception of things regularly includes my "sizing them up" in relation to me, here. At a most obvious level, this means that things are perceived as off to my left, or in front of or behind me. As Castaneda puts it, I am the geometrical origin of my experienced world.[20]* And their spatial relation to me may also include an element of value, feeling, or expectation,—they are perceived as too close (invading my space), as larger than I need, as intimidatingly large, or as smaller than I expected. Perceiving things *here* means perceiving them under the constraints of physical space but it also means perceiving them under the constraints of psychological space; the meaning they have for me is indexed particularly to the latter. The variability of the spatial content of perceptual meaning is as much a matter of concomitant psychological states as it is a matter of physical coordinates.

What makes this added dimension of indexicality (its non-demonstrative indexicality) so important is its connection with behavior. The demonstrative element of perception is not able by itself to account for the perceiver's ensuing behavior.[21] The precise behavior that is likely to follow on seeing this bear at this time will depend crucially on the psychological and bodily state of the particular perceiver—e.g., whether or not she is looking for entertainment, or hoping to shoot a bear, or aware of her inability to run very fast. So even when the demonstrative element remains constant, the ensuing behavior may well vary as a function of the rest of the meaning that attaches to the perception.

Other philosophers have made reference to an indexical element in perception. [22] But the emphasis in these cases has been on the *logic* of indexical or demonstrative *concepts*, on the role such concepts play in the logical analysis of perceptual language or in propositions that specify the representational content of perceptual experience. My focus is different. I am not concerned with the logical analysis of concepts or statements but with the fact that objects and events are experienced in *actual* relation to a perceiver at a particular time and place. This is the foundation of my claim that perceptual meaning is neither stereotypical nor impersonal.

It has been suggested to me that my claims here could be better captured by saying that perceptual meanings are *idiosyncratic* rather than that they are *indexical*.[23]* The term "idiosyncratic" surely captures the general notion I have in mind, for it suggests something that is peculiar to an individual person. So in that sense the term picks up the heart of my claim. Still there is at least one important reason to prefer the notion of indexicality. To say that perceptual meanings are idiosyncratic is not to specify the respect in which they are unique; designating them as temporally and spatially indexical is an attempt to clarify the respects in which they are idiosyncratic. They could, after all, be idiosyncratic in virtue of being peculiarly and systematically mistaken or peculiarly and systematically associated with evil, etc. Their idiosyncracy has to do with certain psychologically salient temporal and spatial considerations.

Returning to my substantive claim, to say that perceptual meanings are indexical does not mean, of course, that they are incommunicable or that they share no content in common. We regularly talk about them and just as regularly discover commonalities in them. Neither am I arguing here for logically private states or for incorrigibility. With respect to privacy, it is a truism that only I can *have* my experiences; it does not follow that only I can *understand* them. As far as incorrigibility is concerned, psychologists from Freud to the present have given us ample reason to suppose that we can be mistaken about the content of our own experiences. My claims do not entail either of these problematic views. What they do entail is that the full meaning of a perceptual experience can be understood only by taking account of the perceiver, his or her psychological and bodily state at the time, and his or her spatial location at the time.

The parallel with an act of pointing is instructive: abstracted from its time, place, and pointer, it loses the heart of its meaning. Perception is subject to analogous constraints. Indexical elements are clearly relevant to darwinian considerations. If an individual is to survive, his perception of objects and events needs to highlight their relation to his body at this place and time. Impersonal, timeless beliefs won't do the job.

Perceptual meaning differs, then, from (Fregean) linguistic sense in that it instantiates network meaning rather than just signitive meaning, and it incorporates essentially indexical elements. One further difference needs consideration.

(d) Perception and non-cognitive states

Perceptual meaning regularly incorporates non-cognitive as well as cognitive components. Returning to the example of the train whistle, one can see that the elements in the network (the "nodes" in relation to which the perceived object is given meaning) include values, emotions, needs, etc., as well as concepts. That is, perceived objects have meaning for us not simply because they fall under certain general concepts (like "train" or "whistle") but also because they engender certain feelings in us, respond to our needs or interests, have a certain value for us. So the meaning generated in perception is not a purely cognitive meaning.

The claim that perceptual meaning incorporates non-cognitive as well as cognitive elements can be taken in at least two ways. On the strong version, perceptual meanings would *always* include some non-cognitive material. On the weaker version, perceptual meanings would be the sorts of things that always *could* include non-cognitive components—that is, they would be the sorts of things for which non-cognitive elements are *always possible* (though not always actual) components.

My position entails at least the weaker version. The plausibility of the stronger version depends on what is taken to count as "non-cognitive." While we have some intuitive sense of how to distinguish between cognitive and non-cognitive factors, precise definitions for the two are not easily given. Cognitive states could be taken to be states that involve conceptual information processing, or perhaps have truth-functional content. Neither of these characterizations is without its problems, but both of them approximate what we are concerned about when we talk of cognitive states. On this view we find beliefs at one end of the spectrum—paradigmatic cognitive states whose conceptualized contents can be true or false [24*]—and states like moods at the other end of the spectrum, in which conceptualization and truth-value play virtually no role. This view also leaves us with a number of psychological states somewhere in the middle—namely, those involving some conceptualization and having some truth-functional content but also having some non-conceptual and non-truth-functional components. Emotions, involving as they do both beliefs and certain physiological responses of the organism, belong here. Values, attitudes, and desires probably also belong somewhere in this middle range; at the very least, it seems clear that these states are not *purely* cognitive. When I speak of "non-cognitive" psychological elements, I mean to include all those psychological states that have any non-cognitive components, as well as straightforward bodily states (like hunger, sexual arousal, etc.) that can contribute to the meaning one gives to things in one's perceptual field.

My claim, then, is that perceptual meanings are the sorts of things that regularly (and *perhaps* always) incorporate emotions, values, desires, moods, and the like. While I suspect that empirical findings may show that the stronger version is true, I can rest my case on the weaker one since that is all it requires. Notice how far it is at odds with an atomistic approach to perception by way of isolated bits called sense data.

Before considering the consequences of what I have said so far, let me pause to take account of some likely objections.

First of all, one might want to object that what I am talking about is really a series of distinct conscious elements, some cognitive and some non-cognitive, that ought not be lumped together into what I have called perceptual meaning. Why not stick with the classical theories of perception, the objection runs, which take it to be a purely cognitive affair. This cognitive event might then be said to "evoke" certain memories, or to have a certain emotional "impact," etc. But these latter would remain distinct from the perception itself. This is surely the standard way of looking at perception, and it has a long philosophical tradition behind it. One must admit, too, that it is difficult to know just what criteria should be used in deciding what belongs properly to perception and what is a mere accompaniment. As I have said previously, in trying to decide the issue by specifying necessary and sufficient conditions for perception, one runs the risk of begging the question.

However, if one begins with experiences that would obviously count as perceiving—like hearing a train whistle, or seeing a bear in the woods—the grounds for excluding the non-cognitive elements are not persuasive. The grounds that have been used are that philosophical accounts of perception belong in the context of the *justification of truth-claims* about the world. Using such grounds, one quickly pares perception to the conceptual organizing of sense information. The influence of skepticism has been profound here. The accounts of perception offered by Moore and Russell are paradigm cases of this approach.

But, as I have argued, it is at least as plausible to claim that perception plays a crucial role in providing for the *survival and well-being of individual perceivers.* In that context there is no reason to suppose that individual desires or fears or bodily needs would be extrinsic to the perception itself. On the contrary, it is often these non-cognitive states that guide perceptual attention to look for or listen for things that will meet the needs or relieve the fears of the perceiver. It is states like these that "color" the way one sees objects and events.

Standard theories of perception, preoccupied with issues of justification, have paid little attention to cases of perception in which one is *looking for* or *listening for* something. The focus has been on simple *seeing* or *hearing,* cases in which one need not take account of activity on the part of the perceiver. Again, recall the passivity of perception at the heart of Moore's and Russell's accounts. But even the particular object on which one focuses has many more aspects than the few on which attention settles. The portion brought to the foreground of attention is often actively selected. The elements of the perceiving system that might reasonably be thought to guide the process of selective attention surely include not only its beliefs, but also its current bodily needs, affective state, interests, past experiences, etc.

It is also very likely that even the particular concepts that are brought to bear on sensory information are affected by non-cognitive states of the perceiver. A person can be seen not only as "human being" but also as friendly or intimidating, as a sexually attractive partner or as a dangerous threat—all depending to some extent on the physical and psychological state of the perceiver at the time.

In sum, when one recognizes that perception functions on behalf of an organism's struggle for existence, the interaction of cognitive and non-cognitive states in guiding the perceptual process and in interpreting perceived objects and events becomes compelling.

There are, in addition, several other relevant considerations that support my contention that the cognitive and the non-cognitive are profoundly interwoven in perception. Taken individually, these considerations may not be conclusive, but as a group they are, I think, persuasive.

(i) In the hearing of the train whistle as abrasive or pleasing, welcome or annoying, the cognitive and non-cognitive components occur roughly simultaneously, providing them with a *temporal unity.*

(ii) The *focus of attention*—the object to which I respond at all these various levels—is the same (e.g., the bear or the train whistle), and that object is made the focus of attention by perception. If I were glad about the train, worried about the bear, and wondering if I locked the door when I left the house, there would be little temptation to coalesce them. The case of the train whistle is clearly different. In such a case, to insist on treating each element as if it were independent of the others is arbitrary.

(iii) Our *perceptual memories* are most frequently both cognitive and non-cognitive in content. To remember a wedding day or the funeral of a parent or a first success at skiing is hardly to recall a simple conceptualization of sense information. The memory is woven through with feelings,[25]* This blend that appears in memory is probably best accounted for as derivative from the blend of cognitive and non-cognitive elements in perceptual meaning. That is, perceptual memories may be best understood as recalled portions of perceptual meanings.

(iv) There is a *functional unity* of the cognitive and non- cognitive elements. That is, it is the *combination* that functions causally in determining the behavior that accompanies or follows perception. The cause of my subsequent behavior is not simply an isolated belief or judgment. It is generally the beliefs and feelings and desires and expectations, functioning jointly, that generate my behavior. I turn and run or shout for help, or whatever, because I see a bear unexpectedly in a threatening context, I am frightened, I want to survive, I feel confident about my running skills, etc. If any one of the elements were different, the outcome is likely to be affected. It is not simply the belief that a bear is present that makes me run; I see them and believe that they are present in the zoo and am not inclined to run away. Neither is it fear by itself that causes my behavior; fear alone might leave me fixed to the spot, unable to move. My desire to survive, my confidence in my running skills, and my belief that running from bears in the woods is usually wise, are long-standing dispositional states. In order to activate me they need to be joined to some more immediate psychological states—like my belief that this frightening thing is present. None of these elements *by itself* accounts for my response to the situation; it is the unity of them that plays the causal role. You also see the bear, but by contrast you head straight for it, adrenalin pumping, because you perceive him, optimistically, as a long-awaited challenge to your wrestling skills. The complex perceptual meaning you generate differs from mine and causes behavior quite different from mine.

It has been argued by others that mental states like beliefs need to be ascribed and understood holistically, as part of a coherent system.[26] I am pressing that point further and arguing that beliefs often play their causal roles only in conjunction with many other types of psychological states. Further, the connections among these various states are not simply linear, with a belief causing a desire which causes an action, etc. The cause of an action is *standardly* a concatenation of beliefs, emotions, desires, and the like, working together and simultaneously. By itself, this need not be taken as evidence for the psychological integration of cognitive and non-cognitive elements in perceptual meaning, but coupled with the various other considerations I have mentioned, their standard treatment in isolation from one another seems far less plausible.

(v) Finally, there is mounting empirical evidence that the cognitive and non-cognitive functions—in humans, at least—are profoundly interdependent. On the one hand, there is a growing consensus that emotions (but probably not moods) are at least partially cognitive—that is, they include, or are closely related to, cognitive states like beliefs. On the other side, certain cognitive states like memory, learning, and perception have been shown by psychological experiments to be affected by moods, emotions, etc. The functioning of these cognitive capacities as well as the content of such cognitive states are altered by non-cognitive factors.[27]*

Collectively, these considerations provide a good reason to think that cognitive and non-cognitive elements are linked in important ways in perception.

A second objection that one might want to make to my claims about the interaction of cognitive and non-cognitive states in perception is that the philosophic distinction between *seeing* and *seeing-as* needs to be put to work here. One might be inclined to say that the non-cognitive elements in the example of perceiving the bear ought to be analyzed in terms of a purely conceptual version of seeing-as. Thus, the conceptualization of the sense information would include not only recognizing an object as belonging to the class of bears, it would involve in addition the recognition that the object also belongs to the class of frightening things, challenging things, exciting things, etc. On such an analysis, it might be argued, the full content of consciousness could be taken into account without abandoning the purely cognitive model.

But there is a clear difference between seeing an object as a bear and seeing it as challenging or frightening. There are publicly accepted standards that make things fall into the class of bears. For a *perceived* object to belong to a class, fall under a concept, it normally must have certain sensible properties that distinguish it as a member of that class. Specifying such sensible properties can indeed be difficult business in some cases, but this general principle is at the heart of research in pattern recognition for computers.

On the other hand, things that are perceived as frightening or challenging don't have some required shape or set of parts. They are, rather, objects that generate certain responses in us, and their ability to generate those responses may have little to do with their sensible properties. It is likely to have a great deal to do with our individual past experiences or with our current needs, expectations, and capabilities. The perceiving of an object or event as frightening is not a matter of conceptually noting its similarity to other members of some class. It is, rather, an emotively charged taking-account-of this object or event in relation to me and my well-being here and now. Unfortunately, most philosophical discussions of *seeing-as* have attended only to cases of ambiguous figures—seeing a drawing as a duck or as a rabbit. Such cases easily lend themselves to discussion in terms of the simple altering of concepts.

To sum up this first part: I have argued that human perception is a more complex affair than the theories of Moore, Russell, and much subsequent analytic philosophy would suggest. It is more than the impersonal sorting of passively received sense data. And it is more than a meaning construction by an anonymous transcendental ego of the sort proposed by Husserl. Perception should, first of all, be understood within the darwinian context of individuals struggling for life and well-being within a particular environment. This, in turn, suggests an active subject capable of selective attention and able to relate what it perceives to its own needs and interests, its own cognitive and non-cognitive states. What needs to be added to theories of perception is not simply a more complicated version of impersonal conceptual structures (like Minsky "frames"). Rather, what is needed is an account of *perceptual meanings*—essentially indexical, and therefore highly personal, psychological entities that are generated by active perceiving subjects and that regularly incorporate non-cognitive as well as cognitive elements.

Mind And Mental States

If my contentions in the first part of this chapter are correct, they have some significant consequences for philosophy of mind. I have argued that certain tendencies in turn-of-the-century philosophy—perhaps especially in the analytic tradition—provided us with skewed accounts of perception. The approaches were atomistic, timeless, and purely cognitive; they ignored both Subjectivity and the function of perception on behalf of the living organism. I have also said that these approaches to perception have continued, largely unquestioned, to the present.

Much the same can be said about the theories of mind that were formulated during the first half of the century. No one *denied* that mental capacities had evolved in natural ways, but the implications of that point were generally neglected, lost in debates over the mind-body problem. As I noted at the outset, there have been exceptions of course. Some philosophers have attended to the relevance of evolution theory in connection with philosophy of mind. But the issues on which I have focused have not been the center of concern.

In this section I want to suggest that at least one very influential portion of contemporary philosophy of mind, namely Machine Functionalism, continues in the problematic tradition established by Russell. And while I think that the view suffers from each of the problems I have discussed in connection with perception, I shall highlight just two of the factors that mark its continuity with the early analytic tradition: its treatment of mental states in complete abstraction from their function on behalf of the living organism, and its isolation of cognitive states from non-cognitive states.

I should say at the outset that I shall use the language of "folk psychology" although I have no doubt that portions of it will require significant refinement as we learn more about neuroscience. Whatever the ultimate nature of psychological states, our present limited knowledge of them seems to require that we refer to them using the concepts like belief, desire and fear. But my primary concern is not to argue the case for either folk psychology or eliminativism. Rather, my point is that, whatever the final verdict on folk psychology, I believe that our theories of psychological states need to be constructed within a Darwinian framework. Most obviously, psychological states need to be understood as functioning on behalf of living organisms.

In the 1960's the issue of the metaphysical status of the mind, that had so troubled the mind-body theorists, was supplanted by *Functionalist* theories of mind. One might have expected that the emphasis on the *function* of mental states would lead quite naturally to a consideration of evolution. That, however, was not the direction taken.

One of the earliest and most sweeping statements of the view appears in one of Hilary Putnam's papers:

> ... these examples support the idea that our substance, what we are made of, places almost no first order restrictions on our form. And ... what we are really interested in, as Aristotle saw, is form and not matter. *What is our intellectual form?* is the question, not what the matter is. And whatever our substance may be, soul-stuff, or matter or Swiss cheese, it is not going to place any interesting first order restrictions on the answer to this question. [28]

More recently Putnam has reaffirmed his view:

> My 'functionalism' insisted that, in principle, a machine.., a human being, a creature with a silicon chemistry, and a disembodied spirit could all work much the same way when described at the relevant level of abstraction, and that it is just wrong to think that the essence of our minds is our 'hardware.' This much—and it was central to my former view—I shall not be giving up in this book, and indeed it still seems to me to be as true and as important as it ever did.[29]

Jerry Fodor has put the point this way:

> ... there is a level of abstraction at which the generalizations of psychology are most naturally pitched and, as things appear to be turning out, that level of abstraction collapses across the differences between physically quite different kinds of systems. .... , what does seem to provide a natural domain for psychological theorizing, at least in cognitive psychology, is something like the set of (real and possible) information processing systems. ... This is a state of affairs which cries out for a *relational* treatment of mental properties, one which identifies them in ways that abstract from the physiology of their bearers. [30]

These are the claims that concern me: that our theories of mind or of psychological states ought to abstract from the physical makeup of the systems that exhibit such states. For its supporters, such a view makes it possible to formulate an adequate psychological theory that could apply in principle to systems as diverse as human beings, Martians, and computers. That is to say, such a view not only makes it possible, but takes it to be a desideratum that psychological theories be formulated in such a way as to be equally applicable to a specifiable set of both living and non-living systems.

This particular goal of Functionalism is, I shall argue, misguided. The effort to provide a model for psychological states that abstracts from all physiological aspects of the system ignores critical considerations arising from evolutionary biology.

The principal issue here is not the *causal history* of these states. The issue is their *function*. Even if they had arisen through intelligent engineering of some sort, the essential point is that they function on behalf of the living organism in its struggle for existence. So the difficulty with formulating psychological theories that are intended to apply to both living and non-living systems is not that the states of one arose through natural selection while the states of the other did not. The difficulty is that in one case, psychological states function in the service of the system itself; in the other case, they do not.

I shall approach the issue from three different angles. At the outset, I shall consider the restricted set of paradigm cognitive states—beliefs and desires—that are normally the focus of Functionalist theorizing. Even here, I shall argue, one finds darwinian commitments to the *living organism*. My second approach will argue, however, that there are good reasons to think that the context for Functionalist accounts of psychological states needs to be expanded. More precisely, it cannot reasonably exclude certain non-cognitive states like *emotions*. These, in turn, carry with them even more specific commitments to the physiology of the living organism. Lastly, I shall argue that the Functionalist position really incorporates two distinct claims—one about definitions and one about ontology. The former, when suitably expanded, turns out to be acceptable; the latter is unjustified.

Let me begin by considering how beliefs and desires function in living organisms like ourselves. If the darwinian framework is right, an adequate *functional* theory of beliefs and desires ought to take account of the fact that the beliefs and desires of living organisms consistently have a view to the needs of the organism itself. One consequence of this is that when the Functionalist provides an account of the causal relations that link input with the output of the system—and this, of course, is a role that beliefs and desires play—he needs to include two elements that have been consistently omitted.

At the early end of the causal chain, one needs to have an account of why the system *selects* certain inputs for focused attention. We are continually confronted with far more data than we are able to attend to, so, as I argued in my discussion of perception, the perceiver must select some of the data for focused attention. Any datum that has immediate relevance to the organism's survival and well-being needs to be selected for attention if the organism is to endure for long. In human beings at least, beliefs and desires about the environment, about the current state of the individual herself, and about the relationship between the two, play an important role in this process of selection. Obviously, not every input carries information about a threat or a benefit to the organism. But the organism is, and must be, habitually alert to the possibility that any input *could* carry such information. An organism needs to be standardly on the lookout for items that may be relevant to what it believes to be its own well-being (understood in a broad sense). We are not, of course, always successful in our selections. But fallible though the selective mechanism is, we would not last long without it. Thus, the data that become available as the content of conscious states are, to a considerable extent, an outcome of the fact that the system is a living organism concerned with its own survival and well-being.

In social animals like ourselves, that concern for survival and well-being will extend to others who are related to us by biological or social ties. And, as Darwin commented in his *Descent of Man*, the scope of our concern for others—even for the welfare of other species—ought to expand as we learn to see more clearly the long-range consequences of our actions. The point is not to argue for an exclusively self-interested viewpoint on the part of human beings and other living organisms. But it is important to note the fact that a self-interested viewpoint is *part* of our normal and necessary psychological makeup. This decisively differentiates us from non-living systems.

Later in the causal chain, moving toward the behavioral "output" of the system, one needs an account of the factors that motivate the organism to give *differing weights* to individual beliefs and desires, such that some of these but not others will govern its behavior. Within a darwinian framework, beliefs and desires (and other psychological states) will be "weighted" in ways that give persistent importance to concerns about the organism's own well-being or harm (as well as that of relevant others). So, for example, in the process that determines its ensuing behavior, an organism's belief that she is in imminent danger will normally override a belief that her hair needs combing; a desire for a hot dog will normally be overridden by a desire to avoid a mugging. One cannot give a satisfactory account of the causal roles of beliefs and desires if one ignores the "weight" that each has for a particular organism at a particular time. And one cannot adequately account for those weights if one ignores the organism's concern for *its own* well-being.

These two factors, selective attention and the weighting of beliefs and desires, constitute a natural *requirement* for living organisms. Without them, organisms could not survive and provide for their needs for any length of time. Here we have one of the decisive strands in the evolutionary account of our psychological states. Non-living systems like computers have no need of such adaptive mechanisms. Their continued "survival" and well-being is a matter of concern to us, not to them.

But beliefs and desires do not constitute the whole story. Among the psychological states that function on behalf of the organism, non-cognitive states like emotions also count. I shall focus my discussion on just one particular type of emotion—namely, fear. But since I take fear to involve beliefs and desires as well as physiological events, my claims should have some fairly broad implications, and they will extend the points I just made about beliefs and desires.

A few years ago, Georges Rey argued[31] that Functionalists seem to overlook the emotions in their accounts of psychological states and that, since the emotions tie in closely with human physiology, Functionalist theories may need to take the physiological composition of the human system more seriously than they have. More recently, Rey has said (in conversation) that he is less convinced by that argument than he was at the time he wrote it. Rey's original conviction seems to have been weakened by considerations like the following: If one were to remove all the physiological components from an emotion (say, the sweaty palms, the lump in the throat, etc.), what would be lost? Might not the coldly cognitive components (say, a certain set of beliefs) perform precisely the same function that the original emotion did? That is to say, aren't the cognitive components the only functionally relevant ones, and therefore, can't the physiology of the system be bypassed?

The answer to this question is, I think, negative. My argument proceeds in two stages. First I shall consider the *cognitive* component of emotions like fear. Even here the physical makeup of the system is germane. Then I shall turn to the role of the explicitly *physiological* components and shall argue that at least some of these are functionally important for the system's ensuing behavior.

A couple of caveats may be in order. My discussion centers almost entirely on fear. Much of what I say about it will not apply, without modification, to various other emotions. Nonetheless, if it can be shown that there is at least one sort of emotion that is inextricably linked with the status of the system as a living organism as well as with its cognitive states, then the Functionalist claim about the irrelevance of the composition of the system can be challenged. I might point out, too, that I think fear is not idiosyncratic in this respect. In addition to the fact that it incorporates beliefs and desires—states that are common in all sorts of other contexts—it seems clear that a similar sort of case could be mounted for other psychological states, for example, anger and sexual attraction.

Secondly, I shall use a fairly standard model of fear, but I won't argue here for its adequacy since my present argument does not depend on it. I shall assume that fear is a *complex* state that includes one or more beliefs, one or more desires, and one or more physiological changes in the system. On my view all three elements are each necessary and jointly sufficient. But my argument will stand even if one identifies fear simply with the physiological changes in the system (as Jerome Shaffer does[32]) or with the cognitive events (as Robert Solomon seems to do[33]). One crucial aspect of my argument concerns the set of *causal* links that connect the beliefs, desires, and physiological events; whether one identifies fear with just one of these elements or with all three, the relevant causal links remain intact. And for the Functionalist, causal links are crucially important. But more on that later.

Let me begin with a consideration of the cognitive side of fear. And in order to focus attention more directly on Darwin's comments about the "universal struggle for life," consider a case in which the organism takes its life to be in danger. It is widely accepted that conscious fear generally involves some sort of belief, at the very least the belief that some dangerous thing (let's say a bear) is present or is likely to appear.[34]* So as a first approximation one might say that a belief like the following is involved in one's fear of a bear:

B_1: *There is a bear present (or in the vicinity).* But it is clear that the content of the belief must be richer than that. If, for example, I am visiting the zoo, the appearance of a bear does not generally fill me with fear. That is to say, the belief involved in fear is not simply about the surrounding environment. At the very least the belief must be expanded to something like the following:

B_2: *There is a bear present in a way that makes him a threat to my life or well-being.* In addition to the fact that the belief is not simply about the bear, it has two further features. First, it is what John Perry calls "essentially indexical."[35] That is to say, the content is not simply about *someone* being in a dangerous situation; it is a belief about *me*. Secondly, the belief is about me in a very particular way—it is about a threat to my continued life. Here again we have a piece of the evolutionary thread. The content of the beliefs involved in fear includes essential reference to what the organism takes to be relevant to its own life.

Another piece of that evolutionary thread appears in the concomitant *desire*. One of the factors that makes this belief function in the way that it does—e.g., causing me to run or to reach for a rifle—is that it is accompanied by my desire to assure my own continued survival and well-being. Notice that my desires here are not simply that I continue to "function." They include the desire to avoid pain, for example. That is to say, the functional role of beliefs that occur in fear depends on the fact that I am the *kind of system* that I am, namely a living organism capable of pain and death. Rocks and silicon chips, not being threatened with pain or death, have no need for these sorts of beliefs or desires or their related fears.

My first claim, then, is that even the cognitive component of one's fear is tied to the fact that one is a living organism. To this extent, physiology is not a matter of indifference in accounting for cognitive states. So even if one views the emotions as purely cognitive or supposes that the physiological events associated with emotions can be ignored, one is still not justified in disregarding the "stuff" of which the system is composed. Whether it is carbon-based or silicon-based "stuff" is not the relevant issue; whether it is living or non-living is at the heart of the matter.

Let me turn now to the explicitly physiological components of fear. While we do not yet have anything like a complete story on the physiology of emotions, we do have a growing body of data on a number of significant physiological changes that take place in the system undergoing an emotion like fear. Some of these changes seem to have lost their functional significance for human beings. Sweaty palms may be a case in point. Other physiological changes in the system do, however, appear to play an important role in preparing that system for its ensuing behavior. Commenting on patterns of autonomic activation in states of intense aversive emotion, Joseph LeDoux says:

> One of Cannon's most influential proposals was that the arousal of emotion induces an emergency reaction that prepares the organism for struggle, for fight or flight. . . . This emergency response involves diffuse sympathetic activation and, among other things, releases epinephrine from the adrenal medulla, increases respiration, and thereby stimulates the conversion of lactic acid to glucose, and redistributes blood flow away from the viscera and skin and to the active skeletal muscles. Circulating epinephrine, in turn, releases glycogen from the liver, which is then available for consumption as glucose by the active muscles. These adjustments thus mobilize the organism's energy stores, redistribute blood away from the body surface (where cuts and scratches produce hemorrhaging in proportion to the amount of blood available) and toward the tissues most in need of substrate. [36]

These comments are not specifically about fear alone, but are about intense aversive emotions in general, which surely include fear. And while the precise details of the physiological events involved in different emotions are still subject to debate, there seems to be increasing experimental evidence that something close to this story is true for emotions like fear.

My purpose in quoting at some length is to make clear that the physiological changes that occur in these emotions are not all epiphenomenal. They are not simply factors like sweating palms or a lump in the throat that might conceivably be dropped out of consideration with no explanatory loss, as one objection suggests. Increasing the supply of oxygen, re-routing blood resources, etc., are aids to the organism in carrying out what it takes to be its most promising behavioral response. That is to say, many of the physiological changes are highly functional for the organism in that they prepare it to deal with its environment in a way that is most likely to contribute to its own survival. Once again, the evolutionary thread.

One might defend the Functionalist position here in either of two ways—by eliminating emotions like fear from accounts of the psychological, or by arguing that non-living systems like computers are capable of exhibiting such emotions.

First, one might argue that states like fear belong to the natural sciences rather than to psychology, and that they therefore do not pose any difficulty for Functionalist theories of the psychological. This sort of claim can take two forms. It can simply argue, as Shaffer does, that emotions are purely physiological events. If that were true, then it ought to be reasonable to assign them to theories in physiology. Alternatively, one might include emotions like fear among the propositional attitudes but argue that their cognitive components (beliefs and desires) can be adequately separated from their physiological components and can be incorporated into a psychological theory, leaving the physiological events to physiology. Fodor seems to take this position.

If one takes the first view, considering the emotions to be purely physiological events, it is difficult to explain the apparent intentionality of emotions like fear. They do seem to be "about" something.

There is a more pressing difficulty for the Functionalist, however, and it affects both the first and the second way of trying to eliminate emotions from psychological theories. It is widely agreed that whatever the precise nature of the emotion itself, there is at least a causal relation between the relevant beliefs and desires on the one hand, and the physiological changes, on the other. So the attempt to provide a theory of such beliefs and desires, while abstracting from some of their causal relations to other states *that also contribute to the ensuing behavior of the system*—such an attempt would surely seem to run counter to the whole Functionalist project. Their concern is, after all, to provide an account of psychological states in terms of their functional or causal relations. It hardly seems satisfactory from a theoretical point of view to simply ignore some subset of these relations. Notice that if LeDoux's account of the physiological changes that occur in intense aversive emotions is correct, those changes are *functionally* relevant to the organism's ensuing behavior. The changes are not analogous, for example, to the raising of the temperature in a computer by its carrying out a calculation. The latter may indeed be caused by the calculating, but it is functionally irrelevant to the outcome of the calculation (except, perhaps, by some bizarre accident). In the case of the living organism, many of the physiological changes that occur in states like fear assist the organism in carrying out its behavioral response to the perceived threat. They, unlike the heating up of the computer, are not epiphenomenal.

The suggestion, then, that fear or its physiological dimensions can simply be relegated to physiology won't do. Philosophy of mind and particularly a Functionalist philosophy of mind needs to give some account of it. Furthermore, if my earlier claims about the *content* of the beliefs and desires that occur in fear is true, then any attempt to treat these cognitive states separately from the correlated physiological events would still leave the beliefs' and desires' functional relations with the living organism intact.

A second line of defense for the Functionalist might go something like this: while it is true that states like fear *are* appropriate subjects for a theory of psychological states, there is no reason to suppose that non-living systems like computers cannot exhibit them.

Very likely a robot could at least be made to behave *as if* it feared something. But there are several points to notice here. The first is that a living organism would provide the model, the constraints, on what states need to be instantiated and how they need to be related. That is to say, the robot could simulate the functioning of a system quite different from itself. But the functional setup of the robot would not abstract completely from the makeup of the system that it mimics. On the contrary, its functional states would be organized in just the way that a living system requires that they be organized. To duplicate the requirements of a living organism is hardly to abstract totally from the makeup of the system.

In some of the strong versions of Functionalism, the modelling process has been reversed. It is assumed that the computer can be taken as an adequate model for constructing a theory of human psychological states. This assumption may be encouraged by the fact that we know a great deal more about how the computer works than we know about ourselves. Consequently, since we can control the research much more easily, the strategy has pragmatic value. But if the goal is to provide a genuine model for understanding human psychological states, then the research needs to begin with *us* and be constrained by the sorts of causal relations that seem to be functioning in us. The problem with getting the modelling relation reversed is that we get trapped by a false kind of parsimony. One is tempted to suppose that if the computer can get by without recourse to emotions, then it must be possible for a simple belief-desire psychology to give an adequate account of *our* mental workings. However, if our normal functioning incorporates emotions as well as persistent beliefs and desires relevant to our own survival and well-being, and if all these states contribute to the determination of our behavior, then a parsimony that omits them is too costly.

A second point to notice about computer simulations that incorporate some version of emotions is that the latter are gratuitous for the system. A computer functions in *its* environment perfectly well without them. This is one outcome of the fact that the computer does not require friends or pleasure, pain-detectors or sexual satisfaction. We, normally, do. The computer is not a candidate for pain or suffering; we are. The presence or absence of such things causes states in us that motivate us to behave in certain characteristic ways. However well the computer simulates the behavior associated with protecting itself, the computer itself has nothing really at stake. To return to the darwinian point with which I began, the computer is not engaged in a struggle for life. And this, for obvious reasons— neither life nor death are genuine possibilities for it. Perhaps the closest it can come to simulating death is to turn itself off or be unplugged. But unlike death these states are of course, temporary and reversible.

The issue is not whether a non-living system could be made to act on its own behalf; it could, perhaps, be programmed to have persistent self-regarding states. But these are clearly not *required* for its normal operation. A non-living system can deal with data continuously and permanently *without* referencing that data to the well-being of the system itself. By contrast, normal living systems need continually to act on their own behalf. The information they receive about their environment is systematically treated as having some possible bearing on their own well-being. A psychological theory that fails to take account of this distinction between the *requirements for normal function* in living systems and those in non-living systems is missing something vital.

The third point to notice in connection with the computer simulation of fear is that Functionalism defines psychological state-types by their causal relations. So a state can be defined as fear just in case it enters into the appropriate set of causal relations. If, as I have argued, fear plays a causal role in how an organism responds to what it takes to be relevant to its struggle for life and well-being, that fact cannot be arbitrarily discounted when one gives a functional account of fear. To claim, then, that one has the same state in a system in which it does not play that same causal role is a mistake on purely Functionalist grounds.

One of the most significant ways in which Functionalism represented an improvement over classical behaviorism was that it required the addition of causal factors *between* stimulus and response. What emerges from my discussion so far is that these intermediate links in the causal chain include at least two things that have been neglected by certain versions of Functionalism. First, living organisms have a persistent and overriding set of beliefs and desires that concern their own survival and well-being. These exert a causal influence on both selective attention to input and on the weighting of beliefs and desires that govern behavioral output. Secondly, the causal links between input and output often include not only beliefs and desires but also emotions, and these latter incorporate physiological events in the system that are functionally relevant to its ensuing behavior. In cases of fear and similar emotional states, the psychological and the physiological are not causally insulated from one another. And one of the most compelling reasons for their integration has been provided for us by Darwin—living things that have psychological states use them in their struggle for life and well-being. Those psychological states can exert causal influence on the physiology of the organism in such a way that both the psychological states and the altered physiological state contribute to the behavior of the organism. It seems to follow, therefore, that a plausible account of human psychological functions cannot be given in isolation from their role on behalf of the living organism.

So Functionalism must admit some constraints on the sorts of systems that can exhibit certain psychological states. But this is not unusual; functional characterizations of almost anything implicitly acknowledge constraints on the sort of properties a system must have if it is to carry out that function. As someone else has pointed out, pencil sharpeners can't be made of whipped cream. States like fear need occur only in organisms whose body chemistry can be stirred to influence their bodily behavior in ways that might have survival value.

This leads me to my third and final argument against Machine Functionalism. The Functionalist claim with which I began really has two dimensions. One dimension attempts to *define* psychological states by what they do rather than by what they are made of. This adds an important dimension to the largely structural accounts of mental states offered by Russell and Husserl. A second demension of the claim attempts to free psycholgoical theories from all specific *ontological* commitments. The argument of this paper has no serious quarrel with the definitional aspirations of Functionalism. It may be the case that we can construct our clearest and most useful definitions of particular psychological states by describing their causal relations with one another and with a range of other states of the organism.

But the fact that such definitions make no reference to the composition of the state does not entail that they make no *assumptions* about the sorts of systems capable of realizing such functions. A carburetor (a favorite example) might well be given a functional definition that makes no reference to its composition. But notice that the materials capable of carrying out its functions are not unlimited. Peanut butter won't do it; water, smoke, cotton candy, and a host of other things don't have the properties required to carry out the function. Multiple realizability ought not be confused with unlimited realizability.

It may indeed be possible to construct theories of psychological states for a variety of living types, like Martians, chimps, dogs, and human beings. But they will need to differ in critical respects from the theories we construct for the information-processing states of non-living systems like computers. A living organism is not functionally equivalent to a system that is capable only of impersonal, purely cognitive states, because the states that are causally efficacious for an organism are not merely cognitive and impersonal states.

The definitional goals of Functionalism may be unobjectionable; its efforts in the direction of ontological neutrality are not.

It is important to see that my claim here is not the standard one that has already been made by others, to the effect that Functionalism (and strong versions of Artificial Intelligence) overlook the role of such things as emotions in the life of the human person. My concern is not that Functionalism is incomplete in that it has omitted one or two elements that simply need to be appended to the theory. Rather, I am arguing that the very things about which Functionalism *does* theorize—namely, cognitive states—cannot be treated adequately when they are systematically divorced either from their function on behalf of the living body or from their relations with non-cognitive states of the organism.[37*] It is not simply a question of incompleteness; it is a matter of misrepresentation.

Conclusion

I have argued that traditional philosophical theories of human perception are incomplete, that they need to take account of Subjectivity and of a complex psychological entity that I have called "perceptual meaning." That, in turn, requires that they give due consideration to the indexical and non-cognitive components of perceptual experience. Further, I have argued that all of this has repercussions for Functionalist theories of mind. Human mental function is intimately connected with the fact that we are living organisms, pursuing our own well-being and survival. Adequate theories of mind and perception cannot ignore these facts.

At the turn of the century, as philosophy attempted to redefine itself, some enormously important choices were made. They continue to echo through contemporary philosophy. One of the most important of these choices was the elimination of all evolutionary considerations, whether they originated with Darwin or with the Evolutionist philosophers. The reasons that were offered in support of the decision to exclude evolution are open to question, and yet many of the consequences of that decision are still with us. Our theories—following Russell especially, but also to some extent

Moore and Husserl—continue to treat both perception and mind as virtually disembodied, a-temporal, impersonal, and purely cognitive.

I have provided little more than a sketch of how we might pick up the evolutionary thread that was dropped and might begin to formulate theories of perception and mind that take adequate account of some of Darwin's most fundamental insights about living organisms. Philosophical theories that purport to deal with our perceptual commerce with our environment or with the function of our mental states cannot ignore the Darwinian insight that a living organism is engaged in a struggle for existence and well-being. Once that fact has been conceded, then our embodiment, our active Subjectivity, the indexical character of our psychological states, and the integration of our non-cognitive states with our cognitive states, should all be seen as cardinal factors in our philosophical theories about ourselves.

Notes

Introduction

1. Bertrand Russell, *Our Knowledge of the External World* (London: Allen & Unwin, 1914) p. 26.
2. On the importance of naturalism, rather than Hegelianism, in late nineteenth-century Germany, see Hans Sluga, *Gottlob Frege* (London: Routledge & Kegan Paul, 1980), especially chapter 1.
3. Robert Marsh, in Russell, *Logic and Knowledge* (London: Allen & Unwin, 1956) p. 365.

Chapter 1

1. See William Whewell, *The Philosophy of the Inductive Sciences* (London: Parker, 1847) new ed., vol.2, p. 77.
2. Charles Darwin, *The Origin of Species*, 6th ed. (New York: Modern Library, n.d.) p. 98; see also his earlier accounts in the first edition facsimile (Cambridge, MA: Harvard University Press, 1964) pp. 61, 80-81, 470-471.
3. Darwin, *Origin of Species*, 1st ed., p. 81. There has been some debate about the issue of "neutral" variations, but Darwin is quite explicit in this text.
4. Darwin, *The Life and Letters of Charles Darwin*, ed. by Francis Darwin (New York: Basic, 1959) vol.i, p. 284.
5. For a somewhat different view on this, see James Collins, "Darwin's Impact on Philosophy," *Thought*, 34, June, 1959.
6. Darwin, *Origin of Species*, 1st ed., p. 488.
7. Darwin, *Origin of Species*, 1st ed., pp. 62-63; it is perhaps worth noting that these passages remain unchanged in the 6th edition, pp. 52-53.
8. For a discussion of the differences between Malthus' and Darwin's conceptions of the struggle for existence, see Peter Bowler, "Malthus, Darwin, and the Concept of Struggle," *Journal of the History of Ideas*, 37, 1976. In the same paper, Bowler argues that the Darwinian notion of struggle is to be carefully distinguished from the *laissez-faire* economics of Adam Smith.
9. Darwin, *Origin of Species*, 1st ed., p. 62.

10. Peter Bowler makes a similar point in *Evolution, The History of an Idea* (Berkeley: University of California Press, 1984) p. 151.

11. George Daniels makes an even stronger point: "Darwin used the word 'struggle' in a very broad sense—actual cases of conflict among individuals, he thought, were comparatively unimportant. The more meaningful struggle was the effort to gain food, to protect oneself from the weather, or to procreate." *Darwinism Comes to America* (Waltham, MA: Blaisdell, 1968) p. xiii.

12. Darwin, *Origin of Species*, 1st ed., pp. 62-63.

13. I should perhaps point out that I am not concerned here with the issue of the *unit of selection*. Darwin thought that it was the individual, Wallace thought it was the group, and Richard Dawkins thinks that it is the genes. Whatever the correct view is, it seems to be the case that individual organisms are the primary centers at which the struggle is carried on. They perceive their environment, they eat, they fight, they build houses, they mate, etc. The organism may ultimately be acting on behalf of the group or the genes, but both the group and the genes make use of the individual organism with its bodily, mental (and moral) capacities in the struggle for life. This is all I need to assume in the discussion that follows.

14. Unfortunately, Gertrude Himmelfarb is not alone in her remarkably narrow interpretation of Darwin's notion of the struggle for existence as exclusively competitive. She says: "Not only the concept of the survival of the fittest but even that of the struggle for existence has been found to be less obvious and more dubious than might seem to be the case at first sight. For if competition is a primary fact of nature, so is cooperation." *Darwin and the Darwinian Revolution* (New York: Norton, 1968) p. 317. Barry Gale offers a cogent analysis of some of the reasons that Darwin's use of the notion of *struggle*, intended in a "large and metaphorical sense," was so often interpreted quite literally. See his "Darwin and the Concept of a Struggle for Existence: A Study in the Extrascientific Origins of Scientific Ideas," *Isis*, 63 (1972), pp. 321-344.

15. Darwin, *Descent of Man*, 1st ed. facsimile (Princeton, NJ: Princeton University Press, 1981) p. 98.

16. Darwin, *Descent of Man*, pp. 135-137.

17. Darwin, *Descent of Man*, p. 46.

18. See Donald Griffin's work on this issue, most recently *Animal Minds* (Chicago: University of Chicago Press, 1992).

19. Darwin, *Autobiography*, p. 109. Descartes, incidentally, makes comments that suggest his openness to the possibility of evolution. See, for example, his *Principles of Philosophy* 3, #45.

20. It should be noted that Darwin's later work incorporated traces of a Lamarckian account of things—with "use and disuse"—in spite of the fact that in his early thinking he was strongly antipathetic to Lamarck's views. In a letter to J.D. Hooker, in 1844, he says: "Heaven forfend me from Lamarck nonsense of 'a tendency to progression,' 'adaptations from the slow willing of animals,' etc! But the conclusions I am led to are not widely different from his; though the means of change are wholly so." See Darwin, *Life and Letters*, vol.I, p. 384; see also p. 399, 542. And as late as 1863, in a letter to Charles Lyell, Darwin protests

that his view is different from Lamarck's in virtually every respect except that both concern the evolution of species. See Darwin, *Life and Letters*, vol.II, pp. 198-9.

21. Cf. Darwin, *Descent of Man*, pp. 116-121.

22. Charles Darwin,*The Autobiography of Charles Darwin*, ed. Nora Barlow, (New York: Norton, 1969) pp. 88-89; recounted also in *The Life and Letters of Charles Darwin*, vol.i, p. 280.

23. See Michael Bradie, "Evolutionary Epistemology as Naturalized Epistemology," in Kai Hahlweg and C.A. Hooker, eds., *Issues in Evolutionary Epistemology* (Albany: SUNY Press, 1989) p. 408.

24. Darwin, *Descent of Man*, p. 159.

25. Patricia Greenspan gives a particularly good example of a case in which a feeling of uneasiness can in fact be at odds with one's explicit beliefs about a situation. One can feel suspicious before one has any clear evidence that something is amiss. See *Emotions and Reasons* (New York: Routledge, 1988) p. 5-6. See also Joseph LeDoux, "Emotion, Memory, and the Brain," *Scientific American*, June, 1994, 50-57.

26. For some recent experimental evidence regarding the survival value of the interaction of cognitive and emotive systems in the brain, see Joseph LeDoux, "Cognitive-Emotional Interactions in the Brain," *Cognition and Emotion*, 1989, 3 (4), pp. 267-289; and "Emotion, Memory, and the Brain," *Scientific American*, June, 1994, pp. 50-57.

27. Anthony O'Hear argues against what he calls "hyperselectionism"—the view that every variation must somehow be relevant to adaptation and survival. He argues, along with Stephen Jay Gould and others, that some variations are simply neutral and have no direct bearing on survival. (See Darwin, *Origin of Species*, 1st ed., p. 81, for a similar view.) Surely some of our intellectual capacities fit that description. An ability to compose poetry or to enjoy Mozart need not have an immediate link with survival. These contribute to a level of well-being far beyond mere survival. See O'Hear's "Has the Theory of Evolution any Relevance to Philosophy?," *Ratio*, 29, June, 1987. (It is possible, of course, that that level of well-being might itself be a contributor to survival. Current psychological evidence seems to point in that direction.)

28. John Passmore, "Darwin's Impact on British Metaphysics," *Victorian Studies*, 3, 1959, p. 42.

29. John Herman Randall, "The Changing Impact of Darwin on Philosophy," *Journal of the History of Ideas*, XXII, No.4, 1961, p. 436. While Randall's analysis is problematic in a number of ways (e.g., he includes Auguste Comte among the "adjusters" of Darwin's views in spite of the fact that Comte died two years before *Origin of Species* was published), his general distinction between the "adjusters" and the "transformers" is a useful one.

30. See Randall for example.

31. John Passmore locates Spencer in the "agnosticism of the right," by which he means the group of thinkers who acknowledged that God's existence and nature could not be demonstrated by reason, but who concluded that "the true

238 Philosophy and the Darwinian Legacy

Philosophy and the Darwinian Legacy

238

source of such knowledge must be Revelation." John Passmore, "Darwin's Impact on British Metaphysics," p. 45.

32. See Russell's "Pragmatism," in *Collected Papers*, VI, (London: Routledge, 1992), p. 280; the paper was originally published in *The Edinburgh Review* (unsigned) in 1909, and was reprinted the following year in his *Philosophical Essays*.

33. Nietzsche's emphasis on the inner power of the individual to shape things suggests a Lamarckian account of evolution. And some commentators see Nietzsche as rejecting Darwin in favor of Lamarck. The evolution of the *Ubermensch*, for example, is thought to be Lamarckian because it is "consciously striven for." But there is reason to think that this may be an oversimplification of Nietzsche's view. For example, where Nietzsche stressed the centrality of the will, Lamarck insisted on the importance of habit. It may indeed be the case that Nietzsche was influenced by Lamarck's views and was more sympathetic to them than he was to Darwin's account of evolution. But it is probably misleading to simply characterize him as a Lamarckian. See Robert Richards, *Darwin and the Emergence of Evolutionary Theories of Mind and Behavior* (Chicago: University of Chicago Press, 1987) p. 51.

34. Nietzsche, *The Joyful Wisdom*, vol.10 of *Complete Works*, ed. by Oscar Levy (New York: Russell & Russell, 1964 [originally published in 1882]) #349.

35. See Nietzsche, *Will to Power*, vol.II (vol.16 of *Complete Works*), #656-657.

36. Quoted by Walter Kaufmann, from Nietzsche's Ubermensch, in *Nietzsche. Philosopher, Psychologist, Antichrist* (Cleveland: World Publishing/Meridian Books, 1950), p. 142.

37. Nietzsche, *Will to Power*, vol.II, #684, 654, 682, and 685.

38. See, for example, Russell, *The Collected Papers*, XII, pp. 36-37, 68, and 171.

39. J.S. Mill, *System of Logic*, 8th ed. (New York: Harper, 1874) p. 355 footnote.

40. J.S. Mill, *The Later Letters of John Stuart Mill*, vol.XV, ed. by Francis Mineka & Dwight Lindley (Toronto: University of Toronto Press, 1972) p. 695.

41. John Stuart Mill, "Theism," in *Essays on Ethics, Religion, and Society, vol.10 of Collected Works, ed. by J.M. Robson* (Toronto: University of Toronto Press, 1969) pp. 449-50.

42. cf. J.W. Burrow, *Evolution and Society: A Study in Victorian Social Theory* (Cambridge: Cambridge University Press, 1966) pp. 78-81.

43. See Alexander Vucinich, *Darwin in Russian Thought*, (Berkeley: University of California Press, 1988) p. 356.

44. Friedrich Engels, *Socialism: Utopian and Scientific*, reprinted in *Marx-Engels Reader*, 2nd ed., ed. by Robert C. Tucker (New York: Norton, 1978) p. 697.

45. For further discussion of the relationship between the views of Marx and Engels and those of Darwin, see Peter Bowler, *Evolution. History of an Idea*, p. 102, and Alfred Kelly, *The Descent of Darwin*, (Chapel Hill: University of North Carolina Press, 1981) chapter 7.

46. In light of all this, I find puzzling the comment by James Collins in 1959 that "the internal growth of philosophy itself during the past hundred years has been strongly shaped by the current of evolutionism." ("Darwin's Inpact on Philosophy," *Thought*, 34, June, 1959, p. 186.)

47. I don't think that J.H. Randall overstates the case by much when he says that "British empiricism has remained pre-Darwinian in its basic assumptions pretty much down to the present [1961] in A.J. Ayer." Randall, "The Changing Impact of Darwin on Philosophy," p. 438.

48. For some recent discussions of evolutionary epistemology see Henry Plotkin, *Darwin Machines and the Nature of Knowledge* (Cambridge, MA: Harvard, 1994); Nicholas Rescher, ed., *Evolution, Cognition, and Realism* (Lanham, Maryland: University Press of America, 1990); Kai Hahlweg and C.A. Hooder, eds., *Issues in Evolutionary Epistemology* (Albany: State University of New York Press, 1989); Gerard Radnitzky and W.W. Bartley, eds., *Evolutionary Epistemology, Rationality, and the Sociology of Knowledge* (LaSalle, IL: Open Court, 1987); Franz Wuketits, ed., *Concepts and Approaches in Evolutionary Epistemology* (Dordrecht: Reidel, 1984).

49. Most recently James Rachels, *Created from Animals: The Moral Implications of Darwinism* (Oxford: Oxford University Press, 1990); Robert Richards, *Darwin and the Emergence of Evolutionary Theories of Mind and Behavior* (Chicago: University of Chicago Press, 1987) Appendix 2; Matthew Nitecki and Doris Nitecki, eds., *Evolutionary Ethics* (Albany: SUNY, 1993).

50. For a recent commentary on difficulties with some of the work in both evolutionary epistemology and evolutionary ethics, see Bernard Williams, "Evolutionary Theory: Epistemology and Ethics," in *Evolution and Its Influence*, Alan Grafen, ed. (Oxford: Clarendon, 1989); also Anthony O'Hear, "Has the theory of Evolution any Relevance to Philosophy?"

51. Michael Ruse, *Taking Darwin Seriously* (Oxford: Basil Blackwell, 1986) p. 279.

52. Mayr, "Prologue: Some Thoughts on the History of the Evolutionary Synthesis," in *The Evolutionary Synthesis*, ed. by Ernst Mayr and William Provine (Cambridge: Harvard, 1980) p. 30.

53. Ernst Mayr, "Prologue: . . . ," pp. 5-6; Peter Bowler, *The Eclipse of Darwinism* (Baltimore: Johns Hopkins, 1983) p. 7.

54. See William Provine, *The Origins of Theoretical Population Genetics* (Chicago: University of Chicago Press, 1971) p. 5.

55. For a fine recent discussion of sexual selection, see Helena Cronin, *The Ant and the Peacock* (Cambridge: Cambridge University Press, 1991).

56. Vernon Kellogg, in his excellent book *Darwinism To-day* (New York: Henry Holt, 1908), suggests that sexual selection was "in the eyes of most biologists . . . practically discredited." p. 86

57. Kellogg, *Darwinism To-day*, p. 79.

58. Francis Galton and the biometricians were soon to take care of at least a portion of that criticism.

59. See Ernst Mayr, *The Growth of Biological Thought* (Cambridge: Harvard University Press, 1982) p. 113; Mayr, "Prologue . . . ," p. 9; Peter Bowler, *Eclipse of Darwinism*, pp. 13-14.

60. See William Provine, *The Origins of Theoretical Population Genetics*, p. 11.

61. Hugo de Vries, *The Mutation Theory*, trans. by J.B. Farmer and A.D. Darbishire; 2 vols. (LaSalle: Open Court, 1910 [Orig. Pub. 1901-1903]).

62. Mayr contends that Mutation theorists retained an implicit commitment to

essentialism, treating species like clearly defined types rather than simply like biological populations. "Prologue . . . ," p. 6. He continues, "No other concept was as detrimental as the prevalence of typological thinking (essentialism)." pp. 17-18.

63. For an extended discussion of the divisions between the Darwinians and the Mendelians see William Provine, *The Origin of Theoretical Population Genetics.*

64. See Peter Bowler, *The Eclipse of Darwinism*, for an argument that Lamarckism provided no more humane or optimistic view of the future than did Darwinism (pp. 18-19).

65. Bowler, *The Eclipse of Darwinism*, p. 41.

66. Bowler, *The Eclipse of Darwinism*, p. 4.

67. For extended accounts of the period see Vernon Kellogg, *Darwinism To-day;* William Provine, *The Origins of Theoretical Population Genetics;* Ernst Mayr, *The Growth of Biological Thought;* Peter Bowler, *The Eclipse of Darwinism* (Baltimore: Johns Hopkins, 1983).

Chapter 2

1. John Passmore, *One Hundred Years of Philosophy*, (London: Duckworth, 1957) p. 203.

2. G.E. Moore, "Autobiography," *The Philosophy of E.E. Moore*, ed. by P.A. Schilpp (Evanston: Northwestern University Press, 1942) p. 14.

3. Moore, "Autobiography," p. 6.

4. Moore, *Elements of Ethics*, T. Regan, ed. (Philadelphia: Temple University Press, 1991) pp. 36-7; *Principia Ethica* (Cambridge: Cambridge University Press) pp. 47-8.

5. See Peter Bowler, *Evolution. The History of an Idea*, p. 225; Robert Richards, *Darwin and the Emergence of Evolutionary Theories of Mind and Behavior*, p. 244.

6. Tom Regan attributes this insistence on the autonomy of ethics with respect to both science and "common life," to the influence of Kant on Moore. *Bloomsbury's Prophet* (Philadelphia: Temple University Press, 1986) p. 52.

7. J. Schneewind, *Sidgwick's Ethics and Victorian Moral Philosophy* (Oxford: Clarendon, 1977) p. 385.

8. Robert Richards, *Darwin and the Emergence of Evolutionary Theories of Mind and Behavior*, p. 323.

9. "Ethics and the Theory of Evolution," in *Biology and Personality*, I.T. Ramsey, ed. (New York: Barnes and Noble, 1965) p. 107; See also Robert Richards, *Darwin and the Emergence of Evolutionary Theories of Mind and Behavior*, p. 323. And as Thomas Baldwin points out, ". . . for better or worse, twentieth-century British ethical theory is unintelligible without reference to [Moore's] Principia Ethica . . . ," *G.E. Moore* (London: Routledge and Kegan Paul, 1990) p. 66.

10. For a detailed and sympathetic account of Spencer's *whole* view of ethics (Moore deals with only *Data of Ethics*), see Robert Richards, *Darwin and the Emergence of Evolutionary Theories of Mind and Behavior*, p. 302 ff.

11. Herbert Spencer, *Data of Ethics* (New York: William Allison, 1879) p. 36.

12. Spencer published *Data of Ethics* in 1879, later integrating it into his two-volume *Principles of Ethics* published in 1892-3. He was an evolutionary thinker well before Darwin published *Origin of Species*, having published an essay on "The Development Hypothesis" in 1852, a full seven years before *Origin*. And although he strongly supported Darwin's views when they emerged, his own account of evolution retained, as I have said, considerable influence from Lamarck.

13. Moore, *Principia Ethica*, p. 54. Moore had said in his 1898 lectures, "I wished in this lecture to discuss a view which should maintain that the course of evolution, while it shewed us the direction in which we are developing, thereby and for the same reasons shewed us the direction in which we ought to develop." Moore, *The Elements of Ethics*, p. 35.

14. For a spirited attack on anti-naturalism, including Moore's, see Anthony Quinton, "Ethics and the Theory of Evolution," in *Biology and Personality*. In the end, however, Quinton joins Moore in rejecting evolutionary ethics.

15. See C. Lewy, "G.E. Moore on the Naturalistic Fallacy," in *Moore: Essays in Retrospect*, Alice Ambrose and Morris Lazerowitz, eds. (London: Allen & Unwin, 1970).

16. *Social Statics*, (London: John Chapman, 1851) p. 32.

17. Herbert Spencer, "Progress: Its Law and Cause," *Essays Scientific, Political, and Speculative*, vol.i, (New York: Appleton, 1910) p. 10.

18. Moore, *Elements of Ethics*, T. Regan, ed., pp. 36-37; *Principia Ethica*, pp. 47-48.

19. James Rachels, *Created from Animals. The Moral Implications of Darwinism* (Oxford: Oxford University Press, 1990); Robert Richards, "A Defense of Evolutionary Ethics," in *Darwin and the Emergence of Evolutionary Theories of Mind and Behavior* (Chicago: University of Chicago Press, 1987). Anthony Flew rejects evolutionary ethics as such, but argues for "Seeing [Ethics] in an Evolutionary Perspective." A.G.N. Flew, *Evolutionary Ethics* (London: Macmillan, 1960) pp. 52-60. Rachels work, by the way, is a particularly good illustration of how Darwinian evolution and ethics might be linked because he bases his view squarely on *Darwin*. Spencer, of course, did not.

20. Anthony Flew, for example, cites Russell's objection to evolutionary ethics as crucial. Russell says, "If evolutionary ethics were sound, we ought to be entirely indifferent as to what the course of evolution may be, since whatever it is is thereby proved to be the best." *Evolutionary Ethics*, p. 44, quoting from Russell, *Philosophical Essays*, p. 24.

21. Anthony Quinton characterizes evolutionary ethics as attempting "to make a scientifically establishable matter of fact, *the general trend of the evolutionary process*, into the rational criterion for the validity of moral propositions." [italics mine] "Ethics and the Theory of Evolution," in *Biology and Personality*, p. 108.

22. C. Lewy, "G.E. Moore on the Naturalistic Fallacy," in Ambrose and Lazerowitz, p. 297.

23. Moore, *Lectures on Philosophy* Casimir Lewy, ed. (London: Allen & Unwin, 1966) p. 10.

24. Leslie Stephen, for example, had published *The Science of Ethics* in 1882. And at least one historian of the period characterized it as "perhaps the maturest

and best thought-out contribution to establishing morals upon the foundation of an evolutionist philosophy." Rudolf Metz, *A Hundred Years of British Philosophy* (London: Allen & Unwin, 1938) p. 135. Henry Sidgwick, however, apparently had a low opinion of Stephen's philosophical abilities, and this fact may have dissuaded Moore from making any reference to the work. One potential ally to whom Moore might have made reference is T. H. Huxley. He was a confirmed supporter of evolution but an opponent of evolutionary ethics. On some points at least, Moore would have found support for his own views. Huxley had published his Romane lecture, "Evolution and Ethics," first as a pamphlet in 1893 and then in volume nine of his *Collected Essays* in 1894. Huxley was, however, also a confirmed naturalist about ethics.

25. Darwin, *Descent of Man*, 2nd ed., p. 471.
26. For a detailed account of the development of Darwin's views on the relationship between instinct and moral sense, see Robert Richards, *Darwin and the Emergence of Evolutionary Theories of Mind and Behavior*, p. 110 ff.
27. A recent item in *Nature* (1/16/92) notes that even in computer tournaments in which programs work on the "prisoners' dilemma," strategies of reciprocal altruism prove to be more advantageous to all participants than do strategies of constant selfishness. I am grateful to David Ozar for pointing out this article to me.
28. Robert Richards argues that this was the distinctively Darwinian contribution; see *Darwin and the Emergence of Evolutionary Theories of Mind and Behavior*, pp. 214-215.
29. The italicized clause appears in the Sixth Edition of the *Origin*. In the first four editions, the final clause required that the individual benefit; in the Fifth Edition the wording was ambiguous. By the Sixth Edition, in 1872, he had clearly moved to the importance of community benefit. See Robert Richards, *Darwin and the Emergence of Evolutionary Theories of Mind and Behavior*, p. 217, footnote 82.
30. Darwin, *Descent of Man*, p. 100-101.
31. Darwin, *Descent of Man*, 2nd ed., p. 490
32. Darwin, *Descent of Man*, 2nd ed., p. 504.
33. Darwin, *The Autobiography*, ed. by Nora Barlow (New York: Norton, 1958) p. 89.
34. As one commentator put it, "And like every other species, he [the human being] will have been selected to be *comfortable* in his environment. An individual always dissatisfied and attempting to escape is unlikely to persist and reproduce . . . " A.J. Cain, "The True Meaning of Darwinian Evolution," in *Evolution and Its Influence*, ed. by Alan Grafen, p. 10.
35. Peter Bowler notes that very few philosophers were able to distinguish Darwin's view from the progressivism that was so prevalent in nineteenth-century thought. See *Evolution: The History of an Idea*. Unfortunately, the subtitle of Darwin's *Origin of Species* might lend credence to such a progressionist interpretation. His subtitle reads: "The Preservation of Favored Races in the Struggle for Life." But that subtitle can be misleading, and apparently Darwin's original plan did not include it. In a letter to Charles Lyell, dated March 28, 1859, he enclosed a proposed title page for the *Origin*. The title read "An

Abstract of an Essay on the Origin of Species and Varieties" with the subtitle, "Through Natural Selection." When Lyell or the publisher (it is not clear from the correspondence) objected to the phrase "natural selection," Darwin responded: "I hope to retain it with explanation somewhat as thus: 'Through natural selection, or the preservation of favoured Races." Charles Darwin, *Life and Letters*, vol.i, p. 507-8. The context makes it clear, I think, that the phrase "preservation of favoured races" is meant to indicate merely those groups of animals that are "favoured" insofar as they survive the selection process. *Progress* has nothing to do with it.

36. For a spirited defense of the view that Darwin did indeed believe that *evolution* was progressive see Robert Richards, *The Meaning of Evolution* (Chicago: University of Chicago Press, 1992). See also his paper, "The Moral Foundations of the Idea of Evolutionary progress: Darwin, Spencer, and the Neo-Darwinians," in *Evolutionary Progress*, Matthew Nitecki, ed. (Chicago: University of Chicago Press, 1988). Richards says, "From the early period to the late, Darwin thought that evolution gradually produced ever more complex creatures, . . . that the most conspicuous instances of evolutionary progress were greater intelligence and a moral sense in the human species." (p. 135)

37. Darwin, *Descent of Man*, p. 183-184.

38. Even Russell, in his early years, could write, "To feel that the universe may be hurrying blindly towards all that is bad, that humanity may any day cease its progressive development and may continually lose all its fine qualities, that Evolution has no necessarily progressive principle prompting it; these are thoughts which render life almost intolerable." Russell, "A Locked Diary," *Collected Papers*, I, (London: Allen & Unwin, 1983) p. 56.

39. Darwin, *Descent of Man*, p. 178.

40. Darwin, *Descent of Man*, p. 177.

41. Darwin, *Descent of Man*, p. 166.

42. It is remarkable how few commentators on Moore's ethics make any reference to his discussion of "evolutionistic ethics." This may be attributable to the fact that for many, Moore was simply beating a dead horse in his criticism of Spencer. As Thomas Baldwin points out, Spencer's work had been "subjected to criticisms of this kind for at least two decades." *G.E. Moore*, p. 94. At any rate, the publication of Moore's *Principia Ethica*, according to James Rachels, "sounded . . . the death knell [for Spencer's popularity]." *Created From Animals*, p. 66-7.

43. Thomas Baldwin, *G.E. Moore*, p. 40; also Regan, *Bloomsbury's Prophet*, p. 106.

44. Regan argues that "Moore's ethical precepts, . . . offered, and were offered by him as, a cognitively and emotionally satisfying substitute for the discarded belief in a supernatural deity—offered, that is, a religion without god." *Bloomsbury's Prophet*, p. 28; cf. also p. 53 and pp. 275-6.

45. Darwin, *Descent of Man*, 2nd ed., p. 498.

46. I am grateful to Bill Rowe for pointing this out to me.

47. Moore, *Principia Ethica*, p. 3.

48. Herbert Spencer, *Data of Ethics*, p. 32.

49. Casimir Lewy points out that Moore, in notes for a Preface to the Second Edition of *Principia* (written in 1920 or 1921 but never finished or published)

acknowledges several senses of "good," but says that in *Principia* he is concerned solely with one of them—the one related to "right." See "G.E. Moore on the Naturalistic Fallacy" in A. Ambrose & M. Lazerowitz, eds., p. 292.

50. Moore, *Principia Ethica*, p. 9.
51. Harald Hoffding characterizes Spencer's philosophy as "completely unified knowledge." *A History of Modern Philosophy*, vol.2 (Dover, 1955) p. 462.
52. G.E. Moore, *Lectures on Philosophy*, p. 10.
53. "Kant's Idealism," *Proceedings of the Aristotelian Society*, 4, (1903-04) pp. 127-140; reprinted in *G. E. Moore: The Early Essays*, ed. by Tom Regan.
54. See Tom Regan, *Bloomsbury's Prophet*, pp. 78-85.
55. J. Schneewind, *Sidgwick's Ethics and Victorian Moral Philosophy, p. 385.*
56. The Apostles were a highly select, secret group of students (and alumni) at Cambridge, founded in 1820. At the time that Moore and Russell were members, the group met weekly to discuss a paper delivered by one of the members. See Paul Levy, *G. E. Moore and the Cambridge Apostles* (Oxford: Oxford University Press, 1981) for a detailed account of the group and its role in Moore's life.
57. The title was later changed to "Is Ethics a Branch of Empirical Psychology?," *Bertrand Russell. Collected Papers*, I, p. 99 ff.
58. Ironically, by the end of his paper, Russell denies the objectivity of the *good*, saying it is a "matter for purely psychological investigation," (p. 104) and challenges Moore to show how he is mistaken in this. However, he leaves the objectivity of *truth* intact. Russell, in fact, later came to agree for a time with the position Moore took in *Principia Ethica* regarding a non-naturalistic ethics and a platonic account of the good.
59. Anthony O'Hear, "Has the Theory of Evolution Any Relevance to Philosophy?"
60. See Rudolf Metz, *A Hundred Years of British Philosophy*, p. 249.
61. G.E. Moore, *Lectures on Philosophy*, p. 10.
62. In a second lecture from the 1928-29 series, entitled "Are Material Things Real?" Moore does make reference to Darwin's views on the evolution of man, but his point is a purely conceptual one. He suggests that there is a sense in which the term "human body" is a vague term because, if Darwin is right there was a time in our past when some of our progenitors were neither clearly human nor clearly non-human. Thus, the term "human body" might or might not apply to them.

Chapter 3

1. Cf. Nicholas Griffin, *Russell's Idealist Apprenticeship* (Oxford: Clarendon, 1991) p. 4.
2. See, for example, Russell's ruminations in "Greek Exercises," in *The Collected Papers of Bertrand Russell I.*
3. Russell, "Greek Exercises," *Collected Papers*, I, p. 9.
4. Bertrand Russell, "Mechanical Morals and the Moral of Machinery," *Collected Papers*, I, pp. 326-327.

5. Russell, "Mechanical Morals," pp. 325-7.

6. Russell makes no effort here to distinguish between *intelligence* and *reason*. In his later essay, "Mysticism and Logic" he appears to treat them as interchangeable. See p. 31, where he seems to equate Bergson's notion of *intellect* with his own account of *reason*.

7. See Russell's review of George Chatterton-Hill's *Heredity and Selection in Sociology*, "The Politics of a Biologist," in *Collected Papers*, XII, p. 368.

8. Russell, "Mechanical Morals," p. 327.

9. Russell, "What Shall I Read?" in *Collected Papers*, I, p. 348, 355. The title of the list of readings might suggest that Russell merely intended to read *Origin* and *Descent*, but never actually did. However, the editors of the volume note that "The list is confined to books read, rather than to be read." (p. 345)

10. See, for example, Darwin, *Descent of Man*, pp. 163, 165.

11. Indeed, in an 1894 essay on Bacon, Hobbes, and Descartes, Russell had concluded that " . . . in Metaphysics, he [Descartes] made the enormous advance of beginning from the side of mind, from consciousness, instead of trying, as Bacon and Hobbes did, to reach this from the side of physical Science and explain it in terms of mechanical laws." (Russell, "A Comparison of Bacon, Hobbes and DesCartes," *Collected Papers*, I, p. 161.) It seems that Russell at this time had some sympathy for the Cartesian distinction between the mental and the physical. There is evidence that his predilection for a dualistic view continued until 1918 when he became a Neutral Monist. Later, in 1921, he writes, "In this first lecture I shall be concerned to refute a theory which . . . I formerly held . . . : the theory that the essence of everything mental is a certain quite peculiar something called 'consciousness,' conceived either as a relation to objects, or as a pervading quality of psychical phenomena." Russell, *Analysis of Mind*, (New York: Dover, 1954) p. 9.

12. "My original interest in philosophy had two sources. On the one hand, I was anxious to discover whether philosophy would provide any defence for anything that could be called religious belief, however vague; on the other hand, I wished to persuade myself that something could be known, in pure mathematics if not elsewhere." Russell, *My Philosophical Development*, (London: Allen & Unwin, 1959) p. 9.

13. Russell, "Ethical Axioms," *Collected Papers*, I, p. 227. Russell had argued on an 1893 essay that *ought* cannot be derived from *is*. (Russell, "The Relation of What Ought to Be to What Is, Has Been or Will Be," *Collected Papers*, I, *Cambridge Essays*, pp. 213-14.)

14. Russell, *My Philosophical Development*, p. 155.

15. "Psychogony" is "an obsolete term for the science of the historical development of mentality (including the moral sentiments)." Harry Ruja, "Russell on the Meaning of 'Good,' " in *Russell: The Journal of the Bertrand Russell Archives*, n.s., vol.4, no.1 (1984) p. 139.

16. Russell, *Philosophical Essays* (New York: Simon & Schuster, 1966) p. 13. Even the title of the essay is the same as the title of Moore's lectures on ethics in 1899. And the text bears out Russell's claim of indebtedness to Moore. There are, in fact, so many points of similarity between Russell's paper and Moore's

Principia that a reader of both might well wonder why Russell bothered to publish the paper. In fact, the essay was apparently intended originally to be included in a collected volume of essays that were to be expositions of Moore's philosophy in easily accessible form. (See Harry Ruja, "Russell on the Meaning of 'Good' ".) Other essayists were to be R.G. Trevelyan, Sidney Waterlow, and G. Lowes Dickinson. The significant point is that the edited collection was never published, but Russell went ahead and published his "Elements of Ethics" simply under his own name.

17. In addition to the influences I have already suggested, Russell was also unfavorably impressed by the work of L.T. Hobhouse on evolutionary ethics. See his review of Hobhouse's *Morals in Evolution* published in *The Independent Review*, February, 1907; reprinted in *Collected Papers*, XII, pp. 336-340.

18. Russell, *My Philosophical Development*, p. 157.

19. Russell, *My Philosophical Development*, p. 158.

20. Russell, *Philosophical Essays*, Preface to 1966 edition, p. 7. In fact, there was a period in the late 1890's when he also connected the concept "good" with the satisfaction of desire. Difficulties in working out the details of that view may have led him to adopt Moore's position that "good" is not definable. But when George Santayana criticized Russell's Moorean account in "The Elements of Ethics," Russell reverted to his earlier view of good as the satisfaction of desire. For a detailed discussion of this development in Russell's views, see Harry Ruja, "Russell on the Meaning of 'Good,' " pp. 137-156.

21. Russell, *Philosophical Essays*, p. 7.

22. Russell, "Mechanical Morals," *Collected Papers*, I, pp. 325-6.

23. For a careful discussion of some of the important differences between the views of Darwin and those of Malthus, see Peter Bowler, "Malthus, Darwin, and the Concept of Struggle." M.J.S. Hodge argues that " ... while he [Darwin] and Wallace did use the populational arithmetic Thomas Malthus made notorious, it was this, not his political economy, that they, like Malthus himself, reckoned to be true of all species. This point, too, is an obvious one, but none the less fatal to that remarkably persistent thesis, pioneered almost jokingly in letters between Karl Marx and Friedrich Engels, that, in their use of Malthus, Darwin and Wallace were extending the laissez-faire capitalist ethos from society to all nature ... "—"England," *The Comparative Reception of Darwinism*, T.F. Glick, ed. (Chicago: University of Chicago Press, 1974) p. 16.

24. Incidentally, the phrase "red in tooth and claw" was not penned originally with reference to Darwin's views at all. *In Memoriam*, in which the line appears, was published by Tennyson in 1850, nine years before Darwin's *Origin of Species* appeared.

25. Nicholas Griffin suggests that it may have been a psychosomatic illness rather than actual angina. See *The Selected Letters of Bertrand Russell*, vol.1 (Boston: Houghton Mifflin, 1992), pp. 215-216.

26. Bertrand Russell, *Autobiography* (London: Allen & Unwin, 1978) p. 149.

27. It has been suggested that the conversion experience was also related to his rejection of neo-Hegelianism. As one commentator puts it: "With the previous

organic view of social relationships gone, the fabric of society became a much more delicate thing, requiring love and care for its preservation. Social groupings took on less importance, for the basic fact was that each human being was alone in a dangerous, painful and, above all, indifferent universe. Whatever might be achieved in the way of society had to be achieved in despite of this fact. Nor could the pain and suffering be in some way discounted as steps on the route to some higher fulfilment in the Absolute." (Nicholas Griffin, "Bertrand Russell's Crisis of Faith," in *Russell: The Journal of the Bertrand Russell Archives*, vol.4, no.1 (1984) p. 112.) These concerns would be likely to inspire a rejection of a Spencerian, as well as a Hegelian, view of things. Any facile optimism about life, or convictions about the inevitability of progress, of the sort associated with Spencer, were at this point impossible for Russell to accept.

28. Russell, *Freedom versus Organization* (New York: Norton, 1962) p. 144; he acknowledges, however, that "Darwin himself had no such tendencies."

29. The editors of Russell's *Collected Papers*, I, note that the individualism of British Liberals gradually gave way to a "New Liberalism" that took collective interests more seriously and came to have many points of agreement with Socialism. Russell, in an address to the Fabian Society in 1896, urged cooperation between Liberals and Socialists. See p. 310.

30. Russell's concerns about natural selection were echoed in the emerging community of social scientists at the turn of the century. Particularly in anthropology and sociology, people were unwilling to assent to a doctrine that seemed to suggest that efforts to ameliorate the conditions of society were futile. (See Robert Richards, *Darwin and the Emergence of Evolutionary Theories of Mind and Behavior*, chapter 11, especially pp. 509 - 511.) Richards notes that "Many of the fresh recruits who came to the new departments of sociology at Chicago, Pennsylvania, and Columbia had recently shucked off religious fundamentalism, but retained a residual missionary zeal to improve the lot of the wretched. . . ." Franz Boas and his followers rejected the view that biology had anything significant to do with anthropology, so eager were they to deny any claims about racial or cultural hierarchies. Another commentator further notes, "Other movements in anthropology rejected a historical approach altogether and studied societies as though they were static entities, as in the 'functionalism' of A.R. Radcliffe-Brown. It has been argued that the human sciences never adopted a truly Darwinian perspective." (Peter Bowler, *The Non-Darwinian Revolution* (Baltimore: Johns Hopkins, 1988) p. 140.) The similarities with Russell's point of view, and with its consequences for the future of his discipline, are striking.

31. As Elizabeth Eames has pointed out to me, Russell did not really see himself as a pacifist; he was simply a critic of specific wars.

32. Russell, "Elements of Ethics," *Philosophical Essays*, p. 24.

33. Russell, *Human Knowledge: Its Scope and Limits* (New York: Simon & Schuster, 1948) p. 34. For related comments see his *Scientific Outlook* (New York: Norton, 1962) pp. 186-187, and his *History of Western Philosophy* (New York: Simon & Schuster, 1945) p. 726 and pp. 780-781.

34. Russell, *Our Knowledge of the External World*, pp. 33-34.

35. Precise dates for the synthesis are difficult to specify. Ernst Mayr says it began in 1937 and was completed in 1946. William Provine notes that significant steps toward it had been taken as early as 1918. See Peter Bowler, *Evolution: The History of an Idea*, p. 256-265, and *The Non-Darwinian Revolution*, p. 93. Ernst Mayr points out that some "mild" opposition to Darwinian views continued to come from some Mendelians in the 1940s and 1950s. See *One Long Argument* (Cambridge, MA: Harvard University Press, 1991) p. 46.

36. See John Greene, "The Interaction of Science and World View in Sir Julian Huxley's Biology," *Journal of the History of Biology*, 23 (1), Spring, 1990, p. 51.

37. See Russell's comments on Adam Smith in *Freedom versus Organization. 1814-1914*, p. 76. Smith was convinced that a free market economy would ultimately work to the benefit of all, even if individuals were not aware of the social benefits of what they did. (Adam Smith, *An Inquiry into the Nature and Causes of the Wealth of Nations*, Sixth Ed., (London: George Bell & Sons, 1908 [originally published in 1776]) I, pp. 453 and 456. Also see Peter Bowler, "Malthus, Darwin, and the Concept of Struggle," pp. 642-3.)

38. As one commentator puts it, "If the struggle [for existence] is understood as a contest between individuals within a species, as it was by the sociologist William Graham Sumner of Yale, then altruism, any concern whatever for the welfare of others, is a handicap to the man who might otherwise be one of 'the fittest' and therefore entitled to survive. . . . Thus, in Sumner's theory of 'social Darwinism' evolutionary biology is used as the rationale for a predatory and completely competitive capitalism. If, however, the struggle for survival is taken to be a contest among different species, if each species is thought to be vying with every other species for its foothold on earth, as Lester Frank Ward believed, then the identical evolutionary theory can become the justification for a welfare state. Social organization would have as its primary purpose the improvement of the human species by raising the quality of its inferior members, thus giving it a better chance to win out over other species, and to become the fittest to survive of all species." (Joseph Blau, *Men and Movements of American Philosophy*, (New York: Prentice-Hall, 1952) pp. 158-9.) See also A. Kelly, *Descent of Darwin*, chapter 6; and Peter Bowler, *Evolution. History of An Idea*, p. 102, and *The Non-Darwinian Revolution*, p. 152 ff.; and Robert Richards, *Darwin and the Emergence of Evolutionary Theories of Mind and Behavior*, p. 597. For an effort to disassociate Darwin's views from economic theories like *laissez-faire*, see M.J.S. Hodge, "England," in *The Comparative Reception of Darwinism*, pp. 15-16.

39. Russell, *Human Knowledge: Its Scope and Limits*, p. 36.

40. In fact, sometime between 1910 and 1914 Russell seems to have decided that ethical concerns could actually be damaging to philosophy. In his Herbert Spencer lecture of 1914, he begins by noting that philosophers have generally been motivated by either religion and ethics or by science. He continues, "It is my belief that the ethical and religious motives . . . have been on the whole a hindrance to the progress of philosophy, and ought now to be consciously thrust aside by those who wish to discover philosophical truth. . . . It is, I maintain, from science, rather than from ethics and religion, that philosophy

should draw its inspiration." Russell, "On Scientific Method in Philosophy," in *Mysticism and Logic* (Totowa, NJ: Barnes & Noble, 1981) p. 75.

41. Russell, *Religion and Science* (Oxford: Oxford University Press, 1961 [orig. pub. 1935]) p. 72; see also his *The Scientific Outlook*, p. 171.

42. Russell was thoughtful enough to leave to posterity a list of books that he read between 1891 and 1902, the earlier ones with evaluative comments ranging from "magnificent" to "very trifling." Unfortunately, he stopped that practice of entering comments before he reached the material related to evolution. See Russell, *Collected Papers*, I, pp. 347-365.

43. See Russell's *Portraits from Memory* (New York: Simon & Schuster, 1963 [Orig. pub. 1951]) p. 78.

44. Portions of their correspondence can be found in both the Russell Archives at McMaster University and at the Woodson Research Center at Rice University.

45. cf. Colin Dival, "From a Victorian to a Modern . . . " in *Julian Huxley: Biologist and Statesman of Science*, C.K. Waters and A. Van Helden, eds. (Houston: Rice University Press, 1992) p. 37.

46. Divall, p. 43.

47. Many of the book's arguments against Evolutionism also appear, in some cases almost verbatim, in his essays "Mysticism and Logic" and "On Scientific Method in Philosophy," also published in 1914.

48. Russell, *Portraits from Memory*, p. 39.

49. Russell argues that the mathematical notion of infinite numbers and infinite series, propounded by Georg Cantor in the late nineteenth century, opened the way to resolving the difficulties that Idealists like Bradley saw in both notions.

50. Russell notes that he thought Moore was most concerned to reject Idealism as such, while Russell was primarily concerned with its *monistic* dimension. (Russell, *My Philosophical Development*, p. 42.) This may explain Moore's heavy focus on analyzing our common sense beliefs about the external world and their possible relation to sense data, while Russell emphasized logical analysis and the atomic structure of facts.

51. Russell, *Our Knowledge of the External World* (London: George Allen & Unwin, 1914). Page references to this work will appear in parenthesis in the text for the remainder of this chapter.

52. Most recently two excellent studies: Peter Hylton, *Russell, Idealism, and the Emergence of Analytic Philosophy* (Oxford: Clarendon, 1990), and Nicholas Griffin, *Russell's Idealist Apprenticeship*.

53. It is worth recalling that Nietzsche's philosophy was not Darwinian, by his own account.

54. Ironically, when Russell does turn to a consideration of biological evolution in his 1948 book, he characterizes it in decidedly Spencerian terms as "an increase in complexity or heterogeneity." *Human Knowledge*, p. 31.

55. Russell, "Greek Exercises," in *Collected Papers*, I, p. 8.

56. John Passmore, *A Hundred Years of Philosophy*, 2nd ed. (London: Duckworth, 1966) p. 204.

57. By the 1920s Russell became especially interested in Einstein's work and

published several items on relativity theory as well as on atomic theory. See, for example, Russell, "Relativity Theory of Gravitation," *English Review* (1920) 30:11-18; *The ABC of Atoms* (New York: Dutton, 1923); *The ABC of Relativity* (New York: Harper, 1925).

58. It is not clear that at this point in history Russell had in mind a reductive view of the sciences. In a brief essay in the *International Encyclopedia of Unified Science* (Vol.i, Chicago: University of Chicago, 1938) he says: " . . . take a hypothesis that I neither affirm nor deny—that all scientific propositions can be tested in terms of physics, . . ." p. 41. Nonetheless, by the time he published *Human Knowledge: Its Scope and Limits*, in 1948, his view clearly supported reductionism. "The evidence, though not conclusive, tends to show that everything distinctive of living matter can be reduced to chemistry, and therefore ultimately to physics. The fundamental laws governing living matter are, in all likelihood, the very same that govern the behavior of the hydrogen atom, namely, the laws of quantum mechanics." p. 33.

59. Russell, "On Scientific Method in Philosophy," in *Mysticism and Logic*, p. 76.

60. Elizabeth Eames lists, among six of Russell's "prejudices" his "often expressed preference for the viewpoint of physics and astronomy, rather than that of the human, the subjective, and the psychological." *Bertrand Russell's Theory of Knowledge* (New York: Braziller, 1969) p. 50.

61. Many years later Russell reiterates the same sort of position. "We are not in the mood proper to philosophy so long as we are interested in the world only as it affects human beings; the philosophic spirit demands an interest in the world for its own sake." *Outline of Philosophy* (London: Allen & Unwin, 1970) p. 247. The dichotomy he creates here is a false one: we must be interested in the world *only as it affects human beings*, or we must be interested in it solely for its own sake. There is an intermediate position in which we are interested in *both* how the world is *and* how it affects human beings.

62. Russell, "On Scientific Method in Philosophy," in *Mysticism and Logic*, pp. 83-85.

63. Moore, for example, had said that the most important thing that philosophers had tried to do is "To give a general description of the *whole* of the Universe. . . ." *Some Main Problems of Philosophy* (London: Allen & Unwin, 1966 [originally published in 1953, but it was a series of lectures that were delivered in 1910-11]). This, of course, is not quite the same as Russell's claim that philosophy itself must be general, but the ideas are not unrelated. Russell distinguishes his own view from the claim that "philosophy deals with the universe as a whole." ("On Scientific Method in Philosophy," p. 83) The latter is, of course, the view of Idealism, to which both Moore and Russell take exception.

64. For a discussion of the development in Russell's views on the relation between philosophy and logic see Elizabeth Eames, *Bertrand Russell's Theory of Knowledge*, p. 40ff. John Passmore suggests that Russell meant different things by the term "logic" in his earlier and later work. See *A Hundred Years of Philosophy*, p. 219, footnote 2.

65. Given this view of philosophy, one can better understand Russell's response,

much later, to a commentator on his political and economic philosophy. "Mr. McGill's essay on my political and economic 'philosophy' deals mainly with matters which I should regard as lying wholly outside philosophy." "Reply to Criticisms," in Schilpp, ed., *The Philosophy of Bertrand Russell*, (Lasalle, IL: Open Court, 1989) p. 729.

66. Joseph Blau, *Men and Movements in American Philosophy*, pp. 157-8.

67. R. Metz, *A Hundred Years of British Philosophy*, p. 97.

68. See Henry Plotkin, *Darwin Machines*, for an illuminating discussion of recent versions of "universal darwinism."

69. Russell gives a more complete account of his views on Bergson's philosophy in "The Philosophy of Bergson," *The Monist*, XXII (July, 1912). See also his later criticism of Bergson's views in "Philosophy in the Twentieth-Century," in *Skeptical Essays* (London: Unwin Paperbacks, 1977).

70. Some years later, in 1924, after Russell had begun publishing on Einstein's relativity physics, he added a more technical objection to claims about progress. " . . . if the time-order is arbitrary, there will be progress or retrogression according to the convention adopted in measuring time." ("Philosophy in the Twentieth-Century," in *Skeptical Essays*, p. 59; originally published in *The Dial*, October, 1924).

71. In his 1909 book, *Darwin and the Humanities*, James Mark Baldwin says: "If the unfit or less fit are killed off, and so do not propagate at all, and the more or most fit do, then the next generation will be, on the average, *more fit than the preceding was*. That is, there is an advance from generation to generation in those characters upon which Natural Selection is working . . . As nature acts continuously, through her great forces, such elimination and survival continue through ages; and there is thus a progressive evolution of characters of all sorts. . . . This, then, is the theory of Natural Selection, currently called Darwinism." (p. 5).

72. Darwin, *Life and Letters*, vol.2, pp. 198-9.

73. Charles Darwin, *Origin of Species*, First Ed., p. 489; Sixth Ed. p. 373.

74. Darwin, *Origin of Species*, Sixth Ed., p. 367.

75. Darwin, *Origin of Species*, Sixth Ed., p. 374. This concluding statement (without the phrase 'by the Creator') appears also in the First Edition, p. 490.

76. Stephen Jay Gould quotes the letter in his essay, "The Individual in Darwin's World," The Second Edinburgh Medical Address, 1990, p. 3.

77. There was, of course, widespread belief in progress during much of the nineteenth century. On some accounts, one origin of such a belief was Kant's "nebular hypothesis" according to which the solar system had been formed from a great cloud of dust that condensed under the force of gravity. This theory suggested to some thinkers that the forces of nature moved things in an orderly way toward higher levels of development. Biological evolution was then seen as a continuation of this cosmic process of development. See Peter Bowler, *The Non-Darwinian Revolution*, p. 132 ff. The social philosophies of Hegel and Marx can be seen as part of this progressive view of history.

78. For an extensive discussion of the many issues involved in settling the question, see *Evolutionary Progress*, ed. by Matthew Nitecki. In that volume,

John Maynard Smith, David Hull, and William Provine, are among those who argue against any useful notion of biological progress entailed by natural selection; Michael Ruse and Francisco Ayala argue for some limited version of evolutionary progress. See also Michael Ruse, *Monad to Man* (an unpublished manuscript).

79. See also T.A. Goudge, *The Ascent of Life* (Toronto: University of Toronto Press, 1961) pp. 180-191.

80. See also T.A. Goudge, *The Ascent of Life* (Toronto: University of Toronto Press, 1961) pp. 180-190.

81. See Francisco Ayala, "Can 'Progress' be Defined as a Biological Concept?" in *Evolutionary Progress*, Matthew Nitecki, ed.

82. See John Greene, "History of Ideas Revisited," *Revue de Synthese*, 4(3), 1986, p. 221, for similar views on the relativity of the notion of fitness.

83. Russell, *Portraits from Memory* (London: Allen & Unwin, 1956 [originally published in New York, 1951] p. 12.

84. Many of Russell's criticisms of Bergson's views on intellect were originally written for his essay "Mysticism and Logic," which also appeared in 1914. They were then also published as part of *Our Knowledge of the External World.*

85. Gottlob Frege, "Logic," in his *Posthumous Writings* (Oxford: Blackwell, 1979) [essay written between 1879 and 1891]) p. 4.

86. One version of platonism that seems to have had considerable influence on late nineteenth-century thought was the one proposed by Hermann Lotze, particularly in his *Logik* of 1874. He made an effort to save the objectivity that platonism offered without having to make all the strong ontological commitments that classical platonism required. On the influence of Lotze on Frege see Hans Sluga, *Gottlob Frege* (London: Routledge & Kegan Paul, 1980) especially pp. 52-58. It is less clear that Lotze had any great degree of influence on Russell's later philosophy in spite of a brief, early interest Russell had in his views. See Nicholas Griffin, *Russell's Idealist Apprenticeship*, p. 37, footnote 44.

87. Or again, in "On Scientific Method in Philosophy" (1914), reprinted in *Mysticism and Logic*, he says: "It is my belief that the ethical and religious motives in spite of the splendidly imaginative systems to which they have given rise, have been on the whole a hindrance to the progress of philosophy, and ought now to be consciously thrust aside by those who wish to discover philosophical truth. . . . It is, I maintain, from science, rather than from ethics and religion, that philosophy should draw its inspiration." (p. 97-98)

88. Russell, "Mysticism and Logic," *Collected Papers*, XII, p. 174.

89. See his letter to E. Ray Lankester, March 15, 1870, in *The Life and Letters of Charles Darwin, vol.2, p. 301.*

90. See his letter to John Fiske, December 8, 1874, in *The Life and Letters*, vol.2, p. 371. In his *Autobiography* Darwin says of Spencer, "After reading any of his books, I generally feel enthusiastic admiration for his transcendent talents, and have often wondered whether in the distant future he would rank with such great men as Descartes, Leibnitz, etc., about whom, however, I know very little. Nevertheless I am not conscious of having profited in my own work by Spencer's writings. His deductive manner of treating every subject is wholly

opposed to my frame of mind. His conclusions never convince me: and over and over again I have said to myself, after reading one of his discussions,— 'Here would be a fine subject for half-a-dozen years' work.' His fundamental generalisations (which have been compared in importance by some persons with Newton's laws?)—which I daresay may be very valuable under a philosophical point of view, are of such a nature that they do not seem to me to be of any strictly scientific use. They partake more of the nature of definitions than of laws of nature. They do not aid one in predicting what will happen in any particular case. Anyhow they have not been of any use to me." (Charles Darwin, *Autobiography*, p. 108-9.)

91. John Passmore, "Darwin's Impact on British Metaphysics," p. 50.

92. See Russell's "Pragmatism" in *Philosophical Essays*, and "The Philosophy of William James" in *Collected Papers*, VI; the latter was originally published in *The Nation*, 7 (Sept. 3, 1910).

93. Elizabeth Eames suggested just such a worry.

94. Letter to Satyagopal Bhattacharyya in Konnagar, Hooghly, India. October 8, 1962. Russell Archives, McMaster University.

95. Letter #356, February 23, 1912. Russell Archives, McMaster University.

96. Letter # 716, March 5, 1913. Russell Archives, McMaster University.

97. Russell, *Freedom versus Organization. 1814-1914* (New York: Norton, 1934) p. 143. The Philosophical Radicals were the Benthamites, and Russell notes that they included the Mills, Malthus, and Ricardo.

98. Russell, *Freedom versus Organization*, p. 144.

99. See Alfred Kelly, *The Descent of Darwin: The Popularization of Darwinism in Germany, 1860-1914*, pp. 119-122. Haeckel was apparently also seen as a source of Nazism.

100. Bergson he counted among the irrationalist sources of Fascism. See Russell, "The Ancestry of Fascism," in *In Praise of Idleness* (London: Unwin, 1935) p. 68.

101. See his *Marriage and Morals*, (London: Liveright, 1929) chapter 18.

102. Russell, *Freedom versus Organization*, p. 145.

103. Russell makes related claims in his essay, "The Ancestry of Fascism," in *In Praise of Idleness*.

104. Darwin, *Descent of Man*, pp. 100-101.

105. For an extensive discussion of Russell's views on the nature of philosophy, see John Slater, "Russell's Conception of Philosophy," *Russell*, 8 (1988) pp. 163-178.

106. Alan Wood's comments on the relationship between Russell's philosophy and the theory of evolution are revealing. As late as 1957 Wood could say: " . . . I have an uneasy feeling that it is a legitimate criticism of Russell's philosophy to say that it is too static; though I have no more idea than anyone else of how to introduce into a philosophy the facts of evolution and process, without the dangers of bringing in an element of mysticism." *Bertrand Russell. The Passionate Sceptic* (London: George Allen & Unwin, 1957) p. 155.

107. Russell refers to Wittgenstein, in his *Portraits from Memory*, as " . . . the Austrian philosopher . . . who began as my pupil and ended as my supplanter at both

Oxford and Cambridge." (p. 23) A.J. Ayer comments: ". . . it is to his [Russell's] philosophical work, and especially that which he accomplished in his youth and early middle age, that he will owe his place in history." *Bertrand Russell* (New York: Viking, 1972) p. 1. And later, "Russell was chagrined by the comparative lack of attention which professional philosophers paid to this book [Human Knowledge: Its Scope and Limits, 1948], and attributed it to the contemporary vogue for a narrow form of linguistic philosophy of which he disapproved." (p. 23)

108. Rush Rhees, ed., *Ludwig Wittgenstein, Personal Recollections* (Oxford: Blackwell, 1981) p. 174.

109. I am grateful to Garth Hallett who suggested to me the importance of this point.

Chapter 4

1. See Rudolf Metz, *A Hundred Years of British Philosophy*, pp. 259-268. Metz also notes that "it often seems as though Kant and Hegel were called in for no other reason than to help the cause of religion in its fight against the new heresy [Darwinism]." p. 98.

2. Rudolf Metz, *One Hundred Years of British Philosophy*, p. 249.

3. Thomas Baldwin comments that Spencer's work, for example, had been under heavy criticism for at least two decades before Moore published *Principia Ethica* in 1903; *G.E. Moore*, p. 94.

4. Green's critical Introduction to Hume's *Treatise* was published in 1874.

5. Russell, *Autobiography*, p. 64.

6. Russell, *My Philosophical Development*, p. 9.

7. See, for example, Moore's "The Subject-Matter of Psychology," *Proceedings of the Aristotelian Society* 10 (1909-1910) p. 57 ff.; and Russell's "Theory of Knowledge," in *Collected Papers*, VII, p. 54; also *Mysticism and Logic*, p. 124.

8. Russell, *My Philosophical Development*, p. 10.

9. In the Introduction to the Second Edition of *The Principles of Mathematics*, written in 1938, Russell explains some of his reasons for abandoning his belief in "the Platonic reality of numbers." p. x-xiv.

10. Russell, "Mysticism and Logic," p. 41.

11. Everything except the elements in propositions. Russell thought that propositions exhibited a peculiar sort of unity such that their elements could not be adequately treated in isolation from the rest of the proposition.

12. Russell, *Our Knowledge of the External World*, p. 171; he repeats these comments, almost verbatim, in his essay "Mysticism and Logic," p. 38. See also his account of change in the chapter on motion in *Principles of Mathematics*, 2nd ed. (New York: Norton) p. 469ff.

13. Russell, *Mysticism and Logic*, p. 48.

14. Russell, "Philosophy of Logical Atomism," in *Logic and Knowledge*, Marsh, p. 248.

15. Russell, "On Scientific Method in Philosophy," in *Mysticism and Logic*, pp. 103-4.

16. See, for example, Moore, "Is time real?" in *Some Main Problems of Philosophy*, pp. 201-215.
17. In the 1913 manuscript, "Theory of Knowledge," he includes a chapter on the *experience* of time. But his concern is with "all those immediate experiences upon which our knowledge of time is based." (Russell, *Collected Papers*, VII, p. 64.) The discussion has as its goal the clarification of notions like sensation and memory, simultaneity and succession. Thirty-five years later he wrote another chapter on "Time in Experience," in which his purpose is to "consider those features of crude experience which form the raw material of the concept of time. . . ." (Russell, *Human Knowledge: Its Scope and Limits*, p. 210.)
18. Russell, "Philosophy of Logical Atomism," *Logic and Knowledge*, p. 277.
19. Peter Hylton, *Russell, Idealism, and the Emergence of Analytic Philosophy*, p. vii.
20. Russell, *My Philosophical Development*, p. 53.
21. Garth Hallett, commenting on an earlier version of this manuscript, notes a related point: " . . . Russell's disinterest in the details of linguistic usage and his strong reaction to Wittgenstein's later interest in them. Such details are messy, contingent, temporal, historical. They belong to a realm where practical considerations are prominent. . . . Moore, too, . . . showed slight interest in linguistic usage. He was not interested in how people used the word *good*, but in what the good was."
22. See Peter Hylton, *Russell, Idealism, and the Emergence of Analytic Philosophy*, p. 76, for a discussion of Russell's views on Kant's alleged psychologism, and pp. 168 and 179 for discussions of the relation between Russell's logicism and Kant's view of mathematics.
23. The "problem" he refers to here is the inadequacy of William James' theory of Neutral Monism. Russell, "Theory of Knowledge," in *Collected Papers*, VII, p. 22.
24. There are, for example, places in his *Outline of Philosophy* that might suggest such a reading. But there are other statements in that work that reaffirm his insistence on the theoretical character of philosophy (e.g., p. 226). See, too, some of his comments in *Religion and Science*, where he distinguishes normal perception from "abnormal perceptions" like mystical experiences on the grounds that the former, but not the latter, must "have some correspondence with fact" because they "have to be useful in the struggle for life." (p. 188) But the fact of their utility has little more significance for his theory of perception than that it allows him to distinguish the normal from the abnormal.
25. Russell, *Human Knowledge: Its Scope and Limits*, p. 35.
26. Russell, *Human Knowledge: Its Scope and Limits*, pp. 34-5.
27. As early as 1919 Russell was cautiously beginning to side with the possibility of reductionist accounts of living organisms, against the positions of J.B.S. Haldane and Hans Driesch. By 1948, his position had become even firmer. See "Philosophy and the Soul," (1919), and "Materialism, Past and Present," (1924), in *Essays on Language, Mind and Matter: The Collected Works of Bertrand Russell*, IX (London: Unwin Hyman, 1988); also *Human Knowledge: Its Scope and Limits*, p. 199.

28. See Thomas Baldwin, *G.E. Moore*, for a discussion of Moore's views on self and personal identity, pp. 50-55.
29. Metz, *A Hundred Years of British Philosophy*, p. 533.
30. See, for example, G.E. Moore, "A Defense of Common Sense," in J.H. Muirhead, ed., *Contemporary British Philosophy*, 2nd series (London: Allen & Unwin, 1925).
31. I should point out that when I speak of the *subject* in perception, I do not intend any claims about an enduring *self*. The distinction between Subjectivity and personal identity will emerge later when I sketch an account of Subjectivity that takes evolutionary considerations into account.
32. Russell, *My Philosophical Development*, p. 11.
33. The former gives direct, non-inferential access to sense-data and universals (among other things). Knowledge by description allows one to have knowledge of things—most notably physical objects—with which one is not acquainted, by way of acquaintance with the universals that occur in their descriptions. Robert Marsh notes that this distinction "is found in a clear and well developed form in St. Augustine's *De Magistro*; see Marsh's *Logic and Knowledge*, p. 125. A version of it also appears in William James' *Principles of Psychology* in 1890. Russell's first account of it was presented to the Aristotelian Society in 1910.
34. Russell, "Theory of Knowledge," *Collected Papers*, VII, p. 21.
35. In *Our Knowledge of the External World*, also 1914, he uses this issue as a primary illustration of the fruitfulness of his "logical-analytic method in philosophy." See the Preface, pp. 7-8; see, too, Chapter IV, "The World of Physics and the World of Sense."
36. Russell, *The Analysis of Matter*, p. 178.
37. Russell, *Our Knowledge of the External World*, p. 8. A year later he could say: "The supreme maxim in scientific philosophizing is this: *'Whenever possible, logical constructions are to be substituted for inferred entities.'* " (Russell, "The Relation of Sense-Data to Physics," in *Mysticism and Logic*, p. 149.) But it is to be noted that his distinction between inference and construction becomes blurred in his later work.
38. This constructionist period in his philosophy is often characterized as "phenomenalist," a characterization that may make his constructionism sound perilously close to the Idealism he had earlier abandoned. (Russell himself apparently declined to call his view "phenomenalism." See his comments in reply to a paper by C.D. Broad, *Collected Papers*, VIII, p. 310.) But it should be noted that even in this phase, whatever label one chooses to attach to it, Russell was trying to provide a non-Idealist account of perception. In his 1915 paper, "The Ultimate Constituents of Matter," he characterizes his position, with its emphasis on logical constructions, as "realistic." (p. 75) One of the ways in which he maintains his opposition to Idealism is by claiming that sense-data are themselves physical. ". . . sense-data . . . are relevant to physics, being that part of the material world which is immediately given." Russell, *"Theory of Knowledge,"* VII, in *Collected Papers*, p. 54; also "The Ultimate Constituents of Matter," in *Mysticism and Logic*. "I believe that the actual data in sensation, the immediate objects of sight or touch or hearing, are extra-mental, purely

physical, and among the ultimate constituents of matter." p. 124. See also David Pears, *Bertrand Russell and the British Tradition in Philosophy* (New York: Random House, 1967) p. 33. For Russell, these sense-data must be carefully distinguished both from the mental states in which they appear and from ordinary physical objects like tables and chairs.

39. Russell, *Analysis of Matter*, see for example pp. 193,199, and 209. As late as 1940, Russell repeats his argument from simplicity in support of a causal theory of perception. *Inquiry into Meaning and Truth*, (London: Allen & Unwin) p. 234. For Russell, the causal argument proves nothing conclusively, but it offers a reasonable hypothesis against which there is no substantive evidence. It may be false; the external world may be an illusion, (See Russell's *Scientific Outlook*, p. 98), but our best theory is the one that argues for its independent reality and its causal role in generating our sense-data. The caution that Russell makes explicit in these later writings is that we have no reason to suppose that the physical world is anything like the sense-data that we experience except in its structural properties. (See Russell's *Outline of Philosophy*, pp. 154-5; *The Scientific Outlook*, p. 82; *Religion and Science*, pp. 128-30; *Analysis of Matter*, p. 254.) The representational element in his causal theory is considerably weakened.

40. However, in 1931 Russell was apparently worried that, "under the influence of physics" he had "been driven into a position not unlike that of Berkeley. . . . " See his *Autobiography*, p. 395.

41. Russell's early protestations about the irrelevance of biological theories to philosophy eventually gave way to the view that a theory of knowledge needs to take account of the continuity between humans and non-human animals. (See, for example, Russell, *Inquiry into Meaning and Truth*, p. 247; *Analysis of Mind*, pp. 40-41.) Behaviorism influenced him in this and led him to give serious consideration to the role of pre-linguistic states in providing material for knowledge. So there is an important sense in which, in some of his later work, Russell takes some evolutionary insights into account in formulating his theory of knowledge. Unfortunately, when analytic philosophy took its "linguistic turn" Russell's insights about pre-linguistic states were abandoned. The heavy emphasis on the importance of linguistic items overshadowed Russell's point about our continuity with other animals. (See Elizabeth Eames, *Bertrand Russell's Theory of Knowledge*, p. 50.)

42. Stephen Stich offers a slightly different example, relevant to false beliefs in general: " . . . in an environment with a wide variety of suitable foods, an organism may do very well if it radically overgeneralizes about what is inedible. If eating a certain food caused illness on a single occasion, the organism would immediately come to believe (falsely, let us assume) that all passingly similar foods are poisonous as well. When it comes to food poisoning, *better safe than sorry* is a policy that recommends itself to natural selection." Stich, "Dennett on Intentional Systems," *Philosophical Topics* 12 (1981), reprinted in William Lycan, ed., *Mind and Cognition* (Cambridge, MA: Basil Blackwell, 1990) p. 177. See also Stich, *Fragmentation of Reason* (Cambridge, MA: MIT/Bradford, 1990) p. 62.

43. cf. Roderick Chisholm, "Russell on the Empirical Foundations of Knowledge," in *The Philosophy of Bertrand Russell*, ed. Paul Schilpp, p. 421.
44. Russell, "Reply," in Schilpp, p. 707.
45. In his later work Russell will discount the force of *arguments* for realism that rely on passivity. (Russell, *Inquiry into Meaning and Truth*, p. 234.)
46. Moore, in his paper, "The Status of Sense-Data," (1913-14) makes reference to *attention*. But the notion he intends is simply that of alert awareness. He notes, for example, that it seems to be required in cases of "direct apprehension." "The Status of Sense Data," in *Philosophical Studies*, (New York: Humanities, 1951) p. 176. Later, in his *Commonplace Book*, (London: Allen & Unwin, 1962) in the Notebook from 1919, he discusses "discrimination." He is exploring what might be the case when one can discriminate between two shades of a color or between two sounds. The goal of his whole discussion of discrimination, including some remarks on attention, is to get clear about whether or not, when differences are given, one can always discriminate those differences. (See Moore, "Discrimination," as well as the subsequent and untitled entry, in *Commonplace Book*, pp. 63-69.)
47. Russell, *Collected Papers*, VII, p. 123. Note that this way of construing analysis—as requiring that one take account of the whole to which the analyzed part belongs—was not Russell's preferred way. He generally treats analysis as a process of isolating data for purposes of clarification. They may then be related with other data in a process of construction, but that process is subsequent to analysis, not a necessary part of it.
48. Russell, *Collected Papers*, VII, pp. 132-3.
49. Russell, *Collected Papers*, VII, p. 40. His view here appears to be concerned with different ways in which one can be acquainted with objects. Attention is one way. It gives us the capacity to attend to one object from among many. " . . . within the general relation of acquaintance, there are various recognizably different ways of experiencing particular objects. There is *attention*, which selects what is in some sense *one* object. There is *sensation*, which serves to define 'the present time'. . . . There is *memory*, which applies only to past objects; and there is *imagination*, which gives objects without any temporal relation to the subject." (p. 79.)
50. Russell, *Outline of Philosophy*, p. 213.
51. Russell, *Human Knowledge: Its Scope and Limits*, p. 8.
52. See "Knowledge by Acquaintance and Knowledge by Description," in *Problems of Philosophy* (London: Oxford, 1959) pp. 49-51. In his 1917 reprint of the essay he repeats a somewhat more cautious commitment to acquaintance with some version of the self. See also "Knowledge by Acquaintance and Knowledge by Description," in *Mysticism and Logic*, pp. 202-203.
53. Russell, *Collected Papers*, VII, p. 35.
54. Russell, "Knowledge by Acquaintance and Knowledge by Description," in *Mysticism and Logic*, p. 201.
55. Russell adds the notion of *sensibilia*, literally "possible sensory information," in order to account for sensory material that is theoretically available to perceivers but not actually being perceived.

56. "The Relation of Sense-Data to Physics," in *Mysticism and Logic*, p. 144.

57. In 1909, Moore in fact argued for the need for some notion of *I* or *subject*, and he thought it might be the body. He suggested that the unity of our mental acts *may* arise from their common relation to our body. See his paper "The Subject-Matter of Psychology," *Proceedings of the Aristotelian Society*, 10 (1909-10) p. 54. Incidentally, Moore makes no effort in the paper to distinguish between psychology and epistemology. His views on these matters had little impact on much of the theorizing about perception that followed.

58. See Russell, "On Propositions: What They Are and How They Mean," in*Logic and Knowledge*, p. 306.

59. He sees Subjectivity as a necessary element in the notion of *mind*, but it is not sufficient to define it. The latter will require, in addition "mnemic causation," the capacity to be affected by past experience. Mnemic effects distinguish perceptions from appearances where there is no living brain. (Russell,*Analysis of Mind*, p. 131.) Russell was clearly influenced in this last point by his reading of Watson's behaviorism and the "principle of the conditioned reflex." (He had read some of Watson's papers while in prison in 1918.) So a mind is a series of perspectives that can be affected by past experiences. The emphasis is passive, cognitive, and has no concern with bodily well-being.

60. Russell, *Analysis of Matter*, p. 270.

61. Russell, *Analysis of Matter*, pp. 223-225; also *Human Knowledge: Its Scope and Limits*, p. 7.

62. Russell, *Outline of Philosophy*, p. 141.

63. Russell, *Religion and Science*, p. 131.

64. In 1940 he will argue that all emphatic (or "egocentric") particulars "can be defined in terms of 'this.' Thus: 'I' means 'The biography to which this belongs;" And even "this," when his analysis is complete, "is a word which is not needed for a complete description of the world." (Russell, *An Inquiry into Meaning and Truth*, pp. 108; 113.)

65. For convincing evidence that this is a mistake, see the work of Josef Albers, for example his *Interaction of Color* (New Haven: Yale University Press, 1971).

66. Russell, *Portraits from Memory*, p. 39; p. 41.

67. Russell, *Analysis of Mind*, p. 131.

68. Russell, *Analysis of Mind*, pp. 77-78.

69. Russell, *Analysis of Matter*, p. 189-90.

70. Russell, *Religion and Science*, pp. 206-7.

71. Russell, *My Philosophical Development*, p. 158.

72. Moore also uses consciousness as the most fundamental characteristic of the mental. See his paper, "The Subject-Matter of Psychology," *Proceedings of the Aristotelian Society*, 10 (1909-10) pp. 38-39.

73. Russell, "The Ultimate Constituents of Matter," *Collected Papers*, VIII, p. 75.

74. Russell, "Professor Dewey's *Essays in Experimental Logic*," *Collected Papers*, VIII, p. 147.

75. Russell, "Behaviourism and Knowledge," *Collected Papers*, VIII, p. 257.

76. Russell, "On Sensations and Ideas," *Collected Papers*, VIII, p. 255. Russell apparently remained a convinced Neutral Monist to the end of his life.

77. A similar point was made by James Mursell in his review of Russell's *Analysis of Mind* in *Journal of Philosophy*, 19 (1922) p. 165.
78. E.G. Boring, *A History of Experimental Psychology*, 2nd ed., (New York: Appleton-Century-Crofts, 1957) p. 555.
79. Edwin G. Boring, *A History of Experimental Psychology*, p. 243.
80. Russell, *Analysis of Mind*, pp. 121-122.
81. Russell, *Analysis of Mind*, p. 105.
82. Russell, *Analysis of Mind*, p. 255.
83. Russell, *Analysis of Mind*, p. 278.
84. See for example Russell's *Outline of Philosophy* p. 20; pp. 27-28.
85. Russell, "Philosophy of Logical Atomism," *Logic and Knowledge*, pp. 201-202.
86. Russell, *Portraits from Memory*, p. 42.
87. Note, for example, that the two share the same intentional object—a fact about which Garth Hallett reminded me.
88. For a revealing account of the interconnection of the cortical and subcortical activities in the brain during fear states—controlling the organism's cognitive and physiological responses—see Joseph LeDoux, "Cognitive-Emotional Interactions in the Brain," and "Emotion, Memory, and the Brain."
89. Russell, *Outline of Philosophy*, p. 227, p. 230.
90. Russell, *Outline of Philosophy*, p. 226.
91. Bertrand Russell, "Cleopatra or Maggie Tuliver," *Collected Papers*, I. He distinguishes between *passions*—"a body of particular desires coordinated by direction to a single end or to a closely related system of ends"—and *emotions*—"the State of Mind accompanying the fruition or frustration . . . of a Passion, with special reference to its aspect of pleasure and pain." (p. 92) In this early paper Russell defines passion in terms of desires, and says that "Desire and knowledge are separate and independent realms. . . . Knowledge is concerned with fact—Desire can (and does) damn facts, and construct an utterly different world of its own, a self-subsistent world, for which the ultimate and entire justification is that it is desired, and would satisfy desire if it were actual."(p. 97) Both passion and emotion are defined without any reference to the body. This is rectified in his later account.
92. Russell, "Cleopatra or Maggie Tuliver," p. 93.
93. Russell, "Cleopatra or Maggie Tuliver," p. 95.
94. Russell, letter #429, April 30, 1912, Bertrand Russell Archives.
95. Russell, *Outline of Philosophy*, p. 228. Could this final phrase possibly be a gesture of defiance against Marxist views?
96. Russell, *Skeptical Essays*, p. 123.
97. Moore, *Principia Ethica*, pp. 189-190.
98. Moore, "The Character of Cognitive Acts," *Proceedings of the Aristotelian Society*, 21.
99. Russell, "Philosophy of Logical Atomism," p. 181.
100. Russell, *Collected Papers*, IX, p. 43.
101. Russell, *Religion and Science*, pp. 205-206.
102. Russell, *Portraits from Memory*, pp. 153-155.
103. See, for example, Russell's paper, "On Propositions: What They Are and How They Mean," where he *seems* to equate the act of consciousness with the

subject. " . . . Meinong, for example—distinguish[es] three elements in a presentation, namely, the act (or subject), the content, and the object. . . . I have to confess that the theory which analyses a presentation into act and object no longer satisfies me. The act, or subject, is schematically convenient, but not empirically discoverable." *Logic and Knowledge*, p. 305.

104. Russell, *Our Knowledge of the External World*, p. 81. It is worth noting that this way of dividing up the notion of self is suggestive of an analogous distinction made by William James. In his *Principles of Psychology*, which Russell read in 1894 and 1895, James has a chapter on the self in which he makes a distinction quite like the one Russell makes here. James distinguishes between the "me" and the "I," what he also calls the empirical ego and the pure ego or subject. See pp. 279-379 in the *Principles*.

105. Russell, "On Propositions: What They Are and How They Mean," p. 305-306.

106. Russell, *My Philosophical Development*, p. 104.

107. Russell, *Outline of Philosophy*, p. 171.

108. See, for example, his comments in *Religion and Science*, pp. 118-119.

109. Passmore, *A Hundred Years of Philosophy*, p. 209.

Chapter 5

1. Edmund Husserl, "Philosophy as a Rigorous Science," in *Phenomenology and the Crisis of Philosophy*, trans. Quentin Lauer (New York: Harper Torchbook, 1965 [orig. pub. 1910]) p. 140. A small portion of this chapter appears in the 1995 edition of the *Encyclopedia of Phenomenology*.

2. Husserl, "Phenomenology and Anthropology," trans. by Richard Schmitt, in McCormick and Elliston, eds., *Husserl: Shorter Works*, (Notre Dame: University of Notre Dame Press, 1981) p. 317; this lecture was originally presented in 1931.

3. See Husserl's *Idea of Phenomenology*, trans. by W.P. Alston and G. Nakhnikian (The Hague: Nijhoff, 1973 [lectures originally given in 1907]) p. 23; *Ideas*, Vol.I, trans. by W.R. Boyce Gibson (London: Collier, 1962 [orig. pub. 1913]) #84, p. 223; *Cartesian Meditations*, #14, p. 33.

4. Franz Brentano, *Psychology from an Empirical Standpoint*, L. McAlister, ed.; trans. by Rancurello, Terrell, and McAlister (London: Routledge & Kegan Paul, 1973) vol.I, Bk.II, chapter 1, #5.

5. Husserl, "Phenomenology and Anthropology," *Shorter Works*, p. 317.

6. Husserl, *Cartesian Meditations*, #6, p. 15.

7. Husserl, *Formal and Transcendental Logic*, trans. by Dorion Cairns (The Hague: Nijhoff, 1969) #94, p. 234.

8. For an extended discussion of Husserl's theory of meaning, see J.N. Mohanty, *Edmund Husserl's Theory of Meaning* (The Hague: Nijhoff, 1969) and "Husserl's Theory of Meaning," in F. Elliston and P. McCormick, eds., *Husserl. Expositions and Appraisals* (Notre Dame: University of Notre Dame Press, 1977).

9. See Husserl's *Cartesian Meditations*, #41, p. 86; also *Formal and Transcendental Logic #60, p. 162.*

10. Husserl, Formal and Transcendental Logic, #26, p. 81.
11. Husserl's complex and extended argument is given in *Formal and Transcendental Logic*, Part II, Chapter 4, especially #88-93. I have offered an elucidation of that argument in, "Representation: Rorty vs. Husserl," in *Synthese*, 66 (1986), pp. 273-289.
12. For a clear discussion of this issue, see Harrison Hall, "Was Husserl a Realist or an Idealist?" in H.Dreyfus, ed., *Husserl: Intentionality and Cognitive Science* (Cambridge, MA: MIT Press, 1981).
13. See N.R. Hanson, *Patterns of Discovery* (Cambridge: Cambridge University Press, 1958). Paul Teller originally brought this question to my attention in a discussion following my presentation of a paper on Husserl several years ago.
14. Husserl, *Formal and Transcendental Logic*, Appendix II, #2(b), pp. 316-317.
15. Husserl, *Phenomenological Psychology*, trans. by John Scanlon (The Hague: Nijhoff, 1977) #41, pp. 161-162; *Cartesian Meditations*, #32.
16. See, for example, Husserl's *Cartesian Meditations*, #22, p. 54.
17. Husserl, *Phenomenological Psychology*, #3(e), p. 27.
18. It is difficult to be sure whether or not he would have included computers in his claim. When he speaks of "any sort of beings which can count, compute, do mathematics . . . " one is tempted to suppose that computers would be included. On the other hand, he also speaks of "objects of *consciousness* in *subjective* lived experiences," and it is less clear that computers would count among the beings he intends to include in that group. Since he wrote this in 1925, it is unlikely that he saw the ambiguity that his claim harbors. But it is likely that his emphasis on consciousness and Subjectivity would exclude non-conscious systems.
19. Husserl, *Cartesian Meditations*, #5, p. 13; see also *Ideas*, #24, p. 83.
20. Husserl, *Cartesian Meditations*, #5, pp. 13-14.
21. See Husserl, *Phenomenological Psychology*, #9(d), p. 59.
22. See Husserl, *Phenomenological Psychology*, #9(a), p. 54.
23. See Husserl, *Cartesian Meditations*, #34, pp. 70-72; *Phenomenological Psychology*, #9, pp. 54-65.
24. Just as in the description of the data, so also in the step to uncover essences, one can focus on different portions of the data. But one can also operate at a number of different levels of generality. (Husserl, *Phenomenological Psychology*, #9(e), pp. 60-62.) One might be interested in the essence of perception-of-something, where the emphasis is on the act of *perception*. Or one might focus, more generally, on consciousness-of-something, where one would look for commonalities that are essential to perception, memory, imagination, etc. On the other side, one might focus on what is essential to the experience of perceiving-a-tree, where the emphasis is on the perceived *tree* (which will differ in certain discoverable ways from an imagined tree, for example). Or one might be interested in the perceived *object* (of whatever sort). Different elements in the act-object structure, and varying levels of generality, will be relevant to different areas of investigation. One set might be more relevant to the natural sciences, another to psychology, still another to metaphysics, etc.
25. Husserl, *Ideas*, I, Author's Introduction, p. 40.

26. Husserl, *Phenomenological Psychology*, #18; #27, p. 114.

27. See Husserl, *The Idea of Phenomenology*, p. 31; see also the Introduction ("The Train of Thoughts in the Lectures") and Lecture I where he discusses the issue extensively. Husserl's most extensive criticisms of psychologism appear in the Prolegomena to his *Logical Investigations*, Vol. I. trans. by John Findlay (London: Routledge and Kegan Paul, 1970 [orig. pub. 1900]). See also his *Formal and Transcendental Logic*, trans. by Dorion Cairns, #55, p. 149ff. and #65, p. 169ff.

28. Husserl's posthumously published *The Crisis of European Sciences and Transcendental Phenomenology*, trans. David Carr (Evanston: Northwestern University Press, 1979), is an extended argument to this effect.

29. Bertrand Russell, "On the Relation of Sense-Data to Physics," Scientia, 4, 1914; reprinted in *Mysticism and Logic*, pp. 140-172.

30. See especially Merleau-Ponty's *Phenomenology of Perception*, trans. by Colin Smith (London: Routledge & Kegan Paul, 1962).

31. Husserl, "Philosophy as Rigorous Science," p. 80.

32. Husserl, *Ideas*, I, #42, p. 121; see also John Scanlon's Introduction to Husserl's "Phenomenology and Anthropology," *Shorter Works*, p. 311.

33. See his *Phenomenological Psychology*, #14, p. 79; #15, pp. 80- 81.

34. Husserl, *Phenomenological Psychology*, #14, p. 79.

35. Husserl, *The Crisis of European Sciences*, #64, p. 221.

36. Husserl, *The Crisis of European Sciences*, #64, pp. 222-223.

37. See, too, his comments on the work of Rudolf Eucken. In a tribute to Eucken in 1916 Husserl says:

> "There are ... two ways to penetrate to the essential difference between man in nature and man as mind or spirit (Geist), in order to catch sight of the unity of spiritual life increasingly manifest in the course of human history and to trace it back to its primordial sources. Rudolf Eucken has followed the first in his philosophy of spiritual life, and phenomenological philosophy has chosen the second. . . .
>
> Instead of regarding human spiritual life as a mere causal appendage to nature Eucken saw in it the unity of a life-stream sustained by an immanent teleology in which the finality of motivation predominates, not the causality of its nature. . . .
>
> Eucken's philosophy and phenomenological philosophy must ultimately fuse into an harmonious agreement." ("Selected Letters," in *Shorter Works*, p. 353-354.)

The dualism suggested here may not be the substance dualism of Descartes, but there is a sharp distinction made between nature and spirit or mind, between the realm of causality and the realm of motivation. However one is to understand mind (or intellect or consciousness), it is not simply part of the causally governed realm of nature.

38. Husserl, *Phenomenological Psychology*, #15, p. 82. The context suggests a distinction between the "psychic" (which is experienced in conjunction with a body)

and the "mind" (which is "the absolute which the world already presup-
poses"). But Husserl does not continue to make the terminological distinction
carefully himself.

39. Jerry Fodor's work in this area offers an important example.
40. Husserl, *Phenomenological Psychology*, #3(b), p. 18.
41. Husserl, *Phenomenological Psychology*, #3(b), p. 20.
42. For some striking examples that challenge the notion of timeless and universal
    structures of meaning, see George Lakoff, *Women, Fire, and Dangerous Things*
    (Chicago: University of Chicago Press, 1987).
43. Husserl, *The Idea of Phenomenology*, pp. 16-17.
44. G. Frege, "Key Sentences in Logic," *Posthumous Writings*, p. 174.
45. Husserl, *Logical Investigations*, I, p. 111 ff. Husserl also discusses Mill and
    Spencer in connection with the status of properties, pp. 345-347.
46. See Herbert Schnadelbach, *Philosophy in Germany, 1831-1933* (Cambridge:
    Cambridge University Press, 1984) pp. 34-40, for an extended discussion of
    historicism in Germany.
47. Erazim Kohak, "Selected Letters," *Husserl: Shorter Works*, p. 357.
48. Husserl, letter to Arnold Metzger, September 14, 1919, "Selected Letters,"
    Shorter Works, p. 360.
49. Husserl, letter to Metzger, *Shorter Works*, p. 362.
50. Husserl, "Selected Letters," in *Husserl: Shorter Works*, p. 356.
51. Husserl, *Shorter Works*, p. 357.
52. See Husserl's comments in *Phenomenological Psychology*, #3(c), pp. 21-22.
53. Husserl, "Phenomenology and Anthropology," *Shorter Works*, p. 316.
54. Husserl, *Idea of Phenomenology*, pp. 18-19.
55. Husserl, *Ideas*, I, #24, p. 83.
56. See, for example, his *Cartesian Meditations*, pp. 13-14.
57. Husserl, *Ideas*, I, #19 and #20.
58. There is an extensive literature on the mechanisms involved in memory. One
    of the classic sources is Frederic C. Bartlett, *Remembering* (Cambridge: Cam-
    bridge University Press, 1932). For a more recent collection of papers, see
    Henry Roediger and Fergus Craik, eds., *Varieties of Memory and Consciousness*
    (Hillsdale, NJ: Erlbaum, 1989).
59. See Abner Shimony, "Perception from an Evolutionary Point of View," *Journal
    of Philosophy*. 68 (1971), p. 572, for a similar point, but without reference to Husserl.
60. Husserl, *Idea of Phenomenology*, p. 24.
61. For extensive arguments against the notion of intuition, see Charles Peirce,
    "Questions Concerning Certain Faculties," *Journal of Speculative Philosophy*,
    vol. 2, 1868, pp. 103-114.

Chapter 6

1. Husserl, *Phenomenological Psychology*, trans. by John Scanlon (The Hague:
   Nijhoff, 1977) p. 97.
2. Husserl, *Experience and Judgment*, ed. by Ludwig Landgrebe, trans. by James

Churchill and Karl Ameriks (Evanston, IL: Northwestern University Press, 1973) #17, p. 79.

3. See Husserl, *Phenomenological Psychology*, #29-31, pp. 125-128.

4. Husserl, *Ideas*, I, #27, p. 92.

5. Husserl, *Ideas*, I, #44, p. 125.

6. Husserl, *Experience and Judgment*, #8, p. 32; see also *Cartesian Meditations*, #19, p. 45, and *The Crisis of European Sciences*, #48, p. 167.

7. Husserl, *Phenomenological Psychology*, #6, p. 46.

8. Husserl, *Experience and Judgment*, #33, pp. 149-151.

9. Husserl, *Experience and Judgment*, #8, pp. 33-4.

10. Husserl, *Phenomenological Psychology*, #6, p. 45.

11. See Husserl, *Ideas*, I, #27, p. 92.

12. See Husserl, *The Phenomenology of Internal Time- Consciousness*, M. Heidegger, ed., trans. by J.S. Churchill (Bloomington, IN: Indiana University Press, 1964 [lectures orig. given in 1905]) p. 43ff.

13. Husserl, Ideas, I, #83, p. 221.

14. Husserl, *Cartesian Meditations*, #28; #41, pp. 83-88; #11, p. 26; *Ideas*, I, #44, pp. 124 ff.

15. Husserl does discuss the role of certain habits and dispositions as defining a personality. See *Phenomenological Psychology*, #42, p. 164.

16. Husserl, *Ideas*, I, #27, p. 93.

17. Husserl, *Ideas*, I, #95, p. 255.

18. Husserl, *Cartesian Meditations*, #24, p. 58.

19. Husserl, *Cartesian Meditations*, #13, p. 30.

20. See Husserl, *Phenomenological Psychology*, #3(f), p. 31-2.

21. See, for example, his condemnation of theories that see the mind as a causal supplement to physical bodies or as running in parallel with them, *Phenomenological Psychology*, #6, p. 41.

22. Husserl, *Phenomenological Psychology*, #23, pp. 106-107.

23. Husserl, *Phenomenological Psychology*, #14, p. 79.

24. Husserl, *Phenomenological Psychology*, #3(c), pp. 20-21.

25. Husserl, *Phenomenological Psychology*, #23, p. 103.

26. Husserl, *Phenomenological Psychology*, #24, p. 107.

27. Husserl, *Phenomenological Psychology*, #24, p. 108.

28. One might compare his method here to that used by David Armstrong in his *Materialist Theory of Mind*: one begins with an account of mental *concepts* and only later approaches the issue of the metaphysical status of mental states.

29. For a compelling account of the role the body plays in the formation of many of our most basic concepts, see Mark Johnson, *The Body in the Mind: The Bodily Basis of Meaning* (Chicago: University of Chicago Press, 1990).

Chapter 7

1. Substantial portions of this chapter have been published previously in two journal articles: "Perception, Meaning, and Mind," *Synthese*, 80 (1989), and

"A Darwinian Approach to Functionalism," *Journal of Philosophical Research* XVI (1990-91). My paper, "Perceptual Meaning and Husserl," *Philosophy and Phenomenological Research*, 45(4), 1985, contains some relevant background material.

2. An objection suggested to me by Garth Hallett.

3. When the context allows it, I shall use the term "psychological" rather than "mental" simply to avoid the metaphysical issue completely.

4. I shall use the lower case *d* to characterize views that are darwinian in the sense that they are at least consistent with Darwin's views, even if he did not explicitly articulate them himself.

5. James, *Principles of Psychology*, p. 379.

6. James, *Principles*, p. 324.

7. James, *Principles*, p. 317.

8. James, *Principles*, pp. 319-320.

9. See Robert Ehman, "William James and the Structures of the Self," in *New Essays in Phenomenology*, ed. by James Edie (Chicago: Quadrangle, 1969), p. 268. I am grateful to Vincent Colapietro for calling this point to my attention.

10. I suspect that it is often simply taken for granted, but making it explicit can give one's philosophy of mind quite a different direction from the theories currently being proposed. Most contemporary theories treat mind as an "anonymous" repository of information.

11. I owe this objection to Thomas Carlson.

12. There is one additional consideration that supports the view I am proposing. It is commonly claimed, against theories of the self that rely heavily on memory, as this one does, that persons with amnesia would be left with no self, no personal identity. But on the view I suggest, several dimensions of the subject are normally left in tact. For example, the body of the individual is integral to its Subjectivity. And, obviously, amnesia does not cause the loss of one's body, nor does it cause a loss of one's awareness of that body's current state and needs. Second, amnesia may cause one to lose track of portions of the self that James calls the "me"—may cause me to forget my name, my family, where I work, what I did yesterday, etc. That is, it may cause me to lose access to all the objective ways that I and others have come to see me. It may even cause me to lose track of some of the content of my own psychological states over which my Subjectivity normally functions, but it leaves both the functions and the content at least minimally in tact. It does not, for example, cause me to forget that I am here now, that I speak English, that I know how to walk, that I am hungry, that I cannot remember what I did yesterday, etc. That is to say, there remains even in amnesia victims a *core* of Subjectivity, a core of personal identity, upon which the rest is built. This is the foundation on which my continuing identity is built, however much the other dimensions of that identity may change.

13. I use the phrase "perceptual *meaning*" rather than perceptual *sense* primarily because the latter is ambiguous and might suggest sensory mechanisms.

14. For Husserl's best-known extended discussion of the *noema* see *Ideas*, I, trans. by W.R. Boyce Gibson. Dagfinn Follesdal's paper, "Husserl's Notion of

Noema" *Journal of Philosophy*, 66 (1969), was the seminal work in suggesting a Fregean interpretation of Husserl's view. I make no claims to be faithful to Husserl's intentions; and, as will become apparent, my view is directly at odds with that of Follesdal.

15. Barwise and Perry, in *Situations and Attitudes*, have offered a comprehensive theory of meaning (i.e., a theory that covers more than just linguistic meaning) in terms of what I am calling "signitive meaning."

16. I shall confine my claims to cases in which a person perceives an *object* or an *event*. The perception of *language* involves important differences from the other cases, differences which make it unwise to take the perception of language as paradigmatic for all perception. The most obvious assymetry for present purposes is that the "transparency" of perceived language—it generally directs our attention to something other than itself—makes the application of the sense-reference distinction more complex than it is in the perception of objects and events.

17. cf. G.H. Bower, "Mood and Memory," *American Psychologist*, February, 1981.

18. I deliberately construe the term "meaning" broadly here. Note, for example, that an action like pointing will be indexical not only in terms of the object it picks out (its "referent," so to speak) but also in terms of what significance it has in this particular context. It might be a gesture of accusation, it might be an attempt at ostensive definition, it might be giving directions, etc.

19. See David W. Smith, "The Ins and Outs of Perception," *Philosophical Studies*, 49, 1986; "Content and Context of Perception," *Synthese*, 61, 1984.

20. cf. Merleau-Ponty, in *Phenomenology of Perception*: "The word 'here' applied to my body does not refer to a determinate position in relation to other positions or to external co-ordinates, but the laying down of the first co-ordinates, the anchoring of the active body in an object, the situation of the body in face of its tasks." p. 100.

21. See John Perry, "The Problem of the Essential Indexical," *Nous*, 13, 1979, for a discussion of an analogous point in relation to belief.

22. For some recent discussions of indexicality as it relates to perception see David W. Smith, "The Ins and Outs of Perception," *Philosophical Studies*, 49 (1986) and "Content and Context of Perception," *Synthese*, 61 (1984); Jaakko Hintikka, "Objects of Knowledge and Belief," in *The Intentions of Intentionality* (Dordrecht: Reidel, 1985); Colin McGinn, *The Subjective View* (Oxford: Clarendon, 1983); Christopher Peacocke, *Sense and Content* (Oxford: Clarendon, 1983); Izchak Miller, *Husserl, Perception, and Temporal Awareness* (Cambridge, Mass.: MIT Press, 1984); John Searle, *Intentionality*, (Cambridge: Cambridge University Press, 1983); Hector-Neri Castaneda, "Perception, Belief, and the Structure of Physical Objects and Consciousness," *Synthese*, 35 (1977). In addition there is considerable work on indexical and demonstrative concepts, the most relevant for my purposes being, John Perry's paper "The Problem of the Essential Indexical," *Nous*, 13 (1979). The entire issue of *Synthese* 49 (1981) is devoted to the topic of indexicality.

23. By John Haugeland in a commentary on an earlier version of this material, delivered at a meeting of the Indiana Philosophical Association.

24. Although Stephen Stich makes a convincing case that there are some beliefs for which truth-conditions are extraordinarily elusive. See *From Folk Psychology to Cognitive Science* (Cambridge, MA: MIT/Bradford, 1983).

25. There are, of course, two sets of feelings to be distinguished here: those that are remembered and those that are currently generated by that remembering.

26. See Stephen Stich's *From Folk Psychology to Cognitive Science* for example.

27. For a collection of papers addressing this issue, see C.E. Izard, J. Kagan, and R. Zajonc, eds., *Emotion, Cognition, and Behavior* (Cambridge: Cambridge University Press, 1984); more recently a new journal, *Cognition and Emotion*, is devoted to work being done in a variety of disciplines on the reciprocal relations between cognition and emotion. For some of the striking research done in neuroscience, see Joseph LeDoux, "Cognitive-Emotional Interactions in the Brain," *Cognition and Emotion*, 1989, 3 (4); and "Emotion, Memory, and the Brain," *Scientific American*, June, 1994. See also the work of Antonio Damasio, including *Descartes' Error: Emotion, Reason, and the Human Brain* (New York: Putnam, 1994).

28. Hilary Putnam, "Philosophy and our Mental Life," in *Mind, Language and Reality* (Cambridge: Cambridge University Press, 1975) p. 302.

29. Hilary Putnam, *Representation and Reality* (Cambridge, MA: MIT/Bradford, 1988) p. xii.

30. Jerry Fodor, *Representations* (Cambridge, MA: MIT Press, 1981) pp. 8-9.

31. Georges Rey, "Functionalism and the Emotions," in *Explaining Emotions*, ed. by Amelie O. Rorty (Berkeley: University of California Press, 1980).

32. Jerome Shaffer, "An Assessment of Emotion," *American Philosophical Quarterly*. 20:161-173.

33. Robert Solomon, "Emotions and Choice," in *What is an Emotion?*, Robert Solomon and Cheshire Calhoun, eds. (Oxford: Oxford University Press, 1984).

34. I bypass here the refinements suggested by Joseph LeDoux's research, concerning the likely order in which events occur in the case of fear. From LeDoux's point of view, the physiological responses precede the fully conscious cognitive state of belief. There are good evolutionary reasons to think that his account of that order is correct, but the order itself is not germane to the present discussion.

35. John Perry, "The Problem of the Essential Indexical," pp. 3-21.

36. J.E. LeDoux, "The neurobiology of emotion," in *Mind and Brain. Dialogues in cognitive neuroscience*, ed. by Joseph E. LeDoux and William Hirst (Cambridge: Cambridge University Press, 1986), pp. 315-316.

37. John Haugeland made a similar point about Cognitivism in his paper, "The Nature and Plausibility of Cognitivism," *The Behavioral and Brain Sciences* (1978) 1, reprinted in *Mind Design*. Haugeland was, I think, excessively generous in limiting his claim to moods and skills (and "understanding"). cf. also D.A. Norman, "12 Issues for Cognitive Science," in D.A. Norman, ed., *Perspectives on Cognitive Science* (Norwood, N.J.: Ablex Pub., 1981).

Bibliography

Aiken, Henry. 1962. "The Rise of Analytical Philosophy in England," in *Philosophy in the Twentieth Century*, W. Barrett and H. Aiken, eds. New York: Harper & Row.

Albers, Josef. 1971. *The Interaction of Color*. New Haven: Yale University Press.

Ambrose, Alice and Lazerowitz, Morris. eds. 1970. *G.E. Moore: Essays in Retrospect*. London: Allen & Unwin.

Anscombe, G.E.M. 1975. "The First Person," in Samuel Guttenplan, ed. *Mind and Language*. Oxford: Clarendon.

Appleman, Philip, ed. 1970. *Darwin*. New York: Norton.

Armstrong, D.M. 1980. *The Nature of Mind and Other Essays*. Ithaca: Cornell University Press.

Armstrong, D.M. 1968. *A Materialist Theory of Mind*. London: Routledge & Kegan Paul.

Audi, Robert. "The Rational Assessment of Emotions," *Southwestern Journal of Philosophy* 8:115-119.

Ayer, A.J. 1972. "An Appraisal of Bertrand Russell's Philosophy." In D.F. Pears, ed., *Bertrand Russell: A Collection of Critical Essays*.

Ayer, A.J. 1972. *Bertrand Russell*. New York: Viking.

Ayer, A.J., et. al. 1965. *The Revolution in Philosophy*. New York: St. Martin's Press.

Ayer, A.J., ed. 1959. *Logical Positivism*. Glencoe, IL: Free Press.

Baker, Lynne Rudder. 1981. "On Making and Attributing Demonstrative Reference," *Synthese* 49:245-274.

Baker, Lynne Rudder. 1979. "Indexical Reference and *De Re* Belief," *Philosophical Studies* 36:317-327.

Baldwin, James M. 1909. *Darwin and The Humanities*. New York: AMS Reprint.

Baldwin, Thomas. 1990. *G.E. Moore*. London: Routledge & Kegan Paul.

Bar-Hillel, Y. 1954. "Indexical Expressions," *Mind*, 63: 359-379.

Bartlett, Frederic. 1932. *Remembering*. Cambridge: Cambridge University Press.

Barwise, Jon, and John Perry. 1983. *Situations and Attitudes*. Cambridge, MA: MIT Press.

Bedford, Errol. 1957. "Emotion," *Proceedings of the Aristotelian Society*, 57:281-304.

Bergson, Henri. 1944 [1911]. *Creative Evolution*. trans. by A. Mitchell. New York: Random House.

Blau, Joseph. 1952. *Men and Movements in American Philosophy*. New York: Prentice-Hall.

Block, Ned. ed. 1981. *Imagery*. Cambridge, MA: MIT Press.

Block, Ned. ed. 1980-1981. *Readings in Philosophy of Psychology.* 2 vol. Cambridge, MA: Harvard University Press.

Boden, Margaret. 1977. *Artificial Intelligence and Natural Man.* New York: Harvester Press.

Boden, Margaret. 1969. "Machine Perception," *Philosophical Quarterly* 19:33-45.

Boring, Edwin. 1957. *A History of Experimental Psychology.* 2nd ed. New York: Appleton-Century-Crofts.

Bower, Gordon. 1981. "Mood and Memory," *American Psychologist* 36:129-148.

Bowler, Peter. 1988. *The Non-Darwinian Revolution.* Baltimore: Johns Hopkins.

Bowler, Peter. 1984. *Evolution: The History of an Idea.* Berkeley: University of California Press.

Bowler, Peter. 1983. *The Eclipse of Darwinism.* Baltimore: Johns Hopkins.

Bowler, Peter. 1976. "Malthus, Darwin, and the Concept of Struggle." *Journal of the History of Ideas.* 37:631-650.

Bradie, Michael. 1989. "Evolutionary Epistemology as Naturalized Epistemology," in Kai Hahlweg and C.A. Hooker, eds., *Issues in Evolutionary Epistemology.* Albany: SUNY Press.

Brentano, Franz. 1973 [1874]. *Psychology from an Empirical Standpoint.* London: Routledge & Kegan Paul.

Broad, Charles Dunbar. 1924. "Critical and Speculative Philosophy." In J.H. Muirhead, ed., *Contemporary British Philosophy.* First Series: 75-100.

Brown, Harold. 1972. "Perception and Meaning," in *American Philosophical Quarterly* Monograph #6, *Studies in the Philosophy of Mind,* Oxford: Blackwell.

Burge, Tyler. 1979. "Individualism and the Mental," *Midwest Studies,* 4:73-121.

Burks, Arthur. 1948-1949. "Icon, Index, and Symbol," *Philosophy and Phenomenological Research,* 9:673-689.

Burrow, J.W. 1966. *Evolution and Society: A Study in Victorian Social Theory.* Cambridge: Cambridge University Press.

Campbell, Donald. 1974. "Evolutionary Epistemology." In Paul Schilpp, ed., *Philosophy of Karl Popper.* LaSalle, IL: Open Court.

Caplan, Arthur and Jennings, Bruce, eds. 1984. *Darwin, Marx, and Freud.* New York: Plenum.

Castaneda, H-N. 1967. *Intentionality, Mind, and Perception.* Detroit: Wayne State University Press.

Castaneda, H-N. 1966. " 'He': A Study in the Logic of Self-Consciousness," *Ratio,* 8:130-157.

Chisholm, Roderick. 1957. *Perceiving: A Philosophical Study.* Ithaca: Cornell University Press.

Clark, Ronald. 1976. *The Life of Bertrand Russell.* New York: Alfred A. Knopf.

Collins, James. 1959. "Darwin's Impact on Philosophy." *Thought.* 34:185-248.

Colp, Ralph. 1974. "The Contacts Between Karl Marx and Charles Darwin," *Journal of the History of Ideas,* 35:329-338.

Cronin, Helena. 1991. *The Ant and the Peacock.* Cambridge: Cambridge University Press.

Cunningham, Suzanne. (forthcoming) "Dewey on Emotions: Recent Experimental Evidence," *Transactions of the C.S. Peirce Society.*

Cunningham, Suzanne. 1994. "Herbert Spencer, Bertrand Russell, and the Shape of Early Analytic Philosophy," *Russell: The Journal of the Bertrand Russell Archives.* n.s. 14(1):7-29.

Cunningham, Suzanne. 1991. "A Darwinian Approach to Functionalism," *Journal of Philosophical Research*, 16: 145-157.

Cunningham, Suzanne. 1989. "Perception, Meaning, and Mind," *Synthese*, 80: 223-241.

Cunningham, Suzanne. 1986. "Representation: Rorty vs. Husserl," *Synthese*, 66: 273-289.

Cunningham, Suzanne. 1985. "Perceptual Meaning and Husserl," Philosophy and Phenomenological Research, 45: 553-566.

Cunningham, Suzanne. 1983. "Husserl and Private Languages," *Philosophy and Phenomenological Research*, 44: 103-111.

Cunningham, Suzanne. 1976. *Language and the Phenomenological Reductions of Edmund Husserl.* The Hague: Nijhoff.

Damasio, Antonio. 1994. *Descartes' Error.* New York: Putnam.

Dampier, William. 1966 [1929]. *A History of Science and Its Relations with Philosophy and Religion.* 4th ed. London: Cambridge University Press.

Darlington, C.D. 1959. *Darwin's Place in History.* Oxford: Blackwell.

Darwin, Charles. 1981 [1871 facsimile]. *The Descent of Man and Selection in Relation to Sex.* Princeton: Princeton University Press.

Darwin, Charles. 1977. *The Collected Papers of Charles Darwin.* 2 vols., Paul H. Barrett, ed. Chicago: University of Chicago Press.

Darwin, Charles. 1974. *Metaphysics, Materialism, and the Evolution of Mind. Early Writings of Charles Darwin.* [M and N Notebooks], transcribed and annotated by Paul H. Barrett. Chicago: University of Chicago Press.

Darwin, Charles. 1965 [1872]. *The Expression of the Emotions in Man and Animals.* Chicago: University of Chicago Press.

Darwin, Charles. n.d. [1872] *On the Origin of Species.* [6th ed.] and *The Descent Of Man* [2nd ed., 1874] New York: Modern Library.

Darwin, Charles. 1964 [1859 facsimile]. *On the Origin of Species.* 1st ed. Cambridge, MA: Harvard University Press.

Darwin, Charles. 1958 [1887]. *The Autobiography.* Nora Barlow, ed. New York: Norton.

Darwin, Francis, ed. 1959 [1887]. *The Life and Letters of Charles Darwin.* 2 vols. New York: Basic Books.

Dawkins, Richard. 1976. *The Selfish Gene.* Oxford: Oxford University Press.

Dennett, D.C. 1991. *Consciousness Explained.* Boston: Little, Brown, & Co.

Dennett, D.C. 1987. *The Intentional Stance.* Cambridge, MA: MIT/ Bradford.

Dennett, D.C. 1978. *Brainstorms.* Cambridge, MA: MIT/Bradford.

Dennett, D.C. 1969. *Content and Consciousness.* London: Routledge & Kegan Paul.

Deutsch, J.A., and D. Deutsch. 1963. "Attention: Some theoretical considerations," *Psychological Review* 87: 272-300.

De Vries, Hugo. 1910 [1901-03]. *The Mutation Theory.* Trans. by J.B. Farmer & A.D. Darbyshire. 2 vols. LaSalle, IL: Open Court.

Dewey, John. 1988 [1920]. *Reconstruction in Philosophy*, in *Middle Works*, vol. 12. JoAnn Boydston, ed. Carbondale, IL: Southern Illinois University Press.

Dewey, John. 1965 [1910]. *The Influence of Darwin on Philosophy*. Bloomington, IN: Indiana University Press.

Dewey, John. 1929. *The Quest for Certainty*. New York: Putnam.

Dewey, John. 1925. *Experience and Nature*. LaSalle, IL: Open Court.

Dewey, John. 1898. "Evolution and Ethics." *Monist* 8:321-341. Reprinted in *Early Works*, vol.5. Carbondale, IL: Southern Illinois University Press, 1972.

Dewey, John. 1896. "The Reflex Arc Concept in Psychology." *Psychological Review*. 3:357-370. Reprinted in *Early Works*, vol.5, Carbondale, IL: Southern Illinois University Press, 1972.

Dewey, John. 1894-95. "The Theory of Emotion." *Psychological Review*. I:553-569; II:13-32. Reprinted in *Early Works*, vol.4, Carbondale, IL: Southern Illinois University Press, 1971.

Dobzhansky, Theodosius. 1967. *Biology of Ultimate Concern*. New York: New American Library.

Dretske, Fred. 1981. *Knowledge and the Flow of Information*. Cambridge, MA: MIT Press.

Dretske, Fred. 1971. "Perception from an Epistemological Point of View," *Journal of Philosophy*. 68, pp.584-591.

Dreyfus, Hubert, ed. 1982. *Husserl: Intentionality and Cognitive Science*. Cambridge, MA: MIT Press.

Dreyfus, Hubert. 1979. *What Computers Can't Do*. 2nd ed. New York: Harper & Row.

Eames, Elizabeth. 1989. *Bertrand Russell's Dialogue with His Contemporaries*. Carbondale, IL: Southern Illinois University Press.

Eames, Elizabeth. 1969. *Bertrand Russell's Theory of Knowledge*. New York: George Braziller.

Edie, James, ed. 1969. *New Essays in Phenomenology*. Chicago: Quadrangle.

Elliston, Frederick, and Peter McCormick, eds. 1977. *Husserl: Expositions and Appraisals*. Notre Dame: University of Notre Dame Press.

Engels, Friedrich. 1978 [1880]. "Socialism: Utopian and Scientific," in *Marx-Engels Reader*. Ed. by R.C. Tucker. 2nd ed. New York: Norton.

Fay, Margaret. 1980. "Marx and Darwin," *Monthly Review*, March: 40-57.

Fay, Margaret. 1978. "Did Marx Offer to Dedicate *Capital* to Darwin?" *Journal of the History of Ideas*, 39: 133-146.

Flew, Anthony. 1984. "The Philosophical Implications of Darwinism." In Arthur Caplan, ed., *Darwin, Marx, and Freud*.

Flew, Anthony. 1967. *Evolutionary Ethics*. London: Macmillan.

Flew, Anthony. 1966. " 'The Concept of Evolution:' A Comment," *Philosophy*, 41: 70-75.

Fodor, Jerry. 1983. *Modularity of Mind*. Cambridge, MA: MIT Press.

Fodor, Jerry. 1981. *Representations*. Cambridge, MA: MIT Press.

Fodor, Jerry. 1975. *Language of Thought*. Cambridge, MA: Harvard University Press.

Follesdal, Dagfinn. 1969. "Husserl's Notion of Noema," *Journal of Philosophy* 66:680-687.

Frege, Gottlob. 1979. *Posthumous Writings*. Hans Hermes, Friedrich Kambartel, & Friedrich Kaulbach, eds., trans. by Peter Long & Roger White. Oxford: Blackwell.

Frege, Gottlob. 1960. *Translations from the Philosophical Writings of Gottlob Frege.* P. Geach & M. Black, eds. Oxford: Oxford University Press.

Fulton, James Street. 1959. "Philosophical Adventures of the Idea of Evolution, 1859-1959." *Rice Institute Pamphlet.* vol.46.

Gale, Barry. 1972. "Darwin and the Concept of the Struggle for Existence." *Isis.* 63:321-344.

Gardner, Howard. 1985. *The Mind's New Science: A History of the Cognitive Revolution.* New York: Basic Books.

Gauld, Alan. 1966. "Could a Machine Perceive?" *British Journal for Philosophy of Science* 17:44-58.

Girvetz, Harry K. 1959. "Philosophical Implications of Darwinism." *Antioch Review.* 19:9-19.

Girvetz, Harry, et. al. 1966. *Science, Folklore, and Philosophy.* New York: Harper & Row.

Glick, Thomas F., ed. 1972. *The Comparative Reception of Darwinism.* Austin: University of Texas Press.

Gordon, Robert. 1987. *The Structure of Emotions.* Cambridge: Cambridge University Press.

Gosse, Edmund. 1963. *Father and Son.* New York: Norton.

Goudge, T.A. 1961. *The Ascent of Life.* Toronto: University of Toronto Press.

Gould, Stephen Jay. 1990. "The Individual in Darwin's World." Second Edinburgh Medal Address. Edinburgh: Edinburgh University Press.

Gould, Stephen Jay. 1973. *Ever Since Darwin.* New York: Norton.

Gould, Stephen Jay and Lewontin, R. 1979. "The Spandrels of San Marco and the Panglossian Paradigm: A Critique of the Adaptationist Programme." *Proceedings of the Royal Society.* B205. 581-598.

Grafen, Alan, ed. 1989. *Evolution and Its Influence.* Oxford: Clarendon.

Green, O.H. 1972. "Emotions and Belief," in APQ monograph #6: *Studies in the Philosophy of Mind.* Oxford: Blackwell.

Greene, John C. 1990. "The Interaction of Science and World View in Sir Julian Huxley's Evolutionary Biology," *Journal of the History of Biology.* 23(1): 39-55.

Greene, John C. 1986. "The History of Ideas Revisited," *Revue de Synthese.* 4(3): 201-227.

Greene, John C. 1981. *Science, Ideology, and World View.* Berkeley: University of California Press.

Greenspan, Patricia. 1988. *Emotions and Reasons.* New York: Routledge & Kegan Paul.

Griffin, Nicholas. 1992. *The Selected Letters of Bertrand Russell.* vol.I. Boston: Houghton Mifflin.

Griffin, Nicholas. 1991. *Russell's Idealist Apprenticeship.* Oxford: Clarendon.

Griffin, Nicholas. 1984. "Bertrand Russell's Crisis of Faith," *Russell: Journal of the Bertrand Russell Archives.* 4(1): 101-122.

Hahleg, Kai, and C.A. Hooker, eds. 1989. *Issues in Evolutionary Epistemology.* Albany: SUNY Press.

Hall, Harrison. 1981. "Was Husserl a Realist or an Idealist?" in *Husserl: Intentionality and Cognitive Science.* H. Dreyfus, ed. Cambridge, MA: MIT Press.

Hallett, Garth. 1991. *Essentialism. A Wittgensteinian Critique.* Albany: State University of New York Press.

Hamlyn, D.W. 1961. *Sensation and Perception.* London: Routledge & Kegan Paul.

Hanson, N.R. 1958. *Patterns of Discovery.* Cambridge: Cambridge University Press.

Haugeland, John. 1985. *Artificial Intelligence: The Very Idea.* Cambridge, MA: MIT Press/Bradford Books.

Haugeland, John, ed. 1981. *Mind Design.* Montgomery, Vt.: Bradford.

Haugeland, John. 1978. "The Nature and Plausibility of Cognitivism," *Behavioral and Brain Sciences.* 1: 215-226.

Heil, John. 1983. *Perception and Cognition.* Los Angeles: University of California Press.

Himmelfarb, Gertrude. 1968. *Darwin and the Darwinian Revolution.* New York: Norton.

Hintikka, Jaakko. 1985. *The Intentions of Intentionality.* Dordrecht: Reidel.

Hintikka, Jaakko. 1969. "On the Logic of Perception," in *Models for Modalities.* Boston: Reidel.

Hoffding, Harald. 1955 [1900]. *A History of Modern Philosophy.* 2 vols. B.E. Meyer, trans. Dover Publications.

Hookway, Christopher, ed. 1984. *Minds, Machines, and Evolution.* Cambridge: Cambridge University Press.

Hughes, H. Stuart. 1958. *Consciousness and Society. The Reorientation of European Social Thought 1890-1930.* New York: Vintage Press.

Hull, L.W.H. 1959. "The 19th Century and Evolution," in *History and Philosophy of Science.* London: Longmans Green.

Husserl, Edmund. 1981. *Shorter Works.* Peter McCormick and Frederick Elliston, eds. Notre Dame: University of Notre Dame Press.

Husserl, Edmund. 1977. *Phenomenological Psychology.* trans. by John Scanlon. The Hague: Martinus Nijhoff. [1925 lectures.]

Husserl, Edmund. 1973. *Experience and Judgment.* L. Landgrebe, ed., trans. by J.S. Churchill and Karl Ameriks. Evanston, IL: Northwestern University Press.

Husserl, Edmund. 1973. *The Idea of Phenomenology.* trans. by William Alston and George Nakhnikian. The Hague: Martinus Nijhoff. [1907 lectures.]

Husserl, Edmund. 1970 [1931]. *Cartesian Meditations.* trans. by Dorion Cairns. The Hague: Martinus Nijhoff.

Husserl, Edmund. 1970. *The Crisis of European Sciences and Transcendental Phenomenology.* trans. by David Carr. Evanston, IL: Northwestern University Press.

Husserl, Edmund. 1970 [1900-01]. *Logical Investigations.* trans. by J.N. Findlay. London: Routledge & Kegan Paul.

Husserl, Edmund. 1969 [1929]. *Formal and Transcendental Logic.* trans. by Dorion Cairns. The Hague: Martinus Nijhoff.

Husserl, Edmund. 1965. *Phenomenology and the Crisis of Philosophy.* trans. by Quentin Lauer. New York: Harper. ["Philosophy as a Rigorous Science" - 1910; "Philosophy and the Crisis of European Man" - 1935.]

Husserl, Edmund. 1964 [1928]. *Phenomenology of Internal Time-Consciousness.* M. Heidegger, ed., trans. by James S. Churchill. Bloomington, IN: Indiana University Press.

Husserl, Edmund. 1962 [1913]. *Ideas*, I. trans by W.R. Boyce Gibson. London: Collier-Macmillan.

Huxley, Julian. 1942. *Evolution: The Modern Synthesis*. London: Allen & Unwin.

Huxley, Leonard, ed. 1908 [1900]. *Life and Letters of Thomas Henry Huxley*. 3 vols. 2nd ed. London: Macmillan

Huxley, Thomas Henry. 1863. *Evidence on Man's Place in Nature*. London: William & Norgate.

Huxley, Thomas Henry and Huxley, Julian. 1947. *Evolution and Ethics. 1893-1943*. London: Pilot Press.

Hylton, Peter. 1990. *Russell, Idealism, and the Emergence of Analytic Philosophy*. Oxford: Clarendon.

Izard, C.E., and J. Kagan, R. Zajonc, eds. 1984. *Emotions, Cognition, and Behavior*. Cambridge: Cambridge University Press.

Jackson, Frank. 1977. *Perception*. Cambridge: Cambridge University Press.

James, William. 1983 [1890]. *The Principles of Psychology*. Cambridge: Harvard University Press.

Johnson, Mark. 1987. *The Body in the Mind: The Bodily Basis of Meaning, Imagination, and Reason*. Chicago: University of Chicago Press.

Johnston, W.A., and Veronica Dark. 1986. "Selective Attention," *American Review of Psychology*. 37: 43-75.

Kaufmann, Walter. 1968. *Nietzsche: Philosopher, Psychologist, Antichrist*. 3rd ed. New York: Vintage Press.

Kellogg, Vernon. 1908. *Darwinism Today*. New York: Henry Holt.

Kelly, Alfred. 1981. *The Descent of Darwin: The Popularization of Darwinism in Germany, 1860-1914*. Chapel Hill: University of North Carolina Press.

Kenny, Anthony. 1963. *Action, Emotion, and Will*. London: Routledge & Kegan Paul.

Keynes, John Maynard. 1949. *Two Memoirs*. New York: Kelley.

Kohak, Erazim. 1978. *Idea and Experience*. Chicago: University of Chicago Press.

Kohler, Wolfgang. 1947 [1929]. *Gestalt Psychology*. New York: Liveright.

Kohn, David, ed. 1985. *The Darwinian Heritage*. Princeton: Princeton University Press.

Kolakowski, Leszek. 1987. *Husserl and the Search for Certitude*. Chicago: University of Chicago Press.

Krikorian, Yervant, ed. 1944. *Naturalism and the Human Spirit*. New York: Columbia University Press.

Kuhn, Thomas. 1970. *The Structure of Scientific Revolutions*. Chicago: University of Chicago Press.

Lakoff, George. 1987. *Women, Fire, and Dangerous Things*. Chicago: University of Chicago Press.

Lange, F.A. 1892. *History of Materialism*. 4th ed. 3 vols. trans. by E.C. Thomas. London: Kegan Paul, Trench, Trubner.

LeDoux, Joseph. 1994. "Emotion, Memory, and the Brain," *Scientific American*, June: 50-57.

LeDoux, Joseph. 1989. "Cognitive-Emotional Interactions in the Brain," *Cognition and Emotion*. 3(4): 266-289.

LeDoux, Joseph and William Hirst, eds. 1986. *Mind and Brain: Dialogues in Cognitive Neuroscience*. Cambridge: Cambridge University Press.

Leventhal, Howard. 1982. "The Integration of Emotion and Cognition: A View from the Perceptual-Motor Theory of Emotion," in Margaret Clark and Susan Fiske, eds. *Affect and Cognition.* Hillsdale, NJ: Erlbaum.

Levinas, Emmanuel. 1973. *The Theory of Intuition in Husserl's Phenomenology.* trans. by Andre Orianne. Evanston, IL: Northwestern University Press.

Levy, Paul. 1981. *Moore: G.E. Moore and the Cambridge Apostles.* Oxford: Oxford University Press.

Lewy, Casimir. 1970. "G.E. Moore and the Naturalistic Fallacy." In A. Ambrose and M. Lazerowitz, eds., *G.E. Moore: Essays in Retrospect*, pp.292-303.

Lovejoy, A.O. 1936. *The Great Chain of Being.* Cambridge, MA: Harvard University Press.

Lycan, William, ed. 1990. *Mind and Cognition.* Oxford: Blackwell.

Lyons, William. 1980. *Emotion.* Cambridge: Cambridge University Press.

MacIntyre, Alasdair. 1966. *A Short History of Ethics.* New York: Macmillan-Collier.

Malthus, Thomas. 1960 [1798]. *On Population.* Gertrude Himmelfarb, ed. New York: Modern Library.

Mandelbaum, Maurice. 1974. *History, Man and Reason: A Study in Nineteenth-Century Thought.* Baltimore: Johns Hopkins University Press.

Mandelbaum, Maurice. 1964. *Philosophy, Science, and Sense Perception.* Baltimore: Johns Hopkins University Press.

Mandler, George. 1975. *Mind and Emotion.* New York: Wiley.

Mayr, Ernst. 1988. *Toward A New Philosophy of Biology.* Cambridge, MA.: Harvard University Press.

Mayr, Ernst. 1982. *The Growth of Biological Thought.* Cambridge, MA: Harvard University Press.

Mayr, Ernst and William Provine, eds. 1980. *The Evolutionary Synthesis.* Cambridge, MA: Harvard University Press.

Maxwell, Grover. 1972. "Russell on Perception: A Study in Philosophical Method." In D.F. Pears, ed., *Bertrand Russell. A Collection of Critical Essays.*

McGinn, Colin. 1983. *The Subjective View.* Oxford: Clarendon Press.

McGinn, Colin. 1982. *The Character of Mind.* Oxford: Oxford University Press.

Mead, George Herbert. 1936. *Movements of Thought in the Nineteenth Century.* Merritt H. Moore, ed. Chicago: University of Chicago Press.

Merleau-Ponty, Maurice. 1963. *The Structure of Behavior.* trans by Alden Fisher. Boston: Beacon Press.

Merleau-Ponty, Maurice. 1962. *Phenomenology of Perception.* trans. by Colin Smith. London: Routledge & Kegan Paul.

Metz, Rudolf. 1938. *A Hundred Years of British Philosophy.* trans. by J.W. Harvey, T.E. Jessop, H. Sturt. ed. by J.H. Muirhead. London: Allen & Unwin.

Mill, John Stuart. 1972. *The Later Letters of John Stuart Mill.* vol.XV of *Collected Works.* Francis Mineka and Dwight Lindley, eds. Toronto: University of Toronto Press.

Mill, John Stuart. 1969. *Essays on Ethics, Religion, and Society.* vol. X of *Collected Works.* J.M. Robson, ed. Toronto: University of Toronto Press.

Mill, John Stuart. 1958 [1873]. *Autobiography.* London: Oxford.

Mill, John Stuart. 1874. *A System of Logic.* 8th ed. New York: Harper.

Miller, Izchak. 1984. *Husserl, Perception, and Temporal Awareness.* Boston: MIT Press.

Mohanty, J.N. 1964. *Edmund Husserl's Theory of Meaning*. The Hague: Martinus Nijhoff.

Moore, G.E. 1991. *The Elements of Ethics*. ed. by Tom Regan. Philadelphia: Temple University Press.

Moore, G.E. 1986. *The Early Essays*. ed. by Tom Regan. Philadelphia: Temple University Press.

Moore, G.E. 1975. *Ethics*. Oxford: Oxford University Press.

Moore, G.E. 1968 [1903]. *Principia Ethica*. Cambridge: Cambridge University Press.

Moore, G.E. 1966. *Lectures on Philosophy*. ed. by Casimir Lewy. London: Allen & Unwin.

Moore, G.E. 1962. *The Commonplace Book of G.E. Moore. 1919-1953*. ed. by Casimir Lewy. London: Allen & Unwin.

Moore, G.E. 1962 [1959]. *Philosophical Papers*. New York: Collier.

Moore, G.E. 1953. *Some Main Problems of Philosophy*. London: Allen & Unwin.

Moore, G.E. 1951 [1922]. *Philosophical Studies*. New York: Humanities Press.

Moore, G.E. 1920-21. "The Character of Cognitive Acts," *Proceedings of the Aristotelian Society*, n.s., 21: 132-140.

Moore, G.E. 1899. "The Nature of Judgment." *Mind* 8:176-193.

Morris, Charles. 1937. *Logical Positivism, Pragmatism, and Scientific Empiricism*. Paris: Hermann.

Muirhead, J.H., ed. 1925. *Contemporary British Philosophy*. Second Series. London: Allen & Unwin.

Muirhead, J.H., ed. 1924. *Contemporary British Philosophy*. First Series. New York: Macmillan.

Mundle, C.W.K. 1971. *Perception: Facts and Theories*. London: Oxford University Press.

Munro, D.H. 1972. "Russell's Moral Theories." In D.F. Pears, ed., *Bertrand Russell. A Collection of Critical Essays*.

Nagel, Thomas. 1986. *The View from Nowhere*. Oxford: Oxford University Press.

Nagel, Thomas. 1979. *Mortal Questions*. Cambridge: Cambridge University Press.

Natsoulas, T. 1978. "Residual Subjectivity," *American Psychologist*. 33.

Neisser, Ulric. 1976. *Cognition and Reality*. San Francisco: Freeman.

Nietzsche, Friedrich. 1964 [1882]. *The Joyful Wisdom*. vol.10 of *Complete Works of Friedrich Nietzsche*. Oscar Levy, ed., trans by Thomas Common. New York: Russell & Russell.

Nietzsche, Friedrich. 1964 [1909]. *Will to Power*. vol. 15-16 of *Complete Works of Friedrich Nietzsche*. trans. by Anthony Ludovici. New York: Russell & Russell.

Nitecki, Matthew, ed. 1988. *Evolutionary Progress*. Chicago: University of Chicago Press.

Nitecki, Matthew and Doris Nitecki, eds. 1993. *Evolutionary Ethics*. Albany: State University of New York Press.

Norman, D.A. 1981. "Twelve Issues for Cognitive Science," in D.A. Norman, ed. *Perspectives on Cognitive Science*. Norwood, NJ: Ablex Publishing.

O'Hear, Anthony. 1987. "Has the Theory of Evolution any Relevance to Philosophy?" *Ratio*. 29:16-35.

Paradis, James, and George C. Williams. 1989. *Evolution and Ethics*. T.H. Huxley's *Evolution and Ethics* with New Essays on Its Victorian and Sociobiological Context. Princeton: Princeton University Press.

Passmore, John. 1983. "The Mysterious Case of Charles Darwin," in *Evolution from Molecules to Men*, D.S. Bendall, ed. Cambridge: Cambridge University Press.

Passmore, John. 1966. *A Hundred Years of Philosophy*. 2nd ed. London: Duckworth.

Passmore, John. 1959. "Darwin's Impact on British Metaphysics." *Victorian Studies* 3:41-54.

Paul, Leslie. 1953. *The English Philosophers*. London: Faber & Faber.

Peacocke, Christopher. 1983. *Sense and Content*. Oxford: Clarendon.

Pears, D.F. 1972. *Bertrand Russell: A Collection of Critical Essays*. New York: Doubleday Anchor.

Pears, D.F. 1972 "Russell's Logical Atomism." In D.F. Pears, ed., *Bertrand Russell. A Collection of Critical Essays*.

Pears, D.F. 1967. *Bertrand Russell and the British Tradition in Philosophy*. New York: Random House.

Peckham, Morse, ed. 1959. *The Origin of Species by Charles Darwin*. A Variorum Text. Philadelphia: University of Pennsylvania Press.

Peirce, Charles S. 1868. "Questions Concerning Certain Faculties," *Journal of Speculative Philosophy*. 2: 103-114.

Perry, John. 1979. "The Problem of the Essential Indexical," *Nous* 13:3-21.

Perry, John. 1977. "Frege on Demonstratives," *Philosophical Review*. 86:474-497.

Perry, Ralph Barton. 1926. *Philosophy of the Recent Past*. New York: Scribner's.

Petit, Philip. 1972-73. "The Early Philosophy of G.E. Moore." *Philosophical Forum* 4: 260-298.

Pietersma, Henry. 1973. "Intuition and Horizon in the Philosophy of Husserl," *Philosophy and Phenomenological Research*, 34:95-101.

Plotkin, Henry. 1994. *Darwin Machines and the Nature of Knowledge*. Cambridge, MA: Harvard University Press.

Popper, Karl. 1972. *Objective Knowledge: An Evolutionary Approach*. Oxford: Clarendon.

Price, H.H. 1961 [1932]. *Perception*. 2nd ed. London: Methuen.

Provine, William. 1986. *Sewall Wright and Evolutionary Biology*. Chicago: University of Chicago Press.

Provine, William. 1971. *The Origins of Theoretical Population Genetics*. Chicago: University of Chicago Press.

Putnam, Hilary. 1988. *Representation and Reality*. Cambridge, MA: MIT Press/Bradford Books.

Putnam, Hilary. 1975. *Mind, Language, and Reality*. Cambridge: Cambridge University Press.

Pylyshyn, Zenon. 1980. "Computation and Cognition," in *Behavioral and Brain Sciences*. 3(1): 111-134.

Quine, W.V. 1975. "The Nature of Natural Knowledge," in S. Guttenplan, ed. *Mind and Language*. Oxford: Clarendon Press.

Quine, W.V. 1969. "Epistemology Naturalized," in *Ontological Relativity and other Essays*. New York: Columbia University Press.

Quinton, Anthony. 1972. "Russell's Philosophy of Mind." In D.F. Pears, ed., *Bertrand Russell: A Collection of Critical Essays*.

Quinton, Anthony. 1966. "Ethics and the Theory of Evolution," in *Biology and Personality*, I. T. Ramsey, ed. Oxford: Blackwell.

Rachels, James. 1990. *Created from Animals: The Moral Implications of Darwinism.* Oxford: Oxford University Press.

Radnitzky, Gerard and Bartley, W.W., eds. 1987. *Evolutionary Epistemology, Rationality, and the Sociology of Knowledge.* LaSalle, IL: Open Court.

Ramsey, I. ed. 1965. *Biology and Personality.* New York: Barnes & Noble.

Randall, John Herman. 1977. *Philosophy After Darwin.* Beth Singer, ed. New York: Columbia University Press.

Randall, John Herman. 1961. "The Changing Impact of Darwin on Philosophy." *Journal of the History of Ideas.* XXII:435-462.

Randall, John Herman. 1926. *The Making of the Modern Mind.* New York: Columbia University Press.

Regan, Tom. 1986. *Bloomsbury's Prophet.* Philadelphia: Temple University Press.

Rescher, Nicholas, ed. 1990. *Evolution, Cognition and Realism.* Lanham, MD: University Press of America.

Rey, George. 1980. "Functionalism and the Emotions," in Amelie Rorty, ed. *Explaining Emotions.* Berkeley: University of California Press.

Rhees, Rush, ed. 1981. *Ludwig Wittgenstein: Personal Recollections.* Oxford: Blackwell.

Richards, Robert. 1992. *The Meaning of Evolution.* Chicago: University of Chicago Press.

Richards, Robert. 1987. *Darwin and the Emergence of Evolutionary Theories of Mind and Behavior.* Chicago: University of Chicago Press.

Richards, Robert. 1979. "Influence of Sensationalist Tradition on Early Theories of the Evolution of Behavior," *Journal of the History of Ideas,* 40: 85-105.

Ricoeur, Paul. 1967. *Husserl: An Analysis of His Phenomenology.* Evanston, IL: Northwestern University Press.

Roediger, H. and Fergus Craik, eds. 1989. *Varieties of Memory and Consciousness.* Hillsdale, NJ: Erlbaum.

Rogers, James Allen. 1972. "Darwinism and Social Darwinism," *Journal of the History of Ideas,* 33: 265-280.

Rorty, Amelie, ed. 1980. *Explaining Emotions.* Berkeley: University of California Press.

Ross, J.J. 1970. *The Appeal to the Given.* London: Allen & Unwin.

Royce, Josiah. 1892. *The Spirit of Modern Philosophy.* Boston: Houghton Mifflin.

Ruja, Harry. 1984. "Russell the the Meaning of 'Good'," *Russell: Journal of the Bertrand Russell Archives.* n.s. 4(1): 137-156.

Ruse, Michael. *Monad to Man.* (unpublished manuscript)

Ruse, Michael. 1989. "The View from Somewhere: A Critical Defense of Evolutionary Epistemology," in Kai Hahlweg and C.A. Hooker, eds., *Issues in Evolutionary Epistemology.* Albany: SUNY Press.

Ruse, Michael. 1986. *Taking Darwin Seriously. A Naturalistic Approach to Philosophy.* Oxford: Basil Blackwell.

Ruse, Michael. 1979. *The Darwinian Revolution.* Chicago: University of Chicago Press.

Russell, Bertrand. 1994. *The Collected Papers of Bertrand Russell,* vol.4, *Foundations of Logic, 1903-1905.* Alasdair Urquart, ed. London: Routledge.

Russell, Bertrand. 1993. *The Collected Papers of Bertrand Russell.* vol.3, *Toward the Principles of Mathematics, 1900-1902.* Gregory Moore, ed. London: Routledge.

Russell, Bertrand. 1992. *The Collected Papers of Bertrand Russell.* vol.6, *Logical and Philosophical Papers, 1909-1913.* John Slater, ed. London: Routledge.

Russell, Bertrand. 1990. *The Collected Papers of Bertrand Russell.* vol.2, *Philosophical Papers, 1896-1899.* Nicholas Griffin and Albert Lewis eds. London: Unwin Hyman.

Russell, Bertrand. 1988. *The Collected Papers of Bertrand Russell.* vol.13, *Prophecy and Dissent, 1914-1916.* Richard Rempel, ed. London: Unwin Hyman.

Russell, Bertrand. 1988. *The Collected Papers of Bertrand Russell.* vol.9, *Essays on Language, Mind, and Matter, 1919-1926.* John Slater, ed. London: Unwin & Hyman.

Russell, Bertrand. 1986. *The Collected Papers of Bertrand Russell.* vol.8, *The Philosophy of Logical Atomism and Other Essays.* John G. Slater, ed. London: Allen & Unwin.

Russell, Bertrand. 1985. *The Collected Papers of Bertrand Russell.* vol.12, *Contemplation and Action.* Richard Rempel, Andrew Brink, Margaret Moran, eds. London: Allen & Unwin.

Russell, Bertrand. 1984. *The Collected Papers of Bertrand Russell.* vol.7, *Theory of Knowledge. The 1913 Manuscript.* Elizabeth Eames and Kenneth Blackwell, eds. London: Allen & Unwin.

Russell, Bertrand. 1983. *The Collected Papers of Bertrand Russell.* vol.1, *Cambridge Essays, 1888-1899.* Kenneth Blackwell, et. al., eds. London: Allen & Unwin.

Russell, Bertrand. 1981 [1917]. *Mysticism and Logic.* Totowa, NJ: Barnes & Noble.

Russell, Bertrand. 1978 [1967-69]. *Autobiography of Bertrand Russell.* London: Unwin Paperbacks.

Russell, Bertrand. 1977 [1928]. *Skeptical Essays.* London: Unwin Paperbacks.

Russell, Bertrand. 1970 [1927]. *An Outline of Philosophy.* London: Allen & Unwin.

Russell, Bertrand. 1966 [1910]. *Philosophical Essays.* New York: Simon & Schuster.

Russell, Bertrand. 1964 [1st ed. 1903]. *Principles of Mathematics.* 2nd ed. New York: Norton.

Russell, Bertrand. 1962 [1931]. *The Scientific Outlook.* New York: Norton.

Russell, Bertrand. 1962. *Freedom versus Organization. 1814-1914.* New York: Norton.

Russell, Bertrand. 1961. *Religion and Science.* London: Oxford University Press.

Russell, Bertrand. 1960. "Introduction" to Ernest Gellner's *Words and Things.* Boston: Beason Press.

Russell, Bertrand. 1959. *My Philosophical Development.* London: Allen & Unwin.

Russell, Bertrand. 1959 [1912]. *The Problems of Philosophy.* London: Oxford University Press.

Russell, Bertrand. 1956. *Logic and Knowledge.* ed. by R.C. Marsh. London: Allen & Unwin.

Russell, Bertrand. 1956. Review of Urmson's *Philosophical Analysis,* in *The Hibbert Journal.* 54: 320-329.

Russell, Bertrand. 1954 [1927]. *An Analysis of Matter.* New York: Dover.

Russell, Bertrand. 1953. *The Impact of Science on Society.* New York: Simon & Schuster.

Russell, Bertrand. 1951. *Portraits from Memory and Other Essays.* New York: Simon & Schuster.

Russell, Bertrand. 1950. *Unpopular Essays*. London: Allen & Unwin.

Russell, Bertrand. 1948. *Human Knowledge: Its Scope and Limits*. New York: Simon & Schuster.

Russell, Bertrand. 1945. *A History of Western Philosophy*. New York: Simon & Schuster.

Russell, Bertrand. 1940. *An Inquiry into Meaning and Truth*. London: Allen & Unwin.

Russell, Bertrand. 1938. "On the Importance of Logical Form." In *Encyclopedia of Unified Science*. Chicago: University of Chicago Press.

Russell, Bertrand. 1935. *In Praise of Idleness*. London: Unwin Paperbacks.

Russell, Bertrand. 1932. "Reformulation of the Nature of Mind" in Charles Morris, ed. *Six Theories of Mind*. Chicago: University of Chicago Press.

Russell, Bertrand. 1929. *Marriage and Morals*. New York: Liveright.

Russell, Bertrand. 1926. Review of C.D. Broad's *Mind and Its Place in Nature*. *Mind*. 35:72-80.

Russell, Bertrand. 1926 [1914]. *Our Knowledge of the External World*. 2nd ed. London: Allen & Unwin.

Russell, Bertrand. 1925. *The ABC of Relativity*. New York: Harper.

Russell, Bertrand. 1925. "Introduction: Materialism Past and Present." In Frederick A. Lange's *The History of Materialism*. 3rd English ed. New York: Harcourt Brace.

Russell, Bertrand. 1924. *Icarus or the Future of Science*. New York: Dutton.

Russell, Bertrand. 1923. *The ABC of Atoms*. New York: Dutton.

Russell, Bertrand. 1922. "Dr. Schiller's Analysis of *The Analysis of Mind*," *Journal of Philosophy*, vol.xix, 645-651.

Russell, Bertrand. 1922. "Introduction" to L. Wittgenstein's *Tractatus Logico-Philosophicus*. London: Kegan Paul.

Russell, Bertrand. 1921. *An Analysis of Mind*. London: Allen & Unwin.

Russell, Bertrand. 1920. "Relativity Theory of Gravitation," *English Review*. 30: 11-18.

Russell, Bertrand. 1912. "The Philosophy of Bergson." *Monist* 22: 321-347.

Russell, Bertrand and Whitehead, A.N. 1910-13. *Principia Mathematica*. Cambridge: Cambridge University Press.

Russell, Bertrand. 1910. "Elements of Ethics." Reprinted in *Philosophical Essays*.

Russell, Bertrand. 1904. Review of G.E. Moore's *Principia Ethica. Independent Review*. 11: 328-333.

Russell, Bertrand. 1900. *A Critical Exposition of the Philosophy of Leibniz*. London: Allen & Unwin.

Savage, C. Wade. ed. 1978. *Perception and Cognition*. Minnesota Studies in the Philosophy of Science. vol.ix. Minneapolis: University of Minnesota Press.

Schilpp, Paul, ed. 1989. *The Philosophy of Bertrand Russell*. 5th ed., Library of Living Philosophers. LaSalle, IL: Open Court.

Schilpp, Paul, ed. 1942. *The Philosophy of G.E. Moore*. Library of Living Philosophers. Evanston, IL: Northwestern University Press.

Schnadelbach, Herbert. 1984. *Philosophy in Germany 1831-1933*. trans. by Eric Matthews. Cambridge: Cambridge University Press.

Schneewind, J.B. 1977. *Sidgwick's Ethics and Victorian Moral Philosophy*. Oxford: Clarendon.

Schwartz, B. 1986. "Evolutionary Biology and Human Nature," in *The Battle for*

Human Nature: Sciencem Morality and Modern Life. B. Schwartz, ed. New York: Norton.

Scriven, Michael. 1964. "The Mechanical Concept of Mind," in *Minds and Machines.* A.R. Anderson, ed. Englewood Cliffs, NJ: Prentice-Hall.

Searle, John. 1992. *The Rediscovery of the Mind.* Cambridge, MA: MIT Press.

Searle, John. 1984. *Minds, Brains, and Science.* Cambridge, MA: Harvard University Press.

Searle, John. 1983. *Intentionality.* Cambridge: Cambridge University Press.

Searle, John. 1964. "How to derive *ought* from *is.*" *Philosophical Review* 73: 43-58.

Shaffer, Jerome. 1983. "An Assessment of Emotion." *American Philosophical Quarterly* 20: 161-173.

Shimony, Abner. 1971. "Perception from an Evolutionary Point of View," *Journal of Philosophy.* 68:571-583.

Sidgwick, Henry. 1902. *Lectures on the Ethics of Green, Spencer, and Martineau.* ed. by E. Constance Jones. London: Macmillan.

Simpson, George G., ed. 1982. *The Book of Darwin.* New York: Washington Square Press.

Simpson, George G. 1951. *The Meaning of Evolution.* New Haven: Yale University Press.

Slater, John. 1988. "Russell's Conception of Philosophy," *Russell: Journal of the Bertrand Russell Archives.* 8: 163-178.

Sluga, Hans D. 1980. *Gottlob Frege.* London: Routledge & Kegan Paul.

Smith, Adam. 1908 [1776]. *An Inquiry into the Nature and Causes of the Wealth of Nations.* 6th ed. London: Geo. Bell.

Smith, David. 1986. "The Ins and Outs of Perception," *Philosophical Studies.* 49: 187-211.

Smith, David. 1984. "Content and Context of Perception," *Synthese.* 61: 61-88

Smith, David. 1982. "What's the Meaning of 'This'?" *Nous.* 16, 181-208.

Smith, David. 1981. "Indexical Sense and Reference," *Synthese.* 49:101-128.

Smith, David. 1979. "The Case of the Exploding Perception," *Synthese.* 41:239-270.

Smith, David, and Ronald McIntyre. 1982. *Husserl and Intentionality: A Study of Mind, Meaning, and Language.* Dordrecht: Reidel.

Sober, Elliott. 1985. "Panglossian Functionalism and the Philosophy of Mind, *Synthese* 64, pp.165-193.

Sober, Elliott. ed. 1984. *Conceptual Issues in Evolutionary Biology.* Cambridge, MA: MIT Press.

Sober, Elliott. 1981. "The Evolution of Rationality." *Synthese.* 46:95-120.

Solomon, Robert. 1977. "Husserl's Concept of the Noema," in F.A. Elliston and P. McCormick, eds., *Husserl: Expositions and Appraisals.*

Solomon, Robert. 1977. "The Logic of Emotions," *Nous* 11:41-49.

Solomon, Robert. 1977. "The Rationality of the Emotions," *Southwestern Journal of Philosophy.* 8:105-114.

Solomon, Robert, and Cheshire Calhoun, eds. 1984. *What is an Emotion?* Oxford: Oxford University Press.

Spencer, Herbert. 1978 [1897]. *The Principles of Ethics.* 2 vols. Indianapolis: Liberty Classics.

Spencer, Herbert. 1950 [1884]. *The Man Versus the State.* Boston: Beacon Press.

Spencer, Herbert. 1910 [1883]. *Essays Scientific, Political and Speculative.* 3 vols. London: Appleton.

Spencer, Herbert. 1910. "Progress: Its Law and Cause." in *Essays Scientific, Political and Speculative.* [Orig. pub. in *The Westminster Review*, 1857].

Spencer, Herbert. 1904. *An Autobiography.* 2 vols. New York: D. Appleton.

Spencer, Herbert. 1879. *Data of Ethics.* New York: William Allison.

Spencer, Herbert. 1851. *Social Statics.* London: John Chapman.

Spiegelberg, Herbert. 1960. *The Phenomenological Movement.* 2 vol. The Hague: Martinus Nijhoff.

Stephen, Leslie. 1882. *The Science of Ethics.* Freeport, NY: Books for Libraries Press.

Stich, Stephen. 1990. *The Fragmentation of Reason.* Cambridge, MA: Bradford/MIT Press.

Stich, Stephen. 1983. *From Folk Psychology to Cognitive Science.* Cambridge, MA: MIT Press/ Bradford Books.

Stich, Stephen. 1981. "Dennett on Intentional Systems," *Philosophical Topics* 12: 167-184.

Stocker, Michael. 1987. "Emotional Thoughts." *American Philosophical Quarterly* 24:59-69.

Tucker, D.M. 1981. "Lateral Brain Function, Emotion, and Conceptualization," *Psychological Bulletin.* 89: 19-46.

Urmson, J.O. *Philosophical Analysis.* Oxford: Clarendon.

Vorzimmer, Peter. 1969. "Darwin, Malthus, and the Theory of Natural Selection." *Journal of the History of Ideas.* XXX:4, 527-542.

Vucinich, Alexander. 1988. *Darwin in Russian Thought.* Berkeley: University of California Press.

Warnock, G.J. 1958. *English Philosophy Since 1900.* London: Oxford University Press.

Waters, C.K. and A. Van Helden, eds. 1992. *Julian Huxley: Biologist and Statesman of Science.* Houston: Rice University Press.

Whewell, William. 1847. *The Philosophy of the Inductive Sciences.* London: Parker.

White, Alan. 1964. *Attention.* Oxford: Blackwell.

Williams, Bernard. 1989. "Evolutionary Theory: Epistemology and Ethics," in *Evolution and Its Influence*, Alan Grafen, ed. Oxford: Clarendon Press.

Williams, Bernard, and Alan Montefiore, eds. 1966. *British Analytic Philosophy.* New York: Humanities Press.

Wittgenstein, Ludwig. 1922. *Tractatus Logico-Philosophicus.* London: Routledge & Kegan Paul.

Wood, Alan. 1957. *Bertrand Russell. The Passionate Sceptic.* London: Allen & Unwin.

Wuketits, Franz. ed. 1984. *Concepts and Approaches in Evolutionary Epistemology.* Dordrecht: Reidel.

Zajonc, R.B. 1980. "Feeling and Thinking: Preferences Need No Inferences," *American Psychologist.* 35, pp.151-175.

Index